Revisiting the Kerala Model of Health

Revisiting the Kerala Model of Health

Edited by

Dr. Manju S. Nair

KALPAZ

First Published, 2021

Published by

Kalpaz Publications
C-30, Satyawati Nagar,
Delhi – 110052
Ph.: 011-47034999, 9811692060
www.kalpazpublications.com
E-mail: kalpaz@hotmail.com

Printed at: Gyan Press, Delhi.

Cataloging in Publication Data—DK
Courtesy: D.K. Agencies (P) Ltd. <docinfo@dkagencies.com>

Revisiting the Kerala model of health / edited by
Dr. Manju S. Nair.
pages cm
Contributed articles.
Includes bibliographical references and index.
ISBN 9789353246228

1. Health surveys—India—Kerala. 2. Medical policy—India—Kerala. I. Nair, Manju S., editor.

LCC RA407.5.I4R48 2021 | DDC 614.42095483 23

Dedication

Dedicated to my parents, Sri. M. Rajasekharan Nair and Smt. Saraswathy Bai who has always stood with me as a source of incredible support, guidance and motivation

– Manju S.Nair

Contents

Part IV: Human Development status/Quality of Life of the Marginalised

Part V: Economic Burden of Diseases

Foreword

Scholars of health sector in Low and Middle Countries are hungry for successes to celebrate, as they are few and far between. Countries like Sri Lanka, Costa Rica, China and the state of Kerala were celebrated as successes in Bellagio in 1985 because they had health indictors which were better than expected given their economic development. The paradox of Kerala's good health indicators (especially maternal and infant mortality rates) and economic backwardness had already been highlighted by a series of publications from the Centre for Development Studies. The moniker of 'Kerala Model' must have been retrofitted to describe this paradox. A model presupposes predesigning and execution based on the design. But, as has been highlighted in many papers including in this book, Kerala's health outcomes were the result of historical factors, some by design and others by serendipity. I would argue that the fascination with the appellation, ignoring the context in which it was developed, had created complacency and resistance to introspection and change needed to confront a situation that was already changing when the term was coined. As in most social aspects, in health sector, by virtue of actions taken in one time period and the response of other actors to such action, the scenario changes by the next time period. A strategy that succeeds at a point of time may no longer be appropriate in the next as the success has altered the context where it succeeded. To continue to be effective sector manages have to understand the emerging situation and respond to it, not persist with strategies merely because they worked in the past.

Kerala's achievements are by no means insignificant. Substantial reduction in mortality from infectious diseases, childbirth, death of children, control of birth rate, availability of formal health care in most parts of the state at affordable cost, were creditable compared to what existed before and what other states in India have achieved. Farsightedness of an enlightened monarchy, progressive social movements, munificence of missionaries keen in incentivising conversion to their faith, increase in wealth due to globalisation of commerce were all factors that contributed to good health. Many of these have been discussed in the following articles. Education, social reform and women's empowerment appear to have moved in tandem with improvements in health, even though the direction of causality is not entirely clear. Kerala had a head start in health indicators at the time of independence; a pole position the state has not relinquished so far. But comparing Kerala to the performance of other states, which continues to be embarrassingly poor, has only served to create a false sense of complacency and worked against taking the health system to the level achieved by comparable states like Thailand or Sri Lanka. It has also blinded policy makers and researchers to some glaring fault lines of Kerala's health sector, highlighted in this book.

The shortfalls have been largely at system-level. Kerala's health system has retained a dichotomous and disjointed structure with an inadequately funded government health system and an unregulated private sector paid almost entirely by out-of-pocket as fee for service paid at the point of consumption. Stewardship of the sector is needed to ensure good health of the population, achieved through good quality health services with patient satisfaction and little financial risk to the families. This has largely been absent. Systems have not been created to ensure that government and private sector are held accountable to achieve the objectives of good health status, patient satisfaction and financial risk protection efficiently while ensuring quality. Cost of this inefficiency is borne by the public through rising cost of health care and inadequate returns to expenditure. In government this is characterised by poor organisation, (e.g., failure to develop skills in management, such as public health cadre and hospital administrators) leading to sub optimal management and lack of agility to anticipate and adapt to changing demands of the health sector.

While keeping abreast with knowledge generated elsewhere (even while ignoring research in the state) Kerala has been resistant to internalise advances made in organisation of health care in other countries. Attempts to try out reforms are decried as arising from external agenda (the oft cited culprits were the World Bank and IMF) while entrenched vested interests implement their agenda unchecked. An example is the failure of government to implement transparency in pricing by private hospitals in spite of being mandated to do so by a bill unanimously approved by the Kerala legislature. Similarly, government has failed to implement the public health cadre even in the face of the worst public health emergency the world has faced in recent times. Reorganisation of services, including creation of a health network with primary care as the foundation with referrals to higher levels, task shifting, quality control of services and digitisation of hospital management which would have improved quality and reduced costs have also not been done. Kerala does not have a health observatory that can alert us to emerging disease profiles and a data analytics system that can support policy making. Small and medium sized private hospitals, the main stay of health care provision since mid-seventies who are facing existential threat from corporate hospitals, can be protected only by a new method of financing and provider payment system, which is not even under consideration. In short, Kerala is stuck with a twentieth century health system to manage the problems of the 21st century. It is time for an upgrade to the Kerala model of health.

A system change that holds much promise is the decentralisation of the control of health institutions to local governments. After a shaky start this has commenced showing positive impact and can be further refined, learning from other sectors and other nations. Market interventions to control prices has been effective not only in drugs but also in other areas. The investments made in diagnostic and therapeutic infrastructure through Aardram and KIIFB, if managed efficiently, can help reduce predatory pricing by the corporate sector. A new breed of specialised physician administrators that is emerging in the state, if allied with the local governments and given sufficient delegation of powers and administrative support, will be able to improve administration of hospitals. Technical quality in government hospitals have always been high. If service quality is also improved these hospitals will go a long way to improve health status while ensuring patient satisfaction. New initiatives like monitoring and preventing anti-microbial resistance through one health approach, quality assurance (on the input side), electronic health records and digitisation of treatment, collaboration between private and public sector in such areas as cochlear implant, detection and management of congenital heart disease and provision of services under the government funded health insurance augur well for the health sector. The private sector has also been an active partner in the state's successful efforts to further reduce maternal and infant mortality rate.

The Kerala model of health which had leveraged social development to achieve good health outcomes, has not been able to replicate this for socially and economically disadvantaged groups. Health conditions of two such groups, tribal and costal population, are discussed in this book highlighting the health differentials between them and rest of the population. Kerala has also not been able to bridge the nutrition gap leaving a significant percentage of the population stunted and underweight. This has a negative impact on morbidity and mortality. Even Kerala's ability to manage infectious diseases has been called into question by the failure to prevent vector and water borne diseases. The failure to upgrade the capacity of the health system to deal with emerging challenges is highlighted by the poor management of non-communicable diseases, mental health issues and geriatric care.

The essays that follow deal with both the successes and failures of Kerala's health trajectory. They discuss areas where Kerala has done well and where we have fallen short. Such an examination could lead to identifying strategies that could lead to improvement of indicators in many areas. But what Kerala needs to work on is building the capacity of its physician managers, policy makers and political leaders to develop and manage a health system capable of not only comprehending but anticipating and preparing for emerging challenges. This would require a deeper understanding not only of technical areas such as clinical care, epidemiology and public health but also other areas such as organisation, regulation and financing of the health sector as well as the social and environmental determinants of health.

Rajeev Sadanandan I.A.S.

Former Additional Chief Secretary
(Health and Family Welfare)
Government of Kerala &
Chief Executive Officer
Health Systems Transformation Platform
New Delhi

Acknowledgement

Researching more than two decades in the area of health studies, I have always felt the need to publish a book to invite attention and discuss on the happenings after the famous conference in Bellagio, Italy in 1985 where Kerala was held up as a model for 'good health at low cost'. Thirty-five years after the conference, the landscape of health sector has changed drastically in Kerala which needs to be researched on myriad fronts including policy initiatives, governance aspects, status of marginalised, food and nutrition security, economic burden of diseases, morbidity and mortality trends etc. The book is such an attempt at revisiting the Kerala Model of health with focus on its current status, achievements and challenges. I would like to place on record my gratefulness to all those who made this work possible.

Sri. Rajeev Sadanandan, I.A.S, Former Additional Chief Secretary (Health and Family Welfare, Government of Kerala) has spent his valuable time in reading the book and writing a foreword. As a bureaucrat he has rich experience in working in the health sector and has been Chief Minister's advisor on actions to be taken during the Covid pandemic. I place on record my deepest gratitude to him for his efforts and also for the valuable time he has spent for writing a befitting foreword for the book.

The academic environment provided by the University of Kerala to its faculty members to engage in research and extension needs to be recorded with appreciation. Sincere respect and thanks to Prof. V.P. Mahadevan Pillai, Hon'ble Vice Chancellor who has been motivating faculty members to publish and to Dr. S. Nazeeb, Research Convenor of the Syndicate for providing all necessary guidance and to Dr. Gopchandran K.G., Member Syndicate for being a model in academics. Adv. K.H. Babujan, Finance Convenor of Syndicate needs to be specially mentioned for always providing constructive landscape for linking university departments to society and economy. Gratitude also to the faculty and students of the Department of Economics who has always stood with me in my academic activities.

Special thanks to reputed health economist and epidemiologist Dr. V. Ramankutty, Emeritus Professor at the Sree Chitra Tirunal Institute for Medical Sciences and Technology who promoted me to embark upon this study on Revisiting the Kerala model of health in the current context. He has also been kind enough to contribute an article in the book. I would like to place on record my indebtedness to all other authors who have spent a considerable part of their research life in examining the area on which they have contributed in this work. Finally, thanks are due to my family members who have always stood with me during all my academic endeavours.

Dr. Manju S.Nair

List of Tables

List of Figures

Part - I
Introduction

1

Introduction and Overview

Manju S. Nair

Since the 1960s, the South Indian state of Kerala has attracted a considerable amount of interest because of its remarkable achievements in enhancing the quality of conventional life indicators. Kerala's Figures on life expectancy, male and female literacy, child mortality, crude death rate etc. are close to those of developed countries and has been attained at much lower costs. Kerala's achievements in health, in spite of its economic backwardness has prompted many analysts to talk about a unique 'Kerala Model of Health' providing 'good health at low cost' worth emulating by other developing parts of the world. The widely acclaimed Kerala's model of health implied that it was possible, at low levels of resources, to achieve, commendable health status. However, over the last few years doubts are raised about the sustainability of Kerala model of health exemplified by the simultaneous presence of the diseases of poverty (infectious diseases) and diseases of affluence (life style diseases), decay in Public Health System, uncontrolled growth of private sector resulting in escalation of health care cost etc. Realising these aspects the government of Kerala has attempted to revamp the health sector through a plethora of intervention programmes to make healthcare in Kerala accessible, affordable and available to all sections of the population. The book on 'Revisiting the Kerala Model of Health' enquires upon the multiple facets of the Model, the challenges in terms of escalating expenditure and increasing morbidity, health status of the marginalized, interventions in terms of new initiatives at the governance and implementation levels, evaluation of attempts at providing food and nutrition security etc. The book consists of fifteen articles aimed at analysing the above said aspects, an overview of which is provided below.

India since independence has achieved much progress in many fields: space exploration, atomic energy, and even agriculture, within this, however, health continues to be a problem area as evidenced by the low rank among nations when ordered by our health indicators. Speaking of Kerala Model in Health, it is not difficult to see the paradox: 'success' of Kerala within the larger narrative of a failure in India. The 'Kerala model' in health has been discussed in a number of scholarly publications since Kerala became a 'model' for the right kind of social policies to be pursued by developing societies, which will ensure balanced, equitable development, and steady improvement in health indices. The article entitled **'The Kerala Model' in Health: A Review of its Current Status'** examines the current status of the model and answers the question whether it is possible to construct a new Kerala 'model' in health care? The article also defines the features of the model that is to be build and elaborates the components that are to be seen in an ideal health sector. The article argues that this new Kerala model in health cannot be built by focusing on the health sector alone; it should ensure there is social security for the poor, protecting them from economic catastrophe. It should also be one where there is employment guarantee, gender equity and controls on exposure to harmful substances in the environment. Above all it should ensure the rights of the people to question the quality of service that they receive from both government and private players.

The paper titled **'Kerala Model of Health: Features, Twin Challenges and New Initiatives'** is an examination of the trajectory of health sector progress in Kerala with implications on two important aspects, morbidity and health care financing and the policy changes adopted off late. The important factors that contributed to the Kerala Model of Health are explored and data authenticating the Model are also examined. The paper confirms that by 1984, doubts were expressed regarding the desirability of Kerala Model of Health. Surveys found that even though mortality is low in Kerala, the prevalence of morbidity is very high. Since the new century, Kerala has to encounter a rising prevalence of non-communicable chronic diseases including diabetes, cancer and cardiovascular problems. Since last decade some communicable diseases like Hepatitis and Typhoid fever have re-emerged and some new epidemics like dengue fever, chikunguinia, H1N1 flue, Nipah has emerged in the state. Mental health problem including higher suicide rates and death due to accidents and injuries are increasing. Kerala has the highest out of pocket expenditure (OOPE) among the states in India due to the spread of unregulated private health providers. Catastrophic health expenditure is reported to be high in Kerala and falling sick is now a major reason for falling into poverty trap. Keralites' health treatment now depends on ability to pay, although with no assurance to quality. This is against a model where people had access to good health facilities whatever be their socio-economic status. Recognising these pertinent issues in association with the Kerala model of health, the Government of Kerala has come up with several programmes to improve the accessibility, affordability and utilisation of health care services to the common man, the most important one being Aardram Mission. The article examines the features of Kerala Model of Health, identifies the twin challenges that have emerged and examines the interventions made to restore the Model. In particular, the article is an examination of the trajectory of health sector progress in Kerala with implications on three important aspects, morbidity, health care financing and the policy changes adopted off late.

Kerala responded to COVID-19 pandemic through a set of systematic interventionist policies and guidelines, because of which the pandemic remained within reasonable control and negative effects being reduced. The article titled **'Kerala's Response to Covid-19 Pandemic: Lessons to Learn'** tries to understand the unique experience of Kerala in handling the pandemic and the internationally celebrated strategies envisioned to effectively minimize its vulnerabilities to the pandemic. The article analyses the trends in the spread of the pandemic, the immediate responses adopted by Kerala to the pandemic and the reasons behind the containment of the pandemic. The unique experience of Kerala can be traced towards the timely, well-planned and active measures taken by the state such as the Break the Chain campaign, contact tracing, reverse quarantine, COVID Brigade and the formation of rapid response team. The efficiency of these measures in containing the disease got boosted by the strong public health foundation and other historical factors that characterize the development path adopted by Kerala.

Section II: Effectiveness of Intervention Policies in Health Sector Governance

Kerala's success in the health front is because of the continued interventions the state has made in the health and allied sectors, learning from experiences and incorporating good governance. The Section examines the implications of interventions in governance by looking into the ground level realities, by collecting primary data on interventions made as part of Aardram Mission, decentralisation initiatives in health sector, state's association with civil society organisations, interventions to regulate drug prices etc. The section on **'Effectiveness of Intervention Policies in Health Sector'** comprises of three articles focusing on the above said aspects.

Kerala, the state that witnessed vivacious civil society activism, exemplifies the narrowing borders between political society and civil society and the impact that associative projects can create in social development, especially in health and educational sectors. Civil society organisations are engaged in health service delivery and health promotion activities, especially in backward areas of the state, as their presence is valuable to deal with vulnerable populations. Being a place of historical and political significance, partly due to its unique geographical location and partly because of the complex and diverse population specific characteristics, Wayanad qualifies to be a suitable terrain to learn various aspects relating to involvement of civil society- state in health and health care system, since the district has the most number of civil society organisations and joint initiatives, yet continue to be the a poor performer with regard to health and health care service delivery. The complexities resulted from the change in structure and nature of state - civil society association over the past three decades are more visible and evident in Wayanad than any other districts in Kerala, and the article titled '**Involvement of Civil Society and State in Health and Health Care System in Wayanad with special focus on Sickle Cell Disease**' tries to explore the dynamics with respect to Sickle Cell Disease, a major public health threat, as far as the district is concerned. The research article looks into the structure, nature and participation of Health Department (Allopathy), Indian System of Medicine (ISM), Swami Vivekananda Medical Mission and Sickle Cell Anaemia Patient's Association in relation to health care service delivery, information exchange, policy setting, monitoring quality of care and resource allocation. The different strategies deployed by both civil society and state including, strategies of co-option, confrontation and selective collaboration are narrated. The article reveals the benefits as well as disadvantages relating to involvement of state and civil society in health system pertaining to sickle cell disease.

Decentralization of health care sector was viewed by experts as a solution to Kerala's health care crisis, since theoretically it enables greater interagency coordination, ability to respond to local needs, discretion to allot more finance and increased accountability of Local Self Government Institutions and Local Health Care Institutions. Grama Panchayats are the lowest tier of the decentralized system which is expected to function effectively to initiate plans and projects that suits the local needs. Regarding health, Grama Panchayats have adequate participatory spaces and institutions where health issues are discussed and programmes are chalked out. Primary Health Centre (PHC) is an important institution through which the health programmes are implemented by the Grama Panchayats. Considering these aspects, the paper entitled **'Decentralised Health Care System at Grama Panchayat Level: An Effectiveness Analysis'** attempts at analyzing the effectiveness of decentralized health care delivery system at the Grama Panchayat level. The main focus of the study is to understand the institutional mechanism under health sector decentralization and to examine the effectiveness of decentralized health care system at Grama Panchayat level. The institutional mechanisms that support the decentralized governance mainly include Grama Sabhas, that holds the credit of being a constitutional assembly that encourages the participation of people in the local governance. Likewise, the committees such as Hospital Management Committee and Health Standing Committee were established with a purpose of providing a democratic platform to the PHI and PRIs to discuss and analyze the issues prevailing in health sector. The article looks into the effectiveness of these institutional mechanism and also evaluates the health sector initiatives undertaken by the Grama Panchayat and the finance devoted for these initiatives. The nature of health programmes and the frequency of implementation, the opinion of beneficiaries and providers were compared to understand the situation. Eight Grama Panchayats were selected for the study, with data collected from beneficiaries and providers.

Government of Kerala has initiated various measures to reduce out of pocket expenditure and improve access to medicine situation in the State. Recognizing the importance of procurement in reducing medicine prices, Kerala formed a centralized procurement agency called Kerala Medical Service Corporation Limited (KMSCL), to procure and distribute medicines for the public health facilities in the State. Additionally, the government constituted Kerala State Drugs and Pharmaceuticals (KSDP) to produce selected medicines locally and thereby increasing availability of medicines in the State. In the initial years of establishment of KSDP, it was the main supplier of medicines to the public health facilities. Later with the constitution of KMSCL, more suppliers came into picture through open tender. Given this context, the article on '**Fair Price Medical Shops in Kerala : An Exploratory Study**' is designed to find answers to some basic questions on the operations of FPMS in retail medicine market setting in Kerala. In particular the paper examines the structural and operational dimensions of FPMS in Kerala, facilities for monitoring of their operations and regional spread. The paper also examines whether there are any significant price differences among the different FPMS in Kerala and also compares the price differences with the prices in the open market. The study covers three FPMSs – Neethi Medical Stores (NMS), Karunya

Community Pharmacies (KCP) and Jan Aushadhi Stores (JAS). Clearly, they make medicines more affordable and are bolstering the affordability component of Access to Medicine. Relevance of FPMS in the retail medicine market is ultimately determined/evaluated by those who purchase from such stores. So, along with various supply side aspects of functioning of the stores, the demand side realities must also be incorporated in a study of FPMS. Understanding the same along with consumer perceptions regarding FPMSs is materialized through household survey regarding the utilisation pattern of FPMS and the determinants.

Section III: Food and Nutrition Security in Kerala

'Food and Nutrition security' exists when all people, at all times, have physical, social and economic access to sufficient, safe and nutritious food to meet their dietary needs and food preferences for an active and healthy life. (FAO, 1996, 2009). Kerala has a universal public distribution coverage which has been instrumental in providing food security to most of its population. In addition, state run Supplyco is mandated to control the prices of 13 essential commodities by distributing it at subsidised prices through its 1406 stores spread across the state. The state has implemented the National Food Security Act in 2018, incorporating several radical changes in assuring accessibility and utilisation. Inspite of the progress achieved in ensuring food and nutrition security to the majority of the population, there has been insecurities reported from the tribal dominant areas of the state in terms of malnourishment and related diseases and deaths. Taking cue from the crisis in the sector, the Government of Kerala has come up with provision of nutrition security through Community Kitchen, as part of the National Rural Livelihood Mission. The session on Food and Nutrition Security in Kerala includes two articles, one evaluating the performance of Community Kitchen in the tribal block of Attappady and the other evaluating the National Food Security Act in Kerala.

The unceasing occurrence of malnourishment and infant deaths in Attappady, Kerala points to the fact that the tribal community in Kerala remained neglected from the developmental process of the state. High infant fatality due to malnutrition in Attappady implies the inefficiencies in the design and operation of the various development programmes meant for the upliftment of tribal community. On this ground, government has implemented Community Kitchen under National Rural Livelihood Mission in 2013, with the objective to ensure food security and nutritional status. Community Kitchen is the only component under NRLM that directly serve food to the beneficiaries. The paper on '**Nutritional Security through**

Community Kitchen: An Analysis Based on National Rural Livelihood Mission in Attappady' tries to analyse the efficiency of Community Kitchen to assure food and nutritional status of tribes in Attappady, Palghat district, Kerala. Data is collected from nine tribal hamlets in Attappady and an efficiency index of Community Kitchen is worked out and an attempt at delineating the factors contributing to efficient performance of Community Kitchen is also done.

The National Food Security Act, 2013 was notified on 10th September, 2013 with the objective to provide for food and nutritional security in human life cycle approach, by ensuring access to adequate quantity of quality food at affordable prices to people to live a life with dignity. Par with the central government, the state of Kerala adopted NFSA in November 2016. Due to its substantial progress in various developmental spheres, Kerala could adopt the policy in a remarkable manner. The new additions of NFSA into the food security policy like, inclusion of bio-metric authentication (ICT), portability of services, Supply Chain Management, door step delivery etc are efficiently implemented in the state. Unlike the national pattern, considering the higher dependency of its population on Public Distribution System (PDS) the state government included non-NFSA beneficiaries also into the food security net. The paper '**Evaluation of National Food Security Act in Kerala, 2013**' in this context, attempts to understand the historical trajectory of NFSA and its features in India along with analysing the effectiveness of NFSA in the state of Kerala. It also tries to examine how PDS infrastructure were made use to respond to the situation of Covid-19 pandemic in Kerala. Five Fair Price Shops (FPSs) from different village/ urban areas in different taluks are randomly selected from eight districts of Kerala. From each village/urban area 15 sample NFSA beneficiary households (10 PH and 5 AAY, total 75 beneficiary households from each district) under single FPS are selected using systematic random sampling method to elicit primary data.

Section IV: Human Development Status/Quality of Life of the marginalised

Kerala model of development has been acknowledged as a situation where it was possible for a state to achieve high levels of human development with inadequate level of resources evidenced by the internationally comparable levels of literacy rate, life expectancy rate, infant mortality rate, maternity mortality rate etc. which Kerala achieved with a growth rate of less than 1.97 percent, 2.87 percent during the 70's and 80's. This phenomenon of low growth and high human development has been documented as human development lopsided in development literature. Of late, Kerala experienced turnaround in her growth rates as evidenced by around 6.12 percent and 8.05 percent growth during the 1990 to 2000 and 2000 to 2015 respectively, along with maintaining high levels in human development indices. The situation of high growth and high human development is reported as virtuous phase in development literature and scholars now examine whether Kerala has moved on to a virtuous cycle pattern. Ample literature exists to the fact that human development indices are averages which tend to under report the relative deprivation of marginalised communities. During the human development lopsided phase, data shows that the status of Scheduled Tribes and Scheduled Castes and fisher folk in human development, particularly regarding health and education was very low compared to the general population, i.e. Kerala model of development has eluded some communities. Human development status/Quality of Life of the earlier eluded population, particularly Scheduled Tribes and Fisherfolk in the seemingly virtuous cycle path needs to be explored. When two or more categories of deprivations intersect, the issues faced by the concerned group is much severe as in the case of Female Headed Tribal Households in Kerala. The Section on **'Human Development Status/Quality of Life of the marginalised'** includes three articles in these areas, each focussing on Particularly Vulnerable Tribal Groups, Fisherfolk and Female Headed Tribal Households.

There are thirty-four tribal categories in Kerala, and the question of whether the development of ST communities in the state across the groups has taken place equitably gains attention: out of the thirty-four categories of ST, five are classified as Particularly Vulnerable Tribal Groups (PVTGs); they are Kadar, Kattunayakan, Koraga, Kurumbar and Cholanaickan. The article **'Human development status of Particularly Vulnerable Tribal Groups and other tribes in Kerala: A Comparative Analysis'** attempts at a comparison of development indicators of these PVTGs with reference to all other tribal groups to understand the relative position of the PVTGs. A brief profile of the five PVTGs, the demographic details, the educational attainments, health status, livelihood levels and gender related aspects of the PVTGs in Kerala is compared with other tribal groups.

The state of Kerala has indisputably the best social indicators of health, education and other standard of living indices. The women in Kerala account for 52 percent of the total population and Kerala is the only state with a positive sex ratio. Considering the physical quality of life indicators such as HDI and empowerment indicators such as the GDI, Kerala is not only better off to other Indian states, but stands steadfastly at par with the developed countries of the world. However, a critique of this experience is often documented in terms of a section of population including tribals being eluded from the development process. The case of Female Headed Households (FHH), particularly FHH within the scheduled tribe population in Kerala has not been subjected to detailed analysis. The paper '**Quality of Life of Females in Female Headed Tribal Households in Kerala'** is an attempt at researching the quality of life of Female Headed Tribal Households in Kerala against Male Headed Tribal Households relying upon primary data collected from 330 Tribal Households in Kerala belonging to four major tribal categories. The analysis of the same proves the comparative deprived position of FHHs to MHHs and provides argument for an inclusive policy that aims to mitigate and empower the tribal population with distinct emphasis on distressed FHHs must be formulated in Kerala.

Kerala, which is situated in the south west corner of Indian peninsula and one of the smallest states in India with an area of 39 thousand square kilometers, has a coastline of 590 kilometers and a continental shelf of 40 thousand square kilometers rich in marine fauna. Fishing has naturally been the major occupation of the inhabitants of its coastal belt from time immemorial. Kerala which occupied the pride of place in fish production in India for long periods in the past, still accounts for a quarter of the country's marine production and fishermen population and one fifth of its fishing fleet. Fishery is of vital importance to the state's economy judged in terms of its contribution to employment, income, foreign exchange earnings and protein intake of its people. In spite of its importance to economy, the fishery sector had been facing severe problems of widespread misery and poverty of the fishermen, erratic and violent fluctuations in output, and exploitative practices by money lenders, and low output prices. Against the central tendency of the Kerala model of development, many studies attempts to plot the fishing communities as outliers and provides explanations for the same. Some of the factors that condition the fishermen communities to be outliers of the Kerala model of development include low incomes in the fisheries sector, poor condition based upon the land holding and housing, poor health condition, illiteracy and low educational attainment. He also explored some of the economic, social, and cultural characteristics specific to fishing communities that have placed restrictions on its members achieving high level of capabilities. The Kerala Development Report of the Planning Commission, Government of India also observed that the fishermen communities in Kerala are the outliers of Kerala model of development. Their standard of living, educational attainment, and per capita income are very low compared to general communities. Besides, the fisher folk communities are facing a lot of socio-economic problems such as poor living condition, poor quality of housing, lack of access to sanitation and drinking water etc. There has been numerous developmental intervention programmes aimed at improving the socio-economic and human development status of the fisher folk and it becomes important to understand how this vulnerable section fare in terms of human development. The article on '**Human Development status of Fisher Folk in Kerala: A Study Based on Rights Based Approach**' aims to understand the human development status of traditional marine fishermen community in Kerala, and a novel methodology based on a rights-based approach to human development is used. The analysis of human rights approach to human development is based on the perception of the people about the aspects of availability, adequacy, accessibility, affordability, possession, quality, and usage and maintenance. The formal process includes components such as availability, adequacy, accessibility, affordability and possession while the effective process includes two components such as quality, and usage and maintenance.

Section V: Economic Burden of Diseases

Illness strikes households on many angles, spanning from the financial to the emotional facets which are often under-estimated. However, the most visible is the economic burden or financial hit. Out of pocket expenditure on health debilities households financially. In addition to the 'direct' financial expenditures that households incur in obtaining the health services and goods that they need; there is also a more 'indirect' set of consequences that may potentially befall on households. Most notable are the losses in production or income which then translate into lost current consumption, and possibly lost future consumption. An important line of enquiry underlying both the direct and indirect costs of disease at the microeconomic level has been articulation of the 'coping strategies' that households utilize in order to mitigate the unwanted consequences of illness, including substitution of labour within the household (to preserve production and income flows) and the disposal of assets (to pay for health care). Another important aspect refers to the impoverishing and consumption impact of disease and injury. In the absence of social security and other forms of formal / informal compensating mechanisms, increased health expenditures and lower productivity capacity can cause or accentuate household poverty and reduce the amount of resources available for non-health consumption, food-items in particular. The Economic Burden of Diseases needs to be explored in depth to initiate policy interventions including financial risk mitigation due to illness and adoption of social security measures. The Section on **'Economic Burden of Diseases'** includes three articles in these areas, focussing on Vector Borne Diseases in Kerala, Chronic Kidney Diseases and Catastrophic Health Care Expenditure due to Non-Communicable Diseases in Kerala.

Vector borne diseases are illnesses caused by infectious microbes transmitted to people by arthropods. They have long impacted human affairs and cause a significant fraction of the global infectious disease burden. In India, many vector borne diseases occur in epidemic form almost on an annual basis and cause considerable morbidity and mortality. The Kerala morbidity scenario has witnessed the staging back of traditional vector borne diseases for the new and emerging diseases. Over the recent years, the vector borne diseases have assumed alarming proportions in the state even making it impossible for the public authority to combat these diseases. Vector borne diseases result in huge morbidity and cause significant economic burden. The estimation of the economic burden imposed by these diseases can be evaluated by the cost of treatment. A number of studies have illustrated that much of the burden of ill health falls on households. The households have to bear the soaring treatment costs of vector borne diseases and this appears as a domain of distress for the economy. The treatment by providers of care and the resulting cost differences exhibit another intriguing aspect of vector borne diseases in the state. The public care system was the preferred provider of care in the state because of its intrinsic characteristics. But of late, Kerala has been manifesting its preference for private provision of care over public care. The malady associated with this trend is that it makes the poor and the marginalised poorer and more marginalised. The need for the development of a robust public health care system becomes inevitable during times of epidemics like vector borne diseases as it only can provide more and better health provisions to the majority of the population at affordable prices. The paper titled **'Vector Borne Diseases in Kerala: An Analysis of Economic Burden at Family Level'** captures the VBD scenario in Kerala with special attention to dengue in Thiruvananthapuram district. The cost difference between public provider of care and private provider of care is apparent from the study.

Catastrophic health care expenditure has been documented as the major cause of impoverishment for people suffering health shocks. The experience of catastrophic healthcare expenditure differs for people belonging to different socio-economic categories. Factors relating to the pre health shock period like being from lower socio-economic status, past financial losses etc., factors relating to the event including diagnosis, expenditure for treatment and hospitalization and post event factors like loss of employment and distress financing determine the magnitude of catastrophe incurred. These factors determine the pathways to catastrophic health care expenditure and consequent poverty. Delving in to the trends of extent and depth of catastrophic health care expenditure over time across different asset groups and quantifying the incidence, intensity, becomes imperative to have a proper understanding of the whole scenario of catastrophic health care expenditure and its impact on living standards. The increasing prevalence of non-communicable diseases in the disease pattern accentuates catastrophic health care expenditure spread over a long period of time. Tracking the pathways to poverty as a result of catastrophic health care expenditure from non-communicable diseases requires evaluation over a span of time which needs micro panel data. This is necessary in order to facilitate an understanding of where and when the different strategies to address catastrophic health care expenditure are to be targeted. Based on this background, the article on **Extend and Depth of Catastrophic Health Care Expenditure due to Non-Communicable Diseases in Kerala** using micro panel data intends to unravel the extent and depth of catastrophic health care expenditure due to two major NCDS in Kerala, accidents/injuries and cardiovascular diseases. Micro panel data from 120 patients is used for the study.

The central issue discussed in the article '**Economic Burden of Chronic Kidney Diseases in Kerala**' is the financial stress resulting from treatment associated with Chronic Kidney Disease. End stage Kidney disease has only two solutions either kidney transplantation or dialysis. To understand the economic implications of Chronic Kidney Disease, the researcher has selected End Stage Renal Disease and the medical solution of the kidney transplant, since this transplant involves cost of economic and non-economic dimensions including finding an available donor whose kidney matches the recipient, identification of hospitals where the surgery can be performed, mobilizing finance for the transplant, complication after the surgery, adjusting the changed situation both for the donor and recipient, follow up activities both medical and non-medical etc. The direct and indirect cost of kidney transplantation associated with Chronic Kidney Disease and the source of financing in relation to kidney transplantation and other costs is estimated. Direct costs are classified into three : Direct cost I - Cost before transplantation which includes the cost of dialysis and lab/scanning charge and Direct cost II - Cost of kidney transplantation split into medical expenditure which includes special package amount cost of drugs, and scanning charge and non-medical expenditure which includes the cost of room rent, cost of food and transplantation charge and Direct cost III - Current expenditure on treatment. Indirect cost comprises of two components: Indirect cost I - It includes the income loss because of illness and Indirect cost II which involves the income loss of the caretaker. Distress Financing for treatment and the different sources of financing is also examined.

Thus, the articles incorporated in the book provides insights into the myriad aspects of the Kerala Model of health, its challenges, the interventions made to revamp the sector in terms of government policies including Aardram Mission, decentralisation, Fair Price Medical Shops, the health and quality of life status of the marginalised, nutritional status and attempts at ensuring nutritional security and also evidence on the economic cost of diseases. The articles call for a New Model of Health in Kerala highlighting the necessity for more policy initiatives and government interventions in the sector. The New Model of health in Kerala should ensure that everyone, whatever be their place in the social ladder should have access to quality health care at affordable prices.

2

The 'Kerala Model' in Health: A Review of its Current Status

V. Raman Kutty

The 'Kerala model' in health

Kerala, China, Costa Rica, Cuba and Sri Lanka, were held up as models of 'good health at low cost', in a famous conference held in Bellagio, Italy in 1985 under the auspices of the Rockefeller foundation (Halstead, Walsh and Warren,1985). This conference gave rise to a series of discussions and papers on why health was achieved at a comparatively low cost in these places, and the echoes of these can still be found in the development literature. The 'Kerala model' became an object of discussion among scholars studying health. The conference emphasized that it is possible, with very low levels of resources, to achieve commendable health status, at least by the measures of mortality and gross morbidity readily available to us, and these were celebrated as examples. It is to be noted that of the regions mentioned, all except Kerala are sovereign nations; Kerala is only a state in a country, India, which, as a nation, by no means stood apart from other underdeveloped countries in the matter of health. A fresh look at 'good health at low cost' after 25 years of the Bellagio conference threw up new models of good health at perhaps relatively low cost (Balabanova, Mills and Conteh,2013). At this time, it was the Indian state of Tamil Nadu which was picked as a model, along with Kyrgistan, Bangladesh, Thailand, and Ethiopia. This is not surprising, since Tamil Nadu shows relatively robust health indices in India and has put up good performances in the health sector in recent years.

The 'Kerala model' in health has been discussed in a number of scholarly publications. Kerala became a 'model' for the right kind of social policies to be pursued by developing societies, which will ensure balanced, equitable development, and steady improvement in health indices. None other than Nobel laureate Amartya Sen remarked on Kerala as an example of development through public action. What he meant was that by emphasizing health and education as areas of public investment, the governments in Kerala had pursued the right policies.

Kerala's health system came into the limelight again during 1996, when it boldly experimented with 'democratic decentralization', the handing over of more power to the local governments, which now control the health and educational institutions. This was hailed as an experiment in participatory government, though there were criticisms as well. With the onset of the Covid-19 pandemic, Kerala and its health care has again come under focus, as a place where the pandemic was held at bay. The pandemic was relatively well handled in the state, especially in the early stages. This achievement has also been hailed as an outcome of the right policies.

Kerala's mortality statistics show a steady improvement through the twentieth century, even before the state was officially born. This is evident in available estimates from records regarding the princely states of Travancore and Cochin which became integrated into the State of Kerala along with the district of Malabar from the erstwhile Madras presidency. This area provided a striking contrast to the rest of India, even as early as the beginning of the twentieth century. The available indicators show a sex ratio in favour of the female, indicating longer survival of women. The decline in mortality which came first, is augmented by a sharp decline in fertility starting around late sixties and early seventies. Census and SRS (Sample Registration System) reports indicate that this decline in mortality followed by decline in fertility is also taking place elsewhere in India, but at a much slower pace. India's southern states have progressed much in this regard, at a faster pace compared to the northern states. This trend represents the 'demographic transition' that happened in Europe, North America and Japan much earlier, along with large scale industrialization, and in China more recently as a result of coercive policies. In Kerala it seems to have happened without the social cost of either disruptive industrialization or coercive government intervention. This is the remarkable aspect of the 'Kerala model' in health.

It is not difficult to see the paradox in this story: 'success' of Kerala within the larger narrative of a failure in India. India since independence has achieved much progress in many fields: space exploration, atomic energy, even agriculture. Within this, however, health continues to be a problem area: we occupy a low rank among nations when ordered by our health indicators.

Criticism of the Kerala model in health is also old. In a book by Panikkar and Soman, titled appropriately 'the paradox of economic backwardness and health development', the authors pointed out that though mortality was low in Kerala, high levels of morbidity prevailed (Panikar and Soman, 1984). This view was very soon corroborated by a statewide study, undertaken by KSSP, a statewide NGO, which showed that reported sickness in Kerala was indeed high. This led to a debate on the meaning and interpretation of morbidity, especially 'perceived' morbidity: it was contented that people perceive sickness differently, and that such a subjective phenomenon cannot be compared. Later, Chen and others pointed out that in Kerala, perhaps owing to the high levels of education, more people may perceive themselves to be sick, compared to other states in India (Murray and Chen, 1992). However, several micro-studies in various districts of Kerala did report a high prevalence of chronic non-communicable diseases like coronary heart disease and diabetes, somewhat substantiating the view that it was not merely a question of perception (Kutty, Balakrishnan, Jayasree and Thomas, 1993); (Kutty, Soman, Joseph, Pisharody and Vijayakumar, 2000)

A number of later studies have focused on the increasing burden of disease in Kerala. Besides heart disease and diabetes, road traffic accidents and their consequences were on the rise, as were suicides. Suicides were the most frequent cause of death among young females, contributing to perhaps one of the highest rates of suicide in young females in the world (Soman, Safraj, Kutty, Vijayakumar and Ajayan, 2009). In causes of death, Kerala resembled more developed parts of the world: about a third of the deaths were attributable to heart disease, and deaths due to infections were only a small proportion (Soman, Kutty, Safraj, Vijayakumar, Rajamohanan and Ajayan, 2011).

Kerala more recently has also witnessed the re-appearance, or even the resurgence, of infectious diseases: epidemics of dengue, chicken-guinea, rat fever and hepatitis became an annual feature in the state. This is attributed to large-scale environmental degradation. Most water sources are polluted, and garbage disposal in urban areas pose a nearly insurmountable problem. This seems to indicate the transition in health was not the result of conscious policy decisions; rather, it occurred as a consequence of societal transformation.

Many micro-level studies point to the high expenditure in health care, which drove many families to debt and financial ruin. However, economic indicators show that by the turn of the millennium, Kerala was no longer a poor state in India. Its per capita GDP was better than the national average. A large proportion of families both in rural and urban areas reported depending on private health care (Kutty, 2000). Data also indicated that Kerala had become one of India's topmost states if we rank them for inequality. In health as in many other things, Kerala had become a 'non-model'.

What is the current status of the Kerala model?

Has Kerala's health become worse in around fifty years? Kerala has a score of 70 out of the possible 100 in the latest report by the NITI- Ayog (2019) of Indian states' performance in achievement of Sustainable Development Goals (SDGs), and occupies the top slot among large states. The SDG report confirms that the state has maintained the path of progress in health, despite many setbacks.

Most early writers on the low mortality and fertility in Kerala attribute the fall in mortality and the fall in fertility to the social and political influences. High levels of women's literacy, general acceptance of schooling across all castes and creeds, a political ecosystem prioritizing equity, with governments ready to intervene strongly in education and health, and a population ready to respond to perceived injustice. Changes in the health system also contributed to improving health status. By 1970's, Kerala had a network of government health institutions in almost all rural areas accessible to all the population. Most national health programs were vigorously implemented. Within no time, fuelled by the demand for medical care created by government health institutions, there was a booming private sector in health care ((Kutty, 2000).

Large- scale privatization of health created a big market in health-related goods and services, often unproven and perhaps unnecessary. Growing international tourism in health and the successful marketing of Ayurvedic 'health promoting' products became part of the story. Many people in the know allege that the diagnostic imaging and clinical laboratory industry thrived through unethical practices such as cutbacks to referring doctors, though this could never be proved. There was no serious attempt by the policy makers in any coalition ruling the states by turn to regulate the health sector, because of various reasons. Thus, the private sector boomed in an environment of lax or non-existent laws, high demand for services, and availability of investible funds. This growth, however, probably contributed only marginally to both quality of life and improvement in health.

While the private sector grew in leaps and bounds, the government health sector suffered. The almost exclusive emphasis on curative care in the state meant that public health functions were neglected, except in the case of the national programmes such as Pulse-Polio initiative, which were more or less directly run according to Central Government norms. The situation led to conditions ripe for outbreaks of infectious epidemics that the state has seen in the last two decades. Public health training of doctors was de-emphasized, medical specialization was over-emphasized, with a health sector dominated by specialists and procedures. There was no systematic attempt at creating a cadre of public health practitioners. This was largely the result of a complete lack of policy leadership on the part of successive governments of the left (the left democratic front, or the LDF) and the right (the united democratic front, or the UDF) who ruled the state by rotation. But Kerala continued to do well at the national level in the health sector, largely due to the woefully inadequate performance of the other states. This was unfortunately accepted by the policy makers and the health system executives as proof of a system that is functioning well.

The exceptional policy initiative

Kerala has initiated one bold policy move that chose to move in a totally untrodden path as far as India was concerned. In 1996, the LDF government in Kerala brought institutions such as primary health centres (PHCs) and community health centres (CHCs) under local governments (LG). The expectation was that this would result in more accountable and efficient running of health institutions and may thus address many of the ills in the system. It also envisaged giving more power in decision making to all citizens residing in their respective LG. This was part of a broader policy of decentralized planning and governance, whereby powers of the state government were passed on to the LSG. This gave rise to a wide range of quality in services offered by these institutions: while some thrived under responsible political management, others suffered from the conflicts between local political leaders and the staff of the health institutions.

The 'metamorphosis' of the model

As we have seen above, the lead that Kerala had in low infant and crude mortality has been maintained in spite of many of these other deviations.

However, it is doubtful whether it could still be called good health 'at low cost': studies point out that Kerala now has one of the highest per capita payments for health and hospitalization (NSSO, 2006). The Kerala 'model' in health is currently dominated by privatized health care, where services of doubtful quality are offered to an unsuspecting public through advertising and other inducements, many of them unethical, purely as a profit- making venture. The public sector in health largely caters to only to the poorer sections of society. The public seems to have lost trust in the health system, both public and private. Medical care is reduced to shopping around for services of doubtful quality, constrained only by one's purse. The Kerala model was once characterized by health security: whatever one's station in life, one had reasonable assurance of the state that one would receive health care. Moreover, the quality of this care did not depend on one's status. In recent times health care availability is dependent on one's ability to pay for it. Though the poor are more likely to get poor quality care, paradoxically, for the rich, the ability to pay does not assure quality.

Partly to address the lack of access to aspirational levels of care for the poor, and partly as a part of the larger health policy shift towards insurance globally and by the central government, the state instituted health insurance coverage for poor families. This started as a state project under the labour department (because of the affiliation of Employees' State Insurance scheme -ESI- with the labour department) and had an upper limit for coverage. The families registered under the scheme were issued with an insurance card that ensured access to care from private as well as public facilities that were empanelled for the purpose. This provided free though limited private care to those who couldn't previously afford it; it also provided a source of revenue for the government facilities, thus offering an option different from the unpopular 'user fees'. These kinds of schemes started up parallel to various states, and in some of the south Indian states, they were touted to be a huge success, as in the case of the Rajeev Arogyasree of Andhra Pradesh and the Vajpai scheme in Karnataka. These schemes turned into vote-gathering efforts for ruling politicians, whereby they could claim that the 'best of private care' has been made available to the poorest.

In Kerala, the government offered an augmented scheme where families on the verge of poverty, though not officially labelled 'Below Poverty Line (BPL)', could also join the scheme with a nominal premium. Very soon other departments of the government started schemes for assistance for catastrophic health events. The scheme started by the finance department was linked to lotteries. All these happened outside the budgetary allocation for health; it becomes more and more difficult to assess the exact expenditure incurred by the government for health. These schemes primarily served the purpose of building up political capital for the initiators.

More recently, the Government of India consolidated various health insurance schemes such as RSBY under the Ayushman Bharat - PMJAY (Pradhan Mantri Jan Arogya Yojana) scheme (Prime Minister's People's Health Scheme). This has a dual purpose: health insurance for catastrophic events and strengthening of primary health care for health promotion. Kerala is also part of this initiative. It is broadly under the objective of universal health coverage (UHC) which was set up as a goal for the country by the health policy of the new government in the policy document of 2017. However, it is to be noted that the earlier 'high level commission' on UHC had recommended that state funding for health be routed through taxes, and not insurance, to prevent the problems of moral hazard in a country with lax regulation.

The shift from a cheaper, but more equal care in the public system accessible to everyone, to highly technologically intensive curative care available to the better off sections, and neglect of universal primary health care, has been the hall mark of the health system in the last 15-20 years in Kerala. It remains to be seen whether the new initiative in line with Central Government Policy and the shift towards insurance will bring in more equity.

Where are we headed?

The present government of Kerala set a high priority on the health sector. It promulgated its health policy early on in the course of its tenure. As part of the 'Nava Kerala Mission' (mission for a new Kerala), it announced several initiatives not only in health, but in education and other service sectors [10]. In health, the 'Ardram' mission envisaged upgrading primary health centres into 'Family Health Centres', with extended facilities and round the clock service, meeting all primary health care needs of the people. The government is dedicated to extending FHCs to all PHC areas. Besides this, several Community Health Centres (CHCs), Taluk Headquarters Hospitals (THQs), and district hospitals (DHs) have seen infrastructure as well as service improvement. Specialty care is available in the public sector at district and sub district levels now.

With the announcement of the PMJAY scheme from the centre, all earlier insurance schemes have been merged with Ayushman Bharath and the state has opted for a mixed mode in insurance (using both private insurers and a government fund for the public sector hospitals, or the 'trust' mode), with the government acting as a gate keeper. More money is channelled into health, with the help of the local governments who can access their own funds. Availability of drugs has improved at the PHC level, and the government has been recruiting manpower in health in spite of several financial set- backs induced by successive years of flood and the onset of the recent pandemic of Covid-19.

Unfortunately for the current government, it had to function at a time of many adversities. First there were unprecedented floods in two successive years, followed by the Covid-19 pandemic. It is to be noted that the state earned encomiums from all over the world for its handling of the pandemic in its early stage. Supportive institutions such as the Kerala Institute of Virology have been set up to improve the capabilities in the public sector to deal with catastrophes and emergencies in health. Recent statistics indicate that there has been a shift of about ten percent in the proportion of population accessing the public sector in preference to the private sector in recent times.

The fall in mortality has almost reached a plateau; achieving further falls in infant mortality, for instance, from the current levels of 10-12, will involve heavy investment in hospital care for very small birth weight infants to see that they survive into adulthood. Likewise, having achieved near universal institutional pregnancy care and delivery, bringing down maternal mortality further involves investment of a high order in complex systems such as ambulances and blood storage and delivery. An increasingly aging population inevitably faces a huge burden of non-communicable diseases, and treatment facilities for these would put more and more stress on the health services. Health is also influenced in a negative way by developments in other sectors: growing traffic congestion, booming consumption of alcohol, environmental damage, and behavioural traits like an increasingly sedentary society are bound to take their toll. These trends indicate that the state will have to substantially increase its spending on health in the public sector.

The renewal of the Kerala model

Is it possible to construct a new Kerala 'model' in health care? To answer this question, we need to define the features of the model that we want to build. What are the components that we would like to see in an ideal health sector? Do we need to ensure that the 'latest' in health technology will be available in the state, albeit at a high cost and only to a few selected by possession of resources? Are we satisfied by 'distributional equality', which ensures that everyone has a chance, within a resource use limit set by the government, to choose any fancy health intervention that he or she (or the doctor) 'wants' (but may not need)?

The health system that I would like to see in Kerala would ensure that everyone, however humble her station in life and wherever she might choose to live, has access to a qualified physician and reasonable range of health care options and medications within easy reach. Such a system would also ensure that should the need arise, even complex high cost medical interventions like a coronary by-pass graft, cochlear implant or cancer therapy would not be beyond the reach of even the poorest; while protecting them from a predatory market to make sure that these same interventions are not thrust on them unnecessarily, driving them to financial desperation.

This new Kerala model in health cannot be built by focusing on the health sector alone; it should ensure there is social security for the poor, protecting them from economic catastrophe. It should also be one where there is employment guarantee, gender equity and controls on exposure to harmful substances in the environment. Above all it should ensure the rights of the people to question the quality of service that they receive from both government and private players.

What shall be the mainstays of such a model? To name a few:

1. Increased funding for health and health care. This has to be spent on improving the primary health care institutions such as the family health centres (FHCs), PHCs, and CHCs, as well as THQH and DH, and to a lesser extent on the medical colleges. The money for this can be raised from taxes, or from cess on certain items according to the families' ability to pay, such as a designated health cess.
2. Building a system of reference. Each family has to be registered with a primary health care provider such as FHC, PHC or a private clinic. There should be a gate-keeping system which guides them to the next level of care.
3. More regulation on hospitals, with accreditation and quality control. The population should be protected from predatory practices
4. Respecting peoples' choice: families should be able to choose the health care provider of their choice, provided they are legitimate and registered.
5. Protection from catastrophic expenditure: there should be state supported insurance for the poor, and compulsory insurance for

the employed, so that they need not fear catastrophic expenditure for health

6. Availability of drugs: Since Kerala has a large number of people suffering from chronic diseases such as cardiovascular disease and diabetes, drug availability in the public sector at fully or partially subsidized rates is crucial in building up their health

Policy makers have to be proactive in building such a health system, and there should be a conscious effort towards it. Kerala has a tough time ahead living up to the image of the 'Kerala model'.

References

1. Balabanova, D., Mills, A., Conteh, L., (2013). Good Health at Low Cost 25 years on: lessons for the future of health systems strengthening. Lancet (London, England), 381(9883), 2118–2133.
2. Halstead, S. B., Walsh, J. A., and Warren, K. S. (1985). Good health at low cost: Proceedings of a conference held at the Bellagio Conference Center. Bellagio, Italy (The Rockefeller Foundation, New York, 1985), 184.
3. Kutty, V. R. (2000). Historical analysis of the development of health care facilities in Kerala State, India. Health policy and planning, 15(1), 103-109.
4. Kutty, V. R., Balakrishnan, K. G., Jayasree, A. K., and Thomas, J. (1993). Prevalence of coronary heart disease in the rural population of Thiruvananthapuram district, Kerala, India. International journal of cardiology, 39(1), 59-70.
5. Kutty, V. R., Soman, C. R., Joseph, A., Pisharody, R., and Vijayakumar, K. (2000). Type 2 diabetes in southern Kerala: variation in prevalence among geographic divisions within a region. National Medical Journal of India, 13(6), 287-292.
6. Murray, C. J., and Chen, L. C. (1992). Understanding morbidity change. The Population and Development Review, 481-503.
7. NSSO. (2006). Morbidity, health care and the condition of the aged. NSS Sixtieth round, January–June 2004 (Report No. 507).
8. Panikar, P. G. K., and Soman, C. R. (1984). Health status of Kerala: the paradox of economic backwardness and health development. Centre for Development Studies, Trivandrum.
9. Soman, C. R., Kutty, V. R., Safraj, S., Vijayakumar, K., Rajamohanan, K., Ajayan, K., and PROLIFE Study Group. (2011). All-cause mortality and cardiovascular mortality in Kerala State of India: results from a 5-year follow-up of 161 942 rural community dwelling adults. Asia Pacific Journal of Public Health, 23(6), 896-903.
10. Soman, C. R., Safraj, S., Kutty, V. R., Vijayakumar, K., and Ajayan, K. (2009). Suicide in South India: a community-based study in Kerala. Indian Journal of Psychiatry, 51(4), 261.

3

Kerala Model of Health – Features, Challenges and the New Interventions

Manju S. Nair

Since the 1960s, the South Indian state of Kerala has attracted a considerable amount of interest because of its remarkable achievements in enhancing the quality of conventional life indicators. Kerala's Figures on life expectancy, male and female literacy, child mortality, crude death rate etc are close to those of developed countries and has been attained at much lower costs. Kerala's achievements in health, in spite of its economic backwardness has prompted many analysts to talk about a unique 'Kerala Model of Health' providing good health at low cost worth emulating by other developing parts of the world. However, by 1984, doubts were expressed regarding the desirability of Kerala Model of Health. Surveys found that even though mortality is low in Kerala, the prevalence of morbidity is very high. Since the new century, Kerala has to encounter a rising prevalence of non-communicable chronic diseases including diabetes, cancer and cardiovascular problems. Since last decade some communicable diseases like Hepatitis and Typhoid fever have re-emerged and some new epidemics like dengue fever, chikunguinia, H1N1 flue, Nipah has emerged in the state. Mental health problem including higher suicide rates and death due to accidents and injuries are increasing. Kerala has the highest out of pocket expenditure (OOPE) among the states in India due to the spread of unregulated private health providers. Catastrophic health expenditure is reported to be high in Kerala and falling sick is now a major reason for falling into poverty trap. Keralites' health treatment now depends on ability to pay, although with no assurance to quality. This is against a model where people had access to good health facilities whatever be their socio-economic status. Recognising these pertinent issues in association with the Kerala model of health, the Government of Kerala has come up with several programmes to improve the accessibility, affordability and utilisation of health care services to the common man, the most important one being Aardram Mission. Against this background, the article examines the features of Kerala Model of Health, identifies the challenges that have emerged and examines the interventions made to restore the Model. In particular, the article is an examination of the trajectory of health sector progress in Kerala with implications on three important aspects, morbidity, health care financing and the policy changes adopted off late.

Section I: Features of the Kerala Model of Health

Kerala can be said to have made the transition from a society with high population growth rate, high crude death rate and high infant mortality rate (IMR) to one with moderate population growth rate, low crude death rate and relatively low infant mortality rate. This 'health development' has been variously heralded as being the result of a great stress on sound development (Nag, 1983), greater social justice (Ratcliff, 1978), a combination of a great emphasis on female education and an improved health care system (Paniker, 1979; Caldwell, 1886; Soman 1992) or the existence of a political elite dedicated to radical reform and redistribution of wealth (Franke and Chasin 1992).

At the time of formation of the Kerala state on 1 November, 1956, the foundation for a medical system accessible to all citizens were already laid. One indicator of the government's commitment to health services provision is the proportion of government expenditure set apart for health. From the time of state's formation, the government's budget allocation for health was considerable. Social sectors mainly comprising health and education accounted for a large share of the government development expenditure. The period from the formation of the state to early 1980s was characterized by great growth and expansion of the government health services. Figures show that the annual compound growth rate of government health expenditure for the period at 13.04 percent outstripping both the annual compound growth rate of total government expenditure at 12.45 percent and the annual compound growth rate of the state domestic product at 9.81 percent. From 1961 to 1986, the state generally expanded its government health facilities. The number of beds and institutions increased sharply.

Progress in Health indicators

The progress that the state has achieved with regard to life expectancy,

IMR, birth rate, death rate and literacy rate etc. is given in Table 3.1. The decadal population growth has declined from 26.3 during 1971-81 to 4.86 during 2001-2011. The literacy rate has also made a steady progress during the period from 60.4 in 1971 to 93.91 in 2011. The crude birth rate has fallen from 31.1 in 1971 to 14.62 in 2017. The progress in life expectancy is also noticeable.

Table 3.1: Progress in health indicators

Indicators	*1971*	*1981*	*1991*	*2001*	*2011*
Population (in crores)	2.13	2.54	2.90	3.18	3.33
Decadal population growth	26.3	19.2	1 4.3	9.42	4.86
Density (population /Km2)	547	655	749	819	859
Sex ratio	1016	1032	1036	1058	1084
Percent Literate	60.4	70.4	89..8	91	93.91
Male	66.6	75.8	93.6	94	96.02
Female	54.3	65.7	86.2	88	91.98
Crude birth rate	31.1	25.6	17.7	18	14.8
Crude death rate	9.0	6.6	6.3	6	7
Total fertility rate	4.1	2.8	1.8	1.8	1.7
Infant mortality rate	58	37	17	14	13
Male life expectancy	NA	65.2	66.8	71	71.04
Female	NA	69.9	72.3	75	76.03

Source: Census of India, Various years.

The comparative performance of Kerala in terms of health indicators can be understood from the data that both India and Kerala had the same level of infant mortality rate at 228 per 10,000 births during 1930-31 which reduced to 7 for Kerala whereas for all India level the rate is high at 32. Regarding birth rate, there has been a fall from 32.3 to 13.9 against the all India Figures of 41.7 and 20 respectively. During 2013-17, the life expectancy of a male Keralite was 4.7 years greater than the all India average and the corresponding difference with respect to females was 7.4 years.

Table 3.2: Infant Mortality Rates in India and Kerala

Year	*India*	*Kerala*
1930-31	228	228
1950-51	148	120
1960-61	138	61
1970-71	120	37
1980-81	110	21

(Contd...)

1990-91	80	11
2000-01	63	12
2010-11	50	14
2011-12	47	13
2012	42	12
2013	40	12
2014	39	12
2015	37	12
2016	34	10
2017	33	10
2018	32	7

Source: Economic Review, (various years), SRS Bulletins (various years)

Table 3.3: Birth Rate in India and Kerala

Year	*India*	*Kerala*
1960-61	41.7	32.3
1970-71	41.2	25.5
1980-81	37.2	20.3
1990-91	32.5	16.0
2000-01	25.8	14.6
2010-11	22.5	14.7
2011-12	22.1	14.8
2012	21.6	14.9
2013	21.4	14.7
2014	21.0	14.8
2015	20.8	14.8
2016	20.4	14.3
2017	20.2	14.2
2018	20	13.9

Source: Economic Review, (various years), SRS Bulletins (various years), RBI (2019) https://m.rbi.org.in/Scripts/PublicationsView.aspx?id=18804

Table 3.4: Life expectancy in India and Kerala

	Kerala		*India*	
Period	*Male*	*Female*	*Male*	*Female*
1960-61	46.17	50.00	43.2	41.3
1970-71	60.62	62.08	50.1	48.5
1980-81	64.70	69.00	55.9	55.5
1990-91	67.50	72.90	59.3	60.0
2000-01	68.23	73.62	61.4	63.6
2010-11	71.4	76.3	63.8	67.3

(Contd...)

2011-12	71.4	76.3	62.6	64.2
2011-15	72.2	78.2	66.9	70.0
2012-16	72.2	77.9	67.4	70.2
2013-17	72.5	77.8	67.8	70.4

Source: Economic Review, (Various Years), RBI (2019),SRS report(various years)

The remarkable fall in birth rates, IMR and progress in life expectancy is attributed to social and political influences; prominent among these were the high levels of literacy among women, general acceptance of schooling without any class caste difference and a political situation suitable to support the rights of the disadvantaged people.

Thus, if we use the general indicators of IMR, birth rates and Life Expectancy, Kerala's achievements remain remarkable, but it is only one dimension of the changing health experience in the state. In many other dimensions, particularly in the provision of 'good health at low cost', Kerala shows tremendous deviations as is discussed below.

Section II: Challenges in Kerala's health Sector

The widely acclaimed Kerala Model of Health started showing a number of disturbing trends from the 1980s. Doubts remain on the one hand about 'good health' as evidenced by the increasing burden of diseases and on the other hand about 'low cost' when Kerala has one of the highest per capita payments for treatment and hospitalisation. Both these aspects are described below.

(a) Increasing burden of diseases

Although mortality is low, morbidity (those suffering from disease) is high in Kerala compared to other states. Hence the Kerala situation was described as 'Low Mortality High Morbidity Syndrome' (Paniker and Soman 1985). This result was further substantiated by a state wide study undertaken by the Kerala Shasthra Sahitya Parishad. After the year 2000, a number of studies focussed on the increasing burden of diseases in Kerala. Kerala is passing through the third stage of epidemiological transition and fourth stage of demographic transition, which results in the dominance of non-communicable life style diseases in its disease pattern. But Kerala's situation is different in that along with the high prevalence of non-communicable diseases, some new communicable diseases have emerged in the state.

Table 3.5: Trends in communicable diseases in Kerala

Years / Diseases	2011		2012		2013		2014		2015		2016		2017		2018		2019	
	Case	*Death*	*Case*	*Death*	*Case*	*Death*	*Case*	*Death*	*Case*	*Death*	*Case*	*Death*	*Case*	*Death*	*Case*	*Death*	*Case*	*Death*
Dengue Fever	1304	10	4056	16	7938	29	2548	13	4114	29	7218	21	21993	165	4090	32	4651	14
Malaria	1993	2	2036	3	1634	0	1751	0	1549	4	1540	3	1194	2	908	0	656	1
Confirmed Chikungunya	81	-	62	-	247	0	264	0	152	0	124	0	54	0	76	0	109	0
Suspected Chikungunya	183	-	81	-	273	0	271	0	175	0	95	0	87	0				
(AES)(Sus.JE)	37	2	41	10	51	6	9	2	29	3	18	6	5	4	28	15	59	5
(JE)	102	8	3	1	2	0	3	2	0	0	1	0	1	0	5	2	11	2
Leptospirosis	944	70	736	18	814	34	1075	43	1098	43	1710	35	1408	80	2079	99	1211	57
Hepatitis – A	4583	10	6305	8	6166	8	2831	6	1980	10	1351	10	988	24	1369	5	1620	7
Hepatitis – B	852	15	1578	22	1107	20	1319	15	1015	16	1085	16	817	7	759	7	828	6
Cholera	18	1	30	2	20	0	8	1	0	0	10	0	8	1	9	0	9	0
Suspected Cholera	125	5	113	3	67	3	13	0	0	0	118	0	10	0	7	0	20	0
Typhoid	2291	2	2849	1	2930	0	1956	0	1772	0	1668	2	314	1	109	0	27	0
ADD	261178	4	357252	8	411819	2	442104	5	467102	4	493973	14	463368	8	540814	12	544027	6
H1N1	210	10											1411	76	823	50	853	45
Fever OP	1843147	-	2301100	11	2922351	23	2655507	29	2676842	26	2641311		3417968	76	2935627	63	2862375	51
Fever IP	84537	-	105529		119998		85959		96189		80049	18	109974		59983		60080	
Scrub Typhus			39	4	68	0	433	6	1149	15	633	3	340	5	400	6	579	14
(HFMD)			115	-	256	0	43	0	176	0	215	0	408	0	222	0		
Lyme Disease					8	1	0	0	0	0	0	0	0	0				
Kysanur Forest Disease					1	0	6	0	102	11	9	0	0	0	0	0	8	2
Diptheria											69	2	79	5	23	1	32	2
Nipah															18	16	1	0
Chicken Pox																	29583	20
HIV AIDS	2160		1909		1740		1750		1494		1438		1299		886			

Source: Data on communicable diseases, Govt.of Kerala (various years) India HIV Estimation, (2017)

Note: ADD (Accute Diarrhoela Disease) Hand Foot and Mouth Disease (HFMD) Acute Encephalitis Syndrome (AES)(Sus.JE) Japanese Encephalitis (JE)

Communicable Diseases

Water borne diseases like diarrheal diseases, Hepatitis and Typhoid fever had become a threat to Kerala's health sector since last decade. Prevalence of diarrhoea increased from 261178 in 2011 to 544027 in 2019. Leptospirosis is another threat that resulted in morbidity and mortality to many people in previous years. Deaths due to leptospirosis had increased from 70 to 99 during the period of 2011 to 2018 and it was 57 in 2019. Despite the measures taken by the state government, diseases like Dengue fever, Malaria, Chikungunia, H1N1 and Japanese Encephalitis are still remaining as seasonal threats. HIV prevalence rate in the state is 0.05 percent (Economic Review, 2019). The estimated number of people living with HIV in Kerala is 22800 and 880 new cases and 750 deaths were reported in 2017. Out of this 0.08 percent are adults. (India's HIV estimation report, 2017). HIV prevalence in adults was 0.08 percentage and PLHIV was 0.228 lakh as per 2017 estimation. AIDS related death reported in Kerala was 0.75 and new HIV infection had 0.88 (per thousand) as on 2017 (India HIV Estimation, 2017).

Non Communicable diseases

Kerala is witnessing a rising incidence of non-communicable diseases (NCDs) and old age diseases. In the age group between 30 and 59, more than 52 percent of death occurs as a result of NCDs. These include cardiovascular diseases, stroke, high blood pressure, cancer etc (Economic Review, 2019).

Studies made by Cardiological society of India show that on an average 110 individuals are dying of cardiovascular diseases daily in the state. Kerala has the highest prevalence of coronary artery diseases in India. (ie. 7.5 in rural areas and 12 percent in urban areas). 52.1 percent of males and 61.4 percent of females in Kerala have a cholesterol level greater than 200 milligrams per decilitre (mg/dl). Kerala has the highest number of diabetic prevalence in India with 27 percent of adult males and 19 percent of the adult female as diabetic. In India it is 15 and 11 percent respectively. The percentage level of patients from Kerala for the diseases hypertension, CVDs, stroke, and common cancers are 2.67, 2.81, 10.12, 1.52, and 6.18 respectively. (Economic Review, 2019). A survey conducted by Achutha Menon Centre for Health Science Studies states that one out of every three individuals in Kerala has hypertension and one out of five has diabetics.

Table 3.6: Non communicable diseases in Kerala

Diseases \ *Years*	*2018*	*2017*	*2016*	*2015*	*2014*
Diabetes	58,174	108,759	31677	25053	29768
Hypertension	107,995	98,362	43350	57121	61973
HTN & DM (Both)	31,140				
CVDs	20,120	2,778	1631	498	1766
Stroke	1,061	730			
Common Cancers*	10,404	589	1030	116	35

Sources: National health profile (various years)

A total adult hypertensive patient in Kerala are 40.6 percent and females are 38.5 against Indian rate of 30.7 and 31.9 percent respectively. Diseases like diabetes and cancer had increased the level of mental stress in the state which resulted in the prevalence of hypertension in Kerala. Cancer shows an ever-increasing trend in recent years; more than 35,000 new cases of cancer are reported annually.

(b) Accidents and Injury

World Health Organisation has termed road accidents as a health problem and has called for zero tolerance for accidents. Within India, Kerala has one of the worst accident records in terms of deaths per vehicle registered (www.morth.in.com).

The incidence of accidents since year 2000 is shown in table below.

Table 3.7: Accident details of Kerala

Year	*Number of accidents*	*Number of persons*			
		Killed	*Seriously injured*	*Minorly injured*	*Total*
2000	37072	2710	19713	29686	55109
2001	38361	2674	20343	2933	52349
2002	38762	2792	21683	27776	52251
2003	39496	2905	23573	25067	51545
2004	41124	3059	25630	25598	54287
2005	42363	3203	27060	24064	54327
2006	41647	3589	27279	22602	53470
2007	39917	3778	26977	21269	52024
2008	37208	3810	25479	17994	47283
2009	35388	3831	24706	16749	45386
2010	35013	3942	25029	15968	44939
2011	35309	3990	25174	15535	44699
2012	23957	2731	17186	9716	29633

(Contd...)

2013	35215	3972	22627	6941	33540
2014	36282	4049	26219	14877	45145
2015	39014	4196	29096	14639	47931
2016	39420	4064	27263	6445	48395
2017	38481	3996	29783	12902	46681
2018	40260	4069	31672	13786	49402
2019	41153	4355	32414	13726	50495

Source: Crime Records Bureau, Police Department, Government of Kerala, Kerala Road Safety Authority (KRSA), Road accidents in India (various years)

Road accidents either take the lives of individuals or make them disabled. In both the cases the debilitating effect on the family in terms of direct costs (loss of income due to death or disability medical expenditure incurred for treatment etc) and indirect cost (caretaker's income loss) and psychological stress is tremendous. Majority of road accident victims are in the age group of 20 to 55, implying that it is the young who lose their productive life because of accidents.

(c) Ageing

Because of the demographic features of the state, from 1961 onwards, the number of aged people in Kerala shows an increasing trend. The proportion of aged in total population had increased from 5.1percent in 1961 to 12.9 percent (12.2 percent of male and 13.7 percent of females in total population). As per the projected Figures, by the year 2021, the proportion of aged people in the population will reach 16 percent and by, 2051, the same will reach 30 percent. Among all age groups, the fastest growing group is the old (66 – 79 years). The oldest old (80 and above) also shows an increasing trend.

Ageing population necessarily involves addressing several health issues as evidenced by the high morbidity rate among this category. The incidence of non-communicable diseases particularly diseases of life style among this group is imposing a challenge to the Kerala health system.

(d) Mental Health

Recent studies of Kerala State Mental Health Authority (KSMHA) show that 4.5 lakh people in Kerala have mental illness like schizophrenia, mood disorder, profound mental retardation and severe personality problems. Social stigmatization of mental patients is also a problem faced by the health care sector in the state. Suicide rate in Kerala is increasing at an alarming rate. In Kerala 0.4 to 0.9 percent of all deaths in the hospitals and

0.3 to 1 percent of all casualty admissions are following suicidal attempt (KSMHA, 2009). The suicide rate in Kerala in 2018 is 23.5 per lakh with an aggregate registered case of 8237. Alcohol and drug related health problems are very high in the state.

Table 3.8: Mental disorder in Kerala

Mental disorder	*Percentage*
Overall prevalence of any mental disorder	11.36
Prevalence of common mental morbidity	11.0
Depressive disorder	2.49
Neurotic and stress related disorder	5.43
Mental and behavioural problems due to psychoactive substance use	10.12
Prevalence of severe mental disorder	0.44
Psychotic disorders	0.19
Bipolar disorder	0.17
Severe depression with psychotic symptoms	0.08
Neurotic and stress-related disordersPhobic anxiety disorders	3.19
Other anxiety disorders	1.62
Panic disorder	0.89
Panic disorder with limited symptoms	0.45
Generalized anxiety disorders	0.28
Obsessive compulsive disorder	2.48
PTSD and adjustment disorder	0.36
Substance use disorders/Alcohol use disorders	4.82
Tobacco use disorders	7.22
Other substance use disorders	0.08

Source: National Mental Health Survey of India Report- 2015-16

Crisis in Kerala's Health Sector – whether low cost?

Kerala's health care system which satisfied the qualification of affordability because of the supremacy of public health services has become unaffordable over the last decade to the majority because of the dominance of the private sector. Health care services even from the public sector were witnessing cost escalation because public sector itself is being subjected to internal privatisation. Patients seeking medical treatment from the public sector were forced to depend on outside sources for medicines and other materials. Also, the laboratory facilities were quite inadequate in the government hospitals and patients have to depend upon private labs for getting investigation done in time (Ekbal, 2006). In addition to this, on the aegis of fiscal crisis the government has been trying to cut down the expenditure incurred for health.

(a) Fiscal crisis in the Government and its effect on health expenditure

Fiscal crisis is referred to as a situation when government expenditure outpaces government revenue by a critical amount leading to policy shifts involving reduction in government expenditure. Kerala state witnessed fiscal crisis during the period from late 1970s to the early 1990. (George K K, 1993). The beginning of 1990s also marked the ushering of new economic policy with focus on more liberalization and privatisation. These factors led to the withdrawal of government from the scenario as an agent to that of a regulator. These policies had ramifications in the health sector by government cutting down its expenditure. The following tables prove the arguments.

Table 3.9: Public Expenditure on Health in Kerala during five year plans

(Rs. Lakh)

Plan period	State's total outlay	Outlay on health	% of health outlay on total outlay
First Plan	3003	192	6.39
Second Plan	8700	874	9.74
Third Plan	17000	1340	7.94
Annual Plan	14437	495	3.43
Forth Plan	25840	1044	4.04
Fifth Plan	56890	1249	2.19
Annual Plan	42870	903	2.11
Seventh Plan	155040	3595	2.32
Annual Plan	210000	5050	2.40
Annual Plan	66020	1700	2.57
Eighth Plan	77500	1955	2.52
Ninth Plan	546000	12000	2.20
Tenth Plan	1610000	30940	3.06
Eleventh Plan	2400000	40840	2.60
Twelfth Plan	404220	96569	3.29
2017-18	2650000	131495	4.96
2018-19	2915000	141930	4.86
2019-20	3061000	140594	4.59

Source: Economic Review, (various years)

A broad picture of the trend of public expenditure on health in Kerala represents the priority given to health sector out of the total plan outlay. Table shows that the percentage of health outlay has not increased after the fourth five year plan. State's total outlay increased by 1346.05 times from the first five year plan to the twelfth five year plan, and it was 1019.31 times in 2019-20 whereas the health outlay increased only by 502.96 times in twelfth five year plan and 732.26 times in 2019-20. The years of new economic reforms have witnessed a stagnation of the percentage share of health outlay around 2.5 percentage of total outlay. From 2017 onwards there is a significant increase in the percent of health sector outlay.

Table 3.10: Allocative Pattern of Health Expenditure in Kerala Budget (Rs in crores)

Year	*Health Expenditure (Rs. Crore)*		
	Revenue	*Capital*	*Total*
1990-91	176.97(97.69)	4.18 (2.31)	181.15
1991-92	186.90 (97.18)	5.42 (2.82)	192.32
1992-93	283.6 (97.43)	7.47 (2.57)	291.07
1993-94	239.27 (96.23)	9.38 (3.77)	248.65
1994-95	285.91(92.96)	18.33 (9.56)	307.57
1995-96	337.56 (94.85)	23.25 (6.53)	355.89
1996-97	368.32 (94.06)	21.38 (5.46)	391.57
1997-98	419.62 (95.15)	29.89 (6.78)	441.00
1998-99	694.86 (95.88)	24.56 (3.39)	724.75
1999-2000	870.36 (97.25)	18.79 (2.10)	894.94
2000-01	837.04 (97.80)	26.77 (3.13)	855.83
2001-02	861.21 (99.22)	26.67 (3.07)	867.98
2002-03	923.11 (97.19)	45.75 (4.82)	949.78
2003-04	954.78 (95.43)	22.68 (2.27)	1000.53
2004-05	1062.06 (97.91)	30.28 (2.79)	1084.68
2005-06	1156.76 (97.70)	58.07 (4.90)	1184.04
2006-07	1168.47 (96.18)	46.34 (3.82)	1214.81
2007-08	1703.51 (92.10)	21.85 (1.18)	1849.65
2008-09	1802.56 (97.58)	44.74 (2.42)	1847.30
2009-10	2008.15 (88.47)	261.68 (11.53)	2269.83
2010-11	2353.69 (91.73)	212.16 (8.27)	2565.84
2011-12	3163.01 (93.82)	208.47 (6.18)	3371.48
2012-13	3709.57 (94.27	225.43 (5.73)	3935.00
2013-14	4419.46 (94.82)	241.51 (5.18)	4660.97
2014-15	4035.10 (95.43)	193.19 (4.57)	4228.29
2015-16	4551.57(95.39)	219.66 (4.61)	4771.24
2016-17	5499.42 (94.11)	344.10 (5.89)	5843.52
2017-18	6504.91 (95.28)	321.17 (4.72)	6826.70

Source: Government of Kerala, Budget documents, National health account cell document 2015-16 to2017-18.

Budget allocation in Kerala divides the expenditure into revenue accounts and capital accounts. Capital account lists mainly the expenditure on buildings and structures which are one time investment. Revenue accounts include all recurring expenditure such as salaries, wages, expenditure on consumables items etc. The trend of government expenditure on health sector according to capital and revenue throws lights on allocative pattern. During the 1980s, capital expenditure was very high and the ratios stood at 19.5 and 14.67 in 1980 and 1985 respectively (Ravi Duggal et. Al., 1992). Figures from 1991 show the declining priority given to capital expenditure.

(b) Dominance of Private sector

The private sector now dominates the health care provision in Kerala with regard to density of beds and employment of personnel. More significantly private hospitals have outpaced government facilities in the provision of sophisticated modalities of diagnosis and therapy (Eqbal, 2006). The growth of this sector is attributed to many factors including rising disposable incomes and lack of barriers to opening a private hospital. The ageing of the population with its concomitant increase in chronic diseases with demand for more hospital care was also exploited by the private sector.

It is known that out of pocket expenditure in private hospital is more than that in a public hospital. As per the NSSO, the out of pocket medical expenditure of hospitalisation is Rs. 5694 crore in a public hospital and Rs. 17889 crore in a private hospital. Kerala is having the highest Monthly Per Capita (MPC) expenses of institutional and non-institutional medical care as per the recent NSSO data (68th round) shown in table.

Table 3.11: Monthly per capita (MPC) expenses of institutional and non-institutional medical care for 2011-12

States	*MPC for medical care in rupee terms*			*MPC for medical care in rupee terms after adjusting for inflation*		
	MPC institutional expenses	*MPC non institutional expenses*	*Total*	*MPC institutional expenses at 2007-08 price*	*MPC non institutional expenses 2007-08 price*	*Total*
Bihar	9.14	40.28	49.42	6.93	30.52	37.45
Chattisgarh	4.35	40.96	45.31	3.30	31.03	34.33
Gujarat	48.04	49.27	97.31	36.40	37.33	73.73
Hariyana	20.42	68.99	89.41	15.47	52.27	67.74
Himachal Pradesh	27.53	73.87	101.4	20.86	55.97	76.83
Jharkhand	1.89	30.95	32.84	1.43	23.45	24.88
Kerala	96.65	148.12	244.77	73.23	112.23	185.46
Punjab	23.26	132.27	155.53	17.62	100.22	117.84
Uttar Pradesh	22.1	69.74	91.84	16.74	52.84	69.58
Uttrakhand	4.41	49	53.41	3.34	37.13	40.47
West Bengal	16.13	68.94	85.07	12.22	52.23	64.45

Source: Rajesh Kumar Sinha and Keya Chatterjee (2014) International Journal of Humanities and Social Science Vol. 4 No. 5

Table 3.11 shows that, both the institutional and non institutional expenses have been tremendously high in Kerala both at current prices and at 2007-08 prices. Kerala has Rs 244.77 as the monthly per capita health expenditure at current prices and Rs 185.46 as the monthly per capita health expenditure at real prices. Punjab stands second to Kerala in health expenses both at current and constant prices. Keralites on an average spend Rs. 89.24 more than Punjabis in money terms and Rs. 67.62 more in real terms as health expenses. The average medical expense during hospital stay in private hospital is Rs. 28775 whereas it is Rs. 4469 in public hospitals as per NSSO 75th round. (Table 3.12)

Table 3.12: Average medical expenditure incurred for treatment during stay at hospital per case of hospitalization, by state/UT, separately for public and private hospitals in each sector

State/UT	*Average medical expenses (Rs.) during hospital stay per case of hospitalization in*								
	public hospitals			*private hospitals*			*all (incl. NGO, trust-run)*		
	R	*U*	*R+U*	*R*	*U*	*R+U*	*R*	*U*	*R+U*
Andhra Pradesh	1453	1208	1358	22415	32847	25692	16717	22479	18665
Arunachal Pradesh	3793	4810	3952	13966	23497	15469	4504	6092	4754
Assam	4545	7842	4991	28785	71657	44204	9826	38935	15661
Bihar	4064	4027	4061	16479	25052	17518	11595	17861	12298
Chhattisgarh	3303	4618	3537	65288	28151	51622	26123	19873	24521
Delhi	3378	2217	2285	27868	64075	63500	6797	25896	25094
Goa	1818	3466	2894	41351	35512	36199	7765	16742	14333
Gujarat	1151	3529	1936	25027	29281	27361	14924	22418	18530
Haryana	7242	7215	7236	26346	34109	29458	19177	30337	23107
Himachal Pradesh	12797	12738	12792	37797	36003	37639	20308	17791	20098
Jammu & Kashmir	4720	9203	5714	50043	39718	43098	6371	15678	8789
Jharkhand	3971	15699	8147	28229	33058	30353	17288	26055	20741
Karnataka	3445	4195	3624	17085	31462	23149	12768	26575	17900
Kerala	4395	4589	4469	25949	32746	28775	17054	22123	19109
Madhya Pradesh	2093	2030	2073	25086	31094	27037	14325	17365	15278
Maharashtra	5606	7189	6177	23821	42540	32566	19383	36612	27096
Manipur	5932	9051	6944	60361	39541	49784	14170	17505	15366
Meghalaya	1894	7668	2385	14870	35687	27375	2790	22711	6041
Mizoram	5622	7528	6415	19558	47740	39578	7260	17371	12109
Nagaland	4648	5089	4748	13098	19699	16953	6020	12109	7978
Odisha	5098	6698	5283	29974	33935	30947	11159	18748	12295
Punjab	15093	10293	13277	40303	37502	39208	31805	29338	30869
Rajasthan	7332	6707	7174	25788	35228	28226	16268	20824	17435
Sikkim	3339	2915	3266	24805	19168	23201	7180	7703	7282
Tamil Nadu	520	433	485	28412	41566	35581	12362	23260	17570
Telangana	1278	6922	3367	26019	35191	30336	19887	30082	24471
Tripura	3314	6077	3752	64017	67139	65326	5161	13400	6574
Uttarakhand	2774	22376	7372	25502	41647	32372	15945	37038	23421

(Contd...)

Uttar Pradesh	6914	10239	7765	29768	40706	33071	23144	33339	26089
West Bengal	2726	3954	3061	45023	57549	50380	13310	25235	17141
A & N Islands	39	228	98	106015	107038	106800	7316	36642	18686
Chandigarh	9061	23819	23585	126090	120145	120165	19777	55286	54870
Dadra & Nagar Haveli	103	424	230	7224	17081	16449	474	9599	5769
Daman & Diu	270	34	137	43206	24012	27143	26479	20702	21949
Lakshadweep	512	175	287	40943	41432	41347	7940	12984	11380
Puducherry	216	2668	1516	27246	71865	60818	5354	29453	19804
All-India	**4290**	**4837**	**4452**	**27347**	**38822**	**31845**	**16676**	**26475**	**20135**

*excluding hospitalization for childbirth

Source: NSO 75th Round report on Key Indicators of Social Consumption in India-Health (2018)

(c) Catastrophic Health Expenditure

Catastrophic Health Care Expenditure is concerned with high levels of out of pocket health expenditure which might affect household's standard of living. In literature, catastrophic expenditure is defined as that level of out of pocket health expenditure which exceeds some fixed proportion of household capacity to pay. Xu et.al.(2003) defines household's capacity to pay as income after accounting for median level of food consumption in society, in actual practice capacity to pay is treated equal to non food expenditure. Details regarding health expenses as percentage of total expenses and non food expenses are provided in table as per the recent NSSO round.

Table 3.13: Percentage of MPC expenses of institutional and non-institutional medical care to total MPC expenses and total MPC non food expenses

States	*Percentage of MPC institutional expenses to total MPC expenses*	*Percentage of MPC non-institutional expenses to total MPC expenses*	*Percentage of medical expenses to total MPC expenses*	*Percentage of MPC institutional expenses to total MPC non-food expenses*	*Percentage of MPC non-institutional expenses to total MPC non-food expenses*	*Percentage of medical expenses to total MPC non food expenses*
Bihar	0.91	4.01	4.92	1.90	8.39	10.29
Chattisgarh	0.49	4.65	5.14	0.97	9.17	10.14
Gujarat	3.29	3.37	6.66	6.43	6.60	13.03
Hariyana	1.09	3.67	4.76	2.21	7.48	9.69
Himachal Pradesh	1.48	3.97	5.45	2.57	6.88	9.45
Jharkhand	0.21	3.45	3.66	0.47	7.67	8.14
Kerala	3.85	5.90	9.75	5.96	9.14	15.1
Punjab	1.12	6.37	7.49	1.97	11.19	13.16
Uttar Pradesh	2.11	6.66	8.77	4.28	13.51	17.79
Uttrakhand	0.28	3.15	3.43	0.54	5.99	6.53
West Bengal	1.41	6.03	7.44	3.21	13.70	16.91

Source: Rajesh Kumar Sinha and Keya Chatterjee (2014) International Journal of Humanities and Social Science Vol. 4, No. 5.

It is seen that percentage of expenses for medical care is highest in Kerala among the Indian states, it is as high as 9.75 percent. Within the total medical care expenses, the proportion spend as percentage of MPC institutional expenses is highest in Kerala. This is because of the dominance of private sector in providing medical care. Health expenditure is said to be catastrophic if it exceeds 10 percent of the total non food expenditure. Kerala has a very high percentage of non food expenditure (15.1 percent) being spent on medical expenses. This is catastrophic for resource poor families, and increases the risk of impoverishment due to health expenses.

Thus, the widely accepted Kerala model of health started deteriorating for the last two decades with respect to morbidity trends reflected in increasing incidence of communicable and non-communicable diseases and also with respect to increased health care expenditure, particularly out of pocket health expenditure. Realising these issues, the Government of Kerala decided to revamp the health sector as part of the Nava Kerala Mission, the details of which is elaborated below.

Revamping the Kerala Health System

In order to navigate through the multiple challenges faced in the health sector and to reassess the role of the Government in the sector, the Government of Kerala articulated the policy framework under which all the stakeholders can develop their strategies. A recent development in Kerala which facilitate a more active role for Government is the transfer of more powers to the local councils at the panchayat and district level, with the recognition that health is one area where such local control can work most effectively. The Government took efforts to keep on the mantle of the guardian of quality maintenance and standards in health care, catering to the needs of the people irrespective of their social or economic background. It is done by framing stringent policies and by concentrating on providing top quality care at both public and private institutions. The state government takes the lead in setting priorities which ensure that the goal 'good health based on social justice and equity' are met.

Initiatives to Strengthen Kerala's Public Health Care System

The major initiatives to strengthen Kerala's Public Health Care System include introduction of Aardram Mission, Clinical Establishment Act and E-Health Project, schemes for Health Care for the Differently Abled and the programmes under Care for Everyone.

Aardram Mission

Aardram, an initiative taken up by the state on a mission mode, aims at creating "People Friendly" health delivery system. The mission follows need based approach and aims at treating every patient with dignity. The Government is committed to deliver people-friendly public health care system by making quality specialist health care facilities accessible to the poorest of the poor. Aardram Mission is implemented in three stages in Government Medical College hospitals, District hospitals and Taluk hospitals, and PHCs. It envisages restructuring the public health system by transforming all PHCs into FHCs as a first level health delivery point so that Government hospitals are equipped to deliver optimum level of care. Through providing better primary care facilities and hassle-free administration at the secondary and tertiary care levels, the hospitals are equipped as better out patient service providers. Thus the Government aims at making quality improvement at public health care institutions at primary, secondary and tertiary level of care, raising both human and financial resources in health sector, addressing inequity in health care provision, strengthening and refining PHCs, and improving the efficiency of services and facilities in Government hospitals with a view to extend treatment at a reasonable cost, time and satisfaction.

Clinical Establishment Act

The object of the Act is to provide for the registration and regulation of clinical establishments with a view to prescribing minimum standards of facilities and services provided by such establishments. The act will assist in the generation of a reliable and comprehensive database of all Clinical Establishments in the state. This will enable curtailing of unhealthy practices visible in the private health care provision in the state.

Health Care for the Differently Abled

Projects are implemented to assist the differently- abled population of the state. Paediatricians are given special training to detect mental health problems in children, if any, at an early stage of childhood. Anganwadis for children in need is already in effect in Calicut, Kannur, Kasargode and Wayanad. Starting special centres in all medical colleges for autistic children is also under the consideration of the government.

E-Health project

The e-Health programme envisages to create an effective IT-enabled integrated framework to ensure effectual health care delivery model that will ensure that every citizen is connected and a centralized database of healthcare information is created.

In addition to this the Health Policy adopted by the state of Kerala 2019 aims to increase state government expenditure on healthcare from the current 0.6% of the Gross State Domestic Product to at least 5%, by increasing it by 1% every year. The policy also includes measures to curb treatment expenses, improve human resources in the health sector and policies to control spread of communicable and non-communicable diseases and also addressing the issues of the tribals, children and marginalised section of Kerala population.

Section IV: Conclusion

Kerala is widely recognized for her particular pattern of development experience in health sector which reflected in high attainments of general indices of mortality and fertility even in the context of low resources. Hence Kerala was held up to the world as a model of 'good health at low cost'. But the sustainability of this model became questioned form the 1990's when government withdrew from this sector, opening up the way for the dominance of private sector. Since the beginning of this century, the burden of diseases, both communicable and non-communicable has been increasing at an alarming rate in Kerala due to a host of problems including environmental degradation, sanitation failures, life style changes etc. Chronic diseases including diabetes, cardiovascular diseases, cancers, hypertension etc is on an increasing prevalence rate in Kerala. Many communicable diseases have re-emerged and some new diseases like Dengue fever, chikunguinia have emerged in the state. Suicide rates and road traffic accidents are also highest in Kerala.

Given the above scenario, the existence of good health in Kerala has become a misconception. To avail treatment, majority of Keralites now increasingly depend on private health care facilities where the out of pocket health expenditure is very high. Health expenses have become catastrophic and people are being pushed into poverty. The Government of Kerala has recognised these issues and come with a series of policy changes and programmes to make health care affordable, accessible and available to all section of the population.

References

1. Cald Well, J.C (1986), 'Route to Low Mortality in Poor Countries', Population and Development Review, Vol: 12. P-171-220.
2. Clifton D' Rozario, (2013), 'Deaths of unnamed children: Malnutrition and Destitution among Adivasis in Kerala' accessed online at www.righttofoodindia.org
3. Ekbal, B. (2006), 'Kerala's Health sector: Crying for Cure', Kerala Calling, May 2006, pp 37-39.
4. Franke R, Chasin B (1992, 'Kerala state, India, radical reforms as development', International Journal of Health Services 22:139-156.
5. George, K.K. (1993), Limits to Kerala Model of Development: An Analysis of Fiscal Crisis and its Implications. Centre for Development Studies, Monograph series.
6. Government of Kerala (2011), Working Group Report on Medical and Public Health, State Planning Board.
7. Nag, Moni, (1983), 'Impact of social and economic development on mortality: Comparative study of Kerala and West Bengal', Economic and Political Weekly, Vol. 18.
8. Panikar, PGK (1979), 'Resources Not the Constraint on Health Improvement', Economic and Political Weekly, Vol 14, No.4.
9. Paniker, PGK and Soman, CR (1984), 'Health Status of Kerala: Paradox of Economic Backwardness and Health Development, Centre for Development Studies.
10. Rajesh Kumar Sinha, and Keya Chatterjee, (2014) 'Assessing Impact of India's National Health Insurance Scheme (RSBY): Is There Any Evidence of Increased Health Care Utilisation?' International Journal of Humanities and Social Science Vol. 4 No. 5.
11. Ratcliff, JW (1978), Social justice and the demographic transition: lessons from India's Kerala State. International Journal of Health Service, Vol. 8.
12. Ravi Duggal, S. Nandraj, S. Shetty, (1992), State Sector Health Experiences: A Database; All India and the States, 1951-85, FRCH, Bombay.
13. Soman CR. (1992), 'Nutrition and health development- Lessons from Kerala'. Proceedings of the Nutrition Society, Vol.51: 81-92.
14. Xu, Ke, et al (2003), 'Household Catastrophic Health Expenditure: A Multi-country Analysis', The Lancet, Vol 362, July 12
15. websites
16. www.ksmha.org
17. www.morth.in.com

4

Kerala's Response to COVID-19 Pandemic: Lessons to Learn

Kavya Nair P.J. & Santhosh Kumar S.S.

Introduction

Kerala immediately responded to its first case of COVID-19 reported as early as 30th January 2020 through a set of systematic interventionist policies and guidelines. Persons who returned from hotspots were identified, their contacts tracked and quarantined to prevent the spread of the pandemic. This timely action delayed the fatal outbreak of the disease in the state and helped it to contain the spread of the pandemic till the end of June 2020.

Later, facing demands to bring back Keralites stranded in COVID hotspots within and outside the country, Kerala expressed its willingness to embrace those wishing to return to their home state and with the massive inflow of Non- Resident Keralites there occurred an increase in the number of positive cases, although at a controlled rate till August 2020. With the repeal of the lock down and opening up of the economy, there occurred a massive spike in the cases during September and October 2020. By November and December, the transmission rate shows lower progression and the test positivity rate also has declined to become below 10 percent. During all these phases the case fatality rate remained less than that of the national average at 0.36 percent.

Kerala with its vulnerabilities at multiple fronts should have been the worst affected by COVID pandemic and its success in managing the crisis without clogging its health sector can be traced to many factors. These include the path of development chosen by Kerala over the years, strengthened resilience gained through the proper understanding of lessons learnt from previous disasters and visionary measures adopted right from the outbreak of COVID -19 in Wuhan to prepare the state machinery to face the inevitable but unknown crisis. The article, against this backdrop, tries to understand the unique experience of Kerala in handling the pandemic and the internationally celebrated strategies it envisioned to reduce the associated vulnerabilities. The study relies on secondary data retrieved from government websites, newspaper articles, journals and relevant government documents. The data is systematically collected to analyze the experience of Kerala in tackling COVID-19. Section I details with trends in the spread of the pandemic in terms of active, recovered, confirmed cases and the number of deaths ever since its first reporting in the state. Section II examines the reasons behind the containment of the pandemic – the historical factors are looked into in this section and Section III assesses the immediate responses adopted by Kerala to the pandemic and the final Section concludes the study.

Section 1: Trends in the spread of Covid-19 in Kerala

	30-01	20-02	31-03	30-04	31-05	30-06	31-07	31-08	30-09	31-10	25-11
CUMULATIVE SUMMARY OF COVID-19 CASES IN KERALA (30/01/2020 - 25/11/2020) RECOVERED	0	3	24	383	590	2304	13023	51542	128224	340324	511008
CUMULATIVE SUMMARY OF COVID-19 CASES IN KERALA (30/01/2020 - 25/11/2020) ACTIVE CASES	1	0	215	111	670	2112	10495	23488	67061	91190	65107
CUMULATIVE SUMMARY OF COVID-19 CASES IN KERALA (30/01/2020 - 25/11/2020) CONFIRMED	1	3	241	497	1269	4442	23613	75385	196106	433105	578363
CUMULATIVE SUMMARY OF COVID-19 CASES IN KERALA (30/01/2020 - 25/11/2020) DEATHS	0	0	2	3	9	24	73	294	742	1484	2121

Source: Directorate of Health Services, Government of Kerala.

Figure 4.1: Cumulative Summary of COVID -19 Cases in Kerala

From January 2020, since the outbreak of the pandemic in Wuhan region of China, Kerala started its preparations to handle a possible outbreak. The Government declared a health emergency, as soon as cases from Wuhan were reported. The State Emergency Operations Centre (SEOC) and the office of Kerala State Disaster Management Authority provided support to the Health Department for response and mitigation efforts which enabled an early response mechanism. The standard operating procedures issued by the state covered such areas as infection prevention and control for ambulances, management of biomedical waste, handling the spill of body fluids, disinfection and sterilization, hand washing, management of dead bodies, use of personal protection equipment, sample collection and transportation. A set of consolidated guidelines covering testing, quarantine, hospital admissions, treatment and discharge was also issued and revised often to accommodate changes in perception and strategies (Thomas Issac, and Sadanandan, 2020)

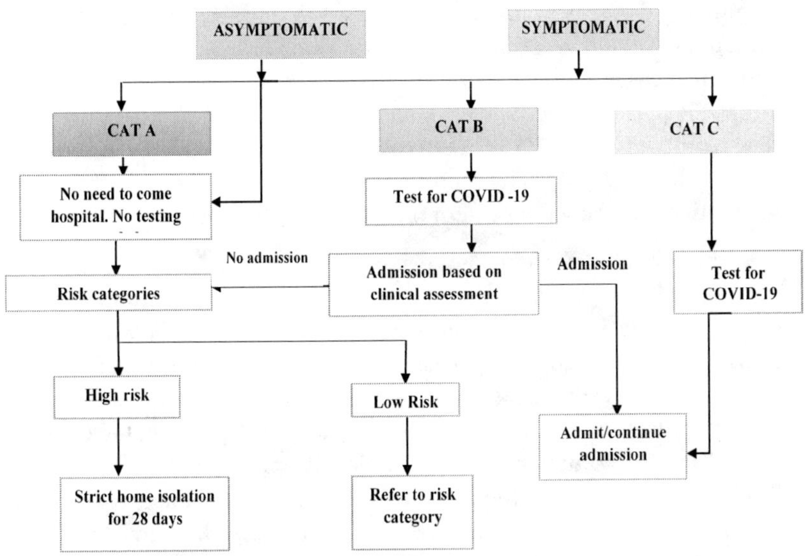

Source: Directorate of Health Service, Government of Kerala

Figure 4.2: Protocols for Examination and Surveillance of People Returning from COVID -19- hit Countries

Every symptomatic patient were tested and the contacts of those found positive were placed under observation. The people arriving from hotspots were thus quarantined and placed under observation. The scale of the exercise is visible as the persons under observation went up to around 1,71,355 persons during April, 2020.

By April, the number of positive cases fell with high recovery rate. On 13th April, reported recoveries surpassed active cases. As of 14th April 2020, the total number of COVID-19 cases in the country crossed 10,000 mark and the death toll reached 325; Kerala saw only around 378 positive cases with high rates of recovery and low fatality rate. Kerala, thus managed to flatten the curve of COVID-19 infections at a time when US, Italy, UK and other developed and emerging economies with sophisticated health infrastructure remained clueless on how to reduce the momentum of the pandemic. On 1st May 2020, Kerala has the lowest case fatality rate of 0.8 percent and highest recovery rate at 78.71 percent whereas for India, the case fatality rate was 3.23 percent and recovery rate was very low at 26.52 percent.

The easing of national lockdown measures coupled with the return of migrants from COVID hotspots in Europe, Iran and Gulf Cooperation countries and other regions of India gave way to the second phase of sporadic spread. Following surge in return migrants towards Kerala, the number of confirmed cases which was around 16 on May 8th increased to 26 on May 14, the highest number since March end. By July 2020, the active cases rose rapidly to 10,495, confirmed cases to 23,613 and deaths to 73. Kerala strictly enforced post-arrival protocols as well as made the 14-day home quarantine mandatory for return migrants and their primary contacts.

The spread of the virus got centered around some clusters during the third stage with super spreading being reported from Poonthura which is a coastal village in Thiruvananthapuram where the crisis was managed through strict containment measures. The health authorities focused on control and prevention measures on the active clusters along the coastal areas in Thiruvananthapuram, Ernakulam and Malappuram. On October 2 2020, Kerala recorded the highest single day spike of 9,258 positive cases forcing the government to prohibit assembly of more than five people to control the spread of the virus. By October 2020, the number of active cases were 91190, the total confirmed cases were 4,33,105 and the reported number of deaths were 1484. The festival season can also be seen as a reason for this spike in numbers.

As of now, Kerala is in the fourth stage of transmission, the state manages to have high recovery rate, low death rate and slow progression of COVID-19 cases in the country. In Kerala, when over four lakh COVID-19 cases were reported around 3,25,166 persons have recovered. During

November 2020, the State's weekly increase in cases dipped by 5 percent, the cumulative case doubling period increased to 40 days, and the case fatality rate remains at 0.34 percent ; much lower than the national average of 1.49 percent. At the current growth rate, the case graph had hit a plateau and it would take weeks for the State's active case pool to cross the one lakh mark. The test positivity rate has started to decline and has fallen below 10 percent for the first time in months to touch 9.68 percent on November 12, 2020.

Active surveillance, setting up of district control rooms for monitoring, capacity-building of frontline health workers, risk communication, strong community engagement, addressing the psychosocial needs of the vulnerable population, social security measures to safeguard the population and those adversely affected by the lockdown restrictions helped to keep the disease under control. Samples were taken from high-risk groups like health care workers as part of the sentinel surveillance in all 14 districts in the state to check the prevalence of a disease in a community or population. True NAAT and CB NAAT (Xpert-SARS-CoV testing) has been initiated in eight government institutions and nine private institutions for testing samples for patients undergoing an emergency surgery, symptomatic health workers, sick patients or COVID suspected death (WHO, 2020). Thus, Kerala has experienced a special case where it managed to flatten the curve during the first wave, witnessed a surge in the number of cases following the opening up of Indian economy and the easing of travel restrictions and finally has reached the stage of gradual dip in the number of reported cases.

Section 2: Pandemic Containment in Kerala: Reaping the benefits of a strong Foundation

Kerala's experience of development has been termed in literature as 'Kerala Model of Development' with focus on social sector-oriented policies, even without adequate resources. Also, Kerala has been very enthusiastic in adopting several policies which had its direct effect on improving the health and education status of the population, examples being Decentralised system of Governance, Poverty Eradication Mission titled Kudumbashree etc. This section examines the historical factors contributing to a strong foundation in Kerala which played a role in the reasonable containment of the pandemic.

Impressive Human Development Indicators

Kerala's rating of HDI of 0.790 is the highest in India which speaks volumes about its impressive performance in the quality of life indicators. Kerala has a very high literacy rate of 94 percent here female literacy is as high as 92 percent. High literacy rate especially female literacy plays an important role in utilization of health services. Thus, there is always demand for better health services by people which lead to more investment in the health infrastructure of the state.

Strong Public Health System

The strong foundation of public health system has a historical trajectory right from the establishment of first public dispensary in 1819 by Maharaja of Travancore which has made a continuous progression throughout his rule towards establishment of state. Even, after establishment of the state of Kerala, public funding for health and education has received considerable attention. Over years, Kerala has developed a strong healthcare foundation and network at local level which has helped in the war against COVID-19. This foundation is spread across three tier health structure with Primary Health Centres, Community Health Centres and District Hospitals. The state also has general hospitals and Medical Colleges which provide tertiary health care services. Primary Health Centers (PHCs) are institutions providing comprehensive primary care services while Community Health Centers (CHCs) and taluk level institutions form the basic secondary care institutions. District hospitals, general hospitals and maternity hospitals provide specialty services and some super specialty services. There are 1,286 health institutions with 38,018 beds and 5,510 doctors under Health Services Department consisting of 568 PHCs, 114 (24*7) PHCs, 170 FHCs, 224 CHCs, 86 taluk headquarters hospitals, 18 District hospitals, 18 general hospitals 3 mental health hospitals, 8 women and children hospitals, 3 leprosy hospitals, 18 TB clinics, 5 other specialty hospitals and 51 other hospitals (Kerala Economic Review, 2019). Kerala has the largest public health system consisting of 6,000 doctors, 9,000 nurses and another 15,000 health workers. The13th Five Year Plan, focus on the implementation of the specialty cadre in all health care institutions up to the level of community health centres and modernisation of the functioning of the PHCs as FHCs. The bed population ratio is 880 and the average doctor bed ratio is 6.9. This data substantiates the strong foundation Kerala has in its public health system against the national scenario.

Aardram Mission

Aardram Mission has the objective to completely transform the public health sector in the backdrop of the Sustainable Development Goals 2030 of UN; the Mission focuses on SDG three – 'Good Health and Well-being'.

The main objectives of Mission Aardram are a) People friendly outpatient services b) Re-engineering Primary Health Centres into Family Halth Centres c) Access to comprehensive health services for the marginalized/ vulnerable population and d) standardization of services from primary care settings to tertiary settings. The Mission focuses on preventive, promotive and rehabilitative health care interventions for all family members in a household. For this programmes has been launched to make Government hospitals people-friendly by improving their basic infrastructure and services. This ensures minimal waiting time for outpatient medical checkup and other investigation facilities, adequate attention to inpatient services and providing quality health care at reasonable cost, time and satisfaction. Aardram Mission is being implemented in three stages in Government medical college hospitals, District and taluk hospitals and Primary Health Centres (PHCs). The percentage of persons using government facilities increased from 34 percent in the 71st round of National Sample Survey Office (NSSO) in 2014 to 48 percent in the 75th round in 2017-18 is a testimony to the efficiency of the public health system in the state.

Decentralized Governance

The first phase of decentralized planning was initiated in Kerala during the 9th Five Year Plan. This led to devolution of 30 percent- 35 percent of state's development budget to local government and brought the primary and secondary health care under the purview of local government. Kerala's People's Plan Campaign created strong accountability, better facilities and service delivery through Primary health centers. The government has empowered the local self-government as the agency to prepare the local-level disaster management plan. Local government coordinates a volunteer force (one volunteer for 100 people) for disaster management. This involvement of local government in primary health care got a boost through Aardram mission. They are involved in the maintenance of health infrastructure, personnel, palliative care as well as prevention of infectious diseases. Their involvement strengthened the Break the Chain campaign, community kitchens and ensuring welfare of people under isolation as well as migrant labourers.

Kudumbashree

Kudumbashree, the State Poverty Eradication Mission is an innovative, women based, participatory poverty alleviation programme launched by Government of Kerala in 1998 with a special focus on women empowerment and has the participation of 43.93 lakh women. Neighbourhood Groups

(NHGs) are the primary units of the Kudumbashree community organization and the activities are done in close partnership with local government. With a vast network across states, Kudumbhashree imparts a strong sense of citizen centric governance and community based action at local level. Kudumbhashree has done a remarkable job in the management of community kitchens and in the popularization of the break the chain campaign. Many of the initiatives undertaken during the pandemic to protect the livelihood of the population has been done under the auspices of Kudambasree.

The Nipah Virus: A Dress Rehersal for COVID

Following the Nipah Virus experience, the government put various measures and protocols in place to ensure better preparedness in the event of a similar crisis in future. During the Nipah outbreak in Kozhikode and Malappuram, over 2000 people were quarantined and kept under observation. Malaysia witnessed the first known global case of the virus. Kerala requested a medical advisory from the Malaysian Health Department and set up The Institute of Advanced Virology and a temporary ban was placed on all social gatherings and interactions. The outbreak was effectively contained within less than a month. A total of nineteen cases were reported in the state, including seventeen deaths. The successful efforts earned praise from Robert Gallo of the Institute of Human Virology, Baltimore.

A basic public health strategy was built during the Nipah outbreak. Every contact of each person 14 days prior to them showing symptoms is identified, contacted and placed under home quarantine. There is follow up by health workers and ASHA workers via phone or in-person. The incorporation of the lessons acquired from Nipah experience helped in tailoring the successful strategies for fighting COVID -19.

Section III: Immediate Responses to Covid-19 Pandemic

Kerala responded to Covid-19 pandemic through a vast set of systematic interventionist policies and guidelines. The section elaborates the strategies that formed the strong chain of defense developed by Kerala against COVID -19.

Strong Communication and Implementation Logistics

Proactive and visible local action is necessary to assure people that all preventive and curative actions are being taken. This is only possible with a strong communication network across levels of government and robust implementation logistics to ensure appropriate course of action is taken swiftly. The government declared the COVID-19 as a state disaster. A 24-member State Response Team consisting of senior officials from various departments such as epidemiology, community medicine and food safety were constituted. They worked along with 18 state-level teams to coordinate surveillance, call centres, and human resource management. This helped to trace people, their travel history and place required people under quarantine effectively. DISHA, Direct Intervention System for Health Awareness is the 24-hour tele-health helpline number. It is backed by a team of trained social workers and counsellors who answers questions about COVID-19 from across Kerala, other Indian states and abroad. NORKA Roots played a commendable role in managing the influx of NRKs and emigrants within the country. NORKA Roots also provide consultation of reputed doctors via video conference and phone for NRKs staying around the globe and rehabilitation assistance to those who lost their jobs due to COVID induced crisis.

Break the Chain Campaign

Despite the variety of infectious agents, germs can spread from person to person through a common series of events. The Break the Chain campaign tries to break the chain of infection and thus prevent spreading of the disease. The chain can be broken at six points which include infectious agent, reservoir, portal of exit, mode of transmission, portal of entry and susceptible host, as shown in Fig 3.

Kerala popularized this novel measure through the slogan 'SMS', which stands for - wash hands using soap or sanitizer, wear masks and keep social distancing.

As a part of the campaign, the Government has installed water taps at public spots and has declared the use of sanitizers as mandatory. The campaign sensitized the public about the importance of hand hygiene, physical distancing and cough etiquette to prevent the spread of COVID-19. Tailoring units of prisons in the state are made responsible to make masks. Kerala State Drugs and Pharmaceuticals (KSDP), a public sector undertaking based in Alappuzha, were instructed to produce one lakh bottles in 10 days for the Kerala Medical Services Corporation. Kerala has started a new chapter in this campaign by introducing Break the Chain Diary to improve the efficiency of contact tracing.

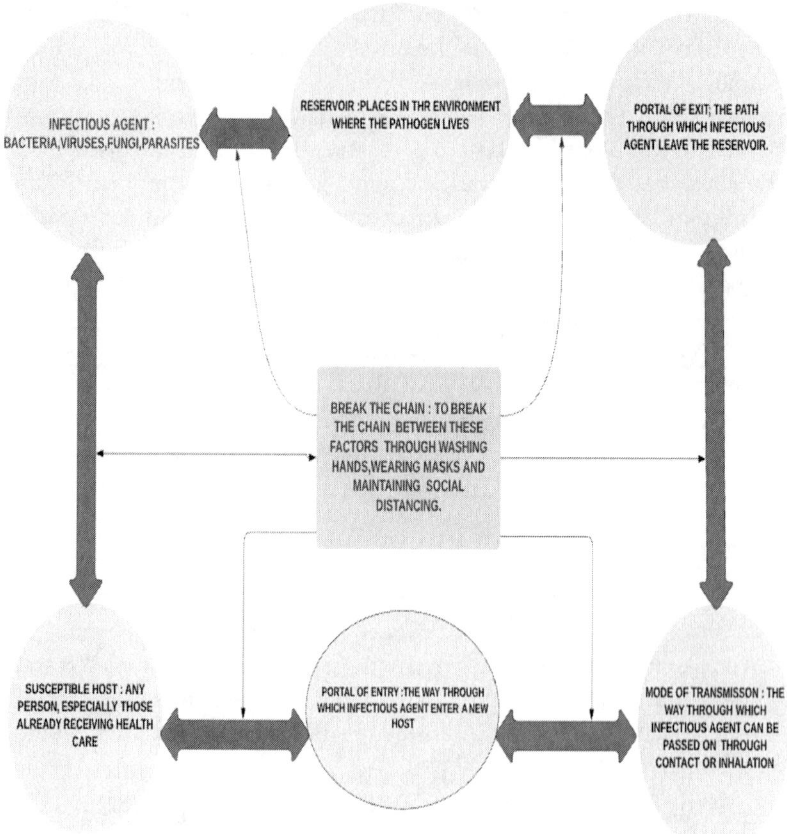

Figure 4.3: Break the Chain of Infection

COVID Brigade

To tackle a massive spike in COVID cases in Kerala with the phasing out of lockdown and opening up of borders, Kerala has begun to build up the human resources, both medical and non-medical, to meet the demand at hospitals and first-line treatment centres (FLTCs) popular as the COVID Brigade. Young professionals from the backgrounds in medicine, nursing, pharmacy, business administration, data-entry and social work are being recruited on a first-come-first-serve basis by the state, trained by experts and then deputed to Covid -19 hospitals and FLTCs in rural areas of districts suffering from an acute lack of manpower. A team of 26 comprising doctors, nurses, pharmacists and lab technicians after extensive training set off from Thiruvananthapuram for Kasaragod to curtail an emerging health crisis.

Training is imparted in infection control, basic life support, advanced life support and extending motivation. More batches are scheduled to undergo training in a decentralized manner across the state's 14 districts. This is an exceptional example of utilizing the existing skilled manpower of the state properly to tackle a health crisis. The Brigade, can always be there for rescue whenever the state may face such crisis in future and can also be deployed to manage challenges in any part of the country.

Proper Information Dissemination

From March, 2020 the measures were taken by government for creating proper awareness among the public. Telephone counseling services for psycho-social support to families of those under quarantine and a YouTube channel for creating awareness on the new disease were initiated. GoK Direct provide updates on COVID-19, quarantine protocol and guidelines for travellers. Collective for Open Data Distribution - Keralam (CODD-K) by a group of technologists, academicians, and students released first bilingual (Malayalam and English) online dashboard to provide real-time analysis, and daily updates of COVID-19 cases in Kerala by leveraging publicly available data from the Department of Health Services (DHS), Government of Kerala, and various news outlets. The Kerala Arogyam portal and the Covid Jagratha also provide comprehensive information on COVID-19. These measures were essential to avoid unnecessary panic about a new disease while ensuring that people take adequate protection as envisioned in the slogan "No Need to Fear, Just Be Cautious" (*Bhayam Venda, Jagratha Mathi*).

Citizen First Approach

COVID -19 has strained the economy and society of Kerala deeply with an estimated contraction in the state's Gross Domestic Product of approximately 1 lakh crore and estimated fall in the growth rate from around 7 percent to less than 2 percent. Citizen First approach gains significance as even after being under financial constraints, the state has planned to finance Rs 20,000 crore package to ensure people have sufficient money in their hands and no one goes hungry due to livelihood disruptions caused by lockdown. The package includes Rs. 500 crore for healthcare, Rs 2,000 crore for loans and free rations, Rs 2,000 crore for creating jobs in rural areas, Rs 1,000 crore for families with financial difficulties, and Rs 1,320 crore for paying two months pensions in advance. Welfare pension payments of Rs 1,200 per month (which has been increased to Rs 1,300 from April) for 55 lakh beneficiaries, clearing four months' arrears and one month's pension in advance to ensure that the majority of households in Kerala get an income transfer of Rs 7,300 before mid-April. Transfer of food to families is ensured through Anganwadis providing cooked food to children and other beneficiaries to their homes. Special food kits were supplied to all families in Kerala in addition to the normal ration. Community Kitchens were organized by the local governments along with Rs 20 meals for takeaway from hotels attached to the kitchens. Street pavement sleepers were accommodated in marriage auditoriums and given free food. Migrant workers were ensured food at the place of accommodation in partnership with the contractor. The state government has also started providing interest subvention for the loans of about Rs2000 given to Kudumbashree as additional consumption loans for member families. The government also envisages food self-sufficiency for the state through Subiksha Keralam. The government recently announced '100 days, 100 projects' scheme to boost employment opportunities in the state.

Reverse Quarantine

Reverse quarantine is a solution to reduce the morbidity and mortality associated with COVID-19 (Raveendran, and Rajeev Jayadevan, 2020). Reverse quarantine involves separating the vulnerable population (all persons above 65 and those suffering from chronic illness) from the general public. The vulnerable population, if infected, can face very adverse consequences and thus has to stay indoors or in isolation rooms at home. This is an important component of Exit Strategy of Kerala. Active grassroot level participation and local planning helped in promoting Reverse Quarantine in the state. It is argued that the lesser number of case fatality in the state is because of reverse quarantine practiced in the state.

Rapid Response Teams

COVID Rapid Response Teams comprising officers of revenue, police and health departments were deployed in areas where clusters have developed such as in Chellanam in Kollam. In the light of heavy restrictions in containment zones, the force ensured smooth functioning of essential activities while restricting unnecessary movement of people.

Strengthening Health Infrastructure

During the pandemic, the state government set-up at least two dedicated COVID-19 hospitals in each district, recruited new staff and constituted first and second line treatment centers to ensure access of health services to all. State and District Medical Boards were constituted to bring out treatment and discharge protocols as well as assess each positive case. COVID-19 hospital was built at Kasaragod in record time to fill the gap in health infrastructure of the district. The hospital with 541 beds is the first fully COVID-19 hospital for infected people in the state. In addition to physical infrastructure, human infrastructure was also improved by appointing junior doctors, nursing staff etc. to the total pool of health workers.

Conclusion

Even under financial constraints, Kerala has diligently utilized and strengthened its existing capabilities to tame an unknown disease whose basic characteristics are yet to be fully discovered. Break the chain, contact tracing, reverse quarantine, COVID Brigade are classic examples of practical solutions to control a pandemic for which there is a lack of effective antiviral agents and vaccines. Kerala has been successful in containing COVID-19 and in achieving a low rate of spread, high recovery, and low fatality. The importance of the public health system, social capital and the active involvement of the people through local governments have led to this success. The systematic, well-planned and active measures taken by the state strengthened by the strong public health foundation has defended Kerala to maintain its momentum of success in managing this vast crisis.

References

1. COVID-19 recovery rate in Kerala lowest among worst-hit states (2020, October 30).The New Indian Express. https://www.newindianexpress.com/states/kerala/2020/oct/30/covid-19-recovery-rate-in-keralalowest-among-worst-hit-states-2216879.html
2. Isaac, T. T., and Sadanandan, R. (2020), 'COVID-19, Public Health System and local Governance in Kerala', Economic & Political Weekly, 55(21): 35-40.
3. Menon JC, Rakesh P, John D, et al. (2020) , 'What was right about Kerala's response to the COVID-19 pandemic?', BMJ Global Health, 1-5.
4. Ramakumar, R. (2020), 'Agriculture and the Covid-19 Pandemic: An Analysis with Special Reference to India', Review of Agrarian Studies, 10 (1) : 72-110.
5. Ramakumar, R. (2020), "Introduction: The Impact of the Covid-19 Pandemic," Review of Agrarian Studies,10 (1) : 57 -60
6. Raveendran A.V, and Rajeev Jayadevan. (2020), 'Reverse quarantine and COVID-19', Diabetes & Metabolic Syndrome: Clinical Research & Reviews ', 14 (5): 1323-1325.
7. State Planning Board. Kerala Economic Review 2019. Thiruvananthapuram: Government of Kerala, 2019.

8. Vijayan, P. (2020), 'Challenges in the Midst of the COVID-19 Pandemic,' Economic & Political Weekly, 55 (24), 11-13.

9. With Covid Brigade, Kerala is building up human resources to combat spike. (2020, September 3). The Indian Express. https://indianexpress.com/article/india/kerala/kerala-covid-brigade-pinarayi-vijayan-6582037/

10. World Health Organization: WHO. (2020, July 2). Responding to COVID-19 - Learnings from Kerala. Https://Www.Who.Int/India/News/Feature-Stories/Detail/Responding-to-Covid-19—Learnings-from-Kerala. https://www.who.int/india/news/feature-stories/detail/responding-to-covid-19—learnings-from-kerala

Part - II
Effectiveness of Intervention Policies in Health Sector

5

Involvement of Civil Society and State in Health and Health Care System in Wayanad with special focus on Sickle Cell Disease

Anupama Augustine

Kerala, the state that witnessed vivacious civil society activism, exemplifies the narrowing borders between political society and civil society and the impact that associative projects can create in social development, especially in health and educational sectors. Of the many factors, the contributions of civil society including missionaries and social activists were very important in helping the state to achieve high health indices without waiting for economic growth to take place (Ekbal, Narayana, Thankappan, and Ajithkumar, 2012). Civil society organisations are engaged in health service delivery and health promotion activities, especially in backward areas of the state, as their presence is valuable to deal with vulnerable populations.

Wayanad, with presence of aboriginal community, is one district that witnessed strong civil society activism. There are about forty-four NGOs working in the district aiming at health and education sector development. Foundation for Educational and Innovations in Asia, Global Ayurvedics Centre For Traditional Health Care and Responsible Tourism, JVALA, Jyothinivas Charitable Society, Muslim Cultural Society, Manavaseva Charitable Trust, Mannam Social Service Society, Neethivedi, Wayanad Girijan Seva Sangh Thanal, etc. are examples. Many of these NGOs are receiving grant in aid from government or act as implementation agency of government projects. In addition, Arogya Keralam, introduced in 2006, to provide accessible, affordable, and accountable quality health services to the poorest households in the remotest rural regions is being implemented in the district. Along with these, independent experimentations such as 'Kanavu', 'Thudi', parallel schools for Adivasi students are working in Wayanad.

In spite of all these, health indices of tribal people continue to stay low, compared to the general population and studies shows that the community experiences rising infant and maternal mortality rates, child malnutrition and steeply falling living and working conditions (Mohindra, Narayana, and Haddad, 2010). This dismal situation in Wayanad naturally raises question about the effectiveness of civil society state initiatives in addressing health inequities and in bringing in structural changes where these communities are not streamlined. Against this context, the article explores the grass root level activities of both civil society and state and their joint initiatives in Wayanad, in the health sector, with reference to Sickle Cell Disease, a genetic disease which is prominent among both tribal communities and Chetty community (a backward community), that pose a great public health threat to the district.

The article is divided into four sections. Section I states the objectives and methodology. Section II explores the prevalence, features and clinical manifestations of SCD. The first objective, organisational structure and nature of civil society and state in addressing sickle cell disease in Wayanad is dealt in Section III. Section IV deals with the contribution of organisations to health systems in Wayanad, particularly with reference to Sickle Cell Disease.

Section I: Objectives and Methodology

Objectives

1. To examine the organisational structure, nature, cohesion and environment of civil society and state organisations and the impact of it on health and health care service delivery with respect to Sickle Cell Disease in Wayanad.
2. To explain the involvement of civil society and state and their association in influencing health and health care system in relation to Sickle Cell Disease in Wayanad.

Methodology

The involvement of civil society in determining health and health care systems in Wayanad with respect to activities related to SCD, the genetic disease seen in both tribal and non-tribal communities is discussed; the findings largely derive from in-depth interview conducted with various stake holders in Wayanad including social activists, journalists, health professionals and patients. In order to validate the information from interviews, secondary sources related to the context was considered. Government orders and reports, minute book of civil society groupings, newspaper articles, books, working papers, unpublished articles, manuscripts, letters, information received from RTI, brochures, leaflets and palm let, website content, articles in blog, Government orders, report of various meetings at government level, copy of applications submitted/ complaints filed against particular organisations, recorded audio and video, dairy writings and information from other social media platforms including whatsapp groups were used for the purpose. In addition, collecting oral history from old people who are associated with the incidents gave valuable insights into the narration of contextual factors.

The narration of organisational structure and environment is based on the in depth and semi structured interviews conducted with management and staff of each organisation and from the insights received from observation of intervention style and participation in the activities conducted by each organisation during the period of field visit.

Section II: Sickle Cell Disease

Sickle Cell Disease (SCD) is a single gene disorder causing a debilitating systemic syndrome characterized by chronic anaemia, acute painful episodes, organ infarction and chronic organ damage and by significant reduction in life expectancy (Williams, 2011). Initially the SCD gene originated as a natural protection against threat of malaria in people residing in the tropical region, but later, the same protective gene itself became a threat to their lives. Sickle cell disease refers to that state in which the red blood cells undergo sickling when it is deoxygenated. The sickle cell disease includes sickle cell HbC disease, sickle cell a-thalassemia, sickle cell HbD disease etc. (Firoze, 2006)

Clinical features of SCD includes painful sickle cell crisis, acute chest syndrome, bacterial sepsis, sequestration crisis, aplastic crisis, acute ischemic stroke, girdle syndrome, and priapism. Common standards of treatment mechanisms are universal/targeted screening programs, vaccination and anti-biotic prophylaxis, regular follow up in specialist clinics and improved parental education. Specific therapies for SCD include hydroxyurea, blood transfusion, Allogeneic HSCT (stem cell transplant) and gene therapy (Williams, 2013). The highest incidence of SCD is in

Africa, where among particular tribal groups the prevalence rate is forty to fifty percent. SCD is also seen in North and South America, Turkey, Saudi Arabia, Israel, Greece and in India.

Sickle Cell Disease in Kerala

Authentic data regarding Sickle Cell Disease in Kerala is seen in the research papers and working reports published by Medical College, Calicut. SCD patients in Kerala are concentrated in the districts of Wayanad and Palakkad. According to Disability Census, the total patients reported of SCD is 738, however data from Medical College shows that around 815 patients are registered in Medical College. The pilot project, conducted by Medical College in Wayanad showed that the prevalence rate is about 25% among tribal people, particularly among Paniyas, Kattunaikkars, Kurumas and Adiyas and the nontribal group, Wayanadan Chetty has a higher prevalence rate of 38%.

It was the volunteers of Solidarity who were working in tribal hamlets as a part of the literacy program who identified instances of death succumbing to severe body pain and fever. Tribal people believed it as Rheumatics and used to treat it with herbal medicines, however volunteers at Solidarity recognized it as SCD and confirmed it with the support of medical team. Dr. Dhananjay Sedge, medical officer at SVMM initiated efforts to bring in more resources, facilities and actors to conduct a scientific study related to SCD. As a result, All India Institute of Medical Sciences (AIIMS) initiated their first pilot project of Sickle Cell Anaemia Control Program in Wayanad with Vivekananda Medical Mission as NGO Partner and more than 70% tribal population were screened. As a second stage of this initiative, a diagnosis and counselling centre was set up in the hospital with a sub centre at Manandavady in 1992. Over these years, patient grouping was formed and registered in 2001, in the name of 'Sickle Cell Anaemia Patients Association' (SCAPA) and C.D Saraswathy became secretary of SCAPA. They demanded government intervention in the issue and raised voices for protecting the right to health of sickle cell anaemia patients. After the public outcry for more than twenty years, State Government institutions became active in creation of special systems for direct health care service delivery for SCD patients in the new millennium. A project for the 'comprehensive health care for sickle cell disease in a primary health care setting' was submitted by Medical College, Calicut and accorded sanction in 2006-07 by European Commission and was implemented in Wayanad and Malappuram and Attapady. Since 2016, India System of Medicine is implementing 'Sickle Cell Disease' project and is focusing on preventive care. In short, the two government agencies- Health Department (Allopathy), ISM (Ayurveda), and the two CSOs- Swami Vivekananda Medical Mission and SCAPA are the major contributors in the health system pertaining to the disease in Wayanad.

Section III: Organisational structure and nature of civil society and state in addressing sickle cell disease in Wayanad

The organisational structure and nature of Health Department (Allopathy), ISM (Ayurveda), and the two CSOs- Swami Vivekananda Medical Mission and SCAPA is narrated in the section.

1. Organisational structure

An organizational structure is a system that outlines how certain activities are directed in order to achieve the goals of the organization. These activities include rules, roles and responsibilities and the level of hierarchy in the organization. Organizational structure is one important feature that determines the efficiency in which each organisation works. Organizational structure of each institutions along with vision and mission with respect to SCD is discussed below.

A. Organisational structure of state (Allopathy)

State government institutions are following a hierarchical system in its functioning. Decision making power stays with the head of each program. There is a written set of rules and regulation already in place and the head is the executer of these rules. Also, other members are selected through formal interviews. The Sickle Cell Disease project is implemented by Pathology Department, Calicut. Head of the Department of Pathology department is the head of the program. One doctor in the Department is given charge for implementation of the program and he is the program coordinator. One counsellor and a field staff are recruited under the project, who are entrusted with maintaining the registry, visiting households of patients and collecting relevant information and recording it. They are also entrusted with coordinating camps, and organising awareness activities for patients with SCD. In addition to it, one person from the tribal community is volunteering in the project, to make the awareness programs effective. 'ArivalKootayma'- a patient grouping was initiated by Medical College to provide a platform for patients so that they can raise their needs to government.

However, it is said that the grouping ceased to function due to the internal conflict among patients and the effort of Medical College to bring in flexibility in the functioning of the program failed. Different stake holders have diverse opinion about the failure of patient group. Some patients who left ArivalKootayma claim that there was not enough freedom to raise voice for their needs or to criticize the way the project was implemented. The volunteer appointed by Medical College to lead the initiatives is not a patient and belongs to a community in which the disease is not prevalent. On the other hand, officials opine that the group was not able to succeed because there was conflict between patients from different communities and the inherent conflict between tribal and non-tribal communities led to the failure of the group. However, implementation of program was decentralized and compared to a centralized system, decentralized implementation ensures better accessibility to services and grievance redressal. Medical Officer in each hospital is entrusted with implementation, monitoring and reporting to higher authorities. The follow up of SCD is reviewed regularly in Block conference and DMO conference each month.

'Comprehensive Health care for Sickle cell disease in primary care setting' is an innovative project proposed by Medical College, since it rightly has emphasized the need for establishing facilities for SCD treatment in a decentralized manner and stressed the need for community participation. The objectives of the project are stated as follows,

(a) To set up the facility for diagnosis and steady state management and management of complications of SCD, and health education for patients in Wayanad, at three levels
    (i) Level I – Primary/ community health care
    (ii) Level II – District/ taluk hospitals in Wayanad
    (iii) Level III – Medical College, Calicut
(b) Enlisting all SCD cases and carriers of Wayanad district through motivated paramedical staff and to develop a disease registry.
(c) Developing and practicing standard practice guidelines for managing SCD and its complications in tribal areas
(d) Determining the presence of other abnormal haemoglobin, if any, and associated inherited haemolytic anaemia among tribals of Wayanad and Wayanadan Chetty.

The objectives clearly state the commitment of Medical College in making a systemic change in health care system by incorporating diagnostic and treatment facilities for SCD patients and to establish standard protocol in treatment and follow up of patients through proper documentation and updates.

B. Organisational structure of State (Ayurveda)- Indian System of Medicine (ISM)

ISM also follows a hierarchical system in functioning. However, interactions with District Medical Officer, ISM and Medical officer in charge of SCD project showed that there is more autonomy in the planning and implementation of the project. The SCD unit is working in the District Ayurveda Hospital, Kalpetta. A team consisting of two specialist doctors, staff nurse, one pharmacist, lab technician, ambulance driver is at service for SCD patients. All the staff except doctors are appointed on contract for one year.

SCD project of ISM in its mission gives importance to preventive care services and hopes that Ayurveda medicine can contribute more to tackling the menace. No conventional therapy available is proven absolutely effective in the cure of Sickle cell disease. Sickle cell disease project has been implemented in the view to fulfil the following objectives:

(a) To analyse the extent to which Ayurvedic drugs and treatment strategies could help in improving the health status of patients.

(b) Proper data collection and documentation which would help in listing, identification of patients and allowing professional exchange of information.

In addition, it aims at improving the awareness among patients and to stress on preventive care by conducting patient meetings and counselling sessions and by giving special attention to pregnant women and children.

C. Organisational structure of NGO hospital: Swami Vivekananda Medical Mission

NGO hospital, SVMM works as a charitable trust. The Managing committee comprises of fifteen persons, there are forty-six members in the General Body of the Society, which is convened twice in a year, besides the Managing Committee which meets on the 11th of every month. Day to day activities are controlled and monitored by a Manager supported by administrative staff. There is one person as volunteer head, to manage the field workers. Medical officer and Nurse Superintendent monitors outpatient and inpatient services offered at hospital. There are fifty-nine workers, including four doctors daily engaged in the hospital in its day- to-day work and twenty field workers daily move around the District, rivetted in the Mission's different engagements. Hundred 'One Teacher School' teachers impart education in the tribal hamlets; and seventy-three amongst them also are

Swasthya Mithras (Villages Health Workers). Researchers and other social workers are given an opportunity to take part in Medical Camps and in other programs.

Control program for SCD implemented by SWMM had two phases. Phase 1: Screening program and Phase II: Control Program.

Major Objectives of the project is stated as,

(a) Curtailing the spread of disease by extensive community counselling with joint efforts by doctors, Anganawadis/tribal department workers.
(b) Preventing the birth case with the disease by identifying carrier couples.
(c) Bringing down the mortality and morbidity of the disease by providing vaccination and other medicines
(d) Organisational structure of MBO: Sickle cell anaemia patient's association (SCAPA)

SCAPA, has a seven-member executive council which meets once in a month. But the decision-making power rests with the general body in which all patients are members. General body meeting is conducted according to need. The meeting usually take place in Oorukootam building or in community halls. Each and every activity is discussed in the meeting and decision is taken based on majority opinion. Executive Council meeting are conducted to discuss and deliberate issues are discussed in general body, in which often doctors, social activists or politicians take part. This helps in getting expert opinion on the issues and how to deal with the issues. The researcher herself participated in the executive council meeting as an invited guest and was able to experience the democratic nature of the organisation. Patients from both tribal and non-tribal communities are members in executive council. President and Secretary is from Chetty community while vice president is from Kuruma Community. One youngster from Adiya community is given the charge of coordinating the meeting. Executive council also have representation of parents of patients. One member in executive council is a parent, and he works as a well-wisher and actively participates in the programs.

The narration clearly shows that except for MBO, decisions are taken by top officials and it is executed in a decentralized way following a hierarchy. Initiatives from the part of government to establish a feedback system to ensure proper communication with patients failed miserably. However, MBO works in a democratic manner and was able to overcome the caste/community consciousness as there were both tribal and non-tribal members in executive council.

SCAPA aims at creating awareness among the patients and instilling them with self-respect and esteem,

(a) To enable each person to speak up of the discrimination they face because of the disease.

(b) Create awareness among patients about the need of pre-marital counselling and blood test to ensure that two patients are not married and regarding the need for timely treatment, especially during pain crisis.

(c) To fight for rights and empower patients to continue life with courage.

(d) Create a harmony and space for good communication among patients form different communities and share knowledge of disease.

(e) Act as a pressure group and monitoring agency to ensure that the policies are beneficial to patients and they are efficiently implemented.

A look in to the vision and mission of various projects throws light in to the priorities of each project. The government project was designed to strengthen prevailing health care system under the Health Department to suit the demands of SCD patients. They mainly concentrate on building infrastructure and standard protocols for treatment which has to be followed. ISM has a more holistic approach to disease in which the project covers not only patients but also their family members and a major thrust is on preventive measures. NGO Hospital follows a more medical approach to disease, main objective is to prevent birth of children with disease and it envisages to use the existing workers such as Anganwadi teachers or tribal promoters for spreading awareness. Unlike NGO, MBO gives prime importance to patients and in giving them a space to share their experience and empower them to fight disease.

2. Organizational Cohesion and Environment

Organizational cohesion is understood by looking into various aspects such as trust among members, scope for personal development of members, shared vision/ nurturing common values and gender diversity. Environment implies status of internal and external environment in the organisation. Internal environment is determined by employee behaviour, leader ship style, culture etc. and external environment are influenced by policies, public opinion and economic conditions prevailing.

Organizational Cohesion and Environment – a comparison

Staff in the project run by Medical College is guided by set of guidelines and rules, imposed by State government. Naturally, not trust, but rules and differentiated responsibilities are at the core. But, in ISM, even though guided by set norms, there is a shared responsibility and team work in the team and the medical officer in charge of project keeps everyone in a satisfactory state, which is evident form the work sharing and friendship shared by the team. NGO Hospital also shows cohesion among its workers, especially amongst the field staff and administrative staff who were with the hospital since its inception. Medical professionals also share a positive vibe in working. Staffs have a say in job division and it is flexible and pre planned. SCAPA exists only because of the trust among patients. Their shared vision for a better future is the one and only factor that holds the organisation intact. Regarding environment, except Health Department institutions, in all other organisations, members are satisfied. Medical and para medical professionals in the department are not satisfied with the concerned authorities, they often complain about the pathetic infrastructure facilities, work load and limited scope for personal development. The staff who has to work for SCD patients in Wayanad is working from Medical College and this leads to coordination failures. The researcher herself experienced difficulty in getting data from the Medical College and had to file an RTI in order to get the information.

Even though, in NGO, some staff and students were complaining about the low wages and poor quality of food provided in the canteen and the work load, especially in conducting the colony visit, majority of the staffs were proud of being the part of hospital, since they feel like they are contributing something to the society. And, the hospital sometimes works in a very flexible way, especially with patents- if they don't have money they are not compelled to pay the full amount, or if a patient is in a situation that he can't any more go to home, the hospital authorities allows him to stay at hospital. All these create a personal relation with doctors and patients. During colony visits also, doctors are getting more exposure to understand the socio-economic situation from which each patient is coming to hospital. The health workers and teachers also share a bond among them and they are taken for trips and trainings.

Similarly, members in SCAPA share a common cause and friendship and all are treated there as equals, as patients. Even the most personal things are discussed in SCAPA and most of the patients see the meetings of SCAPA as place to whistle blow their tension and apprehensions. However, some patients from tribal communities noted the communication gap between the tribal and non-tribal groups.

Table 5.1: Organizational Features of Institutions

No	*Items*	*Name of Organization*	*Characteristics*
1.	Structure	Health Department	Hierarchical
		ISM	Hierarchical
		NGO	Semi Hierarchical, (work arrangement jointly decided)
		MBO	Non-Hierarchical
2.	Nature	HealthDepartment	Rigid in rules and regulations
		ISM	There are fixed rules, but flexible according to patient needs
		NGO	Flexible, Based on practices and custom
		MBO	Based on trust and togetherness
3.	Cohesion	HealthDepartment	Formal/Professional Relationships
		ISM	Good team work in activities
		NGO	Good team work in service provision
		MBO	Very high, works like an extended family
4.	Environment	HealthDepartment	Impartial
		ISM	Positive work environment
		NGO	Good environment
		MBO	Cordial work environment

Source: Estimated from primary data

Civil society structures of participation in Wayanad

Both civil society and state institutions are jointly conducting programs among sickle cell disease patients in Wayanad. Various strategies are adopted by both civil society institutions in their association with state, including co-option, confrontation, selective collaboration and deploying soft power.

Associational activities of civil society and state with respect to SCD State (Allopathy) and NGO

Strategy of NGO to state is of co-option. NGO is receiving huge grant from Ministry of Tribal affairs to provide free health care services to patients from tribal community. It acted as a (Mother NGO) MNGO under the Reproductive and Child Health program, run by Ministry of Health. The sickle cell project implemented by the hospital was with the technical and financial help of central government. Thus, they co-opt in knowledge sharing and advocacy, programme implementation, and resource management. However, with the local self-government and Government of Kerala the relationship is not smooth. The state government tried to curtail freedom of NGO hospital by restricting entries to tribal areas and brining control in receiving financial aids. However, during 2000 the central government enhanced its financial support to NGO and later it was abolished by central government.

State (Allopathy) and MBO

State and MBO has a very peculiar relation of selective collaboration. Both cooperates in programmes where there is convergence of perspectives and mutual benefit. But at the same time MBO conducts protests and demonstrations against state to achieve their demands. MBO act as a partner in the policy dialogues sometimes and supports government policy and inform patients, but at other times they argue with officials and protests. MBO deploys soft power against the state through lobbying, using legal mechanisms and by moral or ethical appealing.

State (Ayurveda) and NGO

State (Ayurveda) keeps a cordial relation with all other stakeholders and takes support from them in implementing the preventive care measures.

State (Ayurveda) and MBO

Unlike to the Allopathic institutions, MBO nurture a good relation with ISM and shares its infrastructure and man power in successful conduction of programs run by them.

Section IV: Contribution of Organisations to Health Systems in Wayanad

The second objective to explain the involvement of civil society and state and their association in influencing health and health care system in relation to Sickle Cell Disease in Wayanad is narrated in the section. The contributions made by Health Department (Allopathy) is narrated below.

(a) Health Department- state (Allopathy)

'Comprehensive Health care for sickle cell disease in a primary health care setting' deploys a strategy for case detention and management of SCD, based on the proven fact that survival and quality of life of SCD patients increase only when they are detected early and primary health care is ensured. The Prevention of Sickle cell crisis is vital to survival of patients and has to be managed at the field level. Since Kerala has a wide network of Health care delivery system existing, it is a perfect setting in which a primary based care can be delivered. The first step towards this attempt was to strengthen the infrastructure facilities in Wayanad so as to provide diagnosis and treatment facilities to patients. The replay to RTI regarding the achievements of the project claims the following:

Infrastructure

Diagnostic facility has been made available at all levels from the sub centre level to PHC, CHC. It includes Solubility test kit (designed and developed by Medical College), Hb electrophoresis system, three Blood cell counters installed in Wayanad district and one in Calicut Medical College), High performance liquid chromatography equipment and PCR testing system in Calicut Medical College.

Management of sickle cell disease is being provided scientifically by, establishing standard protocol for the steady state management as well as complications in sickle cell disease developed during the national level workshop attended by experts in the field and doctors working in Wayanad. Medicines as per the standard protocol are made available free at all centres through the project. Six pulse oximeters are installed in Wayanad district and Medical College, Calicut. Two blood bank refrigerators installed in Taluk Hospital, Sulthan Bathery. A special ward has been renovated for sickle cell disease patients in Nalloornad hospital, Wayanad and in Taluk hospital, Sulthan Bathery.

Equipment purchased

Five Hundred solubility test kits, Sixteen Electrophoresis equipment, four automated blood cell counters, One Densitometer, three computers and accessories, one high performance liquid chromatography, One PCR testing system, two blood bank refrigerators and six pulse oximeters were purchased as a part of the project.

Equipment installed in different institutions

Hb electrophoresis equipments with UPS backup are installed at twelve government hospitals in Wayanad District. Blood cell counters are installed in Sulthan Bathery Taluk Hospital, Amabalavayal PHC and Nalloornad Hospital in Wayanad district and one in Medical College, Calicut. High performance liquid chromatography, PCR testing system are in Medical

College, Calicut. Blood bank refrigerators are installed in Sulthan Bathery Taluk Hospital.

Activities of the project include,

- **Case detection:** The case detection is done by screening for sickle cell gene in the tribal population in Wayanad and Wayanadan Chetties using solubility test. The subjects who are positive for screening test would then undergo further study in the form of Hb electrophoresis done at 14 centres in Wayanad. Five drops of blood will be taken in a filter paper from the positive cases and send to the respective centres. Hb electrophoresis is done by the trained laboratory technicians and it will diagnose the sickle cell anaemia patient who manifest the disease (HbSS genotype) and sickle cell trait who is a carrier of the gene but symptomatic (HbAS genotype). Red cards are issued to the patients and blue cards to the carriers. Treatment based on standard protocol for steady state management and complications in sickle cell disease including free medicines and nutrition is available to all patients in every health centre including the primary health centres on producing the card.
- **Maintenance of registry of all cases:** The record of all cases is maintained in the respective Primary health centres and a copy of all cases in Wayanad is entered into the specifically designed software for sickle cell disease project in Calicut Medical College. A treatment card is maintained for all sickle cell anaemia patients visiting the hospital and monthly follow up are entered thus building a cohort of the cases.
- **Sickle cell disease clinics:** Clinics are run specifically for the sickle cell anaemia patients in 15 PHC/ CHC in Wayanad. The facility is available at least once a month in the centres with some centres conducting the OP once every week. Follow up of the patients, irrespective of whether they are sick or not, is registered. The centres are functioning successfully in PHCs of Cheeral, Ambalavayal, Meenangadi, Chulliyode, Varadoor, Vazhavatta, Chethalayam, Poothadi, Mullenkolly, Noolpuzha, Pulpally, Panamaram, Appappara, Kurukkanmoola and Meppadi in Wayanad district.
- **Creating awareness** among the affected groups and the public is a major activity. This is done by taking classes for the tribal in Wayanad and Attappady and Wayandan Chettis in the meetings organised by voluntary organisations and putting up stalls in

different exhibitions held in the district. Health education is given by the doctors and health workers. Booklets, pamphlets and posters are prepared and distributed among the affected groups. Posters are pasted in health centres.

- **Presentation of the results in national and international conferences:** The work has been presented in many conferences and workshops including 4th International Congress in Sickle cell disease, National Seminar on State Development and the Adivasi question, National conference of Pathologists and Microbiologists, etc. The work has been thoroughly appreciated by the experts working in this field.
- **Research projects:** Research work is being carried out along with this project. Some of the important ones underway and completed are
  1. Sickle cell anaemia in Wayanad – disease characteristics.
  2. A community-based case series study to identify the effect of co-existent alpha thalassemia on the clinical consequences of homozygous sickle cell disease among tribes in Wayanad
  3. Cognitive and psychological function in children with sickle cell anaemia.
  4. Assessment of the knowledge and practice of sickle cell anaemia patients and their care givers regarding the care and prevention of sickle cell crisis in the tribes of Wayanad.
  5. Effect of social support on compliance of sickle cell anaemia patients.

Nutrition supplementation for sickle cell anaemia patients was started in sixteen centres running sickle cell disease clinics. Three kilograms of pulses is given to each patient as protein supplementation. The carbohydrate requirement of the patients is being met by the grains given free through the public distribution system in the state. Nutrition kits are distributed along with medicines from primary health care centres. A total number of 819 patients are receiving nutrition kit and a total amount of Rs.188370/- was spent towards this.

Special Medical camps are arranged for sickle cell anaemia patients to identify presence of medical complications, exclusively for SCD patients. They are attended by specialist doctors from Medical college, Calicut.

- **Summer Camps for school children:** Three summer camps were conducted, two in Sulthan Bathery and other in Thariode. The camps were very successful and it gave opportunity for the children to share their problems and motivate themselves to attend school regularly. A two-day summer camp was conducted in Thariode in 2010 and 2014 and as the part of summer camp 2014, children visited the planetarium and Kappad beach, Calicut.

- **Consultation from other centres.** Consultation material from other centres like Government Medical College, Thrissur and in and around Palakkad district, Kottayam, etc. are received and worked up at Medical College, Calicut.

A total number of 121076 persons were screened which constitutes eighty-six percent of the target population. Eight hundred nineteen patients are attending clinics in Wayanad and benefitting from different schemes. The project has demonstrated a suitable model for development of steady state management as well as complications of the illness and follows up of patients in government health care delivery system. It not only strengthens the health services department but also brings marginalized group of people in to the systems. The project has been recommended and appreciated by national and international experts and has been sighted as a model for developing societies. Studies around the world shows that using projects as parallel system without integration into existing health services has taken significantly longer time to screen subjects. The assessment team of NRHM has rated the project as the best NRHM project in the state and has suggested sharing technical expertise in Kerala with other states to implement this strategy of comprehensive care for SCD. However, interview with beneficiaries shows instances where the installed machines in PHCs are not working and preventive care, especially patient meetings and follow up is not efficient. Even after establishing the facilities in Taluk, CHC and PHC in Wayanad, many patients have to visit Medical college for treating medical complications. And this shows the need for capacity development at the grass root to make the initiatives sustainable.

(b) Contribution of Indian System of Medicine to Health Systems in Wayanad

Sickle cell disease unit is functioning at District Ayurveda Hospital, Kalpetta and Taluk Ayurveda Hospital, Sulthan Bathery. As part of the project, monthly Medical camps are conducted at Ayurveda Hospital, Dwaraka.

Preventive Care Activities

Sickle cell disease project 2016-17 was started in the month of November 2016. Registration camps and awareness class were conducted starting on 2nd November 2016 and successfully completed on 4th February 2017 covering all twenty-three Grama Panchayaths and three Municipalities. Awareness posters were exhibited during each camp. Hand book on general awareness of disease for the patients were issued. Health card were issued to the patients. Solubility test, a screening test for the detection of disease among family members of sickle cell patients were performed. District wide family meet of Sickle cell patients and mega medical camp was conducted at District Panchayath Hall, Kalpetta on 07/02/2017. Medical camps were conducted in 23 dispensaries at Grama Panchayath level.

Infrastructure Development

Solubility test (screening test) kit is made available at District Ayurveda Hospital, Kalpetta and Taluk Ayurveda Hospital, Sulthan Bathery. Hb Electrophoresis machine, used for blood test for the confirmation of disease was installed at District Ayurveda Hospital, Kalpetta for the first time in Wayanad district.

519 patients were registered at Registration camps conducted at various Grama Panchayath and Municipalities in which 394 are tribes and 126 are from Chetty community. Forty-three new subjects were screened during medical camps, of which twenty-five were affected with disease.

Project report for the year 2016-17 was published by ISM in which details of analysis of disease is given and it provides valuable inputs about the demography of patients, disease severity, response to treatment and complication of disease.

(c) Contribution of NGO Hospital (SVMM)

The project document of the NGO Hospital highlights the need to address socio economic problems of patients in order to contain the disease as majority of the patients experience mental stress due to continuous body pain, inability to indulge in hard labour, economic dependency etc. The document suggests that by providing suitable employment opportunity to patients, a drastic shift in the attitude towards the disease is generated which may help the patients to lead a near to normal life. Ensuring nutritious food, financial assistance and proper treatment can improve the well- being of patients.

SCD control program was started in 1998 and the major activities include the following,

1. Counselling Activities: Counselling programs were arranged by taking the support of doctors, and Health Inspector (HI)/ Junior

Public Health Nurse (JPHN)/ Anganwadi/ Tribal development workers in tribal hamlets. About 180 JPHN/HI, 700 Anganwadi workers were trained to provide counselling.

2. Chronic Villus Sampling (CVS): CVS is the method in which unborn child will be tested to find out if it has the disease so that it will be ensured that only normal children are born, thus reducing the burden of disease. The first step of prenatal diagnosis, CVS is done at 10-14 weeks of pregnancy at District Hospital Mandavady and the second step, DNA study at Delhi. A total number of 1.07 lakhs subjects belonging to tribal and Chetty community of Wayanad district were enrolled in the study and the data was systematically entered in a computerized data base. Of these, 60,000 subjects were screened for their sickle haemoglobin status. Carriers (Hb AS) numbering 6830 have been identified. They are being counselled to marry non- carriers; while 215 target couples where both partners are carriers were identified and are being followed up so as to offer prenatal diagnosis to avoid the birth of an effected children. Obstetricians at District Hospital are trained to perform CVS locally in Wayanad. Fortunately, the foetus is found to be unaffected. 1292 subjects were identified as homozygote (Hb SS) and are given appropriate treatment.
3. Treatment: Penicillin, prophylaxis, vaccines consistent with WHO in children and relief of pain and management of complications in older subjects are provided.

A Research project with Kottakkal Arya Vaidya Shala was conducted, in which ayurvedic medicines were given free of cost to patients. An international seminar was hosted by SWMM in February 2007 joining hands with the Indian Medical Association Wayand Unit of Kerala, Government Medical Officers Association (KGMOA) in which eminent professional Dr. Graham R. Serjeant and others participated (SVMM, 2008).

Contributions of SVMM to Health System

SVMM Hospital is a full-fledged hospital with the following facilities,

(a) Outpatient Department
(b) Well-equipped Laboratory and Pharmacy
(c) IP Ward (36 beds and Maternity Ward)
(d) TB Microscopy and Treatment Centre
(e) ECG Units

(f) Pain and Palliative clinic
(g) Sickle Cell Anaemia diagnostic, counselling and treatment centre
(h) Yoga Centre under Department of AYUSH Govt. of India
(i) Two-year training courses for DMLT and Nursing under BSS
(j) Specialty clinics for, Medicine, Cardiology, Paediatrics, Urology, Surgery, Paediatrics, Neurology, Psychiatry, Gynaecology and ENT are at hospital.

SVMM follows a decentralized pattern of service delivery and so six subcentres are working in Cherukara, Kannankode, Muthanga, Chulliyod, Niravilpuzha, and Erumanthoor. Medical camps, awareness classes, literacy classes, Self-employment activities are done in these subcentres. Activities in the subcentre are organized and led under the leadership of Swasthya Mithra Workers (Health volunteers selected from each community). Hospital also provides ambulance facility.

There are four permanent doctors and ten visiting specialist doctors including Homeopathy doctors rendering their service. An average of 200 patients daily comes to hospital for treatment in the OP. Tribal patients and poor patients are given free treatment, medicine and food. About a total number of 63585 patients were treated in the OP last year. Three Thousand Five Hundred patients were admitted in the inpatient ward last year. On an average about thirty persons are admitted in IP wards at a time, out of which thirty percent are patients suffering from SCD.

Sickle Cell Anaemia Diagnostic, Counselling and Treatment Centre

A modernized centre for diagnosis, counselling and treatment is working in SVMM at the new hospital block. The centre has facilities for conducting Sickling/Solubility test and Hb Electrophoresis for diagnosing SCD. Dr. Dhananjay Sagdeo, medical officer has experience of about thirty years in treating the disease provides his service. Patients suffering from sickle cell anaemia crisis are admitted in the hospital and given care. Free food and medicine are given to SCD patients from tribal communities.

Patients also benefit from the other specialty services in the hospital. Main specialty services used by SCD patients includes the following.

Eye clinic, developed with the support of The Comtrust Hospital of Calicut runs daily OP, where vision is being tested by an ophthalmologist and spectacles are issued free of cost to tribal patients, and in a nominal amount to others. There is a monthly eye camp where in cataract affected patients are being referred and given free surgery. Many patients with SCD who have vision impairment are getting treatment from the clinic.

The first ever Pain and Palliative Care Unit in the Wayanad District is working at the hospital. The Mobile Medical Unit of the Hospital moves daily to the hilly hamlets to treat the tribes as they are by habit and superstition hesitant to meet doctors and travel to the hospital at Muttil.

Along with the medical care, SWMM focuses on holistic development of patients, so that livelihood development programs and educational programmes are run by the mission. One important program aimed at generation of self-employment for patients was starting Bamboo Crafts Unit at hospital premises. Training to make handicrafts using bamboo was given by an NGO, Uravu, who specialize in bamboo craft making and marketing. Patients from tribal communities, suffering from Sickle Cell, who are incapable of physical exertion, benefitted from the initiative. The centre was started in 2002 and runs successfully till now. Kerala State Bamboo Mission is supporting the centre. Handicrafts, crockery items made by the patients are sold at different exhibition and fairs, which ensures a permanent income to the patients. One supervisor appointed by the hospital helps the patients in purchasing the raw materials and selling the products.

Swasthya Mithra Project was initiated in 1997 for training tribal youths to visit tribal colonies and to look after health problems and to guide colony dwellers in conducting their lives in clean, neat, and hygienic way. Tribal youths are given training in first aid, hygiene and economic matters and each of the trained volunteer is given charge of a specified area of work. Swasthya Mithra volunteers have worked the reporting year covering 370 different colonies. Medicines were distributed to a total number of 14000 persons last year, in which many SCD patients are included. Patients with SCD are working as Swasthya Mitras which is truly appreciable since, the disease is usually seen with stigma.

(d) Contribution of Sickle Cell Anaemia Patients Association

SCAPA, the member-based organisation works as a pressure group and adopts a strategy of democratic struggle for attaining their rights. Being a social movement and spontaneous actor in the issues of patients, SCAPA does not possess any extensive projects for the welfare of the patients. Following is a narration of the arenas in which SCAPA raised its voice for the patients.

After registering as a society, one important protest was the Dharna organised in front of the secretariat of sickle-cell sufferers to make their plight public in February 2006 (*Indian Express,* Kochi, February 2, 2006) and of their petition to the Chief Minister of Kerala, who announced financial aid of Rs. 20,000/- to each affected person. The demands of the SCAPA are multifaced, that they demand livelihood programs along with good treatment facilities. It includes reservation in education and in jobs, monthly pension, special self-help group, debt relief and allotting special unit for SCD in Wayanad. Each of these demands is justified by the members as essential to attain relief from the disease.

SCAPA has fearlessly approached the government with their demands and many of their demands have been granted by government owing to public pressure. One important among was granting pension for patients. When SCAPA members approached former minister P.K Jayalekshmi, during a function at Wayanad, raising a demand for allowing pension to SCD patients, minister allotted pension for patients belonging to tribal communities only. This policy was questioned by SCAPA, and they approached Chief Minister with a demand to allot pension to all patients with SCD without discriminating patients on caste/community lines. Even though Chief Minister announced pension scheme to all patients irrespective of caste/gender/class in 2013, the government order issued in 2015, limited pension to patients belonging to BPL class only and the authority issuing pension to general community is Social Justice Department. Later after a long struggle, Government was convinced of the need for all patients and Rs. 2000/- was allotted to all patients as pension. Thus, a large segment of patient population, who were outside of the social security benefit were able to receive pension because of the efforts of SCAPA.

Similarly, students who have completed SSLC are not able to study in nearest plus two schools, as admission is done through single window system. SCAPA requested government to ensure spot admission to patients with SCD as they cannot travel long distance and this may affect studies as well. After a long struggle, government issued an order, by which students were able to continue studies.

One important struggle, that is still going on is for opening a special ward for SCD patients, at Manandavady hospital. Government hospitals are overcrowded and admitting SCD patients near to other patients who have communicable diseases, leads to medical complications, as the immunity levels of SCD patents are very low, and they are sensitive to other disease. Hygienic conditions and special care are needed during the time of Sickle cell pain crisis and so the demand for separate ward in District Hospital is justiciable. In addition, if patients have to get specialty treatment they have to travel to Medical College, Calicut, which takes about four-hour journey from Thirunelly, where majority of the patients are staying and they have to travel via nine hair-pins, as it is a high land area. Many patients die on the way to Medical College and many of the patients are reluctant to go up to Calicut as it cost more money and sometimes ambulances are not available. SCAPA has demanded for a separate ward at District Hospital and met all the government officials. As a result, a ward was built in District Hospital, Mannadavady, using M.L.A fund, for SCD patients. However, the ward was built in third floor and it was not suitable for SCD patients since they can't bare much heat or cold (because of the asbestos sheet at roof top) and they find it difficult to reach the ward, as many of them are disabled. SCAPA went on with pressurizing government officials to allow another suitable ward for SCD patients and a favourable G.O was issued. The Government order 429/2011 says that treatment facilities should be ensured in all thaluk hospital and in District Hospital/ Medical college for SCD patients. It was advised that cost of drugs distributed to SCD patients has to be taken form Hospital Development Fund and the money spend for treatment of tribal patients has to be reimbursed from Tribal Department. However, District Hospital authorities has not taken any action to ensure enough treatment facilities for SCD patients. SCAPA members approached, Minister of Health and Director of NRHM to look in to the issue and do the needful. Recently, Minister has announced a project to start Sickle Cell treatment and research centre with international collaboration.

Central government special package was allowed to distribute land for Sickle Cell Anaemia Patients. The nexus of Government officials, local politicians and real estate mafia hijacked the project and made enormous profits. Patients were given uncultivable land, without facilities such as transportation, water or electricity. SCAPA was in the forefront to report the issue in front of the general public and media, and thus an investigation has been ordered into the allegations.

General body meeting of SCAPA is a platform where discussions and deliberations of the issues faced by patients happen. It is a truly democratic space where each patient has a say in any matter and they are considered with almost respect. The discussion topic includes, details of various government schemes, complaints regarding not getting certain benefits, need of better treatment facilities, future plans of the organisation, financial sources, decision on nature of member grouping, formulation of future strategies, evaluation of previous strikes/interventions etc.

SCAPA eases the difficulty of patients in submitting various application forms in order to avail government benefits or files complaints if a member does not get the benefits from government or if anyone misbehaved with its members. SCAPA is platform where quality of treatment from different hospital/doctors are being discussed vivaciously. Especially, there are many uncertified traditional practitioners in Wayanad, discussions in SCAPA empowers the patients to choose quality treatment and counselling facilities. It also gives financial support for treatment and bystander facility to its members. Supportive equipment and self-employment options are given at SCAPA. Along with this they do workshops, seminars, awareness classes, television shows and collect membership fees to raise funds to meet the travel and other working expenses. Contribution of the four organisations are summarised in the table and compared based on the services provided by each of the agency.

Table 5.2: Contribution of civil society to health systems

Health system function	***Organisation/ Association***	***Services provided***
Health services	Health Department (State allopathy)	Decentralised Curative and preventive services Arivalkoottayma, patients grouping initiative, but failed Distributing health resources – nutrition kit, Hydroxyurea and folic acid tablets free of cost Training health workers to conduct essential tests and counselling.
	ISM (State Ayurveda)	Preventive and Curative Services (Outpatient only) Keeping contact with patients through MBOs, ASHAs and other Health workers Distribution of Ayurvedic Medicine
	NGO (SVM)	Decentralised Preventive and Curative Services (Outpatient and inpatients) Keeping contact with patients through Health Volunteers Free food, Medicine and treatment for tribal patients
	MBO (SCAPA)	Financial help to patients Bystander facility to patients Support in getting hospitalised

(Contd...)

Health promotion and information exchange	Health Department (State allopathy)	Obtaining and disseminating health information through decentralised structures Implementing and using health research
	ISM (State Ayurveda)	Building informed public choice on health Popularising need of holistic treatment
	NGO (SVM)	Good feedback system employing volunteers Awareness classes and campaigns
	MBO (SCAPA)	Building informed public choice on health Helping to shift social attitudes; and Mobilizing and organizing for health
Policy setting Representing public and community interests in policy;	Health Department (State allopathy)	Central Government policies; Compartmentalised policies Formulation of standard protocol for steady state management Including CSOs and other stakeholders in review meetings and policy discussions
	ISM (State Ayurveda)	Evaluation reports Including CSOs in conduction of screening programmes and medical camps
	NGO (SVM)	Acting as a partner to Government Popularising government schemes
	MBO (SCAPA)	Promoting equity and pro-poor policies; Negotiating public health standards and approaches; Building policy consensus, disseminating policy positions; and Enhancing public support for policies.
Resource mobilization and allocation	Health Department (State allopathy)	Financing health services; Building transparency and accountability and transparency in raising, allocating and managing resources.
	ISM (State Ayurveda)	Accountability and transparency in system Resources for making additional capacity in Health System
	NGO (SVM)	Raising community preferences in resource allocation; Mobilizing and organizing community co-financing of services;
	MBO (SCAPA)	Raising community preferences in resource allocation; Mobilizing and organizing community co-financing of services; Promoting pro-poor and equity concerns in resource allocation; And Building public accountability and transparency in raising, allocating and managing resources.

(*Contd...*)

Monitoring quality of care and responsiveness	Health Department (State allopathy)	Monitoring responsiveness and quality of health services;
	ISM (State Ayurveda)	Quality care for patients free of cost Feedback to governments
	NGO (SVM)	Quality care to patients
	MBO (SCAPA)	Giving voice to marginalized groups, promoting equity; Representing patient rights in quality of care issues; and Channelling and negotiating patient complaints

Source: inferences from field work

Conclusion

There are multiple civil society organisations working in association and in confrontation with the state, deploying different techniques to achieve their objectives, in the study area. The major stakeholders include state (Allopathy), State (Ayurveda), NGO hospital and MBO. State (Allopathy) provides both preventive and curative services and the special project on SCD has helped in improving the infrastructure facilities at PHCs, and CHCs and there by strengthen the envisaged three tire system of health care service. It has also helped to mobilise additional resources for tackling the menace of SCD and the scientific research paper published by Medical College has helped in inviting academic discourse on the matter and has supported policy setting. Similarly, interventions from the part of ISM has helped in improving the awareness level and has strengthen the bond between patients and health workers, which the Health Department (Allopathy) failed to do. However, joint efforts from Health Department and ISM can increase efficacy of programs conducted by both departments, but the possibility is not practiced. The NGO works supplementing efforts of Government (Allopathy) by providing both preventing and curative services to SCD patients belonging to tribal communities and this helps in providing health services to patients who are either geographically or socially excluded. The MBO, works on aspects related to health promotion and information exchange, represents public and community interests in policy by organising patients and empowering them. Thus, associational action by government departments, NGO and MBO has strengthened health system pertaining to SCD.

References

1. Amendah, Djesika D. et al. (2013), 'Routine Paediatric Sickle Cell Disease (SCD) Outpatient Care in a Rural Kenyan Hospital: Utilization and Costs', **PLoS ONE** 8(4): 1–6.
2. Baiju, K C. (2011), 'Tribal Development under Decentralised Governance in Kerala/: Issues and Challenge', **JOAAG**, 6(1): 11–26.
3. Chatterjee, P. (2008), 'Democracy and Economic Transformation in India', **Economic and Political Weekly**, 53-62
4. Colah, Roshan B., Malay B. Mukherjee, Snehal Martin, and Kanjaksha Ghosh, (2015), 'Sickle Cell Disease in Tribal Populations in India', **Indian Journal of Medical Research** 141: 509–15.
5. Ekbal B, Narayana D., Thankappan K, and Ajith Kumar, K (2012), Social Determinants of Health in Kerala State, **Health Sciencies** 1(2). 1-13.
6. Mohindra, K S, and Ronald Labonté. (2010), 'A Systematic Review of Population Health Interventions and Scheduled Tribes in India', **BMC Public Health**, 10:438.
7. Mohindra, K. S., Narayana, D., & Haddad, S. (2010), "My story is like a goat tied to a hook." Views from a marginalised tribal group in Kerala (India) on the consequences of falling ill: A participatory poverty and health assessment', Journal of Epidemiology and Community Health, 64(6).
8. Nalinam M. (2016), 'Morbidity Pattern of Tribes in Kerala', **IOSR Journal Of Humanities and Social Science** Ver. III 21(4): 30–36.
9. Yale, Steven H et al. (2018), 'Approach to the Vaso-Occlusive Crisis in Adults with Sickle Cell Disease', **American Family Physician**, 1–9.

6

Decentralised Health Care System at Grama Panchayath Level : An Effectiveness Analysis

K. Aruna Anand

Democracy rests on the philosophy that people are the decision makers and ultimate beneficiaries of development. However, the political freedom guaranteed to the people of India by the democratic philosophies was limited to the privilege of electing their representatives to various administrative units. The possibility of stretching people's power from electing governments to actual governance was materialized through democratic decentralization intended to deepen direct democracy. Democratic decentralization evolved space for people to make critical evaluation of policies and strategies and also to participate in policy making. The state of Kerala has been the forerunner among the Indian states to adopt democratic decentralization when it transferred funds, functions and finances to the LSGI in 1994. Of the 28 subjects that were decentralized, the case of health sector receives utmost importance because Kerala's health sector was reeling under crisis owing to the increase in morbidity along with escalation in the cost of treatment (Varatharajan, et al., 2004). Decentralization of health care sector was viewed by experts as a solution to Kerala's health care crisis, since theoretically it enables greater interagency coordination, ability to respond to local needs, discretion to allot more finance and increased accountability of LSGI and local health care institutions. Grama Panchayats are the lowest tier of the decentralized system which is expected to function effectively to initiate plans and projects that suits the local needs. Regarding health, Grama Panchayats have adequate participatory spaces and institutions where health issues are discussed and programmes are chalked out. Primary Health Centre (PHC) is an important institution through which the health programmes are implemented by the Grama Panchayats. Considering these aspects, the present study attempts at analyzing the effectiveness of decentralized health care delivery system at the Grama Panchayat level. The specific objectives of the study includes understanding the institutional mechanism under health sector decentralization and examination of the effectiveness of decentralized health care system at Grama Panchayat level.

Methodology

Health indicators form a major component of Human Development Index (HDI) and hence HDI rank is used to understand the relative health status attained by people of a particular district. Two districts are selected, Ernakulam being the district with maximum HDI and Wayanad being the district with minimum HDI. A detailed study of decentralization of health care is initiated at the Grama Panchayat level. Ernakulam District comprises of 14 Block Panchayats and 82 Grama Panchayats (Census, 2011). Out of these Block Panchayats, Edappally possess the highest HDI and Kothamangalam the lowest. Hence, these two Block Panchayats are selected for analyzing the effectiveness of decentralization of health services at the second tier.

Wayanad District consists of 4 Block Panchayats and 23 Grama Panchayats (Election Commission, 2015), of these Panamaram block is exempted, since the Block got its status only in 2009. The other two Block Panchayats- Sulthan Bathery Block and Mananthavady Block are considered for analyzing the effectiveness of decentralization of health system

From the identified Block Panchayats from each district, two Grama Panchayats are selected randomly for the purpose of analyzing the effectiveness of decentralized health care system at the lowest tier i.e., Grama Panchayat level. The selected Grama Panchayats are Elamkunnapuzha and Mulavukad from Edappally Block Panchayat, Nellikkuzhi and Kuttampuzha from Kothamangalam Block Panchayat, Nenmeni and Noolpuzha from Sulthan Bathery Block Panchayat and Edavaka and Vellamunda from Mananthavady Block Panchayat. Mulavukad is an island Panchayat and Elamkunnapuzha is both an island and a coastal Panchayat comprising of considerable number of fisherman community. Kuttampuzha Panchayat is comprised of dense forests and high ranges which is difficult to reach and supports considerable number of tribal population. Nellikkuzhi Panchayat consists of both plains and highlands and consists of 11 Scheduled Caste colonies. From Wayanad District, all the Grama Panchayats selected for the study viz, Nenmeni, Noolpuzha, Edavaka and Vellamunda Grama Panchayat comprises of Scheduled Tribe population living in a state of deprivation in the remotest areas of district. The PHCs operating in each of these Panchayat is selected for detailed analysis. Five percent of the households (300) from each Panchayat are considered for primary survey. House lists were obtained from the Panchayat office and were arranged continuously starting from ward number one. Every 20th household was selected from the list (systematic random sample) and hence altogether 300 households were identified from each Grama Panchayat. Data was collected from the selected households using interview schedules. Primary survey results revealed that 264 households from Noolpuzha Grama Panchayat availed services from the PHC. However, only 50 households from Elamkunnapuzha Grama Panchayat availed PHC services for the reference period of last one year. To facilitate indexing and comparison, analysis is done only with reference to 50 households, which availed services from the PHC. Hence 50 households were selected randomly using lottery method from each Grama Panchayat.

From the Provider's perspective, 10 health staffs including the Medical officers, Junior Public Health Nurses (JPHN), Health Inspectors (HI), Staff Nurses etc. from each PHCs were interviewed. Likewise, 15 Grama Panchayat officials, including Panchayat President, Vice President, Standing Committee Chairman on development, health and finance and other members and Panchayat secretary were interviewed. Primary Data was collected during the period from June 2018 to June 2019.

Specific Methodology for analyzing the objectives

Decentralization of health care system is made possible by the existence of different committees which act as platform where members from the Panchayat Health Institutions and people have a representation. Hospital Development Committee, Panchayat Standing Committee on health, Ward Sanitation Committee are the examples of such platforms. The functioning of each of these is examined in detail. The institutional mechanism is also understood by examining the conduct of Grama Sabha/Oorukottams at the panchayat level. The opinion of the three stake holders viz, PRI officials, health officials and the beneficiaries on the discussion of health care services during the Grama Sabha meeting, the initiation of health care programmes at the Grama Panchayat level is recorded.

Decision Space Analysis

The level of autonomy is analyzed through the decision space analysis. The decision space of finance analyses the choices about the fiscal autonomy of the local authorities which included the range of autonomy of the local government to raise own revenue source, allocations of expenditures on various priority programmes, choice on setting up of user fees etc. The range of autonomy of local authorities to set priority over different programmes (e.g., immunization, family planning, maternity care) and services, the degree of hospital autonomy, regulation of local health insurance plans etc. is also examined. As far as the decisions on the human resources functions are concerned, the decision space checks the range of choice to fix the salaries, permanent and contractual appointments, dismissal of staffs etc. The access rules deals with the range of decision making power to fix the target population while the governance rules analyses the range of choice on the size and composition of hospital boards, decision making power at the health meetings and the mode of community participation (Bossert, 1998). These functional areas are classified into narrow, moderate and wide range of choice with score 1, 2 and 3 respectively. The weighted scores of the opinions of Block Panchayat officials and Grama Panchayat officials are obtained and the scores are converted into standardized index, so that the index value ranges from 0 to 1. Those values ranging from 0 to 0.33, 0.33 to 0.66 and 0.66 to 1 are classified as low, moderate and wide range of autonomy respectively. The level of autonomy is obtained for the selected Block and Grama Panchayats.

Responsibility Matrix

Responsibility Matrix analysis is conducted from the perspective of PRIs and PHIs. It analyses the nature of relationship shared between the two institutions through the variables measuring co-operation and coordination among the service providers which is a necessary condition for effective decentralized health care delivery system. As per the concept of decentralization, the responsibility over health care should neither be renounced nor monopolized by either of the two stakeholders, but should be shared among them. Both abandoning and domination of responsibility on health care delivery can lead to the emergence of tension between the stakeholders, thereby leading to inefficient delivery of services. Therefore, it is pertinent that these agencies respect each other's significance and coexist in harmony. Responsibility matrix is constructed by analyzing the responsibility felt by the PRIs and PHIs on the initiation of need based programmes, undertaking temporary appointments during the times of staff shortage, fixing target population, supply of medicines, community participation, implementation of new projects and maintenance of existing infrastructure. If both the providers felt it as, not their own responsibility but other's, then the score is given as zero, likewise, if both the providers felt it as their sole responsibility and discards other's significance, then the score is given as one. When both the providers felt it as a shared responsibility and respects each other's significance, the score is given as two. Subsequently the weighted average of the opinion of sample respondents is obtained and converted into standardized index, so that the index value ranges from 0 to 1. Values ranging from 0 to 0.33, 0.33 to 0.66 and 0.66 to 1 are classified as renounced, monopolized and shared responsibility respectively.

Section I: Institutional mechanism involved in decentralization of health care sector at Grama Panchayat

Theoretically decentralization of health care enables greater inter-agency co-ordination, ability to respond to local needs and increased accountability of LSG and local health care institutions. This is made possible by the existence of several institutions which acts as bodies where different stakeholders participate in discussions and decisions are evolved. Grama Sabhas, Panchayat Standing Committee on health and sanitation, HMC etc. are the institutions established to create spaces for discussions and deliberations at different levels to evolve policies suiting the health needs of the population.

Institutional mechanism at the Panchayat level is kick started with the initiation of Grama Sabha which is a forum of discussion by including the Panchayati Raj officials, officials from various local departments and general public. These stakeholders involve in discussion on various topics of interest concerning the Panchayat including health and subsequently identify the priority areas. Similarly there is a Standing Committee on Health and a Hospital Management Committee (HMC) which supplements the health care delivery by enhancing participation and formulating need based public health programmes. The following section discusses the activities related to health of these forums in detail.

Grama Sabha

The Constitutional Amendment Act defines Grama Sabhas as a body consisting of persons registered in the electoral rolls relating to a village comprised with in the area of Panchayat at the village level (Article 243).

'Grama Sabhas are envisaged as a form of direct democracy, where people are given a chance not only in electing their representatives but also in discussing, deciding and participating in the development activities of the Panchayat' (Khan et al., 2001). Powers and functions of Grama Sabhas were enhanced in view of the need for increasing people's participation (1991 amendment). The minimum number of Grama Sabha meeting was raised from 2 to 4 per year. The quorum was raised from 50 persons to 100 persons or 10 percent of the voters, whichever is less. Scope of participation is widened to involve the voter in the process of need assessment, formulation of development programmes and monitoring and assessment of implementation. The voter is empowered to involve in the social audit and performance audit where he/she can question, ask for clarifications and criticize the officers as well as elected representatives. Grama Sabhas as envisaged in Kerala Panchayati Raj Act, 1994 is the people's platform for shedding, individually and collectively their needs, wishes, aspirations, suggestions, plans and solutions to individual and collective problems existing in the village level. Within the conceptual understanding and legal framework in Kerala, Grama Sabhas in Kerala have larger space to involve the citizens in local governance. Frequency of Grama Sabha meetings organized by the Grama Panchayats and health being discussed as a topic shows the success of decentralized spaces in articulating the needs of the population.

As it is mandatory for the Panchayat to convene Grama Sabha meetings quarterly, all Panchayats had followed on to the mandate, however Noolpuzha and Vellamunda has convened Grama Sabha meeting more frequently as and when needs arose. Special Grama Sabhas were also convened in Kuttampuzha Panchayat to discuss health issues.

Discussion with Panchayat members, health officers and the general population reveals that there exists, chance of thirteen health related items being discussed in the Grama Sabha. The discussion on improving resource quality which includes the initiation of training programmes for the PRIs and PHIs is an important topic that should be done in Grama Sabha. Grama Sabha is also a platform where the common people become informed about the number of health care officials to be stationed at each PHI and to place demand to resolve the issues relating to staff shortage. The discussion on preventive measures of epidemics including the initiation of awareness camps and medical camps, ensuring availability of safe drinking water and sanitation should also be important topics of discussion during Grama Sabhas. The monitoring and analysis of working of ward sanitation committee which is operating at the Panchayat level (comprising of an executive body consisting of Panchayat officials and health officials) whose mandate is to maintain proper sanitation facilities can also be done by the Grama Sabha.

Discussion on palliative care programmes providing home care treatment for the bed ridden patients, provision of financial aid for the differently abled patients, discussion of health and other social welfare scheme etc. during the Grama Sabha enables the local community to increase their awareness of health programmes initiated by the Central, State and Local health authorities and thereby gives them an opportunity to question the providers in case of inefficiencies. The planning of health care activities and health budgeting during the Grama Sabhas are noticeable changes since decentralization. Planning at the local level is intended to increase participation of LSGI, local health institutions, various other departments and more importantly the local community who are better informed about the local situation. Therefore, the inclusion of topics related to planning and budgeting of local health facilities during the Grama Sabha discussions are important so that the common public have a platform to ascertain whether the plans are in concurrence with local health demands.

The above-mentioned discussion topics were given a five point grade which included, never, rarely, occasionally, frequently and always with assigned scores of 1, 2, 3, 4 and 5 respectively. Since the average value for any statement was 3, any statement obtaining a mean of 3 meant that the particular issue is being occasionally discussed in the Grama Sabha and a score more than 4 implies that the issues is frequently discussed.

Table 6.1: Discussion of topics of health in Grama Sabha in Ernakulam district

	Elamkunnapuzha		*Mulavukad*		*Kuttampuzha*		*Nellikkuzhi*	
Topics of health	P	B	P	B	P	B	P	B
Initiation of training Programmes for health officials	1.5	1	1.8	1	2.5	1	1.95	1
Recruitment of village health personnels	2.3	1	2.15	1.74	2.65	1	3.1	1.04
Monitoring the working of Ward Sanitation Committee	3.35	1	2.75	1.76	3.7	1.38	4.05	1.34
Coordination of Awareness Camps and Medical camps	4.45	1.2	4	2.28	4	2.66	3.9	1.74
Financial Aid for mentally retarded/disabled people	1.15	1	1.8	1.16	2.1	1	1.05	1.18

(Contd...)

Implementation of Palliative Care Programmes	3.15	1.08	2.85	1	4.4	1.2	4.25	1.02
Health related schemes	4.45	1.2	4.4	2.34	4.35	2.18	4.5	2.14
Enabling Safe Drinking water & Sanitation	3.3	1.4	2.6	2.28	3.65	3.21	3.3	2.5
Implementation of Housing Schemes	1.35	1.24	1	3.12	1.7	4.18	1	3.82
Epidemics	4.05	1.2	4.1	2.48	4	2.87	3.9	1.96
Formulation of Health Plans	1.2	1.02	1.6	1.18	1.9	1.06	1.6	1
Preparation of the Health Budget	1.25	1.02	1.6	1.14	1.65	1	1.6	1

P- Providers, B- Beneficiaries
Source:- Primary Survey

Table 6.2: Discussions of topics of health in Grama Sabha in Wayanad district

Topics of Discussion	*Nenmeni*		*Noolpuzha*		*Edavaka*		*Vellamunda*	
	P	*B*	*P*	*B*	*P*	*B*	*P*	*B*
Initiation of training Programmes for health officials	1	1	1.15	1.02	1	1	1	1
Recruitment of village health personnels	1	1	1.7	1.2	1.1	1.1	1	1.08
Monitoring the working of Ward Sanitation Committee	1.25	1.22	**3.4**	1.26	1.7	1.48	2.8	1.08
Coordination of Awareness Camps and Medical camps	**4.7**	2.16	**4.85**	2.22	**3.2**	1.98	**4.65**	1.52
Financial Aid for mentally retarded/disabled people	1.85	1.28	2.45	0.96	2.2	1.12	**3.35**	1.04
Implementation of Palliative Care Programmes	**4.9**	1.16	**4.9**	2.22	**4.3**	1.58	**4.85**	1.32
Health related schemes	**4.5**	1.6	**5**	2.5	**4.8**	1.96	**4.15**	2
Enabling Safe Drinking water & Sanitation	2.75	1	**3.7**	**3.04**	2.05	**3.5**	2.05	2.66
Implementation of Housing Schemes	2.25	**3.78**	1.1	**3.86**	1	**3.52**	1.15	**3.94**
Epidemics	**4.3**	1.12	**4.65**	2.42	**4**	1.98	**4.3**	2
Formulation of Health Plans	1	1	**3.45**	1	1	1	1.05	1
Preparation of the Health Budget	1	1	**3.3**	1.02	1	1	1	1

P- Providers, B- Beneficiaries
Source:- Primary Survey

Of all the health issues being raised in Grama Sabhas, the frequently raised issue is related to implementation of housing schemes and provision of safe drinking water and adequate sanitation, all these being significant determinants of health. The discussion frequently occurred in Kuttampuzha and Nellikkuzhi Panchayat where majority of the population belonged to Scheduled Tribes. Drinking water and sanitation issues are very important as the quality and availability of these two are the major factors contributing to the control and prevention of communicable diseases. The Panchayats of Ernakulam district including Elamkunnapuzha, Nellikkuzhi and Kuttampuzha faced shortage of safe drinking water, but had better sanitation facilities while the Panchayats of Wayanad district faced both shortage of drinking water and inadequate sanitation facilities. It was observed during the primary survey that these issues were not frequently discussed in Kuttampuzha Panchayat, Elamkunnapuzha Panchayat and Panchayats of Wayanad, where problems of shortage of safe drinking water were acute.

Discussion on imparting health awareness is highly important as the spread of communicable and non communicable diseases has been increasing at a vigorous rate. Hence, the problem of epidemics being discussed in a public sphere like Grama Sabha is highly important for increasing the awareness and in undertaking precautionary measures. According to Panchayat officials, discussion of epidemics was found to be occasional, limited to the rainy season and during the spurt of epidemics. Initiating preventive measures to avoid the incidence of diseases, spread of awareness on the control and prevention of diseases through awareness and medical camps are also important. The camps can be conducted on a need based manner as per the discretion of the health officials and Panchayat officials and the latter played the role of the coordinator of such programme. The beneficiaries' opinion on the conduct of discussion on awareness and medical camps were pessimistic except for Kuttampuzha Panchayat, where the citizens opined of some level of discussion on the issues of epidemics. Health schemes and health education should be an important item of discussion during Grama Sabhas especially, among the Panchayats of Wayanad district as it is comprised of a significant portion of tribal population who are uneducated and ignorant. The transfer of powers to the local government institutions brought the panchayat level institutions under the purview of LSGI and gave them the autonomy to implement developmental programmes. The discussions on the implementation of health schemes gained importance since decentralization and a platform like Grama Sabha is appropriate for imparting such awareness, but unfortunately all the Panchayats except Noolpuzha Panchayat (which conducted very rarely), had not conducted discussions on various health schemes and discussion on health education.

The proposed advantage of decentralization of health care services is the ability of the government system to respond to local needs. This is facilitated by the existence of Grama Sabha where beneficiaries have an opportunity to raise issues of their concern. Panchayat officials are also mandatory to be part in Grama Sabha. Health officials of the Panchayats can also attend Grama Sabha. As regards to the discussion of topics in Grama Sabha, it is clear that only the items of implementation of housing schemes and the issues relating to provision of safe drinking water is discussed at least moderately in Grama Sabha, and that too in three Panchayats out of the eight selected. Other major issues like health care budgets and recruitment of health officials are very rarely raised in Grama Sabha. The enormous space that Grama Sabha has opened for articulation and demanding services remains underutilized in Panchayats with reference to health needs.

Standing Committee on Health and Sanitation

Decentralization also provides organized structures of participation for different stakeholders to evolve and evaluate policies. As such the elected members form Standing Committee on important aspects like finance, development and welfare to enable participation of providers in the formulation of action plans and assessment of their separate sector (Vijayanand, 2009). Standing Committees act as a democratic platform for the elected members of respective departments of the local government institutions (KILA, 2013). Health care planning at the Grama Panchayat level is undertaken by the Health Standing Committee with Panchayat President as the Chairman and Medical officer of the PHCs as the Convener (John, 2012).

Out of the eight sample Panchayats, Health Standing Committees from Kuttampuzha and Noolpuzha had met more frequently. The providers of the sample Panchayats opined that the Health Standing Committee meetings were conducted more frequently during incidences of medical emergencies, like the spurt of communicable and non communicable diseases, endemic diseases or occurrence of health hazards and also during rainy seasons when the chance of experiencing ill health is the most. The effectiveness of the Health Standing Committee from the provider's perspective is portrayed in the Figure 6.1.

The Figure 6.1 shows the effectiveness of the Health Standing Committee meeting of the eight Panchayats from the provider's perspective. It is observed that all Panchayats have constituted a Health Standing Committee and considered it as a significant body in the implementation of local health care delivery. In some Grama Panchayats like Kuttampuzha, Noolpuzha and Vellamunda, both Public Health Institutions and PRI officials consider Standing Committee on health as very effective with a weighted average ranging from 4.4 to 4.8, whereas in Grama Panchayats like

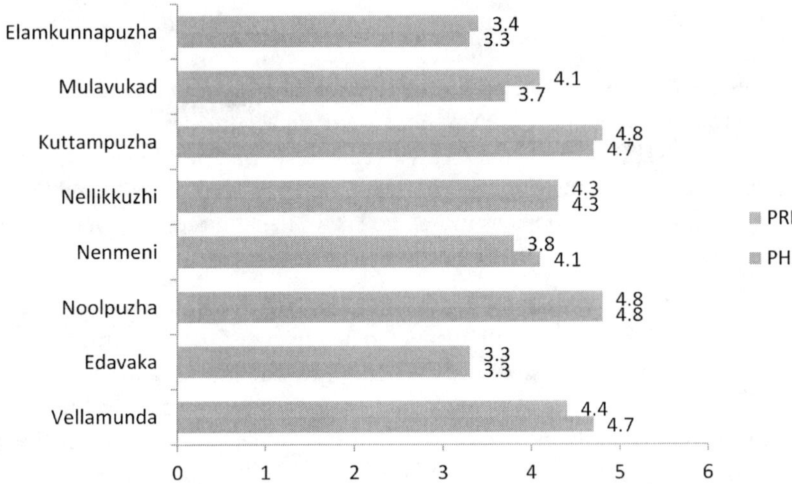

Source:- Primary Survey

Figure 6.1 Effectiveness of the Health Standing Committee from the provider's perspective

Elamkunnapuzha, Mulavukad and Edavaka, both of them considered it to have a neutral effect on health care with a score ranging from 3 to 3.7. It is observed that major proportion of both the providers in Elamkunnapuzha and Edavaka Grama Panchayat considered Health Standing Committee to have a neutral effect on health care. The PRIs of Elamkunnapuzha reported that the health care providers were rarely present during the meetings and had limited opinions on health care delivery. Likewise, the health care institutions in Edavaka were of the opinion that the PRIs were not co-operative in the provision of health care delivery and were not available in most of Health Standing Committee meetings. The officials in Mulavukad however considered Health Standing Committee as a formal body, which possesses limited decision making power with respect to health care delivery in the Panchayat.

Hospital Management Committee

HMC is a similar democratic platform of elected members of LSGI and the medical staffs, constituted for the betterment of the local health institutions. At the Grama Panchayat level, President of Panchayat is the Chairman of HMC with the Superintendent /Medical Officer of PHC as the Convener. It also consists of representatives from PRIs, PHCs, representatives of political parties, professionals and civil society organizations. Main functions of the HMC is the mobilization and management of a separate fund known as HMC fund which is collected from the fees paid by the patients at the time of out-patient and in-patient registration, donations from public funds and from the fund mobilized through NRHM scheme. It also involves in resolving problems concerning public health care institutions and deals with public grievances and health needs of the people. Besides these, the HMC also initiates the appointment of temporary staffs in PHC (John, 2013).

HMCs in the sample Grama Panchayats had undertaken several innovative programmes with respect to health care. HMC of Kuttampuzha Panchayat has constructed a feeding room for the lactating mothers of the Panchayat, Noolpuzha Panchayat had undertaken a programme known as 'Santhvana Sparsham' which was a diversion from the conventional Palliative programme and brought the bed ridden patients to the broad day light. The expenses for the programme were met by the health staffs and Panchayat staffs who voluntarily contributed their one day income for the conduct of the programme. Noolpuzha Panchayat has also initiated the timely distribution of nutritional food for the undernourished children and conducted follow up to evaluate the progress. Successful decentralization depends upon coordination between health providers and Grama Panchayat officials. The Grama Panchayat can provide the community mobilization skills whereas health providers can give their professional skills; whenever these two worked in unison, success emerged.

Responsibility Matrix

It was believed that the responsibility of the LSGI in catering to the needs of population would increase when they were given status of a constitutional body. However, success of decentralization depends on the responsibility felt by the Panchayati Raj officials. Health sector decentralization can work successfully only if the PHI officials also understand their responsibility and work in tandem with the PRI officials. If there exists coordination between the PRI and PHI officials, both consider it as their equal responsibility to improve the health status of the population, the relationship should be harmonious. In conflicting cases, when either of the providers feel that they have increased responsibility over the other, it is an indication to the existence of certain tension between them. Therefore local health care institutions and the LSG should appreciate each other's significance in imparting a healthy environment and thereby carry out a shared responsibility. The nature of their responsibility over the health care delivery is understood with a responsibility matrix.

Responsibility matrix is constructed for PRI and PHI officials. If both felt equal responsibility the score is given as two, if the PRI or PHI felt that it is their responsibility alone, then the score given is one and if PRI or PHI responded that it is the other's responsibility, the score is given as zero. Weighted average of the opinion of sample respondents is obtained with regard to initiation of need based programmes, fixing target population, ensuring supply of medicines, community participation programmes, planning and implementation of new projects and maintenance of existing infrastructure. The mean value of opinion is then converted into standardized index, so that the index value ranges from 0 to 1. Values ranging from 0 to 0.33, 0.33 to 0.66 and 0.66 to 1 are classified as renounced, monopolized and shared responsibility respectively.

Table 6.3: Responsibility Matrix of PHI and PRI in Ernakulam District

	Elamkunnapuzha		*Mulavukad*		*Kuttampuzha*		*Nellikkuzhi*	
Responsibilities	PHI	PRI	PHI	PRI	PHI	PRI	PHI	PRI
Need based Programmes	0.1	0.2	0.9	0.4	1	0.93	0	0.33
Temporary Appointments	0	0	0	0	0.2	0.5	0	0
Fixing Target Population	0	0.2	0.55	0.93	0.9	0.96	0.4	0.46
Supply of Medicines	0	0	0.6	0.46	0.75	0.6	0	0.2
Community Participation	0.2	0.13	0.7	0.73	1	0.93	0.6	0.6
Implementation of new projects	0	0.13	0.4	0.53	1	0	0.3	0
Maintenance of existing infrastructure	0.4	0.66	0.2	0.53	0.8	0.73	0.9	0.26
Average Score	0.05 *	0.09 *	0.42 **	0.25 *	0.78 ***	0.66 **	0.2 *	0.13 *

*renounced responsibility, ** monopolized responsibility, *** shared responsibility

Source:- Primary Survey.

Table 6.4: Responsibility Matrix of PHI and PRI in Wayanad District

	Nenmeni		*Noolpuzha*		*Edavaka*		*Vellamunda*	
Responsibilities	***PHI***	***PRI***	***PHI***	***PRI***	***PHI***	***PRI***	***PHI***	***PRI***
Need based Programmes	0.3	0.33	1	0.6	0.7	0.86	1	0.86
Temporary Appointments	0	0	0	1	0	0	0	0.8
Fixing Target Population	0.5	0.33	0.95	0.83	0.7	0.93	0.7	0.83
Supply of Medicines	0.3	0.26	0.7	0.53	0.7	0.53	0.7	0.93

(Contd...)

Community Participation	0.5	1	1	0.86	0.7	0.86	1	0.96
Implementation of new projects	0.6	0	1	0.83	0.75	0.93	0.9	0.83
Maintenance of existing infrastructure	0.8	0.6	0.95	0.86	0.6	0.53	0.9	0.93
Standardized Score	0.25 *	0.18 *	0.8 ***	0.71 ***	0.62 **	0.36 **	0.74 ***	0.82 ***

*renounced responsibility, ** monopolized responsibility, *** shared responsibility

Source:- Primary Survey.

It is observed that in Grama Panchayats like Mulavukad, Kuttampuzha, Noolpuzha and Vellamunda, the health care institutions pursued shared responsibility over health care delivery and respects each other's significance. In Grama Panchayats like Nellikkuzhi and Edavaka health officials considered it as their sole responsibility alone and declined the significance of PRIs in addressing health issues. However in Panchayats like Elamkunnapuzha and Nenmeni both health institutions and PRIs renounced their responsibilities to the other.

Institutional autonomy

Decentralization which enables people's participation in local planning increases the responsibility and accountability of LSGI and local health care providers towards health issues. Alongside the allocation of the role and responsibilities, decentralization guarantees a certain level of autonomy

Table 6.5: Level of autonomy of PRIs

Functional Areas	*GP 1*	*GP 2*	*GP 3*	*GP 4*	*GP 5*	*GP 6*	*GP 7*	*GP 8*
Revenue	0.05*	0.05*	0.3*	0.25*	0*	0.65**	0*	0.05*
Expenditure	0.3*	0.05*	0.1*	0.15*	0*	0.5**	0*	0.05*
Fees	0*	0*	0*	0*	0*	0.05*	0*	0.05*
Salaries	0*	0*	0*	0*	0*	0*	0*	0*
Decision making autonomy	0.05*	0.6**	0.85***	0*	0.35**	0.8***	0*	0.7**
Hospital autonomy	0*	0.6**	0.85***	0.55**	0.5**	0.9***	0.05*	0.8***
Frame local plans	0*	0.4**	0.65***	0.55**	0.3*	0.8***	0.4**	0.6**

GP 1-Elamkunnapuzha, GP 2-Mulavukad, GP 3-Kuttampuzha, GP 4- Nellikkuzhi, GP 5- Nenmeni, GP 6- Noolpuzha, GP 7- Edavaka, GP 8- Vellamunda

*Low autonomy, ** Moderate autonomy, *** High autonomy

Source:- Primary Survey

over several heads. A decision space analysis is done to understand the level of autonomy of LSGI with respect to health sector and weighted average of the opinion of PRI officials regarding autonomy is obtained. The weighted scores of the opinions of Grama Panchayat officials regarding autonomy is worked out and the scores are then converted into standardized index, so that the index value ranges from 0 to 1. Values ranging from 0 to 0.33, 0.33 to 0.66 and 0.66 to 1 are classified as low, moderate and wide range of autonomy respectively. The Table 6.5 illustrates the level of autonomy as perceived by members of Grama Panchayat.

It is observed from the above table 1.5 that the PRI officials from Ernakulam District felt that they had a narrow decision space over the major functional areas, while the PRI officials of Noolpuzha and Edavaka felt a moderate decision space over the functional areas in health. It could thus be noted that inspite of the decentralization in the health care sector, the degree of autonomy as felt by the LSG officials has been limited on several spheres.

Section II: Effectiveness of Health care programmes

Health providers in a decentralized system act as the technical wing which carries out health care activities with the monitoring of PRIs. The PHCs and CHCs which existed even before the revolutionary Panchayati raj act served as the primary health facility for the people under its purview. The health care activities of these institutions prior to decentralization were limited as it were provisioned with less roles and responsibilities. But since decentralization, the autonomy and sphere of operation of PRIs including health care providers were transferred to the LSGI.

Besides the routine services like outpatient care and inpatient care, the health department has introduced several health programmes which are initiated through the primary health institutions, with a view to improve preventive and promotive care. The public health programmes like immunization, nutritional day programmes, adolescent health programmes, maternal and child health programme, the integrated disease control programme which include the prevention and control of diseases like tuberculosis, leprosy, vector borne diseases etc. are undertaken through the PHC. The Ward Sanitation Committees comprising of health staffs and health workers safeguards the health of the population from the spread of vector borne diseases by frequently checking the breeding of vectors and conducting awareness campaigns that supplements the programmes. The programmes undertaken at the Panchayat level ranges from financing of the local health activities and implementation of centrally sponsored schemes to the initiation of need specific programmes of the Grama Panchayat.

The Grama Panchayat officials and health officials of the eight sample Panchayats opined that decentralization has increased the sphere of influence and their ability to respond to local needs. It has increased the roles and responsibilities of the local governing bodies from a financer to a facilitator. The health care activities at the Grama Panchayat level are currently the shared responsibility of both PRIs and Panchayat health institutions. It was observed during the primary survey that in the situations of medical emergencies like sudden spread of communicable diseases, the health officials with the support of Panchayat officials were able to conduct urgent medical camps and adopt preventive measures. The health officials of Kuttampuzha Panchayat mentioned a recent health crisis created by the spread of typhoid which caused a few casualties and the situation was controlled due to the timely intervention of Panchayat officials by conducting medical camps, increasing the awareness, inspection of local hotels and ensuring the availability of safe drinking water. Table 6.9a summarizes the opinion of stakeholders with respect to effectiveness of health schemes. A five point likert scale is used and a mean score more than 3 indicates that the scheme has been effective.

Table 6.6: Effectiveness of Health care activities undertaken by the stakeholders in the Grama Panchayats of Ernakulam

Health care activities	*GP 1*		*GP 2*		*GP 3*		*GP 4*	
	P	*B*	*P*	*B*	*P*	*B*	*P*	*B*
Monitoring the working of Ward Sanitation Committee	2.92	1.6	3.44	1.94	3.52	3.32	4.08	3.66
Coordination of awareness Camps and medical camps	4.28	2.86	4.08	3.46	3.96	4.16	3.92	3.42
Financial Aid for mentally retarded/disabled people	3.24	1.24	3.04	2.22	3.44	3.24	3.12	1.72
Implementation of Palliative Care Programmes	4.2	3.52	2.48	2.92	4	4.02	4.2	3.04
Health related schemes	4.52	2.06	4.04	2.7	2.68	3.9	4.32	2.8
Enabling safe drinking water & sanitation	4.52	1.54	2.88	2.88	3.92	3.72	3.44	1.24
Control of epidemics	4.04	1.86	3.88	2.08	4.16	3.82	2	3.56

GP 1-Elamkunnapuzha, GP 2-Mulavukad, GP 3-Kuttampuzha, GP 4- Nellikkuzhi P – Providers, B Beneficiaries *Source:-* Primary Survey

Table 6.7: Effectiveness of Health care activities undertaken by the stakeholders in the Grama Panchayats of Wayanad

Health care activities	*GP 5*		*GP 6*		*GP 7*		*GP 8*	
	P	*B*	*P*	*B*	*P*	*B*	*P*	*B*
Monitoring the working of Ward Sanitation Committee	1.32	1	4.28	4.18	3.52	3.44	3.12	3.7
Coordination of awareness camps and medical camps	4.56	3.1	4.12	4.06	3.88	3.22	4.16	3.96
Financial Aid for mentally retarded/ disabled people	3.72	1.52	3.84	3.62	3.52	1.9	3.64	3.4
Implementation of Palliative Care Programmes	4.88	2.84	4.4	4.22	4.56	3.3	4.04	3.84
Health related schemes	4.56	2.1	4.36	4.32	4.8	2.38	4.24	3.92
Enabling safe drinking water & sanitation	2.84	1.62	4.08	3.84	3.48	1.66	3	3.32
Control of Epidemics	4.28	2.72	4.32	4.26	4.12	4.48	3.88	1.94

GP 5- Nenmeni, GP 6- Noolpuzha, GP 7- Edavaka, GP 8- Vellamunda

P – Providers, B-Beneficiaries

Source:- Primary Survey

According to the health officials, the first step taken in the case of a health emergency is the conduct of an urgent medical camp to diagnose the victims and initiating the preliminary treatment thereof. The medical camps at the Panchayat level also become a place to spread awareness regarding precautionary steps to control the emergency. According to the beneficiaries of Kuttampuzha Panchayat, the incidence of communicable disease in the Panchayat was controlled due to the timely intervention of Panchayat and health officials. Both providers and beneficiaries of Kuttampuzha Panchayat felt that medical camps and awareness camps were effective. As far as the health schemes were concerned, beneficiaries representing the Panchayats from Ernakulam district responded positively. The beneficiary opinion of Kuttampuzha Panchayat ranked highest in effectiveness score regarding the implementation of health schemes. It is observed that Panchayat conducted several tribal health programmes including the practical sessions on the nutrition inclusion in the diet and promotion of games which are intended to promote awareness. The non tribal beneficiaries from the Panchayat also opined that the intensive efforts undertaken by the health staffs and Panchayat officials have resulted in the increased institutional deliveries among the tribals.

A major health problem reported by health officials is nutritional deficiency and anemia. The pregnant women, children and the vulnerable sections like tribal population are often victims of under nutrition and anemia. It is observed that the beneficiaries of Noolpuzha Panchayat responded positively to the nutritional day programme conducted at the PHC. According to the respondents, the Panchayat health providers took special care in the case of under nourished children. In addition to this, the people suffering from sickle cell anemia are provided with special nutritional care. The nutritional food distribution at the PHC and the Anganwadi nutrition programme through the ICDS are two parallel programmes aimed at providing adequate nutrition to the needy.

All the above said health programmes undertaken at the Panchayat level are supplemented by the efforts undertaken by the Panchayat on sectors that indirectly influences health like, availability of safe drinking water, maintenance of hygienic environment and ward sanitation programmes intended on the control of vector borne diseases. As far as sanitation is concerned, it is the duty of the Ward Sanitation Committee to keep a constant check on the breeding of mosquitoes and vectors by conducting vector control programmes and the activities like source reduction, distribution of bleaching powder and chlorination of wells and water bodies as a major strategy to control the breeding of vectors. According to the health officials of Vellamunda, they conducted regular check up on the breeding of mosquitoes and stagnant water and iterated the process till the mission was fully accomplished. Similarly, health officials in Nellikkuzhi Panchayat mentioned about the initiation of regular house visits by the sanitation committee members including the health officials such as health inspectors and the health standing committee members representing Panchayat officials. 'Dry day' was celebrated by spreading the awareness on the problems of stagnant water and draining of the water from the flower pots and vessels and drying it under sun. The ward sanitation campaign as observed in the opinion survey of beneficiaries was active in the Nellikkuzhi and Vellamunda Panchayat. The beneficiaries validated the claim of the Panchayat and health officials of Nellikkuzhi on the conduct of dry day campaign and the vector control programmes initiated in Vellamunda Panchayat. It was also observed during the primary survey that the pensioner's association in Edavaka conducted a programme on the cleansing of the Panchayat under the assistance of Edavaka PHC, whereas beneficiaries of Elamkunnapuzha argued that the ward sanitation staffs failed in executing the programmes and only collected the signatures of the people so as to produce an affirmation to the superior authority.

Alongside the health programmes, a major parallel programme initiated at the Panchayat is a palliative care programme which dealt with the home care treatment of bed ridden patients. The health officials of Noolpuzha

Panchayat, initiated a programme called 'Santhvana Sparsham' which mobilized money from the sacrifice of one day income of government employees and other volunteers to organize a day out for the bed ridden patients accompanied by counseling and medication. As far as palliative care programmes are concerned, the beneficiaries of Noolpuzha Panchayat were satisfied by the palliative care programmes and the 'Santhvana Sparsham' programme introduced by the Panchayat.

Conclusion

It is inferred from the study that Grama Sabha holds the credit of being a constitutional assembly that encourages the participation of people in the local governance. However, it is noticed that most of the Panchayats conducted Grama Sabhas only twice a year and failed to include the discussions and deliberations on health and other social factors influencing health. Grama Sabhas were observed to be an assembly, limited only for the selection of beneficiaries in housing programmes and self-employment generating programmes and falling short of minimum majority. It is understood from these observations that, the potential of Grama Sabhas and other local assemblies remain largely underutilized and even violated in certain extreme situation, where the records are manipulated by the coordinators on failing to realize the minimum participation.

Likewise, the committees such as HMC and HSC established with a purpose of providing a democratic platform to the PHI and PRIs, discuss and analyze the issues prevailing in health sector. Although the providers selected for the study acclaimed the constitution of these committees, the actual situation is different as portrayed through the responsibility matrix which depicted the responsibility of the PHI and PRI on the matters of health. It is observed from the responsibility matrix that, except for Grama Panchayats like Mulavukad, Kuttampuzha, Noolpuzha and Vellamunda, most of the providers considered it as either their own sole responsibility or entirely other entity's responsibility. This unaccommodating attitude exhibited by these institutions is destructive to the very essence of decentralization which primarily dealt with the intra agency contribution, cooperation and participation. Besides the responsibility matrix, the autonomy of LSGs on health care is also examined. It is observed that, even after two decades of decentralization, autonomy felt by LSGIs on health care matters remain moderate and often lower in certain functional areas such as finance and appointment of staffs. However, lack of autonomy experienced in other functional areas are either because of the extreme dominance of PHI, reluctance of PRIs on intervening in health matters or due to the worst-case scenarios such as the ignorance of PRIs about the privileges enjoyed in a decentralized governance. To conclude, given its reasonably good track record in the decentralization of power, authority and finances, Kerala provides a good opportunity for PRIs to demonstrate their capability in improving the health service delivery for the benefit of the local community. This, to a great extent, depends upon key factors including the nature and extent of functions decentralized, mechanisms to ensure community participation, sources and distribution of finance at the local levels, approach to planning, professional support, status of intersectoral and interdepartmental collaboration, co-operation, coordination and mutual trust between health bureaucracy and Panchayat leadership etc. Wherever these factors are in affirmative direction, profound success has been materialized. Given this context, the remarkable possibilities that decentralization of health services have opened to solve the public health issues remains under tapped. The need of the hour is concerted efforts from all stakeholders to make the system function effectively.

References

1. Bossert, T. (1998), 'Analyzing the Decentralization of Health Systems in Developing Countries: Decision Space, Innovation And Performance', **Social Science Medicine,** Vol. 47, No. 10, Great Britain, pp. 1513-1527.
2. Buch, N. (2012), 'Gram Sabha and Panchayati Raj', **Social Action,** Vol. 62 January – March 2012. New Delhi.
3. Chaudhuri, S., K.N.Harilal, and P.Heller (2004), '**Does decentralization make a difference? A study of the people's campaign for decentralized planning in the Indian state of Kerala'**, Thiruvananthapuram: Centre for Development Studies.
4. Eapen, M., and S. Thomas (2005), **'Gender Analysis of Selected Gram(Village) Panchayat Plan-Budgets in Trivandrum District, Kerala'**, Discussion Paper series 11, New Delhi, United Nations Development Programme.
5. Franke, R.W., and H.C.Barbara (2000), **'The Kerala Decentralisation Experiment, Achievements, Origins and Implication',** International Conference on Democratic Decentralisation, Thiruvananthapuram, Kerala, India, State Planning Board, Kerala.
6. George, M.S. (2007), **'An Introduction to Local Self Governments in Kerala',** SDC CAPDECK, Swiss Agency for Development and Cooperation p. 51.
7. Government of India (2012), **'Indian Public Health Standards (IPHS) Guidelines for Primary Health Centres',** Directorate General of Health Services, Ministry of Health & Family Welfare.
8. Government of Kerala (1994), **'Kerala Panchayat Raj Act, 1994'**
9. John, J. (2012), '**A Study on Effectiveness of Panchayati Raj Institutions in Health Care System in the State of Kerala',** Planning Commission, Government of India.

10. Kannan KP, Thankappan KR, Kutty VR, et al. Health and Development in Rural Kerala. Trivandrum: Kerala Sastra Sahithya Parishad; 1991.
11. Kerala Institute of Local Administration (KILA) (2009), **'Report of the Committee for Evaluation of Decentralised Planning and Development'**, Government of Kerala.
12. Kerala Institute of Local Administration (KILA) (2013), **'Local Governance System and Students Local Governance System and Students (Handbook for the Students of Higher Secondary Schools)'**, Government of Kerala.
13. Khan, P.M., P. Bava, O. John and L. Kumari (2001), **'Report of the study of Women Component Plan in Kerala'**, UNICEF, Chennai.
14. Nagaraj, K. (1999), **'Decentralisation in Kerala: A Note'**, Discussion Paper No. 2. Kerala Research Programme on Local Level Development, Centre for Development Studies.
15. Narayana, D., and K.K. Harikurup, (2000), **'Decentralisation of the Health Care Sector in Kerala: Some Issues'**, Centre for Development Studies.
16. Padmaja, K. (2005), **'An Evaluation of Primary Health Care System In Kerala'**, Department of Applied Economics Cochin University Of Science And Technology Cochin, Kerala.
17. Raman Kutty, V. (2000), 'Historical analysis of the development of health care facilities in Kerala State, India', **Health Policy and Planning** 15(1): pp.103-109.
18. Thomas, M. B., and K.Rajesh (2011),**'Decentralisation and Interventions in Health Sector: A Critical Inquiry into the Experience of Local Self Governments in Kerala'**, The Institute for Social and Economic Change, working paper 271, Bangalore
19. Varatharajan, R. Thankappan and S. Jayapalan (2004), **'Assessing the performance of primary health centres under decentralized government in Kerala, India'**, Oxford University Press.
20. Varatharajan, R.Thankappan and S.Jayapalan (2004), 'Assessing the performance of Primary Health Centres under decentralized government in Kerala, India', AchuthaMenon Centre for Health Science Studies, SreeChitraTirunaldoi: 10.1093/heapol/czh005 **Health Policy and Planning 19**(1): 41–5, Oxford University Press, 2004.
21. Varatharajan, R. Thankappan, and S. Jayapalan (2004), **'Assessing the performance of primary health centres under decentralized government in Kerala'**, India Oxford University Press.
22. Vijayanand, S. M. (2009), **'Kerala-A Case study of classical democratic decentralization'**, Kerala Institute of Local Administration (KILA) p 80.
23. Vijayanand, S.M. (2001), **'Issues Related to Administrative Decentralization and Administering of Decentralization, Lessons from the Kerala Experience'**, Institute for Social and Economic Change, Bangal

7

Fair price Medical Shops in Kerala: An Exploratory Study

Merin Joy

The state of Kerala is historically famous for its achievements in social developments evidenced by the comparable rates of its health indicators like birth rate, death rate, Infant Mortality Rate, Maternal Mortality Rate, with that of well developed countries. Achievements in the social development despite economic backwardness gave the State's development experience a new title; Kerala Model of Development, with Kerala Model of Health, where quality care was provided at an affordable rate as an important component. Of late the so called Kerala Model of Health is addressing a crisis because, Kerala's health sector today is characterized by low mortality and high morbidity syndrome, prevalence of infectious diseases, high incidence of life style diseases compared to national average, re-emergence of eliminated diseases and alienation of public health system from common people resulting in escalating health care expenditure (Ekbal, 2017).

The demographic features of the state reveal that Kerala is in the final stage of demographic transition with 12.1% of people in above 65 years age category and proportion of elderly population in the State is showing a steady increase over the last 30 years. Ageing population also means ailing population in Kerala because studies show that majority of the elderly population are morbid, particularly with chronic diseases creating financial burden to the entire family (Mukherjee et al, 2012; Loutfi et al, 2018). But in Kerala, the prevalence of non-communicable diseases like diabetes, hypertension, cardio vascular diseases are not confined to elderly population alone, rather population across age groups suffers from the above said diseases. Also, Kerala's disease profile clearly shows a transition from communicable to non-communicable diseases to chronic diseases. Kerala has one of the highest prevalence rate of non communicable diseases and its risk factors (Government of Kerala, 2014). Unlike communicable diseases, non communicable diseases need life long treatment and long term medication. So, ensuring access to essential medicines becomes especially relevant for Kerala due to the demographic and morbidity features described above. On the expenditure side, Kerala follows the same pattern of the country; here also public expenditure is nominal and major share of health expenditure is borne by households as out of pocket expenditure. Among the Indian States, Kerala tops in the share of health in total household expenditure both in rural and urban areas and drugs constitute the largest share of total health expenditure, pushing people to 'medical poverty' (Government of Kerala, 2014).

Government has initiated various measures to reduce out of pocket expenditure and improve access to medicine situation in the State. Like many other States, Kerala too has its own Essential Drug List with 374 medicines. Recognizing the importance of centralized procurement in reducing medicine prices, Kerala formed a centralized procurement agency called Kerala Medical Service Corporation Limited (KMSCL), similar to Tamil Nadu Medical Service Corporation Limited (TNMSCL), to procure and distribute medicines for the public health facilities in the State. Additionally, the government constituted Kerala State Drugs and Pharmaceuticals (KSDP) to produce selected medicines locally and thereby increasing availability of medicines in the State. In the initial years of establishment of KSDP, it was the main supplier of medicines to the public health facilities. Later with the constitution of KMSCL, more suppliers came into picture through open tender (Lekshmi et al, 2014). State Planning Board briefs various measures adopted by the Government to reduce Out of Pocket Expenditure; these include strengthening of primary care service delivery, ensuring comprehensive financial risk protection through various programmes, strengthening of service delivery of public hospitals and strengthening drugs and diagnostic facilities in primary, secondary and tertiary health facilities. Relevant measures pointed out in the report to strengthen access to medicines are constitution of KMSCL and starting of Karunya Community Pharmacies under the Corporation.

Given this context, the researcher would like to examine the Access To Medicine situation in Kerala by focusing on affordability of medicines. WHO (2004) identified affordability of medicines as an important component of Access To Medicines (ATM). Affordability is not an absolute concept, since what is affordable to people with higher income may not be so for others. So, the term 'affordability of medicines' in the present study implies 'provision of medicines at lower prices.' The 'actual' prices (what we pay for medicines may also contain mark ups) of medicines is not known, as they are determined by supply-demand interaction. For practical purpose it is assumed thatmedicines will become more affordable if they are sold at prices less than their Maximum Retail Price (MRP) and hence the study focuses on those medical shops that sell medicines at prices less than their MRP. Medical stores (the terms medical stores/shops and drug stores/shops are used interchangeably) run by government/quasi government agencies that sell medicines at prices less than MRP are consideredsince they try to intervene in drug market.These shops are referred to as'Fair Price Medical Shops (FPMSs)' and hence the researcher attempts to understand the role of FPMSs in ATM situation of Kerala and the study covers three FPMSs – Neethi Medical Stores (NMS), Karunya Community Pharmacies (KCP) and Jan Aushadhi Stores (JAS).

The rest of the study is organized as follows. Section I poses the research questions, objectives and materials and methods of the study. Section II examines the structure and operational aspects of selected FPMS in Kerala along with spatial distribution of FPMS across the State. Section III makes a comparison of prices of selected medicines among the FPMSs, Section IV discusses consumer perception regarding the operations of FPMS andSectionVconcludes the study.

Section I: Research Questions and Objectives

Kerala's pharmaceutical setting is marked with open market retail medical shops as well as fair price medical shops. Even though people have no freedom to choose medicines, they can decide upon 'from where to purchase?' So, people can purchase from FPMS or from any other medical shops according to their choice. This article is designed to find answers to some basic questions on the operations of FPMS in retail medicine market setting of Kerala. As geographical access is a basic determinant of access, the study examines geographical distribution of FPMS across Kerala. The structural and operational elements of the functioning of FPMS is relevant to study as it may help to understand different dimensions of FPMS including discounts for different category of medicines. Relevance of FPMS in the retail medicine market is ultimately determined/evaluated by those who purchase from such stores. So, along with various supply side aspects of functioning of the stores, the demand side realities must be incorporated in a study of FPMS. Considering all these, the researcher arrives at the following research questions;

- o How do the selected FPMSs operate? Who monitor their operations? How are they distributed regionally across Kerala?
- o Is there any significant price difference for same medicines across different FPMSs?
- o To what extent the consumers benefit from FPMSs? What are the perceptions on advantages/disadvantages of FPMSs?

The researcher attempts to answer the above questions and for which the following objectives are set. (a) to understand the structure and organizational/operational aspects of selected FPMSs in Kerala (b) to make a comparison of prices of selected medicines among selected FPMSs and (c) to understand the consumer perception regarding the operations of FPMSs

Materials and Methods

The study relies upon both primary and secondary data sources to meet the specific objectives. In order to understand the structure and operational aspects of FPMSs, available secondary data were used. Key Informant Interviews (KII) with the important stakeholders like physicians, pharmacists and ASHA workers helped to get basic understanding of the issue of access to medicine in the study area. Insights from KIIs added to the information gathered from published sources and helped to meet first objective. The second and third objectives were met through drug shop survey and household survey respectively.

As a case study, Kothamangalam area of Ernakulam district was selected where all the three types of FPMS considered in the study were present. Prices of selected medicines were collected from individual FPMS and from a randomly selected open medical store for comparison. Household survey was conducted at a municipal ward and panchayath ward situated at equidistance from the town (Kothamangalam) where drug shops are situated. The entire households of the wards were surveyed and there were 552 households in the two selected wards. An Interview Schedule was used to collect data. The respondents were mainly the head of households or in their absence the eldest member. The first part of the schedule contained information about socio economic back ground of households, and the second part collected information on disease profile of household members. Details of treatment, choice of health facility, pattern of medication and monthly family health expenditure were recorded. In the third part, questions regarding awareness of FPMSs, and utilization of the same were included.

To make price comparison among selected FPMSs, a list of medicines was prepared. It was done after medical consultation and the list included medicines for common NCDs like diabetes, hypertension, cholesterol and CVDs. Two medicines commonly used for treating these NCDs were selected and insulin was also included in the list, hence the total number of medicines in the list was nine. The prices of these medicines were obtained by visiting branches of selected FPMSs in Kothamangalam. As branded medicines were sold at NMS and KCP, prices of most and least expensive medicines were recorded. In JAS, there was only single price of nine medicines as they sold pure generics.

Section II: Structure and Operational Aspects of FPMSs and Spatial Distribution of FPMS across Kerala

Fair Price Medical Shops (FPMSs) in Kerala

It is a well-recognized fact that medicines constitute major share of household out of pocket expenditure in India as well as in Kerala. As every sphere of health sector is dominated by private players, in the retailing of medicines also the main players are open retail pharmacies. Many open retail pharmacies sell medicines at discounted prices, where the discount varies from store to store. Along with these, medical shops under charitable organizations and some institutions also do this in different places. But this particular study considers a different set of medical shops which are run by governmental or semi-governmental departments or associated with some government programme. Thus, the considered medical stores are part of government efforts to intervene in retailing of medicines in the State. Three categories of medical shops are included under "fair price medical shops"; they are Neethi Medical Stores under Consumerfed, Karunya Community Pharmacies under Kerala Medical ServiceCorporation Ltd and Jan Aushadhi Stores under Pradhan Mantri Bhartiya JanaushadhiPariyojana. The following section details the profiles of the considered FPMS.

Neethi Medical Stores (NMS)

Consumerfed started "Neethi Medical Stores" with the assistance of Government of Kerala from 1st November 1998. Under this scheme, medicines are made available to the consumers at a price less by 18 % to 70% of the MRP. Discount offered can vary between each Neethi store as it is decided by the cooperative society under which the store operates. But discounts will be comparable. The role of Consumerfed in the scheme mainly is to procure and distribute medicines on wholesale basis as per the requirement of the Neethi Medical stores. For this the federation have set up 12 Neethi Medical Warehouses. At present there are 90 Neethi Medical Stores directly run by Federation in addition to the 600 odd stores runby different Primary Co-operative Societies. So, the federation's role is of a wholesaler who purchase, procure medicines on largescale and distribute them to hundreds of medical stores owned and operated by primary cooperative societies to make medicines available at reasonable prices. The active intervention of the Federation in the medicines market is considered one of the important steps of the Federation to control the price levels of medicines, which is a boon to thousands of poor patients in the state. For wholesale buying and distribution of medicines to the Neethi Medical Stores, the Federation has a separate unit at its head office and warehouses at various places in the state.

Karunya Community Pharmacies (KCP)

Karunya Community Pharmacy is a state-run retail chain providing medicines at affordable prices to common people. The pharmacy sells branded generics at steep discounts ranging from 20 to 60 percent. It's a pure for-profit chain of pharmacies, with 52 outlets currently in different parts of the state. The pharmacies are run by Kerala Medical Service Corporation Ltd, which is a fully owned government company started to provide essential medicines and equipment to various public healthcare facilities. Karunya pharmacies compete with other open retail pharmacies on equal terms. The pharmacy manages to offer cheaper prices through bulk procurement for the entire State by the procurement agency KMSCL. So, the reduction in prices is made possible through centralized pooled purchasing directly from the manufacturers and thereby avoiding middlemen margins. Operation of this chain of subsidy medical shops is within government hospitals and primary health care centres. Kerala Government is planning to introduce its own generic brand called "Kerala Generics" to sell through KCPs.

Pharmacists of KCPs communicated with the researcher that the pharmacies face severe shortage of medicines due to payment delay of KMSCL to various drug companies. As per tender agreement, the corporation has to clear the payment within 45 days of supply of medicines. Unlike the initial announcement, expansion of the outlets didn't take place to the targeted number.

Jan Aushadi Stores (JAS)

Jan Aushadhi Stores are started with the intention of making quality medicines available at affordable prices for all, especially the poor and disadvantaged. Since September 2015, the 'Jan Aushadhi Scheme' was revamped as **'Pradhan Mantri Jan Aushadhi Yojana'** (PMJAY). In November, 2016, to give further impetus to the scheme, it was again renamed as "Pradhan Mantri Bhartiya Janaushadhi Pariyojana". Jan Aushadhi Stores sell generic medicines at huge discounted prices but without compromising in quality when compared to expensive branded drugs. It is a part of government initiative to bring down out of pocket expenditure. It is designed as a public programme involving Government, PSUs, Private Sector, NGO, Societies, Co-operative Bodies and other Institutions.

Malayala Manorama Daily (12 October 2018) reported that nearly 60 Jan Aushadhi Stores are either closed or nonfunctional due to lack of stock and delay in getting the offered incentives from the Government. Remedial measures were taken to rectify these complaints. Changes were made in the distribution channel and individual JAS can purchase medicines directly from the Central Warehouse along with the purchase from State Warehouse at Ernakulam. As there is only a single warehouse in the State for the entire JAS all across the State, severe shortage of medicines is experienced by many JAS.

Spatial Distribution of Fair Price Medical Shops across Kerala

Geographical dispersion of fair price medical shops shows a wide disparity among different districts. Also, presence of fair price medical shops differs between categories. Following section gives an overview of regional distribution of fair price medical shops across the State.

Table 7.1: Number of Fair Price Medical Shops in Kerala

Type of FPMS	*Number*
Neethi Medical Store	708
Karunya Community Pharmacies	52
Jan Aushadhi Stores	419

Source: www.dc.kerala.gov.in

It is clear from the table that Neethi Medical Stores are the dominant type of FPMS in Kerala in terms of number. Number of Neethi Medical stores and JAS shows an increasing trend over the time (when compared to the number of FPMS six months back which was recorded by the researcher from the same source) which is not visible in case of KCP.

Table 7.2: Spatial Distribution of FPMS across Kerala in 2019

Sl. No.	*District*	*Neethi*	*Jan Aushadi*	*Karunya*	*District Total*
1.	Trivandrum	56	48	10	114
2.	Kollam	40	32	5	77
3.	Pathanamthitta	56	22	5	83
4.	Alappuzha	61	28	5	94
5.	Kottayam	76	33	3	112
6.	Ernakulam	69	52	6	127
7.	Idukki	30	14	1	45
8.	Thrissur	153	77	2	232
9.	Palakkad	29	33	3	65
10.	Malappuram	35	24	2	61
11.	Kozhikode	67	28	5	100
12.	Wayanad	10	6	2	18
13.	Kannur	58	15	1	74
14.	Kasargod	24	6	2	32
	Total	764	418	52	1234

Source: www.dc.kerala.gov.in

Number of fair price medical shops considerably varies among the districts. But Neethi is the dominant FPMS in all districts except one.Thrissur district has the maximum number of Neethi and Jan Aushadhi. The district leads ahead of other districts in terms of total number of FPMS. The second district with highest number of FPMS is Ernakulam followed by Trivandrum. Wayanad has the least numberof FPMS. Coming to individual presence of each category of FPMS in the districts, Thrissur has the maximum number of Neethi medical stores followed by Kottayam and Ernakulam. But Thrissur has almost double the number of Neethi stores than Kottayam. Wayanad is at the bottom end. In case of Jan Aushadhi Stores also, Thrissur tops the list followed by Ernakulam and Trivandrum. Wayanad and Kasargod has the minimum number of Jan Aushadhi Stores. Palakkad is the only district where there are more number of Jan Aushadhi Stores than Neethi. Number of Karunya Pharmacies are very low compared to other two category. Only Trivandrum district has 10 KCP which is the maximum. Even though there are wide variations in the number of FPMS, there is presence of FPMS in all districts.

To summarise, it is understood that the FPMSs under study procure/ distribute larger quantities of medicines in a centralized manner and try to give a share of the difference between wholesale and retail price to the consumer. This is the core modus operandi of all FPMSs under study; except JAS which tries to give discount by selling and promoting generic than branded medicines. Even in the case of JAS, a Centralized Procurement and Distribution System (CPDS) exist. Based on the stakeholder interaction done by the researcher, it is understood that organizational or operational advantages/disadvantages of FPMSs under consideration can be understood from the efficiency of CPDS of the particular FPMS. JAS face those difficulties as its CPDS could not deliver medicines according to demand in the market. The extent to which CPDSs of FPMSs is able to supply the required medicines on time not only testifies its efficiency, it also determines the sales turnover and long run financial sustainability of FPMSs.Looking at the regional dispersion of FPMSs in Kerala, we can understand that it's highly skewed.

Section II: Comparison of Prices of Selected Medicines among Selected FPMS

Fair Price Medical Shops generally sell medicines at lower price than open market. Primary survey revealed that FPMSs differ in the discounts offered for different category of medicines. Each FPMS offers various discount rates for different category of medicines. The following table compares prices of selected medicines in the selected FPMS and in a randomly chosen open market medical store.

Table 7.3: Price Comparison of Selected Medicines among the FPMS

Medicine Generic Name	*Disease Treated*	*NMS*		*KCP*		*JAS*	*Open Market*	
		Highest Price (Rs.)	*Lowest Price (Rs.)*	*Highest Price (Rs.)*	*Lowest Price (Rs.)*	*Price (Rs.)*	*Highest Price (Rs.)*	*Lowest Price (Rs.)*
Metformin	Diabetes	13.6	7.4	5.4	3.5	4	20	10.42
Glimepride	Diabetes	32.3	21.8	10.4	2.4	4	113.06	24
Insulin	Diabetes	-	120/10 ML	-	70/10 ML	71/10 ML	-	148
Amlodipine	Hypertension	23.6	10	4.9	1.3	5	49.33	23
losartan	Hypertension	51.3	25.2	7.7	6	9	105.69	35.4
Atorvastatin	Cholestrol	49.6	38.4	12.8	4	6	88	50.37
Rosuvastatin	Cholestrol	67.7	34.4	N.A	N.A	10	140	61
Aspirin	CVDs	5	3.4	N.A	N.A	1.42	11.2	4.55
Clopdogrel	CVDs	62.7	38.8	12.3	7.3	13	72.95	46.7

Source: Primary Survey

Price Difference of Selected Medicines among the FPMS - The above table compares the prices of selected medicines in each category of FPMS. Considering the prevalence of non communicable diseases like diabetes, hypertension, Cholesterol and Cardio Vascular Diseases in the State, commonly prescribed medicines for these health conditions are selected for comparison.

Neethi and Karunya pharmacies sell branded medicines at discounted rates. These stores sell different brands of a medicines with different prices. From the various brands with different prices, the highest priced one and lowest priced one are selected for comparison. But in JAS, only pure generics are available meaning, a single price for a single medicine.

Even though, Neethi is the popular and dominant FPMS, maximum prices of the selected medicines (among FPMSs) are observed at Neethi. Even the lowest price in Neethi are higher than the prices in other two stores. This is true in case of all the medicines selected. Some of the selected medicines are not sold at Karunya. Karunya pharmacies offer the best prices for all the selected medicines. The lowest brand price of Karunya is lower than the generic price of JAS. Even some of the highest brand prices of Karunya are lower than JAS prices. Highest prices of all the selected medicines are observed in open retail store.

Price Spectrum of Medicines

Following section describes relevant price spectrums explaining the extent of price difference among different medical shops for each type of medicine considered. Highest prices in the stores are considered for comparison.

Table 7.4: Price Spectrums– Metformin& Glimepiride (for diabetes)

Metformin	*Open Market*	*NMS*	*KCP*	*JAS*	*Glimepiride*	*Open Market*	*NMS*	*KCP*	*JAS*
Open Market	0%	32%	73%	80%	Open Market	0%	71%	91%	96%
NMS	-47%	0%	60%	71%	NMS	-250%	0%	68%	88%
KCP	-270%	-152%	0%	26%	KCP	-987%	-211%	0%	62%
JAS	-400%	-240%	-35%	0%	JAS	-2726%	-708%	-160%	0%

Source: Primary Survey

As there is no difference between price of Metformin in the open market store surveyed, the price difference is 0%. Price of Metformin in open market is 32% higher than that in Neethi stores and 73% higher than KCP prices and 80% higher than JAS price.On the other way, price of Metformin in Neethi stores is 47% lower than that in open market. KCP price of Metformin is 270% lower than open market and that in JAS is 400% lower than open market price. Price of Metformin in KCP is 152% lower than that in Neethi stores but it is 26% higher than the selling price in JAS. Extend of price difference is higher in case of Glimepiride compared to Metformin. Here also, the basic trend is same. Open market prices of drugs are higher than all types of FPMS and maximum price difference is observed between Open market and JAS prices.

Table 7.5: Price Spectrum – Insulin (for Diabetes)

	Open Market	*NMS*	*KCP*	*JAS*
Open Market	0%	19%	53%	52%
NMS	-23%	0%	42%	41%
KCP	-42%	-71%	0%	-1%
JAS	-108%	-69%	1.4%	0%

Source: Primary Survey

Compared to other medicines under consideration, generally, price of Insulin shows lesser variations across the medical shops. Open market price of Insulin is 19% higher than that in Neethi and it is 53% and 52% higher than the prices in KCP and JAS. KCP sells Insulin at a slightly lower price than JAS; KCP price of Insulin is 1% lower than its price in JAS. Compared to open market, JAS price for Insulin is 108% lower and it is 69% lower than the price at Neethi.

Table 7.6: Price Spectrum – Amlodipine& Losartan (for hypertension)

Amlodipine	*Open Market*	*NMS*	*KCP*	*JAS*	*Losartan*	*Open Market*	*NMS*	*KCP*	*JAS*
Open Market	0%	52%	90%	90%	Open Market	0%	51%	93%	95%
NMS	-109%	0%	79%	79%	NMS	-106%	0%	85%	82%
KCP	-907%	-382%	0%	-2%	KCP	-1273%	-566%	0%	-17%
JAS	-887%	-372%	2%	0%	JAS	-1074%	-470%	14%	0%

Source: Primary Survey

The above table shows price spectrum of selected medicines for hypertension. Unlike the cases in previous spectrums, in case of Amlodipine, KCP and JAS shows same price difference with open market and NMS. Open market price of Amlodipine is 52% higher than that in Neethi and 90% higher than prices in KCP and JAS. Extent of price difference between open market and FPMSs in case of Losartan is in comparable range with that of Amlodipine. Price of Amlodipine in Neethi is 109% lower than open market price while the difference in case of Losartan is 106%. KCP price of Amlodipine is 907% lower than that in open market and it is 1273% lower in case of Losartan. JAS price for Amlodipine is 887% and 372% lower than open market and Neethi respectively while the difference in case of Losartan is 1074% and 470%.

The below price spectrum explains extent of price difference among FPMSs and with open market in case of selected medicines for cholesterol.

Table 7.7: Price Spectrum – Atorvastatin& Rosuvastatin (for Cholesterol)

Atorvastatin	*Open Market*	*NMS*	*KCP*	*JAS*	*Rosuvastatin*	*Open Market*	*NMS*	*KCP*	*JAS*
Open Market	0%	44%	85%	93%	Open Market	0%	52%	-	93%
NMS	-77%	0%	74%	88%	NMS	-107%	0%	-	85%
KCP	-85%	-288%	0%	53%	KCP	-	-	-	-
JAS	-1367%	-727%	-113%	0%	JAS	-1300%	-577%	-	0%

Source: Primary Survey

KCP doesn't sell Rosuvastatin, so the relevant columns are left vacant. Open market sells Atorvastatin at a price which is 44%, 85% and 93% higher than the selling prices at Neethi, KCP and JAS respectively. In case of Rosuvastatin, open market price is 52% higher than that in Neethi and 93% higher than JAS price of the medicine. When compared to open market price, KCP sells Atorvastatin at 85% lower price. KCP price of Atorvastatin is 288% lower than selling price at Neethi. JAS sells Atorvastatin at a price which is 1367% lower than open market price and 727% lower than price of the same at Neethi. In case of Rosuvastatin, the difference is 1300% and 577% respectively.

Table 7.8: Price Spectrum –Clopdogrel& Aspirin (for CVD)

Clopdrogel	*Open Market*	*NMS*	*KCP*	*JAS*	*Aspirin*	*Open Market*	*NMS*	*KCP*	*JAS*
Open Market	0%	14%	83%	82%	Open Market	0%	55%	-	87%
NMS	-16%	0%	80%	79%	NMS	-124%	0%	-	71.6%
KCP	-493%	-410%	0%	-6%	KCP	-	-	-	-
JAS	-461%	-382%	5%	0%	JAS	-689%	-252%	-	0%

Source: Primary Survey

As Aspirin is not sold at KCP, the relevant columnsare left vacant. Open market price of Clopdogrel is 14% higher than that in Neethi and 83% and 82% higher than its prices in KCP and JAS respectively. Aspirin is sold at open market at a price which is 55% higher than the price in Neethi and 87% higher than the price in JAS. KCP sells Clopdogrel at the lowest price; their selling price is 493% lower compared to open market, 410% lower than selling price at Neethi and 6% lower than JAS price.

It is evident from the above tables that, in case of the selected medicines, Neethi Medical Stores show a meaningful price difference of 14% to 71% with open market and in case of KCP and JAS the extent of price difference is much wider. The range of price difference with open market and KCP is 73% to 93% for the different medicines considered and it is 80% to 96% for JAS.

To summarise, among the nine medicinesconsidered for the study, the highest discount (on comparison with Open Market Stores (OMS)) was provided for six medicines by JAS and for three medicines by KCP. The prices of all medicines were higher in NMS than KCP/JAS. If we compare the prices of selected medicines in KCP/JAS, it is clear that lowest prices are offered by KCP except in case of Rosuvsatatin and Aspirin which are not being sold at KCP. For these two medicines, JAS offered the lowest price. Among the nine medicines under consideration, KCP offered the lowest price for seven medicines and JAS offered lowest price for two which are not being sold at KCP. Even though NMS is the numerically dominant FPMS in Kerala, it is not providing any one of medicines at lowest price. Thus in an attempt to provide medicines at lower prices, the modus operandi of KCP/JAS is worth emulating than that of NMS.

Any way it is very clear that the FPMSs offered medicines at prices less than OM and there is large variation in price of same medicine among different FPMSs. This variations range from 2% to 708% (refer price spectrums).Hence comesthe issue of the extent to which these differences are made use by the consumers. This aspect along with various aspects of FPMS use by consumers is discussed below.

Section IV: Consumer Perception Regarding Fair Price Medical Shops

Analysis has shown that FPMSs are providing the selected medicines at prices less than OM. Clearly, they make medicines more affordable and are bolstering the affordability component of ATM. But the extent to which consumers benefit from FPMSs depends on the extent to which FPMSs is used by them. Understanding the same along with consumer perceptions regarding FPMSs is the third objective of the study, materialized through household survey. One panchayath ward and municipal ward equidistant from Kothamangalam town was selected and all the households in the wards were surveyed to understand the consumer perceptions on FPMSs. Together there were 552 households with a total population of 2208and they were asked to report if there is at least one household member with any one of the Non Communicable Disease (NCDs) under consideration i.e Diabetes, Hypertension, Cholestrol and Cardio Vascular Diseases (CVDs). If there is any member affected by at least one of this chronic NCDs, they were asked about their sources of purchasing medicines and their perception about FPMS use.

Table 7.9: Income category wise distribution of households

Income Category	*No. of households*
BPL	226(41%)
APL	326(59%)
Total no. of HHs surveyed	552

Source: Primary Survey

The total number of households surveyed in the selected Panchayat ward and Muncipality ward were 552 of which 59% were APL families and the rest was BPL. The households were asked to report the cases of diabetes, hypertension, cholesterol or CVD. Following table shows the disease profile of the sample population. Cases other than the four NCDs mentioned above were not considered.

Table 7.10: Distribution of Chronically ill population

Disease	*Respondents affected by the disease*
Diabetes	358(37.5%)
BP	314(32.9%)
Cholesterol	188(19.7%)
CVD	94(9.85%)
No. of people with atleast one NCD	954

Source: Primary Survey

954 people reported that they are affected by at least one of the non communicable diseases under consideration. Out of the total 954 cases of chronic illness, 37.5% were diabetic cases followed by 32.9% of hypertension, 19.7% of cholesterol and 9.85% of CVD.

Following table explains prevalence of disease in different income categories. This table shows the percentage of respondents in different category (BPL/APL) who are affected by different diseases.

Table 7.11: Income category wise distribution of chronically ill population (%)

Income Category	*Diabetes*	*Hypertension*	*Cholesterol*	*CVD*
APL	35.47%	49.04%	38.3%	46.8%
BPL	64.53%	50.96%	61.7%	53.19%

Source: Primary Survey

BPL category dominates in all types of chronic illness considered. 64.53% of total diabetic population was from BPL families and in case of cholesterol, it was 61.7%, for hypertension it was 50.96% and for CVDs it was 53.19%

The following table describes medicine purchase sources of chronically ill people.

Table 7.12: Choice of medicine purchase

Type of pharmacies	*Respondents purchasing from the pharmacy (%)*
Open Market pharmacies	61.65%
Neethi	16.25%
Karunya	1.26%
Jan Aushadhi	2.4%
Vayomithram	6.8%
Others	11.64%

Source: Primary Survey

The above table reveals people's preference for open market stores over other types of medical stores. The second most preferred option is Neethi. Other types of FPMS ie KCP and JAS, are preferred by only a small share of people. The scheme, 'Vayomithram', an initiative of Social Security Mission to provide free medicines to people above 60 years residing at municipality area is utilized by 6.8% of chronically ill people.The category 'others' include private hospital pharmacies and government hospital pharmacies.

Income (APL/BPL) category wise choice of medical shops is explained in the below table;

Table 7.13: Income category wise choice of medical shop

Income category	*Open Retail*	*Neethi*	*KCP*	*JAS*	*Vayomithram*
APL	53.33%	89.03%	8.33%	69.57%	36.92%
BPL	46.67%	10.97%	91.67%	30.43%	63.07%

Source: Primary Survey

Surprisingly, majority of FPMS users belong to APL than BPL category. So income of respondents is not a significant factor that determines FPMS use. Majority of those who utilize Neethi medical stores were from APL category which is true for those who purchase from JAS also. Majority of the KCP buyers were from BPL category and most of the beneficiaries of Vayomithram scheme were BPL households.

The following section show the people's attitude towards and utilization of different medical shops and rationalization of their choice.

Table 7.14: Choice of medical shop according to disease category

Disease	Open Retail	NMS	KCP	JAS	Vayomithram	Others
Diabetes	36.30%	32.40%	3.07%	6.14%	3.35%	18.67%
Hypertension	34%	22%	2.50%	6%	14.96%	21%
Cholesterol	29%	26.59%	3.19%	3.19%	11.17%	26.55%
CVD	31.90%	37.23%	5.31%	0%	0%	25.52%

Source: Primary Survey

Consistent with the general observation, all categories of respondents prefer open market medical stores over all other types of setting. CVD patients form an exemption with preference of NMS over open retail stores. No CVD patients reported purchasing medicines from JAS or via Vayomithram. 36.3% of total diabetic population purchased their medicines from Open retail store while it was 34% for hyper tension patients, 29% for those who were affected by cholesterol and 31.9% for CVD patients.

It is evident from the above tables that even though FPMS sell medicines at considerable discounts than open market price, most of the sample population reported purchasing from Open market compared to any other medical shops. Among FPMS, Neethi was the most preferred option over KCP and JAS which sell medicines at much lower price than Neethi. There was no APL, BPL difference for this general pattern. An attempt has been made to understand whether this particular preference pattern is due to people's lack of awareness regarding the concept of FPMS.

Table 7.15: Respondents' Awareness about FPMS

Category of FPMS	*Aware/Heard about FPMS (%)*	*Able to locate FPMS (%)*
NMS	96	90
KCP	28	24
JAS	8	5

Source: Primary Survey

96% of the respondents reported their awareness regarding the idea of NMS and in case of KCP, it was 28% and only 8% whoreportedfamiliarity with JAS. Percentage of people who could identify FPMS in their nearby locality was further low. 90% of respondents were able to locate NMS and 24% could locate KCP and in case of JAS, it was 5%. The data clearly reveals low penetration of the concepts of KCP and JAS among public compared to NMS. This might be reflected in the choice of medical shops by different category of people.

Average monthly spending at different medical shops is computed in the below table. Number of people in each category is mentioned in brackets.

Table 7.16: Average monthly spending at different medical shops(Rs.) according to disease category (Numbers)

Disease	*Open Retail*	*NMS*	*KCP*	*JAS*
Diabetes	327.5(130)	294.63(116)	105.4(11)	112(22)
Hypertension	208.46(107)	268.14(68)	108(8)	96.73(19)
Cholestrol	214.25(55)	169.57(50)	172(60)	94.2(6)
CVD	559.42(30)	446.83(35)	196(5)	N.A

Source: Primary Survey

The average spending of those who purchase from OM is generally high.Average monthly spending for diabetes patients was highest in Open market store. Among FPMS, highest spending was observed in NMS. In case of hypertension, monthly spending was highest for those who purchase from Neethi. Highest monthly spending for cholesterol patients was recorded in open market medical shops as in case of diabetes. Unlike previous cases, average spending at KCP was higher than that in NMS for Cholesterol patients. In case of CVD, highest average spending was observed in Open market medical shops.

Generally, average spending at FPMSis found lower than that in open retail store. Among different FPMS, Neethi was most expensive compared to other two as relevant price spectrums indicated.

If low average spending on medicines do not influence FPMS use then what could be the reason for low FPMS use. People who reported purchasing medicines from sources other than FPMS were asked to report reasons for low FPMS use. Those who get medicines at free of cost from Governmentt hospital or through Vayomithram scheme were exempted from this question.Different reasons were cited by respondents for not utilizing FPMS and the relevant answers were the following;

Table 7.17: Reasons for not utilizing FPMS

Reasons	*% of people cited the reason*
Location of FPMS is inconvenient	27.3
Prefer first access points	27.3
Required medicines are not available at FPMS	18.2
Price discount at FPMS is insignificant	15.9
Getting discounts from other medical stores also	11.3

Source: Primary Survey

Inconvenient location of FPMS was the significant reason for non utilization and equal number of people told that they prefer purchasing medicines from the first access points; ie they purchase from the first medical store that they see. 18.2% complained that they do not get the required medicines from FPMS outlets.

The major reasons for low utilization of FPMSs seem to be inconvenient location of FPMS and preference of first access point.

Disease category wise reasons for non-utilization of FPMS is described in the below table;

Table 7.18: Disease category wise reasons cited for not utilizing FPMS (%)

Disease	*Location of FPMS is inconvenient*	*Prefer first access points*	*Required medicines are not available at FPMS*	*Price discount at FPMS is insignificant*	*Getting discounts from other medical stores also*
Diabetes	12.16	7.39	9.76	7.37	3.25
Hypertension	7.22	8.81	-	5	4.8
Cholesterol	4.63	6.22	-	2.43	3.25
CVD	3.31	4.9	8.44	1.1	-

Source: Primary Survey

Here again the major reason for low FPMS use is same as that of previous table i.e inconvenient location of FPMS and preference of first access point.

To conclude, analysis of consumer perception towards FPMS revealed that majority of respondents depends upon Open Market for their drug purchase. There is no difference in respondents having different diseases in this regard. Thus, despite the fact that FPMS offer considerable price discounts, they are not used even by majority of chronically ill people for the medicinal needs. What could be the reason for the same? More FPMS use is reported among APL than BPL category respondents. So, the high income of respondents is not the reason. The respondents might be spending very low amounts per month for medicines and they do not think they can save considerably by depending on FPMSs. But this argument is not valid as average monthly expenditure of respondents on medicines is not very low for people purchasing from various medical shops. Low awareness regarding FPMSs was not the issue as 90% of respondents were able to locate at least one of the FPMSs.

Since supportive evidence could not be found for all the above-mentioned hypotheses regarding low FPMS use, the researcher decided to rely on the perception of respondents regarding reason for not using FPMSs. Inconvenient location of FPMSs and preference of the first access point were the major reasons told by respondents. The disaggregated (disease wise) data pertaining the same also showed more or less similar results. The researcher finds this reason provided by respondents as a solid one as she could not get supporting evidence for other plausible hypotheses to explain the low FPMS utilization by respondents.

Section V: Conclusion

The study was an attempt to explore the operations of FPMSs in Kerala and to understand their role in Access to Medicine situation (ATM) in Kerala. The study had three objectives.

The first objective was to understand the structure and organizational/ operational aspects of selected FPMSs in Kerala. FPMSs operation is based on a Centralised Procurement and Distribution System (CPDS) andtries to give the benefit of bulk purchasing via CPDS as discounts to their customers. The efficiency of FPMSs in improving ATM depend upon efficiency of their CPDSs. The skewed regional distribution of FPMSs may limit their relevance in improving ATM and efforts are needed to make improvements in these aspects.

The second objective was tomake a comparison of prices of selected medicines among selected FPMSs and between open market. There is considerable difference in both respects. Any way there is a scope for patients to get medicines at much lower prices than what they actually pay now. This will definitely help to reduce financial burden of out of pocket expenditure. But the most prevalent FPMS in (NMS) Kerala is not offering maximum discount for medicines. So either enhancing the discount in NMS or spreading the networks of FPMS offering more discount than the NMS (i.e KCP and JAS) can contribute considerably to affordability of medicines and ATM in Kerala.

The third objective was to understand the consumer perception regarding the operations of FPMSs. Many of the respondents do use FPMSs as the source for medicines. The variables pertaining to respondents like income, disease profile, awareness about FPMSs, average monthly spending on medicines etc. could not explain the low FPMS use by respondents. Thus consumers of medicines need not always compare prices (between OM/FPMS and within FPMSs) and purchase medicines from FPMSs. Even FPMS users do not buy from the FPMSs offering highest discount (i.e KCP/JAS). The basic reason for the last two trends is the same. Generally, majority of the consumers of medicines prefer to buy from the medical shop that is located most conveniently or from the first access point. If there is an FPMS having these two features, thentheymay buy medicines from the same. This suggests that to make FPMSs more effective, they should not only provide the medicines that are demanded at a considerable price difference (which they are doing for the medicines considered in the study), but they should be located in such a way that they are easily accessible and preferably be the first access points of consumers. Else the role of FPMSs in improving ATM situation in Kerala may not improve and this matter is to be taken seriously by stakeholders. To conclude, improving procurement/distribution system of FPMSs, reducing skewness in regional distribution and improving their visibility/accessibility can considerably enhance their role in improving access to medicine situation in Kerala.

References

1. Alam, M. & Tyagi, R., P. (2009). A study of out of pocket household expenditure on drugs and medical services: An exploratory analysis of UP, Rajasthan and Delhi.Delhi: Population Research Centre, Institute of Economic Growth.
2. Bhargava, A. & Kalantri, S.P. (2013). The crisis in access to essential medicines in India: Key issues which call for action. Indian Journal of Medical Ethics, 10(2), 86-95.
3. Creese, A., Kotwani, A., Kutzin, J. & Pillay, A. (2004). Evaluating pharmaceuticals for health policy in low and middle income country settings. In N Freemantle & S Hill (Eds.), Evaluating Pharmaceuticals for Health Policy and Reimbursement (pp. 227-43). Massachusetts, USA: Blackwell Publishing.
4. Duraisamy, P. & Mahal, A. (2005). Health, poverty and economic growth in India.In P., G. Lal & Byword Editorial Consultants (Eds.),Financing And Delivery Of Health Care Services In India(pp. 3-17). New Delhi. National Commission on Macroeconomics and Health.
5. Ekbal, B. (2017, August 14). Kerala model of health: From success to crisis.The New Indian Expres, p. 7.
6. Finlay, J. (2007), The role of health in economic development, Programme on the Global Demography of Aging. Working Paper No. 21, Harvard University.

7. Godwin, S., K. &Varatharajan, D. (2006). Drug price differentials across different retail market settings. Health Administrator, 19, 41-7.
8. Government of Kerala. (2014).Twelfth five year plan (2012-2017): Report of the expert committee on health.Thiruvananthapuram: Author.
9. Govt of India. (2016). Economic survey 2015-16. New Delhi: Author.
10. Gupta, I. & Chowdhury, S. (2015). Finances for health in India: Are new sources the way to go? IEG Working Paper No. 356.doi:10.13140/RG.2.1.2300.24.
11. Indranil, M., Sakthivel, S. &Vaidyanathan, G. (2017). Free medicines in Tamil Nadu: Sustainable reforms and effective financial protection. Proceedings of 3rd International Conference on Public Policy.Singapore.
12. Lekshmi, S., Mohanta, G., P., Revikumar, K., G. & Manna, P., K. (2014). Developments and emerging issues in public and private health care systems of Kerala, International Journal of Pharmacy and Pharmaceutical Sciences, 6(2), 92-98.
13. Loutfi D., Levesque J. F. & Mukherjee S. (2018). Impact of the elderly on household health expenditure in Bihar and Kerala, India. Journal of Health Management. 20(1)1-14.
14. Mukherjee, S. & Levesque, Jean-Frederic. (2012). Morbidity and Outpatient Care for the Elderly in Kerala, South India: Evidence from a National Population based Survey. Journal of Population Ageing. 5. 10.1007/s12062-012-9067-7.
15. Roy, V., Gupta, U. & Agarwal, A., K. (2012) Cost of medicines & their affordability in private pharmacies in Delhi (India), Indian Journal of Medical Research, 136, November, 827-835.
16. Sakthivel, S. (2007). Access to essential drugs and medicine. In P., G. Lal & Byword Editorial Consultants (Eds.), Financing and Delivery of Health Care Services in India (pp. 185-212). New Delhi. National Commission on Macroeconomics and Health.
17. Selvaraj, S., Farooqui, H., H. & Karan, A. (2018). Quantifying the financial burden of households' out-of-pocket payments on medicines in India: A repeated cross-sectional analysis of national sample survey data, 1994–2014. BMJ Open, 8. doi:10.1136/ Bmjopen-2017-018020
18. Sharma, S. & Chaudhary, R., R. (2015).Improving availability and accessibility of medicines: A tool for increasing healthcare coverage, Archives of Medicine, 7(5:12).
19. Singh, P., V., Tatambhotla, A., Kalvakuntla, R., R. & Chokshi, M. (2012). Replicating Tamil Nadu's drug procurement model. Economic and Political Weekly, 47(39), 26-9.
20. Thejus et al (2008), Disease Burden and Healh Expenditure of Kerala. Conference Paper, https://www.researchgate.net/publication/259382012
21. World Health Organization. (2004). Equitable access to essential medicines: A framework for collective action. Geneva: Author.

Part III
Food ad Nutrition Security in Kerala

8

Nutritional Security through Community Kitchen: An Analysis based on National Rural Livelihood Mission in Attappady, Kerala

Tanita Eloo Philip

Indian policy makers realize the fact that without considering tribal community who constitute around ten percent of total population, it is impossible to achieve inclusive growth (GOI, 2011). However, in spite of the plethora of developmental interventions programme, the plight of the tribal communities still remains deplorable as compared with general population (Mohindra, 2010). Studies have pointed out that the existing programmes for the upliftment of tribal population could not attain the intended success as they have not taken into due consideration the socio political and cultural background of the tribes, the geographical peculiarities, local specifications, income and asset position and in particular the capability of tribal beneficiaries to handle the implemented schemes (Shyjan, 2008). Of late the need for enhancement of capabilities of tribal population to enable them to effectively take part in the development programmes is increasingly recognised by the policy makers as evidenced by the implementation of National Rural Livelihood Mission (NRLM) in 2011. NRLM is formulated on the philosophy that poor has inborn potential to graduate out of poverty and the only needed support is to foster towards generation of capabilities to unleash their entrepreneurial talent. Taking cue of this understanding, NRLM has put in place a dedicated, sensitive structure at different layers to assist the poor through the institutions which are framed to enhance their capabilities to mobilise credit, savings, livelihood support etc.

The developmental process that the state of Kerala has followed, which resulted in attainment of high human development status has eluded the tribal communities in the process (Shyjan, 2008). The deprivation of tribal people in Kerala is however reported to be non-uniformly dismal, with reference to socio economic status. Also existing literature and empirical evidence points out to the concentration of poverty and deprivation among tribal groups belong to certain geographical areas; Attappady tribal block being the finest example (Kunhaman, 1985). Of late, Attappady has been receiving much public attention because of the continued infant deaths, with the number of new born death tolls reported to be 37 within six months in 2012. Studies on field, reported consecutive infant deaths in Attappady due to the combined impacts of loss of indigenous food items, poor public distribution system, unavailability of alternate nutritious food and the loss of employment opportunities (Ekbal, 2013; and Sathyan, 2014). This crucial circumstances pressed the central and state governments to come with many developmental intervention programmes and was implemented under the title 'Attappady Comprehensive Tribal Development Project'.

Of all the intervention programmes targeted to solve issues in Attappady, National Rural Livelihood Mission (NRLM) deserves special mention because of its multi-pronged approach. The project consists of three aspects – social development, livelihoods (Mahila Kisan Sashaktikaram Pariyojana) and skill development. The major components of NRLM projects are Institution Building, Community Kitchen, Bridge School, Bridge Course, Centre of Excellence, Gender Resource Centre, Youth Resource Centre, Micro Finance and Livelihood Schemes (animal husbandry, goat village, KILA Canteen, Production mill etc.). The project was introduced by focusing on building exclusive tribal women's institutions like NHGs, Oorusamithis and Panchayatsamithi. These institutions would function with the Integrated Development Project of Attappady under the Kudumbashree Mission supported by NRLM among the women in the three tribal communities of Irula, Muduga and Kurumba in Agali, Pudur and Sholayoor Panchayats.

NRLM strategy involves social mobilisation and building exclusive community network of tribal women through its components and institutions. NRLM thus marks a departure from the earlier intervention programmes which were specifically focussed at targeting single incapability of the tribes, may it be housing status, financial status or educational status. Implementation of projects or initiatives among tribal community is not so easy as their initial endowment is low. To overcome this, NRLM implements a participatory approach to make intervention fruitful. NRLM ensures that at least one member from the identified tribal household is brought under the self-help group (SHG) network in a time bound manner. This clarifies that NRLM tries to address poverty through SHGs. Participation in SHGs makes the beneficiaries empowered (Desai & Joshi, 2014; Deininger & Liu, 2013; Banerjee *et al.* 2014). Long term exposure to poverty alleviation programmes (through SHGs) puts positive impact on the consumption, nutritional intake and asset accumulation (or wealth accumulation) of beneficiaries (Deininger & Liu, 2009); which ensures economic and food security of beneficiaries. Additionally, involvement in SHG network increases the social capital of members (Folgheraiter & Pasini, 2009; Nayak, 2015). The social capital is a resource derived from people's social participation. This social participation increases the social awareness that creates more concern regarding basic necessities including education (a component of educational security) sanitation, and drinking water (which are subcomponents of health security). Thus, participation in SHG ensures educational security and health security to tribal communities through the creation of social capital. In nutshell, it can be articulated that through the participation in SHG, beneficiaries could attain five dimensions of livelihood security, i.e., empowerment, health security, economic security, educational security and food security.

NRLM functions through several institutions, of which Community Kitchen is one of the most important one created with an aim to address the malnourishment problem of tribal community. The working base of Community Kitchen is group participation and group efforts taken by members of NHGs among the tribal community. NHGs in each hamlet runs at least one Community Kitchen as self-managed unit, where the executive committee will choose two ladies to cook and manage the kitchen.

Also, the project is implemented with an expectation to nurture the social capital of Community Resource Persons along with protocols and modules developed for deployment wherever needed for supporting and guiding the tribal communities. Community Kitchen acts as a platform for the tribal women to come together and discuss their social issues. The functions of Community Kitchen continue in Attappady since 2014 and the government proposes to implement the same among tribal communities in other parts of the state. This indicates that the very purpose of Community Kitchen has been served.

In this context, the article tries to analyse the efficiency of Community Kitchen that has been initiated as a part of NRLM to guarantee nutritional security to the tribes in Attappady tribal block, Palghat district, Kerala.

Thus, the efficiency of Community Kitchen is determined by observing the magnitude of various factors like availability of infrastructure facilities, continuity of operation, food security and funding system. These factors can be successfully generated by those NHGs who are aware of their rights and who can act collectively in demanding, mobilising and operationalising these determinants.

The paper is divided into three sections. Section I describes methodology and data sources. Section II examines the nature and working of Community Kitchen, Section III examines the efficiency of Community Kitchen in attaining nutritional and Section IV provides the findings and conclusion.

Section I: Methodology

The study aims to examine the efficiency of Community Kitchen under NRLM in Attappady. For analysing this, data regarding the performance of Community Kitchen is collected from selected Community Kitchens in Attappady.

Sample selection

Attappady consists of 192 tribal hamlets located in three panchayats (Agali, Pudur and Sholayur) dominated by 3 communities (Irulas, Kurumbas and Mudugas). The number of Community Kitchen operating in Attappady as on 26th February, 2019 is 137 (54 in Agali panchayat, 31 in Pudur panchayat, and 52 in Sholayur panchayat). 5 % of the Community Kitchen from each hamlet is selected randomly for in depth analysis. Hence the selected Community Kitchens are Nakupathi, Chittoor, Osathiyoor and Melekandiyoor from Agali panchayat (4), Thachampadi and Thazemanikani from Pudur panchayat (2), Chundakulam, Kottamala, Sholayoor and Oothukuzhi from Sholayoor Panchayat (4). In this study, 10 percent of total beneficiaries from each Community Kitchen is selected.

Table 8.1: Details of Sample Selected

Number of Community Kitchen	*Total Beneficiaries*	*Selected sample (10% of total beneficiaries)*
Nakupathi,	40	4
Chittoor	52	5
Osathiyoor	78	8
Melekandiyoor	69	7
Thachampadi	65	6

(Contd...)

Thazemanikani	45	5
Chundakulam	91	9
Kottamala	50	5
Sholayoor	48	5
Oothukuzhi	62	6
Total	600	60

Quantitative techniques

Study relies upon data collected from 60 samples on aspects of efficiency of Community Kitchen. Efficiency of Community Kitchen is measured by using four indicators, they are infrastructure index, funding index, food and nutrition index and Continuity index. Infrastructure index is measured by assessing seating space of Community Kitchen, availability of utensils, firewood, water, warehousing facility, electrification, ventilation system, waste disposal facility, cleanliness condition of community shed etc. Funding index is measured by evaluating the regularity in receiving funds, clearance of reimbursement bills, ability to clear debts, availability of sufficient funds, effectiveness of funding system etc. Food and Nutrition index is analysed by measuring the satisfaction level of quantity and quality of meals served, nutritional value of food etc. Finally, the continuity index is measured by examining operational regularity of Community Kitchen, maintenance and updation of attendance register, regularity of having meals from kitchen etc.

Efficiency Index (EI) is calculated by using four dimensions;

EI1- Infrastructure,

EI2- Funding,

EI3- Food and Nutrition

EI4- Continuity

Each index is computed by $EI = \frac{actual - minimum}{maximum - minimum}$, so that the index lies between 0 and 1.

Finally, a combined efficiency index is worked out by averaging the individual efficiency indices. On the basis of efficiency index, the performance of Community Kitchen is rated as high, medium and low.

If EI is greater than *Mean + SD*, performance of Community Kitchen is high

If EI lies between *Mean + SD*, performance of Community Kitchen is medium

If EI is less than *Mean + SD*, performance of Community Kitchen is low

The secondary data for the study is collected from annual reports of Integrated Tribal Development Programme (ITDP), Attappady tribal block, District census hand book, Report of Attappady Hill Area Development Society (AHADS) of Attappady. Palakkad District Various Census Reports, Population enumeration data, Journals and internet.

Section II: Community Kitchen- Food and health intervention component of NRLM

Attappady Comprehensive Tribal and Particularly Vulnerable Tribal Groups (ACT and PVTG) Development Project was implemented on 3rd September 2014 with the consent of Central and State Government. The Ministry of Rural Development, Government of India had officially sanctioned the project on 18th February 2014 for a duration of seven years. This project has been impended as a model at national level for the tribal community in general and Vulnerable tribal groups in particular. The incident of massive child death due to malnutrition reported in Attappady block during 2012-14 led to the formation of this project.

The aim of this programme is to attain comprehensive social development of the tribal community in Attappady, by focusing on areas like Education, Health, Capacity building of women, Sustainable livelihood opportunities. For this, exclusive tribal women institutions are framed so as to make the absorption and utilization of funds effective. NRLM constitute of three-tier institutional structures like NHGs (Neighbourhood Groups), Oorusamithi, Panchayth Samathi.

NRLM project team comprises 120 Animators, three young professionals, two coordinators- one for social mobilisation and other for institution building and capacity building, and a consultant for Mahilam Kissan Sasaktikaram Pariyojana (MKSP). Animators are selected from the tribal community and a fixed amount of salary is paid by NRLM. The responsibility of animator is to look after the overall activities of NHGs in their respective hamlets.

Therefore, NRLM holds concrete and penetrating administrative structure at various stages to help the deprived to attain sustainable livelihood platforms and raise them out of poverty. The firm institutionalized system of NRLM facilitate in networking, self-help and mutual cooperation, which in turn helps to attain collective action. NRLM comprises components like Institutional structure, Community Kitchen, Bridge Course, Goat Rearing, Resource Hub, Micro Finance, Convergence activities etc. Among these components, Community Kitchen possess a special prominence as this could directly address the problem of malnutrition by providing food for the poor. Thus, this study aims to examine the working efficiency of each Community Kitchen with respect to the level of nutritional security provided.

Origin of Community Kitchen

Community Kitchen was first initiated in 2013 by Social Welfare Department of the Government of Kerala and was implemented through the Integrated Child Development Scheme (ICDS). The infant deaths and pandemic malnourishment trigged the state government to set Community Kitchen to provide least a meal a day for tribes in Attappady, Palakkad district. It is the reappearance of olden days' exercise of having food together in a community. It was aimed to improve the nutritional status of the community and enhanced solidarity.

Moreover, this programme was instigated with the intention to transfer Community Kitchen into nutrition education centre by popularising the traditional form of agriculture like "Panchakrishi". In order to achieve this goal, tribes were encouraged to get back to their traditional food. This programme encourages the young generation of tribal community in Attappady to practice 'Panchakrishi', by understanding the nutritious value of traditional food items like Ragi, Chama, Varag, Chola, Thina, Kambu etc. and pulses like Thomara, Amara, Black gram, horse gram, ground nuts etc. and about 63 varieties of leaves.

Structure of Community Kitchen

In 2014, the management of Community Kitchen was transferred to Kudumbashree mission. Kudumbashree constitute of four-tier institutional structures like NHGs (Neighbourhood Groups), Oorusamithi, Panchayatsamithi and Block samithi. The fundamental form of institution build within a hamlet is Neighbourhood Group. A neighbourhood group will consist of 10 to 15 women members residing in same hamlet. The minimum eligibility age for a woman to be a member of NHG is 18 or above. Subsequently there is a possibility of NHGs having two women members from one family staying under same roof. Also, there can be more than one NHGs in a hamlet. Each NHGs have office-bearers consisting of a President, Secretary, Treasurer, Joint Secretary and other volunteer members. The volunteers would look after areas like agriculture, education, health, skills and self-employment and Mahatma Gandhi National Rural Employment Guarantee Scheme, women and child issues, entitlements and legal aids, decentralization and micro-plan and tribal sub-plan, etc.

The next level of NHG forms Oorusamithi. The Oorusamithi general body represents all women members of NHGs in a particular hamlet. Once Oorusamithi is formed, it is considered that NHGs are affiliated to their respective Oorusamithi. The Oorusamithi would be primarily responsible to ensure that the NHGs are functioning well by retaining proper records and accurate accounts, proper lending and repayment and bank linkages. Also it is their duty to make sure that the most unprivileged are considered and on priority basis that the funds are distributed to overcome their basic vulnerability. The Panchayatsamithi would consist of all the Oorusamithis. Panchayatsamithi would attend meetings of various department by representing NHGs of tribal community. Panchayatsamithi regularly calls Oorusamithi meetings and also review the progress of its activities. However, in some situations it would help Oorusamithi to implement schemes which cannot be taken up on its own. It is the duty of Panchayathsamithi to audit the Oorusamithis accounts and records. On the other hand, Chartered Accountant would audit the accounts of the Panchayatsamithi's and their fund utilization certificate and audit statement would be submitted to the Project Management Unit.

At present, kitchens at each hamlet are managed by their respective Oorusamithis. The Oorusamithi executive committee, the animator and the project management unit of Kudumbashree Mission would be responsible for monitoring the management of the project. The block samithi is the fourth tier institution of the tribal federation under Kudumbashree Mission. The project is managed by the Project management unit under the tribal Block samithi of the Kudumbashree Mission. The PMU works under the 'Comprehensive Tribal and Particularly Vulnerable Tribal Development Project' of Attappady. This project aims at developing institutions and enhancing the capacities to access their rights, entitlements and capitalizing on their resources by building income generating livelihoods.

Working of Community Kitchen

The beneficiaries of Community Kitchen are the pregnant and lactating women, children from 6 months to 6 years of age, adolescent children and senior citizens.. The food is being served in the morning and evening to the beneficiaries. It is the duty of Oorusamathi to allocate regularly the turn of each NHG to manage a particular Community kitchen working in their respective hamlet. The minimum period allotted for each NHG to manage their Community Kitchen is two months. On voluntary basis, two lady helpers from each NHGs are assigned to manage Community Kitchen. It is their duty to manage the working of Community Kitchen like procuring provisions, collecting firewood, storing water, cooking, serving, cleaning etc. At present, this project runs as self-managed unit by the neighbourhood groups where the animators and helpers of each Community Kitchen would procure their provisions from the Civil Supplies store on a monthly basis, whereas firewood would be either bought from shop or collected from forest by the helpers depending on requirements and vegetables from shop. The Community Kitchen has also started using the vegetables grown by the community.

The food is cooked in a kitchen shed constructed adjacent to the community hall. The rations are warehoused in the store room of community hall. The breakfast menu includes aval (rice flakes), broken wheat upma, rice gruel, green gram and idli. A decorum is being made for retaining hygienic condition of kitchen. Utensils are provided for each Community Kitchen by the Project Management Unit. It is the duty of secretary of each NHG to maintain and update the records of stock book. Also he / she has to prepare the bill voucher and need to be submitted to the Project Management Unit of the Kudumbashree Mission. Secretaries make entries on stock book and prepares bill vouchers regularly with the assistance of animators.

Finance

The Social Justice Department, Social Security Mission, Integrated Tribal Development Project, and Kudumbashree Mission jointly mobilise the fund for Community Kitchen Programme. These agencies take turns in granting their share of funds to Kudumbashree Mission, then the Mission transfers the funds to the project. The bill payments are made to each NHG through NEFT transactions. The amount is paid to the civil supplies through cheque and later, civil supplies submits bills to Project Management Unit of the Comprehensive tribal and Particularly Vulnerable Tribal Group development project of Kudumbashree mission. Helpers are paid by the mission based on the number of meals served to the beneficiaries. Cost incurred by the helpers for purchasing vegetables and firewood would be reimbursed against the voucher submitted before Project Management Unit of Mission.

Progress of Community Kitchen

When Community Kitchen was implemented, the food was served to all members in a NHG (both beneficiaries and non-beneficiaries). Later, this system was changed by reframing the beneficiary category. At present, beneficiary category comprises pregnant ladies, lactating women and children (6 months to 6 years, school going students, adolescents). Others are excluded from availing meals from Community Kitchen.

Table 8.2: Year wise details on number of Community Kitchen, beneficiaries, fund received and expenditure

Period	*Number of Community Kitchen*	*Number of beneficiaries*	*Fund received*	*Expenditure*
2014-2015	192	9287	3774921	2398212
2015-2016	192	15049	44462473	17967444
2016-2017	175	15049	58892765	29056520
2017-2018	152	10020	44047394	33537577
2018-2019	137	-	-	-

Source: NRLM Report, 2019.

It is clear from the table 2 that the number of beneficiaries availing meals has drastically reduced to 10020 in 2017-2018 from 15049 in 2016-2017. Initially there was 192 Community Kitchen in 2014-2015 and later the number of kitchens has declined to 137 in 2018-2019. The reason for the decline in number of kitchens is that those hamlets which operates more than one Community Kitchen were made to merge as one as the number of beneficiaries got declined (due to the restructuring of beneficiary category).

Meanwhile, some kitchens were forced to shut down due to mismanagement, delay in receiving funds and scarcity of water. Table shows that over the years fund received and expenditure has increased gradually corresponding to the number of beneficiaries.

Issues of Community Kitchen

Community Kitchen supports the survival of tribal community in Attappady to a great extent during the past couple of years. However, there are certain critical issues that need to be addressed to continue the same. The first and foremost issue is water scarcity. There are barely any initiatives from the authorities to build up a proper infrastructure to provide fresh water supply to the Community Kitchen. Secondly, there is no efficient process to reimburse the amount which in turn result in delay in receiving the funds.

This adversely affects the operations of Community Kitchen. Thirdly, the top level mismanagement affects the coordination and working of institutions involved in the functioning of Community Kitchen. Tribal community in Attappady fears that in long run these issues may result in gradual close down of Community Kitchens.

Section III: Nutritional Security through Community Kitchen

This section examines the provision of nutritional security through Community Kitchen by examining the efficiency of selected Community Kitchens. Community Kitchen is one of the components of NRLM, a developmental programme focused at addressing the problem of malnourishment of tribal community in Attappady, Palakkad district. It is an initiative to run a common kitchen by tribes themselves with the assistance of NHGs and governments to improve their health and nutritional status, by adopting a practise of having food together in a community to enhance solidarity.

Efficiency of Community Kitchen is measured by using four indices, which are identified on the basis of focus group discussion made with NRLM office bearers and animators in Attappady. The indices are Infrastructure index, Funding index, Food & Nutrition index and Continuity index.

EI1- 'Infrastructure index' examines the aspects which enhance the infrastructural capacity required for the smooth functioning of Community Kitchens.

EI2- Funding index scrutinizes whether the funding system under NRLM has served the purpose in a systematic manner over the years.

EI3- Food and Nutrition index considers the variables which measures the quality and quantity of food served among the beneficiaries of Community Kitchen.

EI4- Continuity Index measures whether each Community Kitchen continues their functions regularly without any break.

Efficiency Index 1 of Community Kitchen: Infrastructure Index

Variables like 'Existing seating space' (in1), 'Availability of Utensils' (in2), 'Ease in procuring firewood' (in3), 'Ease in arranging water' (in4), 'Existing warehousing facility' (in5), 'Existing electric facility' (in6), 'Existing ventilation system' (in7), 'Existing waste disposal facility' (in8), 'Existing segregation facility' (in9), 'Existing hygiene and cleanliness condition' (in10), 'Effectiveness of Kitchen Garden' (in11) are used to analyse the strength of infrastructural facility available for each Community Kitchen.

Table 8.3: Infrastructure Index

CK		*in1*	*in2*	*in3*	*in4*	*in5*	*in6*	*in7*	*in8*	*in9*	*in10*	*in11*	*infr*
CK-1	Mean	0.80	1.00	0.75	1.00	1.00	1.00	0.75	0.75	0.25	1.00	0.00	0.75
	SD	0.11	0.00	0.00	0.00	0.00	0.00	0.00	0.00	0.00	0.00	0.00	0.01
CK-2	Mean	0.72	0.75	0.75	0.75	0.75	1.00	1.00	0.75	0.25	1.00	0.75	0.77
	SD	0.16	0.00	0.00	0.00	0.00	0.00	0.00	0.00	0.00	0.00	0.00	0.02
CK-3	Mean	0.61	0.61	0.50	0.54	0.25	0.50	0.25	0.61	0.25	0.61	0.43	0.47
	SD	0.13	0.20	0.00	0.09	0.00	0.00	0.00	0.13	0.00	0.13	0.12	0.03
CK-4	Mean	0.25	0.50	0.25	0.25	0.25	0.00	0.50	0.33	0.33	0.33	0.00	0.27
	SD	0.00	0.00	0.00	0.00	0.00	0.00	0.00	0.13	0.13	0.13	0.00	0.02
CK -5	Mean	0.63	0.67	0.50	0.64	0.61	0.00	0.67	0.50	0.36	0.64	0.00	0.47
	SD	0.13	0.18	0.13	0.13	0.13	0.00	0.13	0.00	0.13	0.18	0.00	0.06
CK-6	Mean	0.35	0.40	0.35	0.35	0.35	0.25	0.50	0.40	0.20	0.40	0.00	0.32
	SD	0.14	0.14	0.14	0.14	0.14	0.00	0.00	0.14	0.11	0.14	0.00	0.07
CK-7	Mean	0.60	0.75	0.65	0.50	0.50	0.60	0.75	0.40	0.40	0.65	0.00	0.53
	SD	0.14	0.00	0.14	0.00	0.00	0.14	0.00	0.14	0.14	0.14	0.00	0.04
CK-8	Mean	0.17	0.63	0.38	0.75	0.63	0.63	0.58	0.67	0.46	0.58	0.00	0.50
	SD	0.13	0.14	0.14	0.00	0.14	0.14	0.13	0.13	0.10	0.13	0.00	0.01
CK-9	Mean	0.50	0.57	0.56	0.38	1.00	0.75	0.75	0.50	0.38	1.00	0.00	0.58
	SD	0.00	0.13	0.13	0.14	0.00	0.00	0.00	0.00	0.14	0.00	0.00	0.01
CK-10	Mean	0.10	0.30	0.20	0.10	0.00	0.00	0.45	0.30	0.00	0.25	0.00	0.15
	SD	0.14	0.11	0.11	0.14	0.00	0.00	0.11	0.11	0.00	0.25	0.00	0.03
Total	Mean	0.49	0.63	0.50	0.55	0.53	0.46	0.62	0.53	0.29	0.65	0.15	0.49
60	SD	0.26	0.21	0.20	0.26	0.30	0.39	0.22	0.18	0.15	0.28	0.28	0.19
(Chittoor- CK-1, Chundakulam- CK-2, Kottamala- CK-3, Melekandiyoor- CK-4, Nakupathi- CK-5, Oothukuzhi- CK-6, Osathiyoor- CK 7, Sholayoor- CK 8, Thachampadi- CK-9, Thazemanchikani- CK- 10)													

Source: Primary Data.

Data on table 3 denotes that, Chundakulam Community Kitchen is endowed with significant amount of all aspects of infrastructure, which projects out that the presence of this dimension i.e. 'infrastructure' is high compared to other Community Kitchens (with mean value-0.77). Moreover, variables like 'Existing electric facility' (in6), 'Existing ventilation system' (in7), and 'Existing hygiene and cleanliness condition' (in10) are sound and predominant compared to rest of the variables influencing this dimension. This position is followed by Chittoor Community Kitchen with mean value of 0.75. The strength of this dimension itself and factors contributing to this dimension are least for Community Kitchen in Thazemanichikani (with mean value of 0.15). The presence of variables like 'Existing warehousing facility' (in5), 'Existing electric facility' (in6), 'Existing segregation facility' (in9), 'Effectiveness of Kitchen Garden' (in11) are completely absent in this Community Kitchen with mean value of 0.00.

Majority of the Community Kitchen lacks sound infrastructural facilities. The members stand critical against the authorities for not taking enough steps to provide basic infrastructure and amenities.

Efficiency Index 2 of Community Kitchen: Funding Index

Variables like 'Regularity in receiving funds' (f1), 'Ease in reimbursement of bills' (f2), 'Availability of sufficient funds' (f3), 'Availability of working capital' (f4), 'Interest rate' (f5), 'Bill clearance' (f6), 'Funding system' (f7) are used to analyse the funding system among the members of community kitchens.

Table 8.4: Funding Index

CK		*f1*	*f2*	*f3*	*f4*	*f5*	*f6*	*f7*	*F*
CK-1	Mean	0.25	0.50	0.75	0.75	1.00	0.90	0.50	0.66
	SD	0.00	0.00	0.00	0.00	0.00	0.14	0.00	0.02
CK-2	Mean	0.50	0.50	0.75	0.75	1.00	0.91	0.60	0.71
	SD	0.00	0.00	0.00	0.00	0.00	0.13	0.13	0.03
CK-3	Mean	0.50	0.50	0.50	0.50	0.68	0.75	0.50	0.56
	SD	0.00	0.00	0.00	0.00	0.12	0.00	0.00	0.01
CK-4	Mean	0.13	0.17	0.50	0.25	0.17	0.42	0.21	0.26
	SD	0.14	0.13	0.00	0.00	0.13	0.13	0.10	0.07
CK - 5	Mean	0.36	0.31	0.53	0.53	0.75	0.67	0.31	0.49
	SD	0.13	0.11	0.08	0.15	0.00	0.13	0.11	0.06
CK-6	Mean	0.30	0.35	0.40	0.25	0.40	0.70	0.35	0.39
	SD	0.11	0.14	0.14	0.00	0.14	0.11	0.14	0.04
CK-7	Mean	0.25	0.55	0.65	0.60	0.60	0.60	0.25	0.50
	SD	0.00	0.11	0.14	0.14	0.14	0.14	0.00	0.05
CK-8	Mean	0.38	0.42	0.58	0.58	0.75	0.63	0.33	0.52
	SD	0.14	0.13	0.13	0.13	0.00	0.14	0.13	0.07
CK-9	Mean	0.50	0.50	0.75	0.31	0.50	0.69	0.31	0.51
	SD	0.00	0.00	0.00	0.13	0.00	0.13	0.13	0.04
CK-10	Mean	0.15	0.05	0.40	0.15	0.15	0.35	0.00	0.18
	SD	0.14	0.11	0.14	0.14	0.14	0.14	0.00	0.06
Total 60	Mean	0.34	0.38	0.58	0.49	0.63	0.67	0.35	0.49
	SD	0.16	0.18	0.15	0.22	0.30	0.20	0.19	0.16
(Chittoor- CK-1, Chundakulam- CK-2, Kottamala- CK-3, Melekandiyoor- CK-4, Nakupathi- CK-5, Oothukuzhi- CK-6, Osathiyoor- CK 7, Sholayoor- CK 8, hachampadi- CK-9, Thazemanchikani- CK- 10)									

Source: Primary Data.

Data clearly Figure out that the satisfaction rate of respondents in Chundakulam Community Kitchen is high with respect to its funding system (with mean value of 0.71). This position is followed by Chittoor Community Kitchen with mean value of 0.66. Meanwhile, the rating of respondents of Thazhemanichikani and Melekandiyoor stands at the lowest level in this regard.

It is observed while interacting with the animators and members that funding is a common problem faced in all kitchens. But then, it is found that the efficiency and cooperative mentality of animators and helpers could manage this problem to some extent. At times due to delay in reimbursement of funds animators give money to the helpers from their pocket to avoid the shutdown of Community Kitchen. In other cases, the helpers pledge their gold and borrow money to meet the financial requirements of Community Kitchen. Once the bill gets reimbursed, the amount may or may not be enough to clear the debt. Even in this scenario the animators and helpers of Chundakulam and Chittoor consider this as a social commitment and this drives them to continue the Community Kitchen without any disruption even if they do not make any money out of it. On the other hand, no such attitude is visible among the animators and helpers of Melekandiyoor and Thazhemanichikani. Throughout the conversation they complain that the work gets hindered due to delay in funds. Moreover, they claim that the earnings from running the kitchen is not as par with their efforts.

Efficiency Index 3 of Community Kitchen: Food and Nutrition Index

Food and Nutrition Index is worked out to analyse the efficiency of Community Kitchen with respect to quantity and quality of food served among the members of each kitchen. Variables like 'Nutritious food' (fn1), 'Quantity of food' (fn2), 'Quality of food' (fn3), 'Availability of raw food products' (fn5), 'Quality of food products supplied by Public Distribution System" (fn6) are used to measure the 'Food and Nutrition Index' of Community Kitchen.

Table 8.5: Food and Nutrition Index

CK		*fn1*	*fn2*	*fn3*	*fn4*	*fn5*	*Fn*
CK-1	Mean	0.95	1.00	0.90	1.00	1.00	0.97
	SD	0.11	0.00	0.14	0.00	0.00	0.05
CK-2	Mean	1.00	1.00	1.00	1.00	1.00	1.00
	SD	0.00	0.00	0.00	.000	0.00	0.00
CK-3	Mean	0.82	0.75	0.75	0.71	0.75	0.76
	SD	0.12	0.14	0.14	0.09	0.14	0.07
CK-4	Mean	0.33	0.50	0.42	0.25	0.25	0.35
	SD	0.13	0.00	0.13	0.00	0.00	0.04
CK -5	Mean	0.67	0.69	0.67	0.58	0.58	0.64
	SD	0.18	0.21	0.18	0.13	0.13	0.08
CK-6	Mean	0.45	0.50	0.50	0.40	0.45	0.46
	SD	0.21	0.25	0.25	0.14	0.11	0.16

(Contd...)

CK-7	Mean SD	0.65 0.14	0.65 0.14	0.60 0.14	0.50 0.18	0.55 0.11	0.59 0.07
CK-8	Mean SD	0.67 0.13	0.83 0.13	0.63 0.21	0.54 0.10	0.54 0.10	0.64 0.11
CK-9	Mean SD	0.56 0.13	0.63 0.14	0.63 0.14	0.50 0.00	0.38 0.14	0.54 0.05
CK-10	Mean SD	0.40 0.34	0.35 0.14	0.55 0.11	0.25 0.00	0.35 0.14	0.38 0.12
Total 60	Mean SD	0.67 0.26	0.71 0.24	0.68 0.23	0.60 0.27	0.61 0.27	0.65 0.23
(Chittoor- CK-1, Chundakulam- CK-2, Kottamala- CK-3, Melekandiyoor- CK-4, Nakupathi- CK-5, Oothukuzhi- CK-6, Osathiyoor- CK 7, Sholayoor- CK 8, Thachampadi- CK-9, Thazemanchikani- CK- 10)							

Source: Primary Data.

It is very much evident from the table 5 that the satisfaction level of members of Chundakulam Community Kitchen is the highest (with mean value of 1.00) with respect to the index 'Food and Nutrition'. The degree of each variable contributing to this level of satisfaction is also very high with a mean value of 1.00. The level of satisfaction possessed by Chittoor Community Kitchen is also high in this regard, with a mean value of 0.97. Each determinant variables occupies a strong presence in Chittoor and thereby it occupies the second position in this regard. While examining all the determinant variables of this index, Melekandiyoor and Thazemanichikani are lagging behind the other Community Kitchens with a mean value of 0.35 and 0.38 respectively. On the whole, majority of the respondents are satisfied with the quality and quantity of food served.

Meanwhile, the respondents revealed an attention-grabbing fact that the tribes are basically lazy to cook and have food on time. Typically, they take only one meal in a day. Tribal men and women take alcohol and drugs which kills their appetite. Even pregnant women in the tribal community are addicted to alcohol. But this situation has significantly got improved by serving cooked food twice a day through Community Kitchen. In effect this indicate that Community Kitchen has served its purpose by directly addressing the issue of malnourishment.

Efficiency Index 4 of Community Kitchen: Continuity Index

Variables like 'Regularity in operation' (c1), 'Attendance Status' (c2), 'Updating of attendance register' (c3), 'Regularity in having food from Community Kitchen' (c4), 'Functional scrutiny' (c5), 'Crosscheck of register', (c6) are used to analyse the 'Continuity' index of Community Kitchen.

Table 8.6: Continuity Index

CK		*c1*	*c2*	*c3*	*c4*	*c5*	*c6*	*C*
CK-1	Mean	1.00	1.00	1.00	0.95	0.90	0.85	0.95
	SD	0.00	0.00	0.00	0.11	0.14	0.14	0.05
CK-2	Mean	1.00	1.00	0.94	1.00	0.94	0.75	0.94
	SD	0.00	0.00	0.12	0.00	0.12	0.00	0.03
CK-3	Mean	0.89	0.82	0.82	1.00	0.82	0.82	0.86
	SD	0.13	0.12	0.12	0.00	0.12	0.12	0.08
CK-4	Mean	0.29	0.20	0.20	0.33	0.13	0.08	0.21
	SD	0.10	0.19	0.19	0.13	0.21	0.20	0.15
CK -5	Mean	0.89	0.69	0.89	1.00	0.61	0.64	0.79
	SD	0.13	0.17	0.22	0.00	0.13	0.13	0.09
CK-6	Mean	0.35	0.35	0.80	0.65	0.50	0.45	0.52
	SD	0.14	0.29	0.11	0.14	0.18	0.21	0.14
CK-7	Mean	0.95	0.85	0.75	0.95	0.65	0.60	0.79
	SD	0.11	0.14	0.00	0.11	0.14	0.14	0.07
CK-8	Mean	0.75	0.67	0.67	0.75	0.63	0.46	0.65
	SD	0.00	0.13	0.13	0.27	0.14	0.19	0.11
CK-9	Mean	0.44	0.44	0.56	1.00	0.44	0.44	0.55
	SD	0.24	0.24	0.13	0.00	0.24	0.24	0.18
CK-10	Mean	0.20	0.20	0.60	0.35	0.15	0.20	0.29
	SD	0.21	0.21	0.14	0.14	0.22	0.33	0.18
Total	Mean	0.71	0.65	0.74	0.82	0.60	0.55	0.68
60	SD	0.32	0.32	0.26	0.28	0.31	0.29	0.27
(Chittoor- CK-1, Chundakulam- CK-2, Kottamala- CK-3, Melekandiyoor- CK-4, Nakupathi- CK-5, Oothukuzhi- CK-6, Osathiyoor- CK 7, Sholayoor- CK 8, Thachampadi- CK-9, Thazemanchikani- CK- 10)								

Source: Primary Data.

Data reveals that the continuity and regularity aspects of working of Community Kitchen is high for Chittoor, followed by Chundakulam with a mean value of 0.95 and 0.94 respectively. Hence it is clear from the data that the degree of each determinant variable is high for both the kitchens. It purely indicates that these two kitchens are working regularly without fail and in a systematic manner. More or less a similar kind of working condition is visible in rest of the Community Kitchens except in case of Melekandiyoor and Thazhemanichikani with a mean value of 0.21 and 0.29 respectively. Data elicited from the respondents of these two Community Kitchen unveils that the level of all the variables contributing for the continuity in working and systematic working conditions of Community Kitchen are very low in these two areas. Wherever the animators and helpers are found to be efficient and responsible, those kitchens are found to be the smooth running ones. Sound administration and cooperation was not present in both Melekandiyoor and Thazhemanichikani. Therefore, they are lagging behind in regularity aspect also. *When the head does not work, the legs suffer- Romanian Proverb.*

Overall Performance of Community Kitchen

Overall performance of Community Kitchen is evaluated by analysing the infrastructural facilities, funding, food and nutrition and continuity factors as reported by the beneficiaries. Table 8.7 shows the overall performance index obtained by taking the averages of four indices, i.e. Infrastructure Index, Funding Index, Food and Nutrition Index and Continuity Index.

Table 8.7: Performance Index of Community Kitchen

CK	*Infrastructure Index*	*Funding Index*	*Food and Nutrition Index*	*Continuity Index*	*Performance Index*
CK-1	0.75 0.01	0.66 0.02	0.97 0.05	0.95 0.05	0.83 0.03
CK-2	0.77 0.02	0.71 0.03	1.00 0.00	0.94 0.03	0.86 0.01
CK-3	0.47 0.03	0.56 0.02	0.76 0.07	0.86 0.08	0.66 0.04
CK-4	0.27 0.02	0.26 0.07	0.35 0.05	0.21 0.15	0.27 0.05
CK -5	0.47 0.06	0.49 0.06	0.64 0.08	0.79 0.09	0.60 0.05
CK-6	0.32 0.07	0.39 0.05	0.46 0.16	0.52 0.14	0.42 0.07
CK-7	0.53 0.04	0.50 0.05	0.59 0.07	0.79 0.07	0.60 0.04
CK-8	0.50 0.04	0.52 0.07	0.64 0.11	0.65 0.11	0.58 0.05
CK-9	0.58 0.01	0.51 0.04	0.54 0.05	0.55 0.18	0.54 0.06
CK-10	0.15 0.03	0.18 0.06	0.38 0.12	0.29 0.18	0.25 0.08
Total 60	0.49 0.19	0.49 0.16	0.65 0.23	0.68 0.27	0.58 0.20
(Chittoor- CK-1, Chundakulam- CK-2, Kottamala- CK-3, Melekandiyoor- CK-4, Nakupathi- CK-5, Oothukuzhi- CK-6, Osathiyoor- CK 7, Sholayoor- CK 8, Thachampadi- CK-9, Thazemanchikani- CK- 10)					

Source: Primary Data.

As mentioned in the methodology, indexing is used to determine the efficiency of Community Kitchen. Efficiency Index (EI) of Community Kitchen is worked out by averaging the sub dimensions of 'Infrastructure Index', 'Funding Index', 'Food and Nutrition Index' and finally 'Continuity Index'. It is obvious from the efficiency index criteria that Chundakulam and Chittoor have the best performing Community Kitchens as the efficiency level attained by these kitchens are the topmost with a mean value of 0.86 and 0.83 respectively, while Thazhemanichikani (with a mean value of 0.25) and Melekandiyoor (with a mean value of 0.27) are the least performing (low efficiency) Community Kitchens among the selected sample. On the other hand, Community Kitchens like Kottamala (0.66), Osthiyoor (0.60), Nakupathi (0.60), Sholayoor (0.58), Thachampadi (0.54) and Oothukuzhi (0.42) belongs to the category of Community Kitchens with medium level of efficiency.

Apart from these four indices, the researcher has identified certain non-quantifiable variables that can influence the overall performance of Community Kitchen. The variables like nature of building, procurement details of cooking utensils, procurement details of firewood, procurement details of water, cost of water, maintenance of kitchen garden, clearance of reimbursement bill, efforts taken to arrange working capital until the bills get cleared, arrangement of working capital, ability to pay back borrowed money, maintenance of attendance register, the custodian of attendance register are observed individually to have an integrated view on the performance of Community Kitchen.

It is observed from the field survey that mainly there are four types of community sheds, such as Bamboo Shed, Kacha Shed, Tarpaulin Sheet, Temporary Aluminium Shed. However, Kacha sheds are found to be the most common type. Community Development Society and NRLM are the main two source through which Community Kitchens procure cooking utensils and in some Community Kitchens, members themselves have fully or partially arranged vessels (from their home).

In the case of procurement of firewood, the main two sources found are forest and shop and data reveals that majority of respondents depend on forest (75 percent) than shop (25 percent). Meanwhile, natural source and panchayat pipeline are the two main source for procuring water. Majority of the respondents (70 percent) depend on natural source than Panchayat Pipeline (30 percent). It is observed from the field survey that no cost is incurred for procuring water. Data derived from the response of members indicate that most of the Community Kitchens lack warehouse facility (60 percent), whereas only 40 percent of Community Kitchens are having warehouse facility. It is clear from the survey that majority of the Community Kitchens are properly electrified (66.7 percent).

Data derived from the survey indicates that majority of Community Kitchens (73.3 percent) have facility to dispose waste. At the same time, the survey observes that there is no mechanism to segregate food waste and non-food waste. The major waste disposal practice is burning (46.7 percent) followed by dumping pits (45.0 percent) and littering away (8.3 percent). Only about 25.0 percent of kitchens maintains their own kitchen garden. All the respondents (100 percent) points out that they face extreme difficulty in getting the bills reimbursed on time. Majority of the respondents (58.33 percent) finds that it is effortless to arrange working capital until the bills get cleared. Borrowing money for working capital is found to be common among all the respondents. About 90 percent of the respondents are able to pay back borrowed money with interest on time.

As insisted by the officials with regard of accountability, the study observed that all Community Kitchens maintain their own attendance register. As a custodian, the attendance register of each Community Kitchen is maintained by their respective animators.

Section IV: Findings and Conclusion

Community Kitchen, as a part of National Rural Livelihood Mission (NRLM), was implemented in Attappady, Palakkad District of Kerala with an objective to bring an effective solution to address the problem of malnutrition by a comprehensive way of intervening into areas like education, health, livelihood and empowerment etc. The researcher focused on analysing the effectiveness of the implementation of Community Kitchen as a nudge to address directly the problem of malnourishment.

The study scrutinised the efficiency of each Community Kitchen by working out its efficiency index and found that among the selected Community Kitchens, two of them are working at high level of efficiency or performance (Chundakulam and Chittoor) and whereas six of them with medium level of performance (Kottamalla, Oothukuzhi, Osathiyoor, Sholayoor, Nakupathi and Thachampadi). Only two Community Kitchens (Thazhemanichikani and Melekandiyoor) are found to be with low level of performance. In short, the performance wise analysis of each Community Kitchen depicts a clear picture that this programme has served its purpose to a great extent.

Apart from the variables taken to derive the efficiency index, the researcher has also analysed certain factors which directly represent the strength of parameters which influences the performance of Community Kitchen like infrastructure, funding, information and communication, etc. In short, it divulges the need to consider certain factors that hinders the working efficiency of Community Kitchen. Lack of factors like concrete and electrified cooking sheds, poor access to basic cooking aids like vessels, fuels, lack of waste disposal facilities, access to safe drinking and cooking water, access to 'information and communication' etc. are some of the major factors which hold back the efficiency of Community Kitchen.

Another important finding of this study is the positive influence of educational qualification of animators on the working efficiency of Community Kitchens. Chundakulam, Chittoor and Osathiyoor Community Kitchens exhibit an impressive level of performance. The animators of these three Community Kitchens are graduates. It can be presumed from the data that the educational qualification of animators has a significant role on strengthening the efficiency level of Community Kitchens. On the other hand, the two common problems faced by the stakeholders of all Community Kitchens are inadequate infrastructural facilities and funding issues. Meanwhile, it is clear from the observation that the voluntary initiatives and helping mentality of non-beneficiaries, animators and helpers are the major factors which made Community Kitchens to function at an impressive standard. The findings point out to the role that social capital play in ensuring successful working of institutions built on community groupings.

The study suggests that the major aspects that the officials need to restructure is the funding system, so as to solve the problem of regularity in receiving funds on time. Apart from this, majority of the respondents are satisfied with the working of Community Kitchen. There is no doubt that people are contented with the food served, whereby it implies the programme could directly address the problem of malnourishment. Hence, it concludes that NRLM could execute and implement Community Kitchen with the help of institutional framework to ensure health and nutritional wellbeing of tribal community in Attappady.

References

1. Banerjee, S., & Dutta, A. (2014). Synergistic effects of microfinance through SHGs: A study of basic health and primary education indicators. In *Microfinance, Risk-taking Behaviour and Rural Livelihood* (pp. 113-129). Springer, New Delhi.
2. Deininger, K., & Liu, Y. (2009). *Longer-term economic impacts of self-help groups in India.* The World Bank.
3. Deininger, K., & Liu, Y. (2013). *Welfare and Poverty Impacts of India's National Rural Employment Guarantee Scheme: Evidence from Andhra Pradash.* The World Bank.
4. Desai, R.M., Joshi, S. (2014.) Collective action and community development: Evidence from self-help groups in rural India, *The World Bank* Economic Review, 28(3), 492-524.

5. Ekbal, B. (2013). Report on the visit to Attappadi by the medical team constituted by the CPI (M) Kerala State Committeee, 18-21 May.
6. Folgheraiter, F., & Pasini, A. (2009). Self-help Goups and Social Capital: New Directions in Welfare Policies? *Social Work Education, 28(3),* 253-267.
7. Government of India. District Census Handbook of Palakkad district, India (over the years)
8. Kunhaman, M. (1985). The tribal economy of Kerala: An intra-regional analysis, *Economic and Political Weekly,* 466-474.
9. Mohindra, K. S., & Labonte, R. (2010). A systematic review of population health interventions and Scheduled Tribes in India. *BMC public health, 10(1),* 438.
10. Nayak, A. K. (2015). Developing Social Capital through Self-Help Groups. *Indore Management Journal*, 7(1), 18-24.
11. Sathyan, E. K. (2014). Report on health assessment camp conducted in Attappady under the leadership of Dr. E. K. Sathyan.
12. Shyjan, D., & Sunitha, A. S. (2008). Changing Phases of Kerala's Development Experience and exclusion of scheduled tribes. Towards an explanation.

9

National Food Security Act in Kerala: An Evaluation

Ancy John

"Food security is.... access to adequate quantity of quality food at affordable prices to people to live a life with dignity and for matters connected therewith or incidental thereto." **(National Food Security Act, 2013)**

Introduction

Food security has been abiding always as a primary concern for all developing nations for many years of planning and development. The enduring importance given to this single target itself points out, its capacity not only to build a healthy population but also, it's potential to ripple progress towards other primary concerns of any developing country. Concepts of food security have evolved in the last thirty years to reflect changes in official policy thinking (Clay, 2002; Heidhues et al, 2004). The term got world policymakers' attention at the World Food Conference (1974) as it is defined as, *Availability at all times of adequate world food supplies of basic foodstuffs to sustain a steady expansion of food consumption and to offset fluctuations in production and prices*. This definition was further modified, by imparting the crucial point, 'access' in 1983 by Food and Agriculture Organization, as *Ensuring that all people at all times have both physical and economic access to the basic food that they need.* However, more recently new lights to focus food security as a human right are made and discussed (UN Declaration of Human Rights in 1948). India's latest improvisation in her prolonged journey for attaining universal food security adapted this concept in National Food Security Act (NFSA) enacted in July, 2013.

In line with the global discussions on the scope of food security, India made a major leap by legally entitling up to seventy percentage of its rural population and fifty percentage of its urban population the basic *right* to have *access to adequate quantity of quality food* by shifting from a welfare-based approach to right based approach. The evolutionary process of this remarkable step dates back to introduction of public distribution system in mid 1960s and expanded the boundaries of coverage from urban scarcity areas to areas of high incidence of poverty including tribal blocks. Further extending the coverage and focusing on area specific programs, Targeted Public Distribution System in June 1997, with exclusively targeting the poor (Lakdawala committee) was introduced. It is these continuous changes, which lead to the revolutionary transition of prolonged welfare programs to National Food Security Act, 2013.

Par with the central government, the state of government of Kerala adopted NFSA in November 2016. Due to its other substantial progress in various developmental spheres, Kerala could adopt the policy in a remarkable manner after four years of implementation. Unlike the national pattern, considering the higher dependency of its population on Public Distribution System (PDS) the state government included non-NFSA beneficiaries also into the food security net. The study, in this context, attempts to understand the effectiveness of implementation of NFSA in Kerala and also tries to examine how PDS infrastructure were made use to respond to the situation of Covid-19 pandemic in Kerala.

The rest of the study is organized as follows. Section I explains the methodology adopted for the study. Section II narrates the evolution of food security policies in India and features of NFSA. Section III gives an analytical explanation of progress of NFSA in Kerala and its evaluation. Section IV elucidates, strategies adopted in Kerala through Public Distribution System to face the unprecedented challenges of Covid-19 pandemic and Section V concludes the study.

Section I: Methodology of the Study

Primary data is made use of to analyze the performance of NFSA in Kerala. Five Fair Price Shops (FPSs) from different village/urban areas in different taluks are randomly selected from eight districts of Kerala. From each village/urban area, 15 sample NFSA beneficiary households (10 PH and 5 AAY, total 75 beneficiary households from each district) under single FPS are selected using systematic random sampling method. Adequate representation of SC/ST poor and vulnerable population is also ensured in the sample.

Secondary data were collected from official websites of Ministry of Food and Consumer Affairs, Government of India and Department of Food and Civil Supplies, Government of Kerala.

Section II: Evolution of Food Security Policies and Progress of NFSA in India

Food is the first among many basic human needs, and it is for this reason that "the human right to food is recognized in several instruments under international law (U N1999)." Food security is said to exist when all people, at all times, have physical, social and economic access to sufficient, safe and nutritious food that meets their dietary needs and food preferences for an active and healthy life (FAO 2009). As a democratic State, is a primary objective of Government of India to ensure adequate access to quality food to each of its citizens. National Food Security Act, (NFSA)which was implemented by the Indian government on September 2013, marks a radical change from its previous food security approach, from *welfare to right based approach.*

India, being a highly populated nation, adopted different policies in this regard and as a result, has achieved considerable improvement after mid-1960's. Today, the country produces 284.83 million tons of total food grains with 112.91 million tons of rice and 99.70 million tons of wheat annually. However, even though the production has massively increased, the issue of achieving universal food security still prevails as a deal for at most concern. The Public Distribution System, was initiated in 1940s to focus on this issue. It was initially started as a system to manage food scarcity, and evolved into a system for the distribution of food grains at affordable prices, and is an important part of the government's policy for food management.

Until 1997, the PDS had provided food security to all without any specific targeting of beneficiaries. Consequently, it was widely criticised for its failure to serve the entire population below the poverty line, its urban bias and the lack of transparency and accountability. It was felt that a substantial part of the PDS benefits accrued to the non-poor and it did not have much of an impact on the nutritional status of those in need. As a result, there were calls for fundamental reforms for targeting the PDS to the poor.

In June 1997, the central government launched the Targeted Public Distribution System, with the focus on the poor. States were required to formulate and implement arrangements for the identification of the poor and the delivery of foodgrains to them. Six crore poor families were to be covered under the TPDS and 72 lakh MT (LMT) foodgrains distributed annually. Allotment to the states was to be made on the basis of the average offtake for the last decade. The most distinctive feature of the new policy was the division of the entire population into the 'Above Poverty Line' (APL) and the 'Below Poverty Line' (BPL) categories, based on the poverty line defined by the Planning Commission. The maximum income limit for the BPL families was kept at Rs 15,000 per annum. The TPDS also had a dual Central Issue Price (CIP) – one for the BPL families and the other for the APL families. The thrust was to include only the really poor and vulnerable sections of society in the BPL category, and the gram panchayats and the *nagarpalikas* were roped in for beneficiary identification. The total number of the BPL families was raised to 652.03 lakh.

In order to make the TPDS more focused towards the very poor, a separate category, under the *Antyodaya Anna Yojana* (AAY), was launched in December 2000 for one crore families. The AAY identified the poorest of the poor families in the BPL category and provided them with food grains at the highly subsidized rates of Rs 2 per kg for wheat and Rs 3 per kg for rice. The total AAY coverage went up to 2.5 crore families (i.e. 38 percent of the BPL category) by 2005-2006. The TPDS, though an important step in ensuring food security in India, was criticized on several counts – of leakage, mis-targeting and inefficient supply chain management – in the first 10 years of its implementation.

The *RashtriyaKhadya Suraksha Adhiniyam*, or the National Food Security Act (NFSA), 2013 (also, the Right to Food Act), was passed by the Parliament of India on September 12, 2013 addressing these criticisms. The Act converts into legal entitlements the schemes such as the Public Distribution System, the Midday Meal Scheme in schools and the Integrated Child Development Services (ICDS). It seeks to provide not only food and nutritional security to the beneficiaries, by ensuring access to adequate quantities of quality food at affordable prices, but also a life of dignity.

The salient features of the NFSA are:

(i) Covers 75 percent of the rural population and 50 percent of the urban population (two-thirds of the total population)

(ii) Persons belonging to eligible households will be able to receive 5 kg of food grains per person per month at Rs 3 per kg for rice, Rs 2 for wheat and Re 1 for coarse grains. The AAY households will continue to get 35 kg per household per month.)

(iii) Special focus on nutritional support to women and children, with emphasis on pregnant and lactating mothers and children up to 14 years of age.

(iv) Grievance redressal mechanisms at the district and state levels.

The NFSA also has some improved management features. It advocates using the ICT in order to improve service delivery and emphasizes grievance redressal and transparency.

Today, it is one of the world's largest social security programmes and makes 810 million Indians legally eligible for subsidised food grains. The Act gives legal rights to approximately 67 percent of the population of India to receive food grains at a fixed price through the PDS and has special provisions for pregnant women, lactating mothers and a few categories of children.

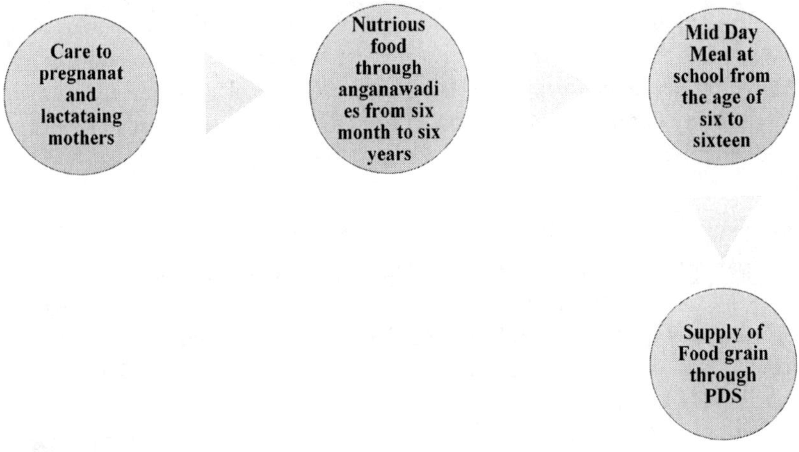

Figure 9.1: Life Cycle Approach in NFSA

Other important features of NFSA are,

1. Women empowerment through, considering eldest woman in the household as head of the family, preferring women or women-self help groups for issuing license for FPS
2. Bio-metric authentication and technology based distribution of food grains
3. Door step delivery to Fair Price Shops and computerized supply chain management

4. States are free to further subsidise the food grains or extend the limits of coverage of the population.
5. More transparency in working of PDS etc.

Thus, NFSA aims at a complete coverage of food and nutritional security to targeted population of all ages. The act was implemented in all states and union territories of the country in India in a uniform basis while, state governments are provided with the power to exclude and include the beneficiaries and extending the coverage of beneficiaries.

The state of Kerala started its food security policies along with central government and managed to acquire faster growth and higher efficiency, in terms of utilization level, access of subsidized food grain through nearby fair price shops, universal coverage etc. The state could efficiently manage and establish the system into a wide network starting from FPS at maximum distance of two kilometer from each household to the ministry of food and civil supplies. FPSs act more like the government machinery reached out to the neighborhood. The success of the system mainly depends on its ability to cover the maximum population and to translate the macro level developmental goals to micro level achievements. The scheme aims to acts as a safety net to enhance food and nutritional security and via this, human development.

Section III: Evaluation of NFSA in Kerala

In par with the activities of the central government the state government has adopted NFSA in November, 2016. Four types of ration cards with different color codes came into practice as part of implementation of NFSA in Kerala. The state has added two sections of additional beneficiaries along with NFSA beneficiaries. The NFSA beneficiaries are Priority Households (PHH) and Andyodaya Anna Yojana households (AAY), their ration cards are issued in pink and yellow colors respectively. The non-NFSA beneficiaries include Non-priority Subsidy (NPS) beneficiaries and Non-Priority Non-Subsidy beneficiaries (Blue and white ration cards respectively). Thus beyond the national coverage the state could assure a universal coverage in an efficient category basis. As of June 2020, under Kerala's population of 36 million, 35740604 beneficiaries are enrolled under NFSA and Non NFSA categories.

From the Figure it is evident that more than half of the Kerala beneficiaries come under the non-NFSA net of NPS (10268769) and NPNS (10058684). The state initiative to expand the food security net by incorporating the middle income group and higher income has increased

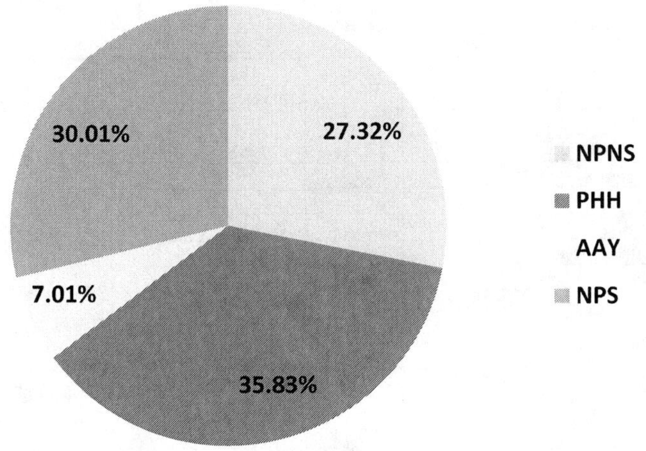

(*Source:* https://civilsupplieskerala.gov.in/)

Figure 9.2: Category wise Distribution of ration cards in the District of Kerala as per August 2020

the coverage from less than half to universal population. This kind of state interventions even from the beginning of introduction of public distribution system has helped in achieving higher efficiency and effectiveness in the state of Kerala's development wheel as food security not only provides a healthy dignified life but it motivates the population to concentrate to betterment of life by achieving education and better standards of life. Thus food security enables the population to less worry about basic needs to survive.

In addition to covering the basic need of the food security these programs have potential to pull other sector developments like health, education etc. and thereby creating skilled work force towards human capital formation.

Rate of Dependence on Public Distribution System

Kerala stands on a unique position compared to other Indian states in human development and progress despite of it lower per capita income and enduring food deficit. The well performing Public distribution System in state has an eminent role in keeping this trend intact. This is evident from the dependency level of Kerala population to public distribution system.

Table 9.1: Share of Public Distribution System to the Consumption of Rice

Quantity of rice	*Alappuzha*			*Pathanamthitta*		
	Total	*Mean*	*Percentage*	*Total*	*Mean*	*Percentage*
Consumed from market	910	12.13	36.63	495	6.6	23.58
Consumed from PDS	1574	20.98	63.36	1604	21.38	76.41
Total	2484	33.11	100	2099	27.98	100
Quantity of rice	*Thiruvananthapuram*			*Kasaragod*		
	Total	*Mean*	*Percentage*	*Total*	*Mean*	*Percentage*
Consumed from market	655	8.73	30.9	656	8.75	28.22
Consumed from PDS	1459	19.45	69.01	1668	22.24	71.77
Total	2114	28.18	100	2324	30.99	100
Quantity of rice	*Ernakulam*			*Kottayam*		
	Total	*Mean*	*Percentage*	*Total*	*Mean*	*Percentage*
Consumed from market	600	8	33.33	450	6	23.71
Consumed from PDS	1200	22.66	66.66	1450	19.33	76.31
Total	1800	33.33	100	1900	25.33	100

Source: Primary Survey

The table 1 shows the dependency of NFSA households to the PDS and Market in eight districts of Kerala. Fifteen NFSA households from eight districts of Kerala are randomly selected. It is evident from the table that the more than sixty percentage share of rice consumption is from PDS. Among the sample districts Pathanamthitta district has reported highest share of dependence to PDS that is 76.41 percent, where as Alappuzha district reported least dependence percent to PDS that is 63.36 percent. However, more than 20 percent of rice consumption in all sample districts is from market. This shows, even though majority share of the consumption is from PDS, people do depend on market also for their monthly rice consumption.

Satisfaction Level of Beneficiaries

Fair price shop is the last end in the supply chain of distribution of subsidized food grains to the beneficiaries. Implementation of NFSA has initiated some technological changes and more transparency to the functioning of FPSs like, introduction of e-pos machine for biometric authentication using finger print or iris, SMS alerts on each month's entitlement to the mobile phone of beneficiaries, printed bills in local languages etc. The act also entitles the right to pose complaints about the functioning of FPSs.

Table 2 shows the satisfaction level of beneficiaries on the functioning of FPSs in eight districts of Kerala. The satisfaction in terms of distribution of food grains at time, time of working of FPSs, incidents of over payment, biometric authentication, display of sample food grains etc. are analyzed here. In all districts the satisfaction level is reported as eighty percent or more that eighty percent. Neutral responses are also reported from seven districts.

The working time of all FPSs are unified as 8:00 am to 12:00 pm and 4:00 pm to 8:00pm. The opening and closing time, monthly entitlement of PHH and AAY category, retail issue price per kilogram for PHH and AAY category, total number of NFSA beneficiaries, toll free number, quantity received and distributed etc are displayed on all sample FPSs. All sample FPSs are accessible by pucca road facilities.

Table 9.2: Satisfaction Level of Beneficiaries

	Ernakulam		*Kottayam*		*Trivandrum*		*Kasargod*	
	No : ofhhs	*%*	*No : ofhhs*	*%*	*No : ofhhs*	*%*	*No : ofhhs*	*%*
Satisfied	62	84.33	60	80	61	81.3	75	100
Neutral	13	15.66	13	17.43	14	18.7	0	0
Dissatisfied	0	0	2	2.56	0	0	0	0
	Wayanad		*Kollam*		*Alappuzha*		*Pathanamthitta*	
	No : ofhhs	*%*	*No : ofhhs*	*%*	*No : ofhhs*	*%*	*No : ofhhs*	*%*
Satisfied	64	85.33	60	80	62	84.33	60	80
Neutral	11	14.66	13	17.33	13	15.66	13	17.63
Dissatisfied	0	0	2	2.66	0	0	2	2.36

Source: Primary Survey

Notes: 1.No: of hhs - Number of Households

Awareness of Eligibility Criteria

High education and high health standards in Kerala compared to its counterparts indirectly owes it development to Public Distribution System that ensures basic necessity for survival. The National Food Security Act implemented in line with the ongoing Food Security programs initiated a large number of changes in the functional structure. The population of Kerala highly adapted to the new scenario and structure of PDS like, portability of card, bio-metric authentication, allocation information through mobile SMS, grievance redressal mechanisms etc. very fast.

Table 9.3: Awareness on the Eligibility Criteria for Availing Benefits

	Ernakulam		*Kottayam*		*Trivandrum*		*Kasargod*	
	No : of hhs	*%*	*No :of hhs*	*%*	*No :of hhs*	*%*	*No :of hhs*	*%*
Awareness	50	66.66	55	73	60	80	55	73
	Wayanad		*Kollam*		*Alappuzha*		*Pathanamthitta*	
	No :ofhhs	*%*	*No :ofhhs*	*%*	*No :ofhhs*	*%*	*No :ofhhs*	*%*
Awareness	75	100	75	100	60	80	55	73

Source: Primary Survey

Notes: 1. No: of hhs - Number of Household

Awareness regarding the eligibility criteria is another benefit of improved literacy rate. From the table: 3 it is evident that in Wayanad district, the sample beneficiaries reported cent percent awareness on their eligibility and entitlement. In Alappuzha and Trivandrum districts eighty percent of sample beneficiaries are aware about their eligibility criterion and entitlement. The least percentage is reported by Ernakulam district as sixty percent.

For a policy to be in function at its best the beneficiaries must be aware of the provisions and eligibility for accessing the provisions, the improved educational standards and literacy rate among the common people has indirectly accelerated the improvement of function of Public Distribution System.

Biometric Authentication through FPSs

Bio-metric authentication is another major change initiated by the implementation of NFSA. It is a method of security measure adopted for verifying identity of the person using their biometric features. Along with this, UIDAI number (Unique Identification Authority of India), bank account number, mobile number are also seeded for the better functioning, transparency and reduced malpractices of PDS. The process started in Kerala, only in late 2016 along with implementation of NFSA. However, the state was able to mark a substantial rate of biometric authentication after four years of inception.

Table 9.4: Biometric Authentication for the sample Districts (January, 2020)

	District	*Total Cards*	*Authenticate % (Against Availed Cards)*	*Manual % (Against Availed Cards)*
1.	Alappuzha	594051	95.40	4.59
2.	Ernakulam	856457	97.25	2.74
3.	Idukki	303548	96.79	3.20
4.	Kannur	628718	98.94	1.05
5.	Kasargodu	315866	98.31	1.68
6.	Kollam	751051	95.63	4.36
7.	Kottayam	520619	98.22	1.77
8.	Kozhikkodu	768889	91.50	8.49
9.	Malappuram	955380	98.64	1.35
10.	Palakkad	756046	98.39	1.60
11.	Pathanamthitta	345339	96.73	3.26
12.	Thiruvananthapuram	956962	94.10	5.89
13.	Thrissur	846722	98.84	1.15
14.	Wayanad	219991	94.74	5.25
	Total	8819639	96.66	3.33

Source: https://epos.kerala.gov.in/

The bio-metric authentication of Kerala as per January, 2020 is 96.66 percentage. These 'ready to adapt' mentality toward technology is a great benefit from higher education and awareness level imparted by the developmental pattern.

Rate of Availing Portability Services

The implementation of NFSA has added another technological change in the function of PDS that is, portability of services. This service provides the beneficiaries with provision of using the ration card at any FPSs inside the state for availing the entitled food grains. Before introducing this provision, the beneficiaries were forced to buy from single FPS to which the card is linked. This has resulted in discontinuous or even cases of stoppage of buying the entitlement due to reasons like migration, unpleasant relationship with FPS dealers etc.

Table 9.5: Rate of Availing Portability Services (January, 2020)

Sl. No.	*District*	*Total Cards*	*Availed Cards*	*Availed Trans*	*Availed Port Cards*	*Availed Port Trans*	*Portability %*
1.	Alappuzha	586277	500766	563554	106526	118194	21.27
2.	Ernakulam	840766	687431	768447	154255	168868	22.43
3.	Idukki	299498	256837	297248	57991	65337	22.57
4.	Kannur	620869	590605	709263	116446	133614	19.71
5.	Kasargodu	311662	297627	348427	62948	71314	21.14
6.	Kollam	741992	602220	654596	146278	157453	24.28
7.	Kottayam	512759	437232	497462	101946	113703	23.31
8.	Kozhikkodu	756407	708218	872707	156855	184097	22.14
9.	Malappuram	937212	902277	1114934	140321	164092	15.55
10.	Palakkad	743229	668198	786808	99280	112557	14.85
11.	Pathanamthitta	340600	286299	333825	70035	79721	24.46
12.	Thiruvananthapuram	942203	816110	917957	230287	254868	28.21
13.	Thrissur	833152	739199	864242	143944	162684	19.47
14.	Wayanad	216334	206647	255902	46422	55406	22.46
Total		8682960	7699666	8985372	1633534	1841908	21.21

Source: https://epos.kerala.gov.in/

The table 5 shows the rate of portability service accessed by the beneficiaries in the month January, 2020. The portability percentage of the districts lies between fourteen percent and twenty nine percent. Highest portability rate is reported in Trivandrum for the month of January that is, 28.21 percentage. The least rate for the month is reported in Palakkad district that is, 14.85 percent, whereas the state average is 21.21 percent.

Nutritional Provision through PDS

Food security acts as an igniting shot to start the engine of growth and development. In order to achieve the benefits of food security reflected to other developmental spheres, the next gateway must be passed, that is nutritional security via food security. The major food grains distributed by public distribution in Kerala are rice and wheat. While a PHH household member is entitled to have 4 kg of rice and 1 kg of wheat the average intake of both food grains per day by a person are 133 gram of rice and 33 gram of wheat.

***The nutrition components present in these are:**

Calories	-512 (required calorie intake for women 2000 and for men 2500)
Fat	- 0.75 grams (required average amount is 44 to 77 grams)
Protein	- 7.52 grams (required level 46 grams to 56 grams)
Carbohydrates	- 28.832 (130 grams per day)

Section V: Strategies adopted in Kerala through Public Distribution System to face the Unprecedented Challenges of COVID-19

Covid-19 pandemic struck India, first in the state of Kerala on 30th January, 2020 in the district of Thrissur. The sudden response from the state government could efficiently keep the situation under control before the pandemic spread in the whole country. The Food and Agriculture Organisation points out, *India, having a denser population comparatively, was forced to take immediate actions to curb the spread of the virus. As the majority of the population is characterized as vulnerable, authorities feared a problem bigger than the pandemic - hunger.*

Kerala being the first hit by the pandemic set an example for the rest of the country through taking immediate action to address the risk of starvation resulted from joblessness following measures like, lockdowns and social distancing to prevent the spread of corona virus. The important measures taken are:

- Other than the entitled food grains (that is 35 kg of food grains for AAY category and 5 kg food grain per members under PHH category) 15 kg of rice were distributed to all under different categoriesthrough the Public Distribution systems (PDS) and Kerala State Civil Supplies Corporation (SUPPLYCO).
- The government also announced free ration for the month of April and people who were under home quarantine were included in priority list.

- An extra step which gained world attention was providing free food kits worth INR 1000 to the whole population of the state. The free distribution was started on started 8th April, 2020 and in order to maintain social distancing separate dates were allotted according to the number series on the card. The free food kit included 17 essential items as given below in the table

Table 9.6: List of Items in the Essential Food Kit Distributed by the State of Kerala.

Sl. No	*Items*	*Quantity*
1.	Sugar	1kg
2.	Tea	250g
3.	Beans	1kg
4.	Coconut oil	500ml
5.	Sunflower oil	1L
6.	Atta	1kg
7.	Cornflour	1kg
8.	Chilly powder	100g
9.	Coriander powder	100g
10.	Dal	250g
11.	Turmeric powder	100g
12.	Fenugreek seeds	100g
13.	Mustard	100g
14.	Urad dal	1kg
15.	Chickpeas	1kg
16.	Soaps	2no.
17.	Wheat Flour	2 kg

(*Source:* Compilation from different News Paper from 8th April, 202)

- These food commodities are sourced from the suppliers registered under Kerala State Civil Supplies Corporation and National Agriculture Cooperative Marketing Federation of India. This project was funded by the Kerala Chief Minister Distress Relief Fund and has allotted about INR 35 crores for this purpose.
- Free hand sanitizers were provided to every Fair Price shops in Kerala so that bio-metric authentication and food distribution is not hindered.

The central government also initiated programs in line with this, like free distribution of food grain for the population under NFSA net. It is found that Kerala's wide coverage and massive dependency of its population to public distribution system played a vital role in reaching out to the local grounds when there is an emergency need. This is why effective inclusion of nutritional security along with food security using the same system is said to be possible to run the development cycle for yielding maximum benefit.

Section VI: Conclusion

Food and nutritional security is a primary concern for every nation who targets in human development and welfare of its population. India's National Food Security act is an adaptation of right based approach to food security. The act entitles food security to 75 percentage of the country's rural population and 50 percentage of its urban population. The act was implemented in all states and union territories in India. Along with this, the state of Kerala enacted the NFSA in November, 2016. Kerala being a forerunner in human development efficiently adopted the central policies and successfully added the state concerns also while implementing the act. The features of public distribution in the state of Kerala are its wide range of coverage and high dependency of vulnerable population, quick adoption of new additions like, biometric authentication, portability of services etc. The effective implementation of NFSA in the state of Kerala is mainly due to its already established social capital. The rate of awareness of eligibility criteria, rate of accessing the provisions like portability services are remarkably high as these are facilitated by the high literacy and awareness levels in the state. The potential of public distribution system to reach out to the poor in times of the pandemic is also evidence to the effectiveness by which the system could respond to the needs of the population.

References

1. Alkire, S. (2002) Valuing Freedoms: Sen's Capability Approach and Poverty Reduction, Oxford University Press, Oxford.
2. C., Mohammed. (2012). Food security and nutrition in Kerala: An exploratory approach, Journal of Rural Development. 31. 513-534.
3. Clay, E (2002): Food Security: Concepts and Measurement: conceptualizing the linkages, FAO Expert Consultation, Rome.
4. De Muro, Pasquale &Burchi, Francesco. (2012). A Human Development and Capability Approach to Food Security: Conceptual Framework and Informational Basis. 2012-9.
5. Food and Agriculture Organization (1983), World Food Security: a Reappraisal of the Concepts and Approaches, Director General's Report, Rome.
6. Food and Agriculture Organization (2001). The State of Food Insecurity in the World 2001, FAO, Rome.
7. Government of India. (2013). The National Food Security Act, 2013. The Gazette of India: Extraordinary (Part II, Sec 1. September.http:// indiacode.nic.in/acts-in-pdf/202013.pdf

8. Government of Kerala (2011), Economic Review 2019. State Planning Board, Thiruvananthapuram. 6. Hossain, Mahabub, Fird

9. Jenkins, J. & Scanlan, Stephen. (2001). Food Security in Less Developed Countries, 1970-1990. American Sociological Review. 66. 718-744. 10.2307/3088955.

10. Jha, S. and Srinivasan (2001).Taking the PDS to the Poor: Directions for Further Reform, Economic and Political Weekly, 36(39), 3779–3786.

11. Joseph AwetoriYaro (2004) Theorizing food insecurity: building a livelihood vulnerability framework for researching food insecurity, NorskGeografisk Tidsskrift - Norwegian Journal of Geography, 58:1, 23-37, DOI: 10.1080/00291950410004375

12. Kannan, K.P. (1995) Declining Incidence of Rural Poverty in Kerala, Economic and Political Weekly, 30(41–42), 2651–2662.

13. Nair, Reshmy. (2011). Public Distribution System in Kerala Reassessed. Indian Journal of Social Work. 72. 23-54.

14. Tanksale, Ajinkya & Jha, J.K. (2015). Implementing National Food Security Act in India: issues and challenges. British Food Journal. 117. 1315-1335. 10.1108/BFJ-07-2014-0239.

15. Teodosijeviæ, S.B. (2003): Armed Conflicts and Food Security, ESA Working Paper No. 03-11, Agricultural and Development Economics Division, FAO.

16. Timmer, C. (2010). Behavioral Dimensions of Food Security. Proceedings of the National Academy of Sciences of the United States of America. 109. 12315-20. 10.1073/pnas.0913213107.

17. https://civilsupplieskerala.gov.in/

18. https://dfpd.gov.in/index.htm

19. https://epos.kerala.gov.in/index.jsp

20. https://www.onmanorama.com/news/kerala/2020/03/29/kerala-government-food-kit-coronavirus-lockdown-list-of-items.html

21. https://www.thenewsminute.com/article/pulses-tea-powder-oil-these-are-17-essentials-food-kits-distributed-kerala-govt-122265

Part IV
Human Development status/Quality of Life of the Marginalised

10

Development Status of Particularly Vulnerable Tribal Groups other tribes in Kerala: A Comparison

Manju S. Nair & Sajeev M.V.

Kerala model of development has been acknowledged as a situation where it was possible for a state to achieve high levels of human development with inadequate level of resources evidenced by the internationally comparable levels of literacy rate, life expectancy rate, infant mortality rate, maternity mortality rate etc. which Kerala achieved with a growth rate of less than 1.97 percent, 2.87 percent during the 70's and 80's. This phenomenon of low growth and high human development has been documented as human development lopsided in development literature. Of late, Kerala experienced turnaround in her growth rates as evidenced by around 6.12 percent and 8.05 percent growth during the 1990 to 2000 and 2000 to 2010 respectively, along with maintaining high levels in human development indices. The situation of high growth and high human development is reported as virtuous phase in development literature and scholars now examine whether Kerala has moved on to a virtuous cycle pattern. Ample literature exists to the fact that human development indices are averages which tend to under report the relative deprivation of marginalised communities. During the human development lopsided phase, data shows that the status of Scheduled Tribes and Scheduled Castes and fisher folk in human development, particularly regarding health and education was very low compared to the general population, i.e. Kerala model of development has eluded some communities. Human development status of the Scheduled Tribes in the seemingly virtuous cycle path needs to be explored. There are thirty four tribal categories in Kerala, and the question of whether the development of ST communities in the state across the groups has taken place equitably gains attention: out of the thirty four categories of ST, five are classified as Particularly Vulnerable Tribal Groups (PVTGs); they are Kadar, Kattunayakan, Koraga, Kurumbar and Cholanaickan. The article attempts at a comparison of development indicators (particularly related to education, health, and livelihood status) of these PVTGs with reference to all other tribal groups to understand the relative position of the PVTGs. Section I gives a brief profile of the five PVTGs, Section II examines the demographic details, Section III the educational attainments, Section IV health status, Section V livelihood levels and Section VI gender related aspects of the PVTGs in Kerala in comparison with other tribal groups.

Section I: A Brief Profile of the five PVTGs

In Kerala five communities, namely; Kadar, Kattunayakan, Koraga, Kurumbar and Cholanaickan are recognised as PVTGs. There are 6771 families with total population of 26,273 consisting of 13,073 males and 13,200 females (Government of Kerala, 2013). Thus the family size is 3.88, registering the sex ratio among them as 1000:1010. The community wise details of PVTGs are discussed below;

Kadar

Kadar population is distributed in Palakkad and Thrissur Districts. In Palakkad they are found in Parambikulam, Kuriyarkutty, Nelliyampathy, Kalchadi and Thaliyakallu areas, while in Thrissur their settlements are found in Vazhachal, Peringalkuthu and Sholayar forest areas. Kadar speaks a form of Tamil with Malayalam elements. The hereditary headman of the settlement is called "Moopan" who deal with the social control mechanism of the community.

They subsist mainly on non timber forest produce collection and forest labour. Traditionally they were expert food gatherers, hunters and trappers. They were adept in making strong rocks required for their honey collection and elephant capturing expeditions. The Britishers had built a tramway deep into their territory and employed Kadar to shift the cut trees from the forests to Chalakudy. The hydro electric and irrigation projects, namely; Parambikulam/Aliyar, Peringalkuthu, Sholayar, Pothundi, Mangalam and Thunakadavu had forced them abandon their habitats and move to resettlement areas which had a direct impact on their social life and economy. Tourism near to their settlements is another threat to their social life. Kadar have 545 families with a population of 1974. Their family size is 3.62. As there are 967 males and 1007 females, the sex ratio is seen as 1000:1041. Kadar population is distributed in Mattathur (269), Athirappally (804), Muthalamada (477), Vandazhy (168) and Kodanchery (126) Grama panchayats.

Kattunayakan

Kattunayakans are distributed in Wayanad, Kozhikode, Malappuram and Palakkad districts. They are also found in the neighbouring states of Karnataka and Tamilnadu. An overwhelming majority of the population is concentrated in Wayanad. The term Kattunayakan is derived from the words 'Kattu' (forest) and "Nayakan or Naickan" (Lord). Thus Kattunayakan literally means lord of forests. They speak a dialect similar to Kannada. They converse with outsiders in Malayalam.

Basically Kattunayakans are forest dwellers and hence their social life and economy are forest based. They were used as mahouts and in elephant capture. Among tribal communities they are found to be the best honey collectors applying different techniques. They were mainly hunters and food gatherers with sporadic shifting cultivation round their settlements. They still subsist on non timber forest produce collection. The headman is called 'Muthan' or 'Muthali' who also officiates as priest.

Kattunayakan is a community with the largest population among the PVTGs in Kerala. Kattunayakan constitute 4.69 percent of the population of Scheduled Tribes in the state. They have 5137 families and majority of them are in Wayanad Disrict (4369). Malappuram (517 families) and Palakkad (218 families) are two other districts which have representation of Kattunayakan. In Kozhikode District there are thirty two families where as one family is located in Idukki District. The total population of Kattunayakan community is estimated as 19995, 9953 being males and 10042 being females.

Kattunayakan families are settled in 51 Grama Panchayats. Idukki (1), Palakkad (5), Malappuram (16), Kozhikode (5) and Wayanad (24) are the districts which have population of Kattunayakan in Grama Panchayats. Besides, Tirur and Kalpetta Municipalities have also nominal population of Kattunayakan. However, majority of the population are in Thirunelli, Noolpuzha, Poothadi, Mullamkolly and Pulpally Grama Panchayats.

Koraga

Koragas are distributed only in Kasargod District and in the adjoining area of Karnataka State. They had a glorious history of having a Koraga region under Hubashika Raja, but later on they were enslaved by their rulers. 'Kora' means sun and it is said that they worship sun and hence the term 'Koraga' originated from it. They speak Tulu.

They live in 'Mathadi' (settlements) and the headman is known as 'Koppu' or 'Guru Kara' who controls the social and cultural practices. They had also a council of elders for decision making and awarding punishments. Koragas were treated as slaves and were sold with the land by their respective masters. They are experts in basketry and weaving a variety of items like winnowing fans, cradles and baskets. They collect the raw materials like bamboos, canes and creepers available from the nearby forests.

Altogether, 445 families of Koraga community are settled in Grama Panchayats and one Municipality in Kasargode district. As the population of Koraga community is 1644, their family size works out to 3.69. The population consist of 802 males and 842 females and hence the sex ratio is 1000:1050.

Kurumbas

Kurumbas are distributed in Attappady Block Panchayat of Palakkad District. They are the earliest inhabitants of Attappady area and are called 'Palu Kurumba' to distinguish them from the 'Alu Kurumba' of Nilgiris in Tamilnadu State. The language spoken by them is a mixture of Tamil and Malayalam. The traditional social organisation of Kurumbas is similar to that of Mudugar and Irular communities residing in that area.

Kurumbas mostly living in reserve and vested forest areas have been practising shifting cultivation called 'Panja Krishi'. They cultivate ragi, thuvara, chama etc. They are experts in cattle rearing. They are also collectors of non timber forest produces. They maintain a community life by sharing land and labour.

Kurumbas were once hunters and gatherers and shifting cultivators of Attappady Valley. However, among the five PVTGs of Kerala, the younger generation of the Kurumba community have shown more interest than others in organising themselves and getting educated.

Kurumba community is settled in Agali and Pudur Grama Panchayats of Palakkad District. There are 543 families with a population of 2251. The family size is 4.14. As the population consists of 1128 males and 1123 females the sex ratio is 1000:996. Ninety eight percent of Kurumba population is settled in Pudur Grama Panchayat and the rest in Agali Grama Panchayat.

Cholanaickan

Cholanaickans are found only in the evergreen recess of the forests of the Ghat section of Karulai and Vazhikkadavu forest ranges of Nilambur Valley of Malappuram District. They have been geographically isolated and leading a life fully with dense tropical rain forest environment. 'Chola' means shade and 'Naickan' or 'Nayakan' denotes leader. They speak a dialect of their own having a mixture of Kannada and Malayalam.

Cholanaickans are distributed in ten hamlets in the deep forest called 'Jemmom' and each 'Jemmom' has a leader called 'Jemmakkaran' who performs both socio political and religious functions. The families associated with each Jemmom do not trespass the rights of other Jemmoms. They practise Jemmom exogamy.

Among the Scheduled Tribes of Kerala, Cholanaickan has unique position in the sense that they are the only community who depends solely on non timber forest produces for their consumption and for exchange or sale. Their territory is blessed with abundance of non timber forest produces. They spend most of their forest life in natural rock shelters. They visit the Kalkkulam co-operative society in Nilambur once in a week and bring the non- timber forest produces in big bamboo basket called 'Poonikotta' they carry on their back. The society has served as a nodal meeting point of all the members belonging to various 'Jemmoms'.

Section II: Demographic Details of PVTGs

Table 10.1: Community wise data on families, population and sex ratio and pattern of settlement of the PVTG in comparison with other tribal groups

Community		*Settlements*			*Population*				
		Numbers	*%*	*Families*	*Male*	*Female*	*Total*	*%*	*Sex Ratio*
PVTG	Kadar	21	0.33	545	967	1007	1974	0.46	1041
	Kattunayakan	479	7.47	5137	9953	10042	19995	4.69	1009
	Koraga	18	0.28	445	802	842	1644	0.39	1050
	Kurumbar	23	0.36	543	1128	1123	2251	0.53	996
	Cholanaickan	10	0.16	101	223	186	409	0.10	834
PVTG Total		551	8.60	6771	13073	13200	26273	6.17	1010
Other Tribal Groups		5858	91.40	101194	196748	203189	399935	93.83	1031
Total		6409	100	107965	209819	216389	426208	100	1031

Source: Government of Kerala (2013), Report on Socio- Economic Status of Scheduled Tribes in Kerala

There are 101 Cholanaickans families with the population of 409 and all are settled in three Grama Panchayts, namely; Amarambalam, Karulari and Vazhikkadavu in Malappuram District. The family size of the Cholanaickan community is 4.05. The population includes 223 males and 186 females. The sex ratio of Cholanaickan works out as 1000:834 which is lowest among the Scheduled Tribe communities.

As depicted in the table, PVTG forms 6.17 percent of the tribal population, Kattunayakan being the major tribe community (4.69 percent). The representation of other PVTGs in the total ST population is less than one percent. They are settled in 551 Oorus and have an average sex ratio of 1000: 1010 as against 1000:1031 for the other tribal groups. Cholanaickan represent a very low sex ratio that is 1000:834.

Section III: Education attainments of PVTGs

Education is a fundamental input for capacity enhancement and major pathway to a life out of poverty. Kerala has always attained a place in development discourse for the achievements the state has made in the field of education and human capacity enhancement. But this becomes a hoax when the educational attainments of tribal communities are considered. Within the tribal groups there exists disparities with regard to different aspect of educational attainments and this section probes into the disparities in the educational attainments of PVTGs against the other ST groups. The indicators selected are literacy levels, education qualification, drop outs etc.

Table 10.2: Community wise data on Male Female Literacy Rate of PVTGs

Community		*Literacy Rate*	*Difference with other tribal groups*	*Difference with general population*	*Male Literacy Rate*	*Difference with other tribal groups*	*Difference with general population*	*Female Literacy Rate*	*Difference with other tribal groups*	*Difference with general population*
PVTG	Kadar	58.74	16.61	35.17	62.20	17.69	31.71	56.09	14.89	37.82
	Kattunayakan	59.37	15.98	34.54	62.35	17.54	31.56	56.54	14.44	37.37
	Koraga	78.35	3.00	15.56	81.63	1.74	12.28	75.23	4.25	18.68
	Kurumbar	56.36	18.94	37.55	63.85	16.04	30.06	48.66	22.32	45.25
	Cholanaickan	39.63	35.72	54.28	36.90	42.99	57.01	42.55	28.43	51.36
PVTG Total		60.02	15.33	33.89	63.27	16.62	30.64	56.93	14.05	36.98
Other TribalGroups		75.35	0	18.56	79.89	0	14.02	70.98	0	22.93
Total		74.44	0.91	19.47	78.90	0.99	15.01	70.15	0.83	23.76

Source: Government of Kerala (2013), Report on Socio- Economic Status of Scheduled Tribes in Kerala

As the table shows the literacy rate of PVTGs is 15.33 percent less than that of other tribal groups and 33.89 percent less than the general population. Within PVTGs Cholanaickan exhibits the lowest literacy rates, the rate is as low as 39.63 percent, exhibiting 35.72 percent difference with respect of other tribal groups and54.28 percent in comparison with general population. Male female literacy rates also shows substantial difference, the difference being highest among Cholanaickan followed by Kurumbar, Kadar, and Kattunayakan. The difference in male literacy of PVTGs with the other tribal groups is as high as 16.62 percent and for the females it is as high as14.05 percent.

Table 10.3: Community Wise data on Illiterates

Community		*Population (Above 5 Years)*	*% to total*	*Illiterates*	*%*	*% to Total population*
PVTG	Kadar	1704	0.44	703	0.71	41.25
	Kattunayakan	17436	4.53	7084	7.20	40.62
	Koraga	1483	0.39	321	0.33	21.64
	Kurumbar	1888	0.49	824	0.84	43.64
	Cholanaickan	323	0.08	195	0.20	60.37
PVTG Total		22834	5.93	9127	9.28	39.97
Other Tribal Groups		362144	94.07	89259	90.38	24.74
Total		384978	100	98386	90.72	25.55

Source: Government of Kerala (2013), Report on Socio- Economic Status of Scheduled Tribes in Kerala.

The percent of PVTGs in the total tribal groups is 5.93; however 9.28 percent of the total illiterates are formed by PVTG. All the five PVTGs have more representation in the percent share of illiterates than their percentage share in total tribal population as is evidenced from Table. Around half of the PVTG still remain illiterates, with Cholanaickan representing the highest percent of illiterates (more than 60%) followed by Koraga, Kadar and Kattunayakan. Educational status of the literates in PVTGs is provided in table 4.

Table 10.4: Community wise data on educational Status of PVTGs

Community		**Population Above 5 Years (%)**	**SSLC**	**PDC/+2**	**Total (% total population)**	**Graduation**	**Post graduation**	**Diploma& certificate courses**
PVTG	Kadar	1704 (0.44)	63	44	6.28	3 (0.07)	-	10 (0.27)
	Kattunayakan	17436 (4.53)	515	243	4.30	16 (0.36)	5 (0.61)	38 (1.03)
	Koraga	1483 (0.39)	77	43	8.09	7 (0.16)	-	6 (016)
	Kurumbar	1888 (0.49)	117	73	10.06	12 (0.27)	1 (0.12)	17 (0.46)
	Cholanaickan	323 (0.08)	9	3	3.72	-	-	-

(Contd...)

PVTG Total	22834 (5.93)	781	397	5.16	38 (0.86)	6 (0.73)	71 (1.92)
Other Tribal Groups	362144 (94.07)	29561	15977	12.57	4437 (99.14)	809 (99.27)	3615 (98.08)
Total	384978 (100)	30342	16374	12.13	4475 (100)	816 (100)	3686 (100)

Source: Government of Kerala (2013), Report on Socio- Economic Status of Scheduled Tribes in Kerala

Of the total tribal groups 12.13 percent have higher secondary as their highest educational qualification, however for the PVTGs, only 5.16 percent of them have higher secondary as their highest educational qualification. Only 3.72 percent of the Cholanaickan come under this category. Regarding higher educational attainments (graduation and post-graduation) although PVTGs forms 5.93 percent of the total tribal groups, they form only 0.86 percent and 0.73 percent of tribal population who have Graduation and Post Graduation respectively. None among Cholanaickan have obtained graduation. From Koraga and Kadar, nobody qualified post graduation also. 99.14 percent and 99.27 percent of those who passed graduation and post graduation belongs to other tribal groups. Same is the case with diploma and certificate groups within the tribal groups. Only 1.92 percent of the diploma and certificate holders belong to the PVTGs and 98.08 percent are from other tribal groups.

Thus the educational status of PVTGs is very deplorable. Around half of them are illiterate and among the literate, majority are below SSLC. Those obtaining higher education are near zero in this group pointing towards their less capability in finding sustainable livelihood.

Table 10.5: Community Wise data on students in Higher Secondary Course

Community		*Students*		
		Children in the Age 15-17	*Students in +2*	*Percentage to Children*
PVTG	Kadar	82	24	29.27
	Kattunayakan	828	153	18.48
	Koraga	85	19	22.35
	Kurumbar	131	34	25.95
	Cholanaickan	22	1	4.55
PVTG Total		1148	231	20.12
Other Tribal Groups		16917	6574	38.86
Total		18065	6805	37.67

Source: Government of Kerala (2013), Report on Socio- Economic Status of Scheduled Tribes in Kerala

Children in the age 15-17 are expected to be studying in secondary courses, but the cases with tribal groups are different. Of all the children aged in the category of 15-17, only 37.67 percent are going to secondary course, the percentage is still less for the PVTGs. Only 20.12 percent of the children in the age group of 15 to 17, are enrolled in higher secondary, the percent for Cholanaickan being very less that is 4.55 percent. It implies that majority of children of PVTGs have less probability of gaining employment opportunities requiring educational qualification.

The Dropout Syndrome

Table 10.6: Community Wise data on Dropout/Discontinuance

Dropout/ Discontinuance	*PVTG*					*PVTG Total*	*Other tribal Groups*	*Total*
	Kadar	*Kattunayakan*	*Koraga*	*Kurumbar*	*Cholanaickan*			
Primary	64	1308	19	38	10	1439	13925	15364
Secondary	74	569	50	32	16	741	12133	12874
Higher Secondary	-	73	10	2	-	85	1390	1475
Graduation	2	4	5	3	-	14	478	492
Post Graduation	-	-	9	-	-	9	185	194
Certificate and Course	-	29	15	2	-	46	779	825
Diploma courses	-	44	28	-	-	72	1124	1196
Others	5	11	1	11	-	28	895	923
Total	145	2038	137	88	26	2434	30846	33387

Source: Government of Kerala (2013), Report on Socio- Economic Status of Scheduled Tribes in Kerala

The dropout or discontinuance of studies by the students is a major concern in the education of ST communities. The average rate of dropout is 36.73 percent of total students. Altogether 33387 students have discontinued their studies of which 2434 (7.89 percent) are form PVTGs. In the general education stream, the rate of dropout is highest in the secondary class. But we see that in the case of PVTG, drop out is dominant right from the primary class itself; 1439 of PVTG students discontinued their studies from the primary class itself, there are drop outs in secondary, higher secondary, graduation and post graduation courses also. Financial constraints, failure / detention, family problems, in accessibility to institution, sense of alienation etc are the reasons attributed for the huge drop out of tribal students (Government of Kerala, 2013).

Section V: Livelihood pattern: Employment Status

The employment pattern of Scheduled Tribes could broadly be classified into three, namely, forestry sector, agriculture and allied sectors and non agriculture and allied sectors. The forestry sector consists of collection of forest produces, traditional occupations, collection of herbal plants and works related to forestry sector. The agriculture and allied sectors include agriculture, animal husbandry and agricultural labour. The non agriculture and allied sectors consist of petty trade, employment under Mahatma Gandhi National Rural Employment Guarantee Scheme (MGNREGS), works under non agricultural sectors, plantation labour, employment under government/ quasi government sector and employment in other sectors including private sector. It has been estimated that 8.17 percent of Scheduled Tribe families are engaged in works under forestry sector, 69.52 percent in agriculture and allied sectors and 20.53 percent in non agriculture and allied sectors. 1.77 percent is no income families.

Table 10.7: Community Wise data on Percentage of Main Workers in Forestry Sector, Agriculture and Allied Sectors, Non Agriculture and Allied Sectors in the Age Group 15-59

Community		*Forestry Sector*	*Agriculture & Allied Sectors*	*Non Agriculture &Allied Sectors*
PVTG	Kadar	81.19	8.29	10.52
	Kattunayakan	16.47	72.84	10.68
	Koraga	41.27	27.94	30.79
	Kurumbar	59.25	24.95	15.81
	Cholanaickan	88.65	4.26	7.09
PVTG Total		27.31	60.39	12.28
Other Tribal Groups		6.83	69.81	23.37
Total		8.13	69.22	22.66

Source: Government of Kerala (2013), Report on Socio- Economic Status of Scheduled Tribes in Kerala.

Table 10.7 shows the distribution of main workers in the three sectors mentioned. Kadar and Cholanaickan are mostly dependent on forestry sector, where as Kattunayakan depends on agriculture & allied sectors. Compared with other tribal groups, data shows that 6.83 percent of the main workers are employed in the forestry sector, for the PVTG as an average, 27.31 percent are employed in forestry sector. 23.37 percent of other tribal groups are employed in non agriculture & allied sectors, whereas only 12.28 percent of PVTGs are employed in non agriculture & allied sectors.

(a) Workers in Forestry Sector

The main workers in forestry sector in the age group 15-59 are 15762, they constitute 8.13 percent of the total main workers in the age group 15-59. Collection of forest products, a subsector supports 3840 workers, whereas the traditional occupation, another subsector offer employment to 1044 persons. 494 persons are engaged in the collection of herbal plants as main occupation. For the tribal groups other than PVTGs forestry sector provides employment only for 6.83 percent, whereas for the PVTGs it is 27.31 percent.

Within the Cholanaickan and Kadar community, majority are engaged in collection of forest products, whereas within Kattunayakan which depend on forestry sector, majority act as workers in the forest area. Koraga and Kurumbar community has traditional occupation in forest sector. Details of main workers in agriculture and allied sectors, non agriculture and allied sectors is given in the table.

Table 10.8: Community wise data on main workers in agriculture and allied sectors in the Age Group 15-59

Community		*Main Workers in Agriculture and Allied Sectors*					
		Total Workers	*Agriculture*	*Animal Husbandry*	*Worker-Agricultural Sector*	*Total*	*% to Total Workers*
PVTG	Kadar	989	13	6	63	82	8.29
	Kattunayakan	9464	128	72	6694	6894	72.84
	Koraga	773	8	-	208	216	27.94
	Kurumbar	930	139	5	88	232	24.95
	Cholanaickan	141	-	-	6	6	4.26
PVTG Total		12297	288	83	7059	7430	60.39
Other Tribal Groups		181668	177	39	99254	126820	69.81
Total		193965	24501	3436	106313	134250	69.22

Source: Government of Kerala (2013), Report on Socio- Economic Status of Scheduled Tribes in Kerala.

The main workers in agriculture and allied sectors in the age group 15-59 are 1,34,250. They are 69.21 percent of total work force, of which 24,501 are farmers, and 1,06,313 are engaged as workers. Within the PVTGs, only 4.26 percent and 8.29 percent of Cholanaikan community are occupied in agricultural and allied sector. Majority of Kattunayakan community are workers in agriculture sector.

Table 10.9: Community wise data on main workers in non agriculture and allied sectors in the Age Group 15-59

	Community	*Main Workers in Non Agriculture and Allied Sectors*								
		Total Workers	*Petty Trade*	*Worker-MGNREGS*	*Worker-Non Agricultural Sector*	*Plantation Labourer*	*Govt./Quasi Govt Employee*	*Others*	*Total*	*% to Total Workers*
PVTG	Kadar	989	2	9	10	11	65	7	104	10.52
	Kattunayakan	9464	5	479	300	62	85	80	1011	10.68
	Koraga	773	-	79	143	-	8	8	238	30.79
	Kurumbar	930	1	77	16	8	37	8	147	15.81
	Cholanaickan	141	-	-	-	8	1	1	10	7.09
PVTG Total		12297	8	644	469	89	196	104	1510	12.28
Other Tribal Groups		181668	292	10471	18536	1201	9409	2534	42443	23.37
Total		193965	300	11115	19005	1290	9605	2638	43953	22.66

Source: Government of Kerala (2013), Report on Socio- Economic Status of Scheduled Tribes in Kerala.

The main workers in non agriculture and allied sectors are 43,953 registering, 22.66 percent of total workers. Petty trade is one of the subsector employing 300 persons, forming only 0.68 percent of the total persons engaged in non agricultural operation. This fact reveals the backwardness of STs in promoting self employment initiatives. The MNREG programmes provide employment to 11,115 workers (25.29 percent). Worker in non agriculture sector is the major subsectors which provide occupation to 19,005 persons (43.24 percent). The plantation labourers are another subsector which has 1,290 workers. The government sector offer employment to 9,605 persons (21.85 percent). The Non Agricultural & Allied Sectors employs 23.37 percent of tribal groups other than PVTGs, but for the PVTGs the corresponding percentage is 12.28 percent. Within the PVTGs, the lowest employment in non agricultural sector is for Cholanaickan followed by Kadar and Kattunayakan. Koraga community has 30.79 percent workers in non agricultural sector.

BPL Families

Half of the tribal families in Kerala belong to BPL category; the corresponding share is 57.22 percent for PVTGs. Within the PVTGs, 75 percent of Koraga, 73 percent of Kadar, 54 percent of Kattunayakan and 52 percent of Kurumbar and Cholanaickan belongs to BPL category.

Table 10.10: Community Wise data on BPL Families

Community		Total Families	BPL	Percentage
PVTG	Kadar	545	401	73.58
	Kattunayakan	5137	2803	54.56
	Koraga	445	334	75.06
	Kurumbar	543	284	52.30
	Cholanaickan	101	53	52.48
PVTG Total		6771	3875	57.22
Other Tribal Groups		101194	51517	50.91
Total		107965	55392	51.31

Source: Government of Kerala (2013), Report on Socio- Economic Status of Scheduled Tribes in Kerala.

Receipt of eligible pension is also low for the tribal groups as a whole. Out of 21,561 widows, only 3,587 get widow pension (16.64 percent) and out of 34,958 old people only 4,526 (12.95 percent) get old age pension.

Table 10.11: Community wise data on status of widow pension and status of old age pension

Community		Total Widows	Pension Bene-ficiaries	% total of Widows	Persons Above 60 Years	Pension Bene-ficiaries	% to persons
PVTG	Kadar	109	17	15.60	82	13	15.85
	Kattunayakan	887	118	13.30	1310	232	17.71
	Koraga	42	8	19.05	147	24	16.33
	Kurumbar	85	13	15.29	81	9	11.11
	Cholanaickan	8	3	37.50	25	2	8.00
PVTG Total		1131	159	14.06	1645	280	17.02
Other Tribal Groups		20430	3428	16.78	33313	4246	12.75
Total		21561	3587	16.64	34958	4526	12.95

Source: Government of Kerala (2013), Report on Socio- Economic Status of Scheduled Tribes in Kerala.

Only very few of the disabled get disability pension (i.e. 8.13 percent). For the PVTGs as such, only 14.06 percent of the eligible widows get pension card and only 3.89 of disabled get disability pension.

Table 10.12: Community Wise data on Status of Pension for Disabled Persons

Community		*Total Number of disabled*	*Pension Beneficiaries*	*% to Total*
PVTG	Kadar	63	1	1.59
	Kattunayakan	454	19	4.19
	Koraga	40	2	5.00
	Kurumbar	1	-	-
	Cholanaickan	7	-	-
PVTG Total		565	22	3.89
Other Tribal Groups		8565	696	8.13
Total		9130	718	7.86

Source: Government of Kerala (2013), Report on Socio- Economic Status of Scheduled Tribes in Kerala.

Indebtedness

Table 10.13: Community Wise Data on Debt Families

Community		*Debt Families*								
		Cooperative Societies	*District/State Cooperative Bank*	*Other Banks*	*Kudumbashree*	*Money Lenders/ Institutions*	*Relatives*	*Other Sources*	*Total*	*% to total*
PVTG	Kadar	2	5	7	20	19	5	25	83	0.13
	Kattunayakan	100	78	92	262	1032	44	97	1705	2.83
	Koraga	11	5	14	6	169	36	75	316	0.53
	Kurumbar	22	3	2	4	95	13	10	149	0.24
	Cholanaickan	6	-	-	-	51	-	-	57	0.094
PVTG Total		141	91	115	292	1366	98	207	2310	3.83
Other Tribal Groups		9445	4765	7445	12330	19140	1618	3377	58120	96.17
Total		9586	4856	7560	12622	20506	1716	3584	60430	100
% to Total		15.87	8.03	12.51	20.88	33.94	2.83	5.94	100	-

Source: Government of Kerala (2013), Report on Socio- Economic Status of Scheduled Tribes in Kerala.

Altogether 60,430 families of ST are in debt. They constitute 55.97 percent of the total population. Details are provided in table 5.13. 2,310 families of PVTGs are in debt, of which 33.94 percent is indebted to money lenders. All the five categories of PVTGs are mostly indebted to money lenders. Out of those indebted, 22.8 percent, 60.52 percent, 53.48 percent, 63.75 percent and 89.48 percent of Kadar, Kattunayakan, Koraga, Kurumbar and Cholanaickan are indebted to money lenders. Formal credit

(Co-operative societies, District co-operative bank and other banks) is accessed by16.89 percent, 15.83 percent, 9.50 percent, 18.12 percent and 10.52 percent of Kadar, Kattunaickan, Koraga and Cholanaickan community respectively.

Section IV: Health Status

Health care is a major problem in far-flung and isolated tribal areas. Lack of food security, sanitation and safe drinking water, poor supply of nutrition, high poverty levels, illiteracy, belief systems and cultural practices and unhealthy life style and new food habits aggravate the poor health status of tribal people.

In the earlier days, fruits, tubers, roots and leaves in forest contributed to maintain the food requirement and nutritional status of tribes. The indigenous health care system prevalent among the tribal communities also helped in providing health care to them. They had their own medicinal system based on herbs collected from nature and processed locally. They had also their own system of diagnosis. But the system has changed very much now.

There are wide variations among different tribal communities and regions in health status and access to health services. In general, the health and nutritional status of the tribal communities in Kerala, especially among children, adolescent girls and women are deficient. The impact achieved by the anganwadies in promoting nutritional status of children and mothers and the mid day meal provided by the educational institutions is minimal.

This section examines the health indicators of PVTGs in comparison with other tribal groups. The health status of a population is affected by their living condition, such as the basic amenities of life including housing condition, sanitation facilities and hence the basic amenities of life are also examined.

Differently Abled Persons and Patients with Chronic Disease

The prevalence of physical disabilities, mental disorder and chronic diseases is higher among ST communities. The number of differently abled persons come to 23,059 from 19,386 families, which is 5.41 percent of the total tribal population (As per 2011, the differently abled population in Kerala forms 2.85 percent of the total population). The percent of members with chronic diseases forms 9.54 percent of the total. Within the PVTGs 10.52 percent of Koraga, 9.68 percent of Kurumbas and 6.94 percent of Kadar are differently abled. 21.99 percent Kurumbar are also with chronic diseases. Table points to the incidence of high rate of disability and chronic diseases among the PVTGs.

Table 10.14: Community wise data on differently abled persons and patients with chronic diseases

Community		*Differently Abled Persons and Patients with Chronic Diseases*				
		Population	*Differently Abled Persons*	*% to Population*	*Patients with Chronic Diseases*	*% to Population*
PVTG	Kadar	1974	137	6.94	167	8.46
	Kattunayakan	19995	1089	5.45	1467	7.34
	Koraga	1644	174	10.52	182	11.07
	Kurumbar	2251	218	9.68	495	21.99
	Cholanaickan	409	18	4.40	23	5.62
PVTG Total		26273	1635	6.22	2334	8.88
Other Tribal Groups		399935	21424	5.36	38703	9.68
Total		426208	23059	5.41	41037	9.54

Source: Government of Kerala (2013), Report on Socio- Economic Status of Scheduled Tribes in Kerala

Malnutrition

Nutritional issues of tribals have received popular attention due to the malnutrition related deaths reported from Attappady and Wayanad. The IMR and MMR of tribals are higher compared to the general population, one reason being malnutrition. The incidence of malnutrition is recorded in the table below. Altogether 14,134 families are apparently affected by malnutrition; they constitute 13.09 percent of the total families. Malnutrition incidence is very high for the PVTGs in comparison with the other tribal groups. PVTGs have 28.25 percent greater incidence of malnutrition compared to other tribal groups. For Koraga, Kurumbar and Cholanaickan, the incidence of malnutrition is to a very high extend of 46.74 percent, 45.86 percent and 40.59 percent respectively. This is sure to enhance the possibility of other communicable and non communicable diseases also. Malnutrition makes them ineligible for any productive livelihood activities.

Table 10.15: Community wise data on families affected by Malnutrition

Community		*Families affected by Malnutrition*		
		Total Families	*Malnutrition*	*% of Total Families*
PVTG	Kadar	545	41	7.52
	Kattunayakan	5137	1374	26.75
	Koraga	445	208	46.74
	Kurumbar	543	249	45.86
	Cholanaickan	101	41	40.59
PVTG Total		6771	1913	28.25
Other Tribal Groups		101194	12221	12.08
Total		107965	14134	13.09

Source: Government of Kerala (2013), Report on Socio- Economic Status of Scheduled Tribes in Kerala.

Preventive Vaccination

Universal Vaccination for children against diseases has been adopted as national health goal. Kerala records very high vaccination rates, however for the tribals, this immunisation rate is low. 17.34 percent of the families with children below 5 years have not been provided with vaccination.

For the PVTGs, the corresponding percentage is 21.96 percent. Within the PVTGs, 90.70 percent of the Cholanaickan children are not administered preventive vaccination and for the Kurumbar, Koraga, Kattunayakan and Kadar community the relative percentages are 44.66 percent, 20.00 percent, 18.33 percent and 12.43 percent respectively.

Table 10.16: Community wise data on non administration of preventive vaccination to children

Community		*Number of Families with Children*				
		Below 5 Years	*Vaccination not fully Administrated*	*Vaccination not Administrated*	*Total*	*% to Children Below 5 Years*
PVTG	Kadar	169	10	11	21	12.43
	Kattunayakan	1604	184	110	294	18.33
	Koraga	100	6	14	20	20.00
	Kurumbar	206	54	38	92	44.66
	Cholanaickan	423	22	17	39	90.70
PVTG Total		2122	276	190	446	21.96
Other Tribal Groups		24643	2448	1826	4274	17.34
Total		26765	2724	2016	4740	17.71

Source: Government of Kerala (2013), Report on Socio- Economic Status of Scheduled Tribes in Kerala.

Basic Amenities

Health status is also affected by basic amenities like shelter, sanitation, drinking water and electrification. A comparative analysis of the basic amenities of PVTGs against other tribal groups is provided below. Status of residential houses and related details are given in table is 17, 18, and 19.

Table 10.17: Community wise data on the status of residential houses

Community		*Families According to Status of Residential Houses*					
		Own House	*Relative House*	*Rental House*	*Side Portion of House (Chaippu/ Charth)*	*Total*	*% to houseless families*
PVTG	Kadar	501	34	3	2	540	0.91
	Kattunayakan	4550	304	16	153	5137	3.29
	Koraga	409	15	1	9	445	2.24
	Kurumbar	509	16	4	11	543	2.76
	Cholanaickan	90	3	-	2	101	1.98
PVTG Total		6059	372	24	177	6771	2.96
Other Tribal Groups		91532	4718	1212	1792	101194	2.96
Total		97591	5090	1236	1931	107965	2.94

Source: Government of Kerala (2013), Report on Socio- Economic Status of Scheduled Tribes in Kerala.

Proper latrine facilities are not available for the tribal communities. Table shows that 47.75 percent of the tribal community do not have latrine, the percent is still very higher for the PVTGs. 78.22 percent of Cholanaickan, and 83.61percent of Kurumbas, 9.45 percent of Kadars, 58.50 percent of Kattunayakan do not have proper latrines. 7.12 percent of the PVTGs depend on others for drinking water.

Table 10.18: Community Wise data on Families without Proper Latrine and dependence on others for drinking water

Community		Families	Families Without Latrine	percentage	Families Without Source of Drinking Water	percentage
PVTG	Kadar	545	324	59.45	16	2.94
	Kattunayakan	5137	3005	58.50	375	7.30
	Koraga	445	160	35.96	90	20.22
	Kurumbar	543	454	83.61	1	0.18
	Cholanaickan	101	79	78.22	-	-
PVTG Total		6771	4022	59.40	482	7.12
Other Tribal Groups		101194	47529	46.97	16211	16.02
Total		107965	51551	47.75	16693	15.46

Source: Government of Kerala (2013), Report on Socio- Economic Status of Scheduled Tribes in Kerala.

Even though the tribal community possess houses, the facilities in the houses are very poor. There are many houses without kitchen, without space for stay of all members of the family, without space for keeping animals, working tools etc. The details on the facilities in houses are given table 19.

Table 10.19: Community Wise data on Facilities in Own Houses

Community		*Number of Houses*								
		Own House (Total)	*Without Kitchen*	*Percentage*	*Not convenient for Stay of the whole Family*	*Percentage*	*No space for Keeping Domestic Animals*	*Percentage*	*No space for Keeping Firewood, Working Tools etc*	*Percentage*
PVTG	Kadar	501	174	34.73	191	38.12	340	67.86	316	63.07
	Kattunayakan	4550	2567	56.41	2873	63.14	4450	97.80	4393	96.54
	Koraga	409	85	20.78	93	22.73	388	94.87	357	87.28
	Kurumbar	509	213	41.84	399	78.39	498	97.83	494	97.05
	Cholanaickan	90	72	80.00	70	77.78	90	100	90	100
PVTG Total		6059	3111	51.34	3626	59.85	5768	95.19	5650	93.24
Other Tribal Groups		91532	38639	42.21	44600	48.72	79532	86.88	77843	85.05
Total		97591	41750	42.78	48226	49.41	85300	87.40	83520	85.58

Source: Government of Kerala (2013), Report on Socio- Economic Status of Scheduled Tribes in Kerala.

Table 10.20: Community Wise data on Construction of Houses with Government /Local Government Assistance

Community		*Constructed with Government /Local Govt. Assistance*				
		Total Own House	*Government /Local Govt. Assistance only*	*More than one Sources including Govt./ Local Govt. Assistance*	*Total*	*% to own Houses*
PVTG	Kadar	501	420	15	435	86.82
	Kattunayakan	4550	3625	153	3778	83.03
	Koraga	409	377	12	389	95.11
	Kurumbar	509	178	39	217	42.63
	Cholanaickan	90	54	4	58	64.00
PVTG Total		6059	4654	223	4877	80.49
Other Tribal Groups		91532	55590	13519	69109	75.50
Total		97591	60224	13742	73986	75.81

Source: Government of Kerala (2013), Report on Socio- Economic Status of Scheduled Tribes in Kerala

It is discerned from the table 5.20 that houses of ST people are constructed with Government /Local Government Assistance. 75.81 percent of ST families constructed their house with Government assistance, for the PVTGs the corresponding percentage is 80.49.

Houseless families and Houses requiring replacement or renovation

Altogether 10,374 families do not own house, they form 9.61 percent of the total families. Of the existing houses, majority are in dilapidated state, 44,540 requires replacement and 30894 requires repair, thus 34.93 percent of the houses are not in good living condition. The same percentage applies to the houses of PVTGs also. 10.52 percent do not own house, 39 percent of the existing houses require replacement and 27.37 percent require repair.

Table 10.21: Community wise data on houseless families and houses requiring replacement or repair

Community		*Total Families*	*Houseless families*	*% to Total*	*Existing Houses Requiring*			
					Replacement	*% to Total*	*Repair*	*% to Total*
PVTG	Kadar	545	44	8.07	162	29.72	92	16.88
	Kattunayakan	5137	587	11.43	2031	39.54	1579	30.74
	Koraga	445	36	8.09	57	12.81	113	25.39
	Kurumbar	543	34	6.26	347	63.90	58	10.68
	Cholanaickan	101	11	10.89	44	43.56	11	10.89
PVTG Total		6771	712	10.52	2641	39.00	1853	27.37
Other Tribal Groups		101194	9662	9.55	41899	41.40	29041	28.70
Total		107965	10374	9.61	44540	41.25	30894	28.61

Source: Government of Kerala (2013), Report on Socio- Economic Status of Scheduled Tribes in Kerala.

Electrification

About 56.59 percent of the total houses are unelectrified, corresponding percent is very high for PVTG that is 81.64 percent. Within the PVTG, all the Cholanaickan houses are unelectrified, for the Kurumbar unelectrified houses forms 97.05 percent of the total. This is because majority of the settlements still remain unelectrified.

Table 10.22: Community wise data on unelectrified houses

Community		Total Houses	Number of Houses				
			Electrified Settlements	Unelectrified Settlements	Scattered Houses	Total Un electrified Houses	% to total Houses
PVTG	Kadar	545	68	311	2	381	69.91
	Kattunayakan	5137	2360	1734	119	4213	82.01
	Koraga	445	107	39	161	307	68.99
	Kurumbar	543	19	504	4	527	97.05
	Cholanaickan	101	-	96	4	100	99.01
PVTG Total		6771	2554	2684	290	5528	81.64
Other Tribal Groups		101194	35060	18168	2342	55570	54.91
Total		107965	37614	20852	2632	61098	56.59

Source: Government of Kerala (2013), Report on Socio- Economic Status of Scheduled Tribes in Kerala.

The unelectrified houses of students deserve special attention. 29,223 houses with students are unelectrified houses, which works out to 47.83 percent of the total unelectrified houses. The ratio of unelectrified houses of students to total number of unelectrified houses is more than 50 percent for Kurumbar and is 46.98 percent and 43.65 percent for Kadar and Kattunayakan community.

Section VI: Gender Status

Kerala has attained high levels of human development without much gender difference. Female education and health status has been the highest recorded by any other state in India. However, human development indices are low for the Scheduled Tribes in general and for the PVTG in particular. It is important to examine whether there is any difference in the human development indicators between the PVTG females and other tribal females. This section enquires upon this question. 2.2 percent of the total PVTGs are single female families whereas it is 1.84 percent for other groups. Cholanaickan families have 5.94 as single female families. Female literacy rate for PVTGs is as low as 56.93 percent, whereas it is 70.98 percent for other tribal groups. Educational status reveals that 5.02 percent of the female PVTGs are having educational qualification of SSLC whereas it is 12.65 for the other tribal groups. Not even a single female from Cholanaickan has gone for degree course. Of the total tribals who have gone for degree course, only 77 percent comes from PVTGs. Same level of deprivation is seen in the case of technical education of female PVTGs. Only three from PVTG has gone for engineering degrees and all belong to the male category, one from Kattunayakan and two from Kurumbas.

Table 10.23: Community Wise data on Women workers aged 15-59 employed in Forestry sector, Agricultural and allied sector and Non agricultural sector

Community		*Women workers in aged 15-59 employed in Forestry sector, agricultural and allied sector and non agricultural sector*						
		Total Women Workers	*Forestry Sector*	*% to total Women Workers*	*Agri-culture and Allied Sectors*	*% to total Women Workers*	*Non Agri-culture and Allied Sectors*	*% to total Women Workers*
PVTG	Kadar	462	388	83.98	31	6.71	43	9.31
	Kattunayakan	4258	691	16.23	2970	69.75	597	14.02
	Koraga	322	180	55.90	68	21.12	74	22.98
	Kurumbar	408	218	53.43	123	30.15	67	16.42
	Cholanaickan	45	40	88.89	2	4.44	3	6.67
PVTG Total		5495	1517	27.61	3194	58.13	784	14.27
Other Tribal Groups		75996	4897	8.36	52579	69.18	18520	24.37
Total		81491	6414	7.87	55773	68.44	19304	23.69

Source: Government of Kerala (2013), Report on Socio- Economic Status of Scheduled Tribes in Kerala.

Women from Cholanaickan and Kadar community are engaged mainly in works in forest sector, whereas those of Kattunayakan are engaged in agriculture and allied workers. Only 14.27 percent of the women workers are engaged in non agricultural sector. The status of women headed families in the tribal colonies is deplorable compared to their counterparts.

Although women headed families forms 6.33 percent of PVTG families, their share in several deprivation measures is very high. 24.48 percent, 20.31 percent.20.24 percent and 24.44 percent of the total female headed tribal families which depend on others for drinking water, without proper latrine, unelecrified houses and BPL families belong to the PVTG. Thus the gender status of PVTGs is not in favour of females with respect to several human development factors.

To conclude, a comparison of the socio economic demographic and human development status of the five PVTGs (namely, Koraga, Kurumba, Kattunayakan, Kadar and Cholanayakan) with that of other tribal groups points to the gross difference in attainments of these five communities. It is also clear that within the tribal communities, there exist wide differences in human development status bringing out the policy relevance of specific policies suited for each tribal community tailored to meet their particular requirements.

Table 10.24 Community wise data on women headed families depending on others for drinking water, without proper latrine, unelecrtified houses and BPL families

Community		*Women Headed Families*				
		%of Women Headed Families	*% to total families depending others for drinking water*	*% to total families without proper latrine*	*% to total families unelecrified houses*	*% to total BPL families*
PVTG	Kadar	8.37	25.00	22.84	18.90	25.19
	Kattunayakan	75.87	23.47	20.87	20.79	24.47
	Koraga	8.53	28.89	28.75	28.01	29.34
	Kurumbar	6.73	-	14.10	14.80	21.13
	Cholanaickan	0.50	-	7.59	7.00	3.77
PVTG Total		6.33	24.48	20.31	20.24	24.44
Other Tribal Groups		93.67	26.92	24.37	24.05	29.37
Total		100	26.84	24.06	23.71	29.02

Source: Government of Kerala (2013), Report on Socio- Economic Status of Scheduled Tribes in Kerala.

References

1. Government of Kerala (2013), **'Scheduled Tribes of Kerala; Report on the Socio-economic Status',** Directorate of Scheduled Tribes Development Department, Thiruvananthapuram.
2. Government of India (2005), **'The Scheduled Tribes and other traditional forest dwellers (Recognition of Forest Rights Act, 2006';** Ministry of Law and Justice (Legislative Department), New Delhi.

11

Human Development Status of Fisher Folk in Kerala

Shameer M.D.

Kerala, which is situated in the south west corner of Indian peninsula and one of the smallest states in India with an area of 39 thousand square kilometers, has a coastline of 590 kilometers and a continental shelf of 40 thousand square kilometers rich in marine fauna. Fishing has naturally been the major occupation of the inhabitants of its coastal belt from time immemorial. Kerala which occupied the pride of place in fish production in India for long periods in the past, still accounts for a quarter of the country's marine production and fishermen population and one fifth of its fishing fleet. Fishery is of vital importance to the state's economy judged in terms of its contribution to employment, income, foreign exchange earnings and protein intake of its people. In spite of its importance to economy, the fishery sector had been facing severe problems of widespread misery and poverty of the fishermen, erratic and violent fluctuations in output, and exploitative practices by money lenders, and low output prices (Ibrahim, 1992)[1].

Kerala boasts of the highest quality of life in the country as measured by human development indicators such as Human Development Index (HDI) and Multidimensional Poverty Index. John Kurian (1995)[2] articulated Kerala state's positive achievements of public action as the major factor in it achieving a relatively high quality of life relative to economic backwardness. However, against the central tendency of the Kerala model of development, he attempts to plot certain communities as outliers, (particularly the tribal people and marine fishing communities) and provides explanations for the same. Some of the factors that condition the fishermen communities to be outliers of the Kerala model of development include low incomes in the fisheries sector, poor condition based upon the land holding and housing, poor health condition, illiteracy and low educational attainment. He also explored some of the economic, social, and cultural characteristics specific to fishing communities that have placed restrictions on its members achieving high level of capabilities. The Kerala Development Report (2008)[3] of the Planning Commission, Government of India also observed that the fishermen communities in Kerala are the outliers of Kerala model of development. Their standard of living, educational attainment, and per capita income are very low compared to general communities. Their income mainly depends upon daily wages and varies with regard to the availability of fish catch. Volume of fish also affect their income; other factors being trolling and climatic changes and these factors lead to lower per capita income of the fishermen community of Kerala. Besides, the fisher folk communities are facing a lot of socio-economic problems such as poor living condition, poor quality of housing, lack of access to sanitation and drinking water etc. There has been numerous developmental intervention programmes aimed at improving the socio-economic and human development status of the fisher folk and it becomes important to understand how this vulnerable section fare in terms of human development. Hence the main objective of the article is to understand the human development status of traditional marine fishermen community in Kerala, and a novel methodology based on a rights-based approach to human development is used.

The study is divided into five sections. Section one elaborates the methodology of the study and Section two deals with conceptual framework of rights-based approach to human development. Analysis of human development status of fisherfolk through rights-based approach is done in Section three and Section five concludes the study.

Section I: Methodology and working definitions

Following are the working definitions used in the study based on literature survey.

Fishermen Family/households

A family in which at least one member is engaged in marine fishing or allied activities or both (Marine Fisheries Census 2010, CMFRI).

Fish Workers

International Conference of Fish Workers and their Supports (ICFWS,

1984)[4] defined Fish workers as "Children, women, and men engaged as crew members, small fishers, processing workers, and settlers"

Fishing Community

A fishing community is a community which is largely dependent on, or largely engaged in, the harvest or processing of fishery resources to meet social and economic needs. (Review of fisheries in OECD countries: Glossary, 1998)[5].

Area of the Study

Kerala is one of the leading fish producing states of India. In addition to its contribution to a flourishing export trade, the fishing industry is capable of providing cheap protein food to fight malnutrition. It also provides employment. Fisheries consist of two sectors - traditional and mechanized, the traditional including two areas, the marine and inland. The fishing economy consists of three operations: harvesting, processing and marketing of fish. There are mainly three fishermen communities in Kerala such as Dheevara community, Latin Catholic and Mappila communities. Latin community fishermen are concentrated in south Kerala consisting of Trivandram, Kollam and Alappuzha districts while Dheevara community is concentrated in Kollam, Alappuzha, Ernakulam, Thrissur and Kasargode districts. The Mappila fishermen community is highly concentrated in Malappuram, Kozhikode, Kannur and Kasargode districts (CMFRI, 2010)[6].

Sample Selection

Thiruvananthapuram district is considered for primary survey as it has the highest number of fishermen families in Kerala. (33,340 families based on marine fisheries census 2010). The coastal belt of Thiruvananthapuram district is situated in three Taluks of the district namely, Chirayinkeezh, Neyyatinkara, and Thiruvananthapuram. There are forty-two fishing villages in Thiruvananthapuram district, out of which six villages are selected randomly, two from each taluk. The fishing villages selected are Vizhinjam and Poovar from Neyyatinkara Taluk, Valiyathura and Beemapalli from Thiruvananthapuram Taluk, and Perumathura and Anchuthengu from Chirayinkeezh Taluk. From each of the fishing villages, thirty samples are selected based on simple random sampling. Thus, on an aggregate, 180 samples are collected from six fishing villages.

The primary data from the above said group was collected on the basis of interview schedule. Secondary data is collected from reports, journals, economic review, economic survey and website. The information so collected is analysed by focusing attention on the human development status of fishermen communities by constructing human development indicators based on human rights approach to human development.

Section II: Conceptual Framework of Human Rights Approach to Human Development

The idea of capability can be very helpful in understanding the opportunity aspects of freedom and human rights, since the two aspects of human rights and capabilities go well with each other. There are many human rights for which the capability perspective has much to offer and also, human rights are the important process in order to analyse the capability approach. Furthermore, both human rights and capabilities have to depend on the process of public reasoning (Sen, 2005)[7].

The human rights literature is not only concerned with political and civil liberties, but also with the rights based on essential needs in human life such as education, adequate health care and other freedoms that have revived the systematic investigation in Human Development Reports. The recent documents, such as the declaration on the Right to Development and the Vienna Declaration and program of action, highlights that economic, social and cultural rights are no less weighty than civil and political rights. The divergence between the two concepts of human rights and human development does not exist, therefore, dishonesty in any basic difference in their subject matter (HDR 2000)[8].

The evaluation of right to development is eventually based on how the opportunities are created. It involves the framing of process indictors on standards of obligations. In the present evaluative mode of the right to development, the approach uses the process indicators in the analytical models employed by the Committee on Economic Social and Cultural Rights (CESCR), the monitoring body of the implementation of the international covenant on economic, social and cultural rights named as United Nations Economic and Social Council (ECOSOC). The general comments of the CESCR have elucidated the right to development in terms of the contents of the rights to food, education, health, water and sanitation in a 4-A's framework such as availability, accessibility, acceptability, and adaptability (OHCHR, 2012[9]).

The process aspect of participation of human rights was highlighted by Osmani. S. R (2005)[10]. He viewed that human development could be achieved by a progressive realisation of human rights. Each state in the world should take immediate action to fulfil all rights that are not much dependent on resources availability. The resources could be diverted from non-essential uses to those uses which that are essential for attaining the human rights. The approach also claims on human rights norms in policy formulation in which it is essential to give special consideration to the deprived groups. The state wants to identify the core obligations and set targets in order to attain human rights in development.

The analysis of human rights approach to human development is based on the perception of the people about the aspects of availability, adequacy, accessibility, affordability, possession, quality, and usage and maintenance. An analysis of these indicators gives an understanding regarding human development in the study area. Each opportunity component of life valued by the people enters the analytical phase of process evaluation. The formal process includes seven components such as availability, adequacy, accessibility, affordability and possession while the effective process includes two components such as quality, and usage and maintenance.

Each opportunity indicator is arranged on a five point scale reflecting the perceptions of people. 1 = Very Bad, 2 = Bad, 3 = neither Bad nor Good, 4 = Good, 5 = Very Good. The analysis of process aspects includes classification into high, medium, and low, the cluster being exclusive in nature. 1 to 3 = Low scores, 3 to 4 = Medium score, and 4 to 5 = High score.

The analysis of the human rights approach to human development could be evaluated towards examining the positions of human development in the study area. There are three indicators used for the analysis of process such as the indicator index (S – index), the facility index (T – index), and the human rights based human development index (U – index). These are explained below.

1. The Indicator Index (S – Index)

All the seven process aspects related to each indicator have values perceived on a 5-point scale by the members of sample household in the study area. The values of all seven process aspects corresponding to each indicator were summed up and divided by seven. Thus,

The S index of an indicator or S_i =

$$\frac{\text{Sum of the scores on 7 process aspects of i}}{7}$$

For each household S_i is calculated in which each value corresponded to the respective indicator. The average S_i value of each indicator was calculated for sample households together. These S indices were divided in to four categories.

1 to 2 = Very low, 2 to 3 = Low, 3 to 4 = High, 4 to 5 = Very high.

2. The Facility Index (T index)

Each facility had one or more than one indicator. The S index values of all indicators under one facility were used to calculate the T index of that facility.

$$T_j = \frac{\text{Sum of the S index values of the indicators under the facility}_j}{Number of indicators under the facility_j}$$

Where, T_j = Index values of the facility j.

The of each household was calculated. The average T index value corresponding to each facility was calculated for the whole of the sample household.

3. The Human Rights based Human Development Index (U index)

This index is derived from T indices. That is,

$$\textbf{U index} = \frac{Sum\ of\ the\ T\ index\ values\ of\ all\ the\ 7\ facilities}{7}$$

For each household in the sample, the U index was calculated and the average of the U index is then worked out. This gives single U index value for the whole sample and then is divided in to the following categories.

1 to 2 = Very low, 2 to 3 = Low, 3 to 4 = High, 4 to 5 = Very high.

The table 1 shows the facilities and the indicators of the human rights approach to human development. There are seven facilities which the researcher identified such as housing, education, occupation, economic opportunities, consumption, health and family welfare, and transport, communication and information.

Housing facility consists of six indicators such as own house, drinking water sources, lighting, cooking fuel, sanitation, and safe and secure residential environment indicators. Education facility consists of educational institutions from primary to higher levels, home environments for studies, and intrinsic skill development indicators. Occupation facility consists of opportunities to work indicator, while economic opportunities facility consists of four indicators such as ownership of asset, income, savings, and credit indicators. Consumption facility consists of food and non-food indicators, while health and family welfare facility consists of three indicators such as health care institutions, health awareness, and programmes for family welfare. The transport, communication, and information facility consists of two indicators such as road and transport facilities and facilities for communication and information.

Table 11.1: Facilities and Indicators of the Human Right Approach to Human Development

Facilities	***Indicators***
Housing	Own House
	Drinking Water Sources
	Lighting
	Cooking Fuel
	Sanitation
	Safe and Secure Residential Environment
Education	Educational Institutions from Primary to Higher Levels
	Home Environment for Studies
	Intrinsic Skill Development
Occupation	Opportunities to work
Economic Opportunities	Ownership of Asset
	Income
	Savings
	Credit
Consumption	Food
	Non Food
Health and Family Welfare	Health Care Institutions
	Health Awareness
	Programmes for Family Welfare
Transport, Communication, and Information	Road and Transport Facilities
	Facilities for communication and Information

Source: Aspects identified by the Researcher

Health is an important component of human development. All indicators and facilities related to both direct and indirect determinants of health are used by the researcher to construct right based human development index. The World Health Organisation (WHO) defines social determinants of health as conditions or circumstances in which people are born, live, work, and age. These conditions are shaped by political, social, and economic forces. The quality, quantity, and distribution of these resources together determine citizen's health and well-being. Opportunities to have an education, a healthy living environment, nutrition, health care, and employment are some of these resources (WHO, 2008)[11].

Section III: Analysis on the Human Development Status of Fisher Folk in Kerala on the basis of Rights based Approach

Facility I - Housing

The table 2 indicates the own house indicator indices of housing facility. The availability aspects of the own house is scored as very high, while other aspects such as adequacy, accessibility, affordability, possession, quality, and usage and maintenance are scored as high. It's found that indicator index of the own house is scored as high.

Table 11.2: Own House and Drinking Water Sources Indicators of Housing Facility

Indicator 1- Own House & Indicator 2 – Drinking Water Sources			
Process	***Process Aspects***	***Score Category (Own House)***	***Score Category (Drinking Water Sources)***
Formal	Availability	4.73 (Very High)	3.89 (High)
	Adequacy	3.92 (High)	2.20 (Low)
	Accessibility	3.92 (High)	2.69 (Low)
	Affordability	3.86 (High)	2.60 (Low)
	Possession	3.70 (High)	1.00 (Very Low)
Effective	Quality	3.54 (High)	2.93 (Low)
	Usage and Maintenance	3.92 (High)	2.99 (Low)
Indicator Index		3.94 (High)	2.62 (Low)

Source: Primary survey.

The table 2 also shows the results of drinking water sources indicator index of housing facility. The availability aspects of drinking water sources are scored high, while possession aspects are scored as very low. The other aspects such as adequacy, accessibility, affordability, quality, and usage and maintenance are scored as low. It's found that the drinking water sources of housing facility are scored as low.

The table 3 shows the results of lighting indicator of housing facility. The availability aspects of lighting indicator of housing facility is scored as very high, mean while the other aspects such as adequacy, accessibility, possession, and quality are scored as high. The affordability, and usage and maintenance aspects of lighting are scored as low. The indicator index of lighting is scored as high.

Table 11.3: Lighting & Cooking Fuel Indicators of Housing Facility

Indicator 3- Lighting & Indicator 4 – Cooking Fuel			
Process	***Process Aspects***	***Score Category (Lighting)***	***Score Category (Cooking Fuel)***
Formal	Availability	5.00 (Very High)	3.64 (High)
	Adequacy	3.00 (High)	2.33 (Low)
	Accessibility	3.00 (High)	2.44 (Low)
	Affordability	2.49 (Low)	1.92 (Low)
	Possession	3.00 (High)	2.83 (Low)
Effective	Quality	3.00 (High)	3.53 (High)
	Usage and Maintenance	2.56 (Low)	2.52 (Low)
Indicator Index		3.15 (High)	2.74 (Low)

Source: Primary survey

The table 3 shows the results of cooking fuel indicator of housing facility. The availability and quality aspects of cooking fuel indicator are scored as high, while affordability aspects are scored as very low. The other aspects of the cooking fuel indicator such as adequacy, accessibility, possession, and usage and maintenance are scored low. The indicator index of the cooking fuel is scored as low. The table 4 shows the indicator indices of the sanitation indicator of housing facility. The availability, usage and maintenance aspects of sanitation indicators are scored very high, while the affordability of sanitation is low. The other aspects of the sanitation indicator are scored as high, and the indicator index of the sanitation indicator is recorded as high.

Table 11.4: Sanitation & Safe and secure residential environment Indicators of Housing Facility

Indicator 5- Sanitation & Indicator 6 – Safe and secure residential environment			
Process	***Process Aspects***	***Score Category (Sanitation)***	***Score Category (Safe and secure residential environment)***
Formal	Availability	4.09 (Very High)	3.62 (High)
	Adequacy	3.51 (High)	2.05 (Low)
	Accessibility	3.19 (High)	2.57 (Low)
	Affordability	2.97 (Low)	3.05 (High)
	Possession	3.45 (High)	3.05 (High)
Effective	Quality	3.18 (High)	2.07 (Low)
	Usage and Maintenance	4.18 (Very High)	2.70 (Low)
Indicator Index		3.51 (High)	2.73 (Low)

Source: Primary survey

The table 4 shows the indicator and aspects indices of safe and secure residential environment indicator of the housing facility. The availability aspects of safe and secure residential environment indicator of housing facility is scored as high, while the adequacy and accessibility aspects of the safe and secure residential environment indicator of the housing facility is scored as low. The affordability and possession aspects of the safe and secure residential environment indicator of the housing facility is scored as high, while the quality and usage aspects of the safe and secure residential environment indicator of the housing facility is scored as low. The Indicator index of the safe and secure residential environment indicator of the housing facility is scored as low.

In Housing facility the researcher has identified that majority of the houses are constructed with tin sheets and bricks. Own house, lighting, and sanitation indicators of housing facility is recorded as high. But drinking water sources, cooking fuel, and safe and secure residential environment indicators of housing facility is low. The researcher observed absence of drinking water sources in the study area. Majority of the houses are situated near by the sea and it eventually leads to unsecure residential environment situation.

Facility II – Education

The table 5 shows indicator and the process indices of the educational institutions from primary to higher level education facilities. In the formal process, availability index is very high. In the other aspects of formal process, the accessibility index is high, while the adequacy, affordability, and possession indices are scored low. In effective process, both the indices such as quality and usage are scored as high. The indicator index of the educational institutions from primary to higher levels is scored as high.

Regarding the indicator and process indices of home environment to studies, the availability index is high, while all other aspects such as adequacy, accessibility, affordability, and possession indices are scored as low.

In effective process, both the indices such as quality and usage are scored as low, while the indicator index of the home environment to studies is scored as low.

The table 5 also shows the indicator and process indices of the intrinsic skill development indicator of education facility. In formal process, the availability index is high, while all other aspects indices such as adequacy, accessibility, affordability, and possession indices are scored as low. In effective process, both the indices such as quality and usage are scored as low, while the indicator index of the intrinsic skill development indicator is scored as low.

Table 11.5: Educational Institutions from Primary to Higher Levels, Home Environment to Studies, & Intrinsic Skill Development Indicator of Education Facility

Indicator 1- Educational Institutions from Primary to Higher Levels & Indicator 2 – Home Environment to Studies & Indicator 3 - Intrinsic Skill Development				
Process	***Process Aspects***	***Score Category (Educational Institutions from Primary to Higher Levels)***	***Score Category (Home Environment to Studies)***	***Score Category (Intrinsic Skill Development)***
Formal	Availability	4.28 (Very High)	3.28 (High)	3.27 (High)
	Adequacy	2.82 (Low)	2.99 (Low)	2.02 (Low)
	Accessibility	3.67 (High)	2.77 (Low)	2.26 (Low)
	Affordability	2.55 (Low)	2.28 (Low)	2.27 (Low)
	Possession	2.72 (Low)	2.77 (Low)	2.03 (Low)
Effective	Quality	3.02 (High)	2.27 (Low)	2.27 (Low)
	Usage and Maintenance	3.24 (High)	2.76 (Low)	2.27 (Low)
Indicator Index		3.19 (High)	2.73 (Low)	2.34 (Low)

In education facility, the researcher explored that home environment to studies and intrinsic skill development indicators are recorded as low. Educational institutions from primary to higher levels indicator of education facility is recorded as high. Hence improvement is essential in education facility, especially enhancing the condition for home environment for study and providing intrinsic skill development.

Facility III: Occupation

The table 6 shows the indicator and aspects indices of the opportunities to work indicator of occupation facility. The availability aspects of the opportunities to work indicator of occupation facility is scored as very high, while the possession aspect is scored very low. The adequacy, accessibility, and affordability aspects of the opportunities to work indicator of occupation facility is scored as low, while the quality and usage aspects are scored as high. Thus the indicator index of the opportunities to work indicator of occupation facility is scored as low.

Table 11.6: Opportunities to Work Indicator of Occupation Facility

Indicator – Opportunities to Work			
Process	***Process Aspects***	***Avg Score Category***	***Score***
Formal	Availability	4.23	Very High
	Adequacy	2.23	Low
	Accessibility	2.90	Low
	Affordability	2.26	Low
	Possession	1.98	Very Low
Effective	Quality	3.08	High
	Usage and Maintenance	3.21	High
Indicator Index		2.84	Low

Facility IV: Economic Opportunities

The table 7 shows the ownership of asset indicator of economic opportunities facility. The availability aspects of the ownership of asset indicator of economic opportunities facility is scored as very high. In the other formal process, accessibility is scored as high, while adequacy, affordability, and possession are scored low.

In effective process, the quality aspects of the ownership of asset indicator of economic opportunities facility is scored as low, while the usage index is scored as high. Overall the indicator index of the ownership of asset indicator of economic opportunities facility is scored as low.

Table 11.7: Ownership of Asset Indicator of Economic Opportunities Facility

Indicator 1- Ownership of Asset & Indicator 4 – Income			
Process	***Process Aspects***	***Score Category (Ownership of Asset)***	***Score Category (Income)***
Formal	Availability	4.20 (Very High)	4.40 (Very High)
	Adequacy	2.31 (Low)	2.16 (Low)
	Accessibility	3.21 (High)	2.82 (Low)
	Affordability	2.21 (Low)	2.17 (Low)
	Possession	2.49 (Low)	2.21 (Low)
Effective	Quality	2.59 (Low)	2.59 (Low)
	Usage and Maintenance	3.04 (High)	2.67 (Low)
Indicator Index		2.86 (Low)	2.72 (Low)

Source: Primary survey

The table 7 shows the indicator and aspects indices of the income indicator of the economic opportunities facility. In formal process, the availability aspect is scored as very high, while the other aspects are scored low. In effective process, all the aspects such as quality and usage are scored as low, and in overall the indicator index of the income indicator of the economic opportunities facility is scored as low.

The table 8 shows the indicator and aspects indices of the saving indicator of the economic opportunities facility. In process aspects, availability aspect is scored as low, while all other aspects such as adequacy, accessibility, affordability, and possession are scored very low.

Table 11.8: Savings & Credit Indicators of Economic Opportunities Facility

Indicator 3- Savings & Indicator 4 – Credit			
Process	***Process Aspects***	***Score Category (Savings)***	***Score Category (Credit)***
Formal	Availability	2.37 (Low)	4.21 (Very High)
	Adequacy	1.49 (Very Low)	2.38 (Low)
	Accessibility	1.49 (Very Low)	2.59 (Low)
	Affordability	1.37 (Very Low)	1.33 (Very Low)
	Possession	1.21 (Very Low)	2.19 (Low)
Effective	Quality	1.32 (Very Low)	2.83 (Low)
	Usage and Maintenance	1.86 (Very Low)	3.12 (High)
Indicator Index		1.59 (Very Low)	2.67 (Low)

Source: Primary survey

In effective process, the quality and usage aspects are scored as very low, and in overall index, the indicator index of saving indicator of economic opportunities facility is scored as low.

The table 8 also shows the indicator and aspects indices of the credit indicator of economic opportunities facility. In formal process, the availability index is very high, while the affordability index is very low. The adequacy, accessibility, and possession indices of the formal aspects are low.

In effective process, the quality index is low, while the usage index is high. Overall, the indicator index of the credit indicator of economic opportunities facility is low.

In economic opportunities facility all the indicators are recorded as low. Majority of fisherman did not have ownership in fishing related equipment such as fishing gear, fishing rod, fishing hook, fishing net, and bait etc. The researcher explored that the interference of intermediaries among fisherman is very high for marketing of fish. So the fisherman did not get the reasonable price. The saving habit among fisherman is recorded as very low due to irregular stream of income and low rate of profit prevailing in fishing. Majority of fisherman have credit liabilities.

Facility V: Consumption

The table 9 shows the indicator and aspects indices of food indicator of consumption facility. In formal process, the availability index is very high, while the other aspects indices such as adequacy, accessibility, affordability, and possession are scored as high. In effective process, the quality and usage indices are scored as high mean while the indicator index of food consumption indicator of the consumption facility is scored as high.

Table 11.9: Food & Non Food Indicators of Consumption Facility

Indicator 1- Food & Indicator 2 – Non Food			
Process	***Process Aspects***	***Score Category (Food)***	***Score Category (Non Food)***
Formal	Availability	4.30 (Very High)	4.23 (Very High)
	Adequacy	3.42 (High)	2.91 (Low)
	Accessibility	3.43 (High)	3.00 (High)
	Affordability	3.09 (High)	2.43 (Low)
	Possession	3.21 (High)	2.52 (Low)
Effective	Quality	3.45 (High)	2.75 (Low)
	Usage and Maintenance	3.95 (High)	3.23 (High)
Indicator Index		3.55 (High)	3.00 (High)

Source: Primary survey

The table 9 shows the indicator and aspects indices of non-food indicator of consumption facility. In formal process, the availability index is very high. The accessibility index is high, while the adequacy, affordability, and possession indices are scored as low. In effective process, the quality index is low, while the usage index is scored as high. In overall, the indicator index of the non-food indicator of the consumption facility is high.

In consumption facility both indicators are recorded as high. But the researcher identified that, the spending for consumption is highly associated with normal goods.

Facility VI: Health and Family Welfare

The table 10 shows the indicator and aspects indices of the health care institutions indicator of health and family welfare facility. In formal process, the availability index is very high, while the other aspects indices such as adequacy, accessibility, affordability, and possession are scored as low. In effective process, the quality and usage and maintenance indices are scored as low mean while the indicator index of the health care institutions are scored as low.

Table 11.10: Health Care Institutions Indicator of Health and Family Welfare Facility

Indicator 1- Health Care Institutions & Indicator 2 – Health Awareness & Indicator 3 - Programs for Family Welfare				
Process	***Process Aspects***	***Score Category (Health Care Institutions)***	***Score Category (Health Awareness)***	***Score Category (Programs for Family Welfare)***
Formal	Availability	4.11 (Very High)	4.12 (Very High)	4.02 (Very High)
	Adequacy	2.56 (Low)	2.03 (Low)	2.02 (Low)
	Accessibility	2.57 (Low)	2.16 (Low)	1.88 (Very Low)
	Affordability	2.25 (Low)	1.74 (Very Low)	1.63 (Very Low)
	Possession	2.13 (Low)	1.89 (Very Low)	1.74 (Very Low)
Effective	Quality	2.39 (Low)	1.90 (Very Low)	1.78 (Very Low)
	Usage and Maintenance	2.67 (Low)	2.08 (Low)	2.05 (Low)
Indicator Index		2.67 (Low)	2.27 (Low)	2.13 (Low)

Source: Primary survey

The table 10 shows the indicator and aspects indices of the health awareness indicator of health and family welfare facility. In formal process, the availability index is scored as high, while the affordability and possession indices are scored as very low. And the adequacy and accessibility indices of the formal aspects are scored as low. In the effective process, the quality index is very low, while the usage index is low. Overall, the indicator index of the health awareness indicator of health and family welfare facility is low.

The table 10 also shows the indicator and aspects indices of the programs for family welfare indicator of health and family welfare facility. In formal process, the availability index is high, while the adequacy index is low. Other aspects indices such as accessibility, affordability, and possession are scored very low. In effective process, the quality index is scored as very low, while usage index is scored low. Over all indicators index of the programs for family welfare is scored as low.

In health and family welfare facility, all indicators are recorded as low. The researcher explored that, there exist inappropriate facility for health care in study area. Health awareness among fisherman is recorded as low, and there exist insufficient programs for family welfare.

Facility VII: Transport, Communication, and Information

The table 11 shows the indicator and aspects indices of road and transport facilities indicator of transport, communication, and information facility. In the formal process, the availability index is high and all other aspects indices such as adequacy, accessibility, affordability, and possession are scored as high.

Table 11.11: Road and Transport Facilities & Facilities for Communication and Information Indicators of Transport, Communication, and Information Facility

Indicator 1- Road and Transport Facilities & Indicator 2 – Facilities for Communication and Information			
Process	*Process Aspects*	*Score Category (Road and Transport Facilities)*	*Score Category (Facilities for Communication and Information)*
Formal	Availability	4.67 (Very High)	3.88 (High)
	Adequacy	3.95 (High)	3.06 (High)
	Accessibility	3.78 (High)	2.96 (Low)
	Affordability	3.77 (High)	2.64 (Low)
	Possession	3.74 (High)	2.45 (Low)
Effective	Quality	2.75 (Low)	2.38 (Low)
	Usage and Maintenance	3.64 (High)	2.75 (Low)
Indicator Index		3.76 (High)	2.87 (Low)

Source: Primary survey

In the effective process, the quality index is low, while the usage index is high. The indicator index of the road and transport facilities indicator is scored as high.

The table 11 shows the indicator and aspects indices of the facilities for communication and information indicator of transport, communication, and information facility. In formal process, the availability and adequacy indices are scored as high, while the accessibility, affordability, and possession indices are scored as low. In effective process, both the quality and usage indices are scored as low. The indicator index of the facilities for communication and information is low.

In transport, communication, and information facility, transportation facility is good while extension or improvement in transportation is essential in study area. The facilities for communication and information indicator is recorded as low. This shows further improvement is essential in study area.

Facility Indices of Human Right Approach to Human Development

The table 12 shows the facility indices of human right approach to human development. Facilities such as the education, occupation, economic opportunities, and health and family welfare are in the low category of the human development, while the facilities such as, housing, consumption, and transport, communication and information have high values of human development.

Table 11.12: Facility Indices of Human Right Approach to Human Development

Facilities	*Facility Indices*	*Score*
Housing	3.11	High
Education	2.75	Low
Occupation	2.84	Low
Economic Opportunities	2.46	Low
Consumptions	3.28	High
Health and Family Welfare	2.37	Low
Transport, Communication, and Information	3.31	High

Source: Primary survey.

Section IV: Human Rights based Human Development Index (U index)

The table 13 shows the human rights based human development index of the sample respondents. For 78.3 percent of the sample respondents, human rights based human development index is low, while for 21.7 percent of the sample respondents human rights based human development is high. In APL category, for 51.9 percent of the sample respondents human rights based human development index is low, while for 48.1 percent of the sample respondents human rights based human development is high. In BPL category, for 89.1 percent of the sample respondents human rights based human development index is low, while for 10.9 percent of the sample respondents human rights based human development is high.

In below 40 category of age, for 93.5 percent of the sample respondents, human rights based human development index is low, while for 6.5 percent of the sample respondents human rights based human development is high. In 40 and above category of age, for 73.1 percent of the sample respondents human rights based human development index is low, while for 26.9 percent of the sample respondents human rights based human development is high.

Table 11.13: Human Rights based Human Development Index (U index)

Dimensions		*The Human Rights based Human Development Index (U index)*		*Total*
		High	*Low*	
Economic Status	APL	25 (48.1)	27 (51.9)	52 (100)
	BPL	14 (10.9)	114 (89.1)	128 (100)
Total		39 (21.7)	141 (78.3)	180 (100)
Age	Below 40	3 (6.5)	43 (93.5)	46(100)
	40 and Above	36 (26.9)	98 (73.1)	134(100)
Total		39 (21.7)	141 (78.3)	180 (100)

Source: Primary survey (The values indicate in brackets are the percents)

Human Rights based Human Development Index (U Index) of the Traditional Fishermen Community

$$\text{U index} = \frac{\text{Sum of the T index values of all the 7 facilities}}{7}$$

Through the above equation, the researcher found the human rights based human development index of each sample respondents and the average value of the u index.

The table 14 shows the human rights based human development index of the traditional fishermen in Kerala.

Table 11.14: Human Rights based Human Development Index of the Traditional Marine Fishermen in Kerala

Index	*Average Score*	*Status*
The Human Rights based Human Development Index (U index)	2.88	Low

Source: Primary survey (The values indicate in brackets are the percents)

The researcher found that, the human rights based human development index of the traditional marine fishermen in Kerala is low.

Section V: Conclusion

The study gives reflection about human rights approach to human development of the fishing communities in Kerala. It elaborates the seven facility indices and indicator indices of each of these facilities. In housing facility, the researcher found that the indicator indices of own house, and sanitation are recorded as high and the indicator indices of drinking water sources, cooking fuel, and safe and secure residential environment are recorded as low. Overall the facility index of housing is recorded as high.

In education facility, the indicator index of the educational institutions from primary to higher levels is recorded as high, however the indicator indices of home environment to studies and intrinsic skill development are scored as low. Over all the facility index of education is recorded as low. In occupation facility, it is discerned that the indicator index of opportunities to work is low and hence the facility index of occupation is also recorded as low. In economic opportunities facility, the indicator indices of ownership of asset, income, and credit are recorded as low, along with that the indicator index of saving is scored as very low. Thus the facility index of economic opportunities is recorded as low. In consumption facility, the indicator indices of food and non-food consumption are recorded as high and hence the facility index of consumption is recorded as high. In health and family welfare facility, the researcher found that, the indicator indices of the health care institutions, health awareness, and programs for family welfare are recorded as low. Thus the facility index of the health and family welfare is recorded as low. In transport, communication, and information facility, the researcher found that, the indicator index of road and transport facilities is recorded as high, while the facilities for communication and information is recorded as low and hence the facility index of transport, communication, and information are recorded as high.

The researcher used the human rights based human development index (U index) to derive human development status of traditional marine fishermen community. It is found that, for 78 percent of the sample respondents human rights based human development index is low.

To conclude, the central issue discussed in this study is the evaluation of the human development status of traditional marine fishermen community in Kerala on the basis of human rights approach. The study reaches the conclusion that based on a rights based approach, the human development status of traditional fishermen community in Kerala is deplorable and requires concerted effort from stakeholders to ameliorate the situation.

12

Quality of Life of Females in Female Headed Tribal Households in Kerala

Megha Radhakrishnan

Female Headed Households (FHHs) refers to units where the main provider is not in attendance owing either to divorce or separation, death, migration or absence of a male adult in the family. Female Headed Households are one of the most deprived categories among population in terms of income, security, opportunities, access to resources and rights. Such cumulative privation makes Female Headed Households the easy victims of poverty and vulnerabilities of varied nature. Most often the younger ones in such households live in exacerbated conditions owing to child rearing and income earning responsibilities of the single woman head along with the added difficulties of single-handedly performing domestic duties. Female Headed Households, lately have received considerable recognition as disadvantaged in numerous aspects such as access to land, labour, credit and insurance market (World Bank, 2011). Furthermore, FHHs suffer from economic immobility, high dependency burdens and lack of economic control over resources (Povel, Lectenfeld, Klasen, 2015) to name a few impediments. Tahmasebi (2006) found that due to women headed households engaging in higher frequency of roles than other women, they experienced more stress and consequently had lower quality of life. Studies also point out that female headed households suffer from difficulties and obstacles both at individual and social levels (Arias and Pallobi, 1999; Rimoz. et.al, 2014).

The phenomenon of feminization of poverty which finds its place in discussions in economic literature have prompted many poverty and vulnerability studies among different nations. This poverty argument rest on the dominant premise that the world is witnessing an increased incidence of women who are poor and households headed by women constitute the majority and enlarge this poverty pool.

A conjunction of a Female Headed Household belonging to an ethnic group can be at great risk of exploitation and privation, resulting in multiple deprivation. Female headed households within the indigenous category face double discrimination, firstly on account of their ethnicity and secondly on account of their status of headship (Meenakshi, et.al, 2000).These two deprivations reinforce upon each other to result in lower labour participation, discriminatory or unequal wage payment, intergenerational transmission of disadvantage, food and nutritional insecurity, social and ethnic alienation, etc. extrapolating into the vulnerable existence of indigenous female headed households.

In the context of Kerala, FHHs constituting both dejure and defacto categories recorded 23 percent incidence according to the 2011 Census of India report. As far as tribal FHHs in Kerala, there is a dearth of analysis and studies on their life and conditions. The Report on the Socio-economic status of Scheduled Tribes in Kerala validates that of the total women Scheduled tribe population in Kerala, 12.33 percent were women in distress constituting the widowed, separated and single mothers. It is also alarming to note that 72 percent of the population of women in distress, were heads of households. In this setting, a study on their poverty dimensions that includes the socio economic status and quality of life becomes relevant. The quality of life scale looks at the larger poverty picture and also captures the well-being and life satisfaction as regards the social, physical, mental, personal and community dimensions of women in FHHs and MHHs, to convey a nuanced perception of deprivation of FHHs in the state of Kerala. This article contains a study conducted on the tribal female and male headed households in Kerala and focus on the disparate accomplishments of household categories across four different tribal communities found in Kerala.

The study is organized as follows. Section I poses the objectives and methods of the study. Section II examines the socio economic status of FHHs and MHHs that conditions the quality of life across the tribal groups studied. Section III assesses the quality of life of FHHs and MHHs on various psychological and social facets in the selected tribal groups and Section V concludes the study.

Section I: Objectives and Methodology

There are polarised generalisations regarding the income poverty of FHHs, the most common reason cited being 'women who head households purportedly fare worse than they would in the male headed households' (Chant, 2015). Numerous studies on income poverty accord FHHs the 'poorest of the poor' space in the general population. A broader multi-dimensional and holistic poverty assessment can impart new dimensions to the gender analysis of poverty, deprivation and differential health attainments. Moreover, well-being measures that examine qualitative life of an individual's relative perceptive position in life beyond pecuniary disadvantage may broaden the horizons of understanding the deprived circumstances of females in FHHs. In this context the study presents two objectives (a) to examine the socio economic status of the females in both male and female headed households (b) to examine the quality of life of tribal females in FHHs and MHHs respectively to elicit comparative attainments of women in respective household categories

The data is gathered from four tribal communities in Kerala spread in three distinct districts based on size of representation, the tribal communities selected being Paniyan, Kanikkar, Mulla Kuruman and Mavilan. Sampling technology used was proportional random sampling, the sample size being 162 from Paniyan, 54 from Kanikkar, 54 from Mulla Kuruman and 70 from Mavilan community. To ensure representation of both gender categories of household head, information from the ST promoters and list of tribal households were utilized. Equal number of female headed households and male headed households are studied for the sake of indexing and comparative analysis. For ascertaining status of poverty, socio economic status measures including income, educational, occupational status, etc. is elicited. The quality of life scale gives information to the individual's perception of deprivation. Flanagan's quality of scale gathers evidence on qualitative life of women in FHHs and in MHHs with respect to physical and material well-being, relationships with other people, social, community and civic activities, personal development and fulfilment, and recreation.

Section II: Socio economic status of tribal male and female headed households

The association between socio economic status of individuals and health outcomes are found to exist throughout the life cycle (Starfeld,et.al,2002) and in multiple measures of health including health status(Fiscella,1999) self-assessed health and disease prevalence(Apter.et.al,1999). Unequal health outcomes are believed to crop from 'discordant social comparisons' (Adler. et.al, 1994; Singh et.al, 2003; Singh. et.al, 2005). This section tries to capture the socio economic status of tribal male and female headed households status of poverty measures on the basis of headship type of tribal households.

Male Headed and Female headed households' distribution in the sample population

In each of the four different tribal communities, for the sake of indexing purpose, equal number of male and female headed households were considered for analysis. Table 12.1 shows the distribution of tribal households on the basis of headship type and tribe type.

Table 12.1: Distribution of MHH and FHH in the sample population

Tribes	*MHH*	*FHH*	*Total*
Paniyan	79	79	158
% within tribe	50.00	50.00	100.00
% within MHH/FHH	47.90	47.90	47.90
Kanikkar	26	26	52
% within tribe	50.00	50.00	100.00
% within MHH/FHH	15.8	15.8	15.8
Mulla Kuruman	26	26	52
% within tribe	50.00	50.00	100.00
% within MHH/FHH	15.8	15.8	15.8
Mavilan	34	34	68
% within tribe	50.00	50.00	100.00
% within MHH/FHH	20.60	20.60	20.60
Total	165	165	330
% within tribe	50.00	50.00	100.00
% within MHH/FHH	100.00	100.00	100.00

Source: Primary Data

Educational attainments

Education is a fundamental indicator of economic development and the level of empowerment of an individual.

Education is the key to opportunities for securing employment and thereby, economic independence. In the tribal community, securing good education is the only means to secure well-paying employment in the Government sector or elsewhere.

Table 12.2 shows the educational status of women in the selected communities on the basis of headship. Within tribal distribution, there exist disparities in educational attainments. In the lower levels of education (illiteracy), the concentration of FHHs was high in all communities. The

Table.12.2: Educational status of females in tribal households based on headship type

Tribes	Illiterate		Primary		Upper Primary		Secondary		Higher Secondary		Degree		PG		Total	
	MHH	FHH	MHH	FHH	MHH	FHH	MHH	FHH	MHH	FHH	MHH	FHH	MHH	FHH	MHH	FHH
Paniya	29	51	19	13	12	15	16	0	1	0	0	0	2	0	79	79
% within tribe	36.2	63.8	59.4	40.6	44.4	55.6	100	0.0	100	0.0	0.0	0.0	100	0.0	50.0	50.0
% within MHH/FHH	76.3	54.8	54.3	41.9	32.4	65.2	37.2	0.0	14.3	0.0	0.0	0.0	100.0	0.0	47.9	47.9
Kani	1	10	6	6	15	6	4	4	0	0	0	0	0	0	26	26
% within tribe	9.10	90.9	50.0	50.0	71.4	28.6	50.0	50.0	0.00	0.00	0.00	0.0	0.00	0.0	50.0	50.0
% within MHH/FHH	2.60	10.8	17.1	19.4	40.5	26.1	9.30	25.0	0.00	0.00	0.00	0.0	0.00	0.0	15.8	15.8
Mulla kuruman	1	12	3	6	3	0	16	8	2	0	1	0	0	0	26	26
% within tribe	7.70	92.3	33.3	66.7	100	0.00	66.7	33.3	100.	0.00	100.0	0.0	0.00	0.0	50.0	50.0
% within MHH/FHH	2.60	12.9	8.60	19.4	8.10	0.00	37.2	50.0	28.6	0.00	33.30	0.0	0.00	0.0	15.8	15.8
Mavilan	7	20	7	6	7	2	7	4	4	2	2	0	0	0	34	34
% within tribe	25.90	74.10	53.8	46.2	77.8	22.2	63.6	36.4	66.7	33.30	100.0	0.0	0.00	0.0	50.0	50.0
% within MHH/FHH	18.40	21.5	20.0	19.4	18.9	8.70	16.3	25.0	57.1	100	66.70	0.0	0.00	0.0	20.6	20.6
Total	38	93	35	31	37	23	43	16	7	2	3	0	2	0	165	165
% within tribe	29.00	71.0	53.0	47.0	61.7	38.3	72.9	27.1	77.8	22.2	100	0.0	100	0.0	50.00	50.00
% within MHH/FHH	100.0	100.0	100.0	100.0	100.0	100.0	100.0	100.0	100.0	100.0	100.0	0.0	100.0	0.0	100.0	100.0

Source: Primary Data

distribution of illiterate females in MHHs and FHHs being 36.2 percent and 63.8 percent in Paniyan, 9.10 percent and 90.9 percent in Kanikkar,7.70 percent and 92.3 percent in Mulla Kuruman, 25.90 percent and 74.10 percent in Mavilan community respectively. Of the total females in MHHs who were illiterate, 76.3 percent belonged to Paniyan, 2.60 belonged to Kanikkar, 2.60 percent belonged to Mulla Kuruman, and 18.40 percent belonged to Mavilan community. Of the total females in FHHs who were illiterate, 54.8 percent belonged to Paniyan, 10.8 percent belonged to Kanikkar, 12.9 percent belonged to Mulla Kuruman, and 21.5 percent belonged to Mavilan community. Illiteracy among Paniyan FHHs was highest, making the community the least empowered category in comparison to other counterpart FHHs. No Paniyan FHHs had secondary or higher levels of education. The high illiteracy among the Paniyan community is due to a number of reasons ranging from indifference towards provision of basic education to inaccessibility or distance to educational institutions from settlements.

The higher levels of education (secondary and above) is concentrated in the females belonging to MHHs as against their counterparts in FHHs. For example, the distribution of higher secondary qualified women in MHHs and FHHs is 100:0 in Paniyan and Mulla Kuruman, and 66.7:33.30 in Mavilan communities. The two women who had post graduate degree in Paniyan community also belonged to MHHs, there was no representation of women in FHHs having secondary, higher secondary, degree or PG level in the Paniyan community. In the Kanikkar community, there was no representation from FHHs in higher secondary education, degree and PG classes. None of the FHHs had a qualification of degree or upwards in all four communities.

Livelihood Arrangements

Employment Status

The main occupation of the tribal community population is categorized into forestry, agriculture and allied sectors, non-agriculture and allied sectors.

Table 12.3 depicts the tribe wise main occupation details disaggregated on basis of headship. The proportion of forest dependence is high for all females in the FHHs (64.5 percent) as compared to females in MHHs (35.5 percent). Agriculture as a source of income was concentrated more among the females in the MHHs as they assist or take part in agricultural activities along with the male members of the family. Non-agricultural activities were concentrated more among the females of the FHHs, their percent share in the total sample being 52 percent against 48 percent for the females

Table 12.3: Percentage distribution of Main occupation of females in tribal households based on headship type

	% within tribe				*% within the main occupation*			
	Forestry	*Agri& allied*	*Non Agri& Allied*	*No Income/ empt*	*Forestry*	*Agri& Allied*	*Non Agri& Allied*	*No Income/ empt*
Paniyan								
MHH	47.6	50.0	47.6	70.0	13.9	11.1	55.6	19.4
FHH	52.4	50.0	52.4	30.0	15.9	11.6	63.8	8.7
Kanikkar								
MHH	0.0	100.0	63.6	0.0	0.0	12.5	87.5	0.0
FHH	100.0	0.0	36.4	100.0	30.0	0.0	60.0	10.0
Mulla Kuruman								
MHH	50.0	75.0	38.1	50.0	4.5	54.5	36.4	4.5
FHH	50.0	25.0	61.9	50.0	5.3	21.1	68.4	5.3
Mavilan								
MHH	0.0	100.0	40.0	52.4	0.0	7.4	51.9	40.7
FHH	100.0	0.0	60.0	47.6	6.1	0.0	63.6	30.3
Total								
MHH	35.5	67.6	48.0	57.8	7.6	17.2	57.2	17.9
FHH	64.5	32.4	52.0	42.2	14.2	8.5	63.8	13.5

Source: Primary Data

in the MHHs. The no income category of females were concentrated more amongst the MHHs in Paniyan and Mavilan community, but for Kanikkar households no income category was concentrated more among FHHs. Within main occupation, the no income category was observably higher among the females in MHH group (17.9 percent) as against 13.5 percent among the FHH counterparts. Of all the families employed in forestry sector, 47.6 percent belonged to MHHs and 52.4 percent belonged to FHHs in Paniyan community. The Figure for Kanikkar for the same sector was zero percent in case of MHHs and 100 percent in case of FHHs. Kanikkar in forest settlements ventured into forests on a daily basis for collecting medicinal plants, plant bark etc. The Mulla Kuruman had very few who reported the forestry sector as their main occupation but had equal representation in MHHs and FHHs. However, in the Mavilan community, only women in FHHs were engaged in the sector.

Within the main occupation, for Paniyan females within the MHHs, the distribution of employment is 13.9 percent, 11.1 percent, 55.6 percent, and 19.4 percent in forestry, agriculture and allied, non-agriculture & allied and not employed categories and for the Paniyan females in FHH, the distribution was 15.9 percent, 11.6 percent, 63.8 percent, 8.7 percent for the respective categories. In the Kanikkar community, the distribution of employment is 12.5 percent and 87.5 percent for agriculture and non-agriculture & allied sectors for females in MHHs and among females in FHHs the distribution of employment was 30 percent, 60 percent and 10 percent in forestry, non-agriculture & allied and no income category. In Mulla Kuruman category, the distribution of employment among MHHs was 4.5 percent, 54.5 percent, 36.4 percent,4.5 percent in forestry, agriculture & allied, non-agriculture & allied and no income category. Among FHHs the same was 5.3 percent, 21.1 percent, 68.4 percent and 5.3 percent in forestry, agriculture & allied, non-agriculture & allied and no income category. In Mavilan category, the distribution of employment among MHHs was 7.4 percent, 51.9 percent and 40.7 percent in agriculture & allied, non-agriculture & allied and no income category. The distribution of main occupation for FHHs was 6.1 percent, 63.6 percent and 30.3 percent for forestry, non- agriculture and allied and no income categories. It was observed in the field study that within main occupation, FHHs in all 4 communities were over represented in non-agriculture and allied sectors (63.8 percent) in comparison with MHHs (57.2 percent). Within the tribal distribution, 67.6 percent MHHs depended on agriculture and allied sectors whereas only 32.4 percent FHHs relied on the sector for livelihood.

Asset details

In the field study, information on asset base of the respondents with regard to holdings of land, building, cash in hand, gold, bank deposit, chitties, post office savings, insurance, provident fund, domestic animals, outstanding savings and other assets were recorded.

Table 12.4 shows asset details of households in all four communities according to gender of household head. In Paniyan community, the ownership of all asset categories in FHHs was less than the MHHs. In the Mulla Kuruman community the proportion of asset holding of gold (52.4 percent), building (54.2 percent) and bank deposit (51 percent) was greater in MHHs. In the Kanikkar community, equal proportion of MHHs and FHHs reportedly had land, building, gold and bank deposits. In Mavilan community, asset holdings of gold (40.5 percent), domestic animals (33.3 percent) was lesser among FHHs.

Table 12.4: Asset details of tribal households based on headship type

Tribe Name	*Headship type*	*Land*	*Building*	*Gold (n)*	*Domestic animals*	*Bank deposit*
Paniyan	MHH	50.7	53.6	51.7	61.1	50.7
	FHH	49.3	46.4	48.3	38.9	49.3
	Total	142	110	58	36	152
	% within tribe	45.5	39.6	33.3	41.9	47.1
Kanikkar	MHH	50.0	50.0	50.0	45.5	50.0
	FHH	50.0	50.0	50.0	54.5	50.0
	Total	52	52	32	11	52
	% within tribe	16.7	18.7	18.4	12.8	16.1
Mulla Kuruman	MHH	50.0	45.8	47.6	51.5	49.0
	FHH	50.0	54.2	52.4	48.5	51.0
	Total	50	48	42	33	51
	% within tribe	16.0	17.3	24.1	38.4	15.8
Mavilan	MHH	50.0	50.0	59.5	66.7	50.0
	FHH	50.0	50.0	40.5	33.3	50.0
	Total	68	68	42	6	68
	% within tribe	21.8	24.5	24.1	7.0	21.1
Total	MHH	50.3	50.7	52.3	55.8	50.2
	FHH	49.7	49.3	47.7	44.2	49.8
	Total	312	278	174	86	323
	% within tribe	100.0	100.0	100.0	100.0	100.0

Source: Primary Data

Table 12.5: Asset ownership details of selected communities based on headship type

Asset Category	*MHH*			*FHH*			*Total*		
	Mean	*N*	*SD*	*Mean*	*N*	*SD*	*Mean*	*N*	*SD*
Land quantity	52.9204	157	101.6061	31.0943	159	46.08678	41.9383	316	79.35724
Cash in hand-quantity	1025.305	164	2834.628	685.0909	165	1395.169	854.6809	329	2235.024
Gold quantity	12.3143	98	11.83452	10.1573	89	10.1957	11.2877	187	11.10803
Bank deposit worth in Rupees	4236.833	162	10518.41	2145.153	163	2863.067	3187.775	325	7757.109
Chitties worth in Rupees	84428	25	275605.8	3416.667	12	2224.178	58154.05	37	228295.1
Domestic animals quantity/number	7.8542	48	10.18967	5.275	40	6.64479	6.6818	88	8.80641
Outstanding savings worth in Rupees	4871.053	38	6639.11	6996.125	32	10465.52	5842.514	70	8601.203

Source: Primary Data

Except the asset constituting outstanding savings, all the asset categories displayed lower averages in FHHs in comparison with MHHs. The mean Figures of land in MHHs was 52.94 cents for all four communities as against 31.09 cents for FHHs; cash in hand average was Rs. 854.68 whereas the average for MHHs was much higher at Rs. 1025.3, the Figure in FHHs was Rs. 685.09. A similar lopsided trend is visible in case of bank deposits and domestic animals. This is a clear validation of the fact that across the four scheduled tribe communities, FHHs are much more prone to asset deprivation and poverty than MHHs.

Basic Amenities

The type of house, floor, roof, house ownership, presence of electrification, source of drinking water, latrine type and fuel type are the amenities that indicate the living standards of a population under study.

Table 12.6: Housing Status (House Type) of tribal households based on headship type

	Within the type of house					*Within the tribe*				
	Paniyan	*Kanikkar*	*Mulla Kuruman*	*Mavilan*	*Total*	*Paniyan*	*Kanikkar*	*Mulla Kuruman*	*Mavilan*	*Total (N)*
MHH										
Pucca	31.6	50.0	42.3	61.8	42.4	35.7	18.6	15.7	30.0	70
Semi pucca	53.2	42.0	42.0	42.0	42.0	57.5	15.1	15.1	12.3	73
Kutcha	15.2	12.0	12.0	12.0	12.0	54.5	9.1	18.2	18.2	22
Total	79	26	26	34	165	47.9	15.8	15.8	20.6	165
FHH										
Pucca	24.1	53.8	30.8	35.3	32.1	35.8	26.4	15.1	22.6	53
Semi pucca	62.0	38.5	65.4	58.8	58.2	51.0	10.4	17.7	20.8	96
Kutcha	13.9	7.7	3.8	5.9	9.7	68.8	12.5	6.3	12.5	16
Total	79	26	26	34	165	47.9	15.8	15.8	20.6	165
Total										
Pucca	27.8	51.9	36.5	48.5	37.3	35.8	22.0	15.4	26.8	123
Semi pucca	57.6	40.4	53.8	42.6	51.2	53.8	12.4	16.6	17.2	169
Kutcha	13.9	7.7	9.6	8.8	11.5	57.9	10.5	13.2	15.8	38
Total	158	52	52	68	330	47.9	15.8	15.8	20.6	330

Source: Primary Data

Table 12.6 shows the type of houses in the selected communities disaggregated on the basis of headship. In the Paniyan community, while 31.6 percent of MHHs resided in pucca, 24.1 percent was the Figure for FHHs. Semi pucca houses were the most common house type in both Paniyan MHHs (53.2per cent) and FHHs (62 percent).

In the Mulla Kuruman and Mavilan community while the MHHs predominant house type were pucca houses, the majority of FHHs reportedly lived in semi pucca houses. A clear divergence in house type was found among MHHs and FHHs in the Mulla Kuruman and Mavilan community. In the Mulla Kuruman community, 42.3 percent of MHHs lived in pucca houses, the corresponding Figure for FHHs was 30.8 percent. In the Mavilan community, 61.8 percent of MHHs lived in pucca houses. Their counterparts in FHHs registered 35.3 percent.

Within the tribal communities, MHHs comprising 54.5 percent Paniyan community resided in kutcha houses. 68.8 percent of Paniyan FHHs constituted the total FHHs residing in kutcha houses. Within the tribe, the semi-pucca and kutcha type houses were much more than pucca houses amongst both headship types in Paniyan community. The presence of kutcha houses was significantly lesser in the other three communities.

Table 12.7: Source of drinking water status of tribal households based on headship type

	%within facilities					*%within tribes*				
	Paniyan	*Kanikkar*	*Mulla Kuruman*	*Mavilan*	*Total*	*Paniyan*	*Kanikkar*	*Mulla Kuruman*	*Mavilan*	*Total*
MHH										
Owntap	15.2	3.8	19.2	5.9	12.1	60.0	5.0	25.0	10.0	20
Own well	2.5	0.0	19.2	8.8	6.1	20.0	0.0	50.0	30.0	10
Commontap	19.0	0.0	7.7	0.0	10.3	88.2	0.0	11.8	0.0	17
Common well	63.3	96.2	53.8	85.3	71.5	42.4	21.2	11.9	24.6	118
Total	79	26	26	34	165	47.9	15.8	15.8	20.6	165
FHH										
Owntap	7.6	15.4	0.0	5.9	7.3	50.0	33.3	0.0	16.7	12
Own well	0.0	7.7	11.5	11.8	5.5	0.0	22.2	33.3	44.4	9
Commontap	29.1	0.0	15.4	0.0	16.4	85.2	0.0	14.8	0.0	27
Common well	63.3	76.9	73.1	82.4	70.9	42.7	17.1	16.2	23.9	117
Total	79	26	26	34	165	47.9	15.8	15.8	20.6	165
Total										
Owntap	11.4	9.6	9.6	5.9	9.7	56.3	15.6	15.6	12.5	32
Own well	1.3	3.8	15.4	10.3	5.8	10.5	10.5	42.1	36.8	19
Commontap	24.1	0.0	11.5	0.0	13.3	86.4	0.0	13.6	0.0	44
Common well	63.3	86.5	63.5	83.8	71.2	42.6	19.1	14.0	24.3	235
Total	158	52	52	68	330	47.9	15.8	15.8	20.6	330

Source: Primary Data

The main sources of drinking water were own tap, own well, common tap and common well. Within tribal distribution, MHHs who used own tap as a drinking water source comprised of 60 percent Paniyan, 5 Percent Kanikkar, 25 percent Mulla Kuruman and 10 percent Mavilan households. Of all households that used common tap among MHHs, 88.2 percent belonged to Paniyan, and 11.8 percent belonged to Mavilan and none in the other two communities. Common well users in MHHs comprised of 42.4 percent Paniyan, 21.2 percent Kanikkar, and 11.9 percent Mulla Kuruman, and 24.6 percent Mavilan community. Common wells were the most common source of drinking water across the selected communities. A similar trend followed in case of FHHs, whereby users of common well comprised of 42.7 percent Paniyan, 17.1 percent belonged to Kanikkar, 16.2 percent belonged to Mulla Kuruman, and 23.9 percent belonged to Mavilan community.

Table 12.8: Housing Status (Latrine type) of tribal house holds based on headship type

	% within facilities					*% within tribe*			
	Paniyan	*Kanikkar*	*Mulla Kuruman*	*Mavilan*	*Total*	*Paniyan*	*Kanikkar*	*Mulla Kuruman*	*Mavilan*
MHH									
Flush/pour Common latrine	6.7	0.0	8.7	3.4	5.2	57.1	0.0	28.6	14.3
Flush/Pour IHHL	88.3	100.0	91.3	79.3	88.8	44.5	18.5	17.6	19.3
Pit Latrine	5.0	0.0	0.0	17.2	6.0	37.5	0.0	0.0	62.5
FHH									
Flush/Pour Common latrine	3.2	0.0	8.0	6.1	4.2	33.3	0.0	33.3	33.3
Flush/Pour IHHL	90.5	100.0	92.0	72.7	88.1	45.2	17.5	18.3	19.0
Pit Latrine	6.3	0.0	0.0	21.2	7.7	36.4	0.0	0.0	63.6
Total									
Flush/pour Common latrine	4.9	0.0	8.3	4.8	4.7	46.2	0.0	30.8	23.1
Flush/Pour IHHL	89.4	100.0	91.7	75.8	88.4	44.9	18.0	18.0	19.2
Pit Latrine	5.7	0.0	0.0	19.4	6.9	36.8	0.0	0.0	63.2

Source: Primary Data

Within tribe, distribution of common latrine in MHHs is 57.1 percent, 28.6 percent and 14.3 percent amongst Paniyan, Mulla Kuruman and Mavilan communities. The common or community latrine and individual household latrine to a large extent was available to the households under the ODF campaign launched under the Swachch Bharat Mission (Gramin) cleanliness campaign. In such toilets, flush or pour flush system prevailed with a sewer system. Every individual household latrine beneficiary of the scheme was eligible for Rs.12,000 which was paid in parts at various stages of construction of one unit of Individual Household Latrine. Unfortunately, it was observed during the field study that some of the common latrines built in toilet complexes were primarily used for storing away firewood from the rains. The distribution of the flush/pour flush latrine was found in 44.5 percent Paniyan, 18.5 percent Kanikkar, 17.6 percent Mulla Kuruman and 19.3 Mavilan. The distribution of Pit latrine was found in the MHHs of the Paniyan community, 6.7 percent used common latrine whereas in FHHs 3.2 percent had common latrines. While 88.3 percent of Paniyan MHHs had flush or pour flush latrine, 90.5 percent FHHs had flush/pour flush latrine

Pit latrines were found only in households of Paniyan and Mavilan community. In the Paniyan community, 5 percent of MHHs and 6.3 percent of FHHs used pit latrine. While 17.2 percent of MHHs in Mavilan community used pit latrines, the corresponding FHHs Figure was 21.2 percent.

Expenditure Pattern of Tribal Household based on headship type

A household's main expenditure may be broadly divided into Monthly Per capita Food Expenditure (MPCFE) and Monthly Per Capita Non Food Expenditure (MPCNFE). MPCFE includes expenses on cereals (rice, wheat, etc.) meat, fish edible oil, vegetables, fruits, pulses, tea/coffee, milk and milk products and liquor. MPCNFE includes expenses made on non-food items such as clothing, entertainment, educational expenses, expenses on medicines, cooking gas/kerosene/ firewood, transport/travel expenses and other expenses (cable/house rent/newspaper/land preparation/foraging expenses).

Table 12.9: Monthly per capita food and non-food expenditure of tribal households based on headship type

Tribe Name	*MHH/FHH*		*MPCNFE*	*MPCFE*
Paniyan	MHH	Mean	423.7135	811.6929
		N	79	79
		Std. Deviation	401.8855	550.9778
	FHH	Mean	425.4497	792.7688
		N	79	79
		Std. Deviation	448.245	628.4871
	Total	Mean	424.628	801.7252
		N	158	158
		Std. Deviation	425.3065	590.8897

(Contd...)

Kanikkar	MHH	Mean	273.3652	836.1413
		N	26	26
		Std. Deviation	103.7635	449.1269
	FHH	Mean	237.8333	575.0208
		N	26	26
		Std. Deviation	117.0353	379.2052
	Total	Mean	258.788	729.015
		N	52	52
		Std. Deviation	109.3333	436.4345
Mulla Kuruman	MHH	Mean	894.9717	1416.625
		N	26	26
		Std. Deviation	386.3339	1128.647
	FHH	Mean	929.102	1087.218
		N	26	26
		Std. Deviation	601.2632	1079.729
	Total	Mean	911.2612	1259.408
		N	52	52
		Std. Deviation	494.7803	1105.294
Mavilan	MHH	Mean	378.3654	863.1155
		N	34	34
		Std. Deviation	175.0842	501.0602
	FHH	Mean	235.501	830.0833
		N	34	34
		Std. Deviation	195.3227	586.0661
	Total	Mean	316.674	848.8516
		N	68	68
		Std. Deviation	195.4579	533.0861
Total	MHH	Mean	470.6851	930.199
		N	165	165
		Std. Deviation	384.296	694.3203
	FHH	Mean	457.1762	820.0364
		N	165	165
		Std. Deviation	477.1827	701.5441
	Total	Mean	464.1401	876.8256
		N	330	330
		Std. Deviation	431.0027	698.6508

Source: Primary Data

Table 12.9 shows the MPCNFE and MPCFE of selected tribes in the year across headship types. MPCFE across the eight sub categories of households showed the Kanikkar FHHs recording the lowest expenditure

(Rs.575.02). The second lowest was observed among the Paniyan FHHs (Rs. 792.768). The highest MPCFE was observed among the MHHs (Rs. 1416.625) and FHHs (Rs. 1087.218) among the Mulla Kuruman community. Within each tribal community, MHHs had comparatively higher expenses in their household when compared with females in FHHs.

MPCNFE across headship types showed the lowest mean among the Mavilan FHHs (Rs. 235.501) followed by the Kanikkar FHHs (Rs. 237.833). The highest MPCNFE was observed among the Mulla Kuruman MHHs (894.9717) and FHHs (Rs. 929.102).

The socio-economic characteristics of the selected sample comprising basic amenities, living arrangement, indebtedness, asset and expenditure pattern and social assistance details depict the disadvantageous position of ST female headed households as against their male counterparts. These factors influences the life opportunities of the respondents which in turn have implications on their quality of life.

Section III: Quality of Life of Female Headed Tribal Households

Quality of life refers to well-being particularly positive aspects constituting physical mental or psychological being, apart from a person's social support and kinship network system that lends a sense of protection and harmony in life. Quality of life not only is the standard of living and achieving the minimum level of comfort and facilities, but also includes the quality of interpersonal and social relationships (Ghaffary, Karimi, Norezi, 2012; Group W, 1998). The females in FHHs face several mental, physical and social poverty which is reflected in their quality of life.

Flanagan's Quality of Life scale (1982) is used to understand how a person evaluates his or her feelings and sense of well-being. These indices are used to ascertain the material and physical well-being, relationships with other people, social, community and civic activities, personal development and fulfilment and recreation activity levels of the sample units. The quality of life of the households in 7 domains have been checked. The physical domain consists of five facets that enquired about aspects such as stress, menstrual problems, and need of medical assistance, sleep and tiredness. The mental domain comprises of control over emotions, ability to think/learn/concentrate, happiness, loneliness, and hallucination/ delusion. The social domain consists of nine facets such as ostracization, threat by anti-socials, theft/robbery, and relationship with in laws, sexual advances, workplace victimization, societal support, and support from friends/relatives, participation in neighborhood functions. Economic domain encompasses four facets such as access to income, difficulty to find regular work, difficulty in getting credit, liability burden. Child Nurturing consists of four facets obedience, child's education, dependence on others and creation of problems by children. Level of Independence and satiation consists of six facets such as dependence, satisfaction of own efficacy, satisfaction with self-care activities, working capacity, self-esteem and self-confidence. Social awareness consists of news awareness, awareness about poverty alleviation programmes and banking habits.

Items are rated on a 5 point Likert interval scale where 1 indicates low, negative perceptions and 5 indicates high and positive perception. Facet scores are the mean of the items in each facet. Domain scores are obtained by adding the facet means in the respective domain and dividing it by the number of facets in that domain. The Quality of Life instrument used here covers respondent's perception of overall quality of life within the above said domains. QOLS used in the study produces a profile of the individual after consideration of 36 facets spread over seven domains. The domains are scored in a positive direction with a higher score indicating a higher quality of life.

Physical Quality of Life

Table 12.10. relates to the physical health of females in MHHs and FHHs. The respondents were asked questions relating to stress related physical problems, menstrual problems, requirement of medicines for daily routine, sleep and work induced tiredness. Paniyan FHHs listed the lowest average, indicating high levels of stress and associated problems across the eight sub categories of households. In all the selected tribes, FHHs were worse off than MHHs. Kanikkar FHHs were found to have a higher incidence of menstrual problems indicated by the lowest mean value of 3, across the eighth sub groups. Kanikkar FHHs, on account of stress and problems related to women's health, conspicuously reported a lower mean of 2.54, implying use of medications very often. A higher incidence of sleeplessness was reported amongst the Kanikkar FHHs, with a mean value of 2.69. The Mavilan FHHs also reported sleeplessness reporting a low average of 2.58. Across the 8 subgroups, the lowest mean implying high level of work induced tiredness was among Paniyan FHHs (2.06). Across the four selected tribes, Paniyan households had lowest mean of 2.19 suggesting high degrees of work induced stress. On comparison between MHH and FHH, the physical quality of life indices were worse off in FHHs in all the communities except Paniyan community wherein FHHs had slightly better physical QOL.

Table 12.10: Physical Quality of Life of tribal women based on headship type

Tribe name	*MHH/FHH*		*Stress related physical problems*	*Menstrual problems*	*Medical assistance for daily routine*	*Sleep*	*work induced tiredness*	*Physical Health Index*
Paniyan	MHH	M	2.38	3.72	3.61	3.41	2.32	3.08
		N	79	79	79	79	79	79
		SD	1.264	1.037	1.091	1.068	1.017	0.86514
	FHH	M	2.32	4.13	3.58	3.59	3.32	3.85
		N	79	79	79	79	79	79
		SD	1.092	1.102	1.183	0.941	0.825	0.74719
	Total	M	2.35	3.92	3.59	3.5	2.19	3.11
		N	158	158	158	158	158	158
		SD	1.178	1.086	1.135	1.008	0.932	0.80934
Kanikkar	MHH	M	3.23	3.5	3.58	3.12	3.27	3.3385
		N	26	26	26	26	26	26
		SD	0.992	0.762	0.703	1.033	0.827	0.74997
	FHH	M	2.54	3	2.54	2.69	2.54	2.6615
		N	26	26	26	26	26	26
		SD	1.104	1.058	0.859	1.087	1.104	0.99079
	Total	M	2.88	3.25	3.06	2.9	2.9	3
		N	52	52	52	52	52	52
		SD	1.096	0.947	0.938	1.071	1.034	0.93473
Mulla Kuruman	MHH	M	3.6	4.36	3.88	3.64	3.12	3.5769
		N	26	26	26	26	26	26
		SD	1	0.952	1.054	0.638	0.781	0.84914
	FHH	M	2.96	4.04	3.4	3.08	2.69	3.2077
		N	26	26	25	26	26	26
		SD	1.113	0.999	1	1.129	1.011	0.73426
	Total	M	3.27	4.2	3.64	3.35	2.9	3.3923
		N	52	52	52	52	52	52
		SD	1.097	0.98	1.045	0.955	0.922	0.80777
Mavilan	MHH	M	3.53	3.62	3.59	3.41	3.56	3.5412
		N	34	34	34	34	34	34
		SD	0.992	0.888	0.925	1.019	1.106	0.94135
	FHH	M	2.85	3.06	2.74	2.88	2.76	2.8588
		N	34	34	34	34	34	34
		SD	1.209	0.886	0.994	1.149	1.13	1.02871
	Total	M	3.19	3.34	3.16	3.15	3.16	3.2
		N	68	68	68	68	68	68
		SD	1.149	0.924	1.045	1.11	1.18	1.03722
Total	MHH	M	3.42	3.76	3.64	3.4	3.21	3.4642
		N	165	165	165	165	165	165
		SD	1.13	0.984	0.996	1.001	0.988	0.85796
	FHH	M	3.04	3.72	3.21	3.22	2.98	3.2315
		N	165	165	165	165	165	165
		SD	1.15	1.152	1.15	1.095	1.015	0.92287
	Total	M	2.92	3.74	3.43	3.31	2.92	3.18
		N	330	330	330	330	330	330
		SD	1.154	1.07	1.095	1.051	1.006	0.89725

Source: Primary Data.

The overall QOL among the selected communities indicating physical well-being was 3.18, the mean score of MHHs recording 3.46, whereas the score of 3.23 was recorded among FHHs.

Mental Quality of Life

To ascertain the mental quality of life, the respondents were asked questions related to difficulty in controlling emotions, Ability to think/ learn/ concentrate, Happiness, Loneliness, delusion/hallucination etc.

Table 12.11: Mental Quality of Life of tribal women based on headship type

Tribe Name	*MHH/FHH*		*Difficulty in controlemotions*	*Ability to think/ learn/concentrate*	*Happiness*	*Loneliness*	*delusion/ hallucination*	*Mental HealthIndex*
Paniyan	MHH	M	2.47	2.37	2.34	3.48	2.73	2.66
		N	79	79	79	79	79	79
		SD	1.084	0.963	1.011	0.984	1.003	0.82558
	FHH	M	2.7	2.73	2.57	2.86	2.69	2.71
		N	79	79	79	79	79	79
		SD	0.925	0.78	0.943	0.845	1.183	0.61797
	Total	M	2.58	2.55	2.46	3.17	2.71	2.69
		N	158	158	158	158	138	158
		SD	1.011	0.893	0.981	0.966	1.095	0.74483
Kanikkar	MHH	M	2.54	2.62	2.5	2.85	2.57	2.62
		N	26	26	26	26	26	26
		SD	0.863	0.797	0.762	0.881	0.896	0.69747
	FHH	M	2.23	2.35	2.46	2.62	2.5	2.43
		N	26	26	26	26	26	26
		SD	1.421	1.023	1.029	1.169	1.147	1.09646
	Total	M	2.38	2.48	2.48	2.73	2.53	2.53
		N	52	52	52	52	52	52
		SD	1.174	0.918	0.896	1.031	1.008	0.90983
Mulla Kuruman	MHH	M	3.76	3.84	3.64	2.92	2.57	3.1769
		N	26	26	26	26	26	26
		SD	0.597	0.473	0.569	0.572	0.896	0.69588
	FHH	M	2.69	2.85	2.62	1.92	1.92	2.5692
		N	26	26	26	26	26	26
		SD	1.158	0.967	1.061	1.093	0.776	0.77911
	Total	M	3.22	3.33	3.12	2.42	2.25	2.8731
		N	52	52	52	52	52	52
		SD	1.064	0.909	0.993	0.868	0.89	0.79314
Mavilan	MHH	M	3.32	3.29	3.18	3.24	3.07	3.1471
		N	34	34	34	34	34	34
		SD	1.007	0.97	1.167	1.103	1.337	1.01062
	FHH	M	2.74	2.71	2.76	2.71	2.56	2.5588
		N	34	34	34	34	34	34
		SD	1.333	1.194	1.075	1.194	1.294	1.12361
	Total	M	3.03	3	2.97	2.97	2.84	2.8529
		N	68	68	68	68	68	68
		SD	1.209	1.12	1.133	1.171	1.33	1.10122
Total	MHH	M	3.02	3.03	3.22	2.53	2.73	2.90
		N	165	165	165	165	165	165
		SD	1.078	0.977	1.009	1.078	1.056	0.85967
	FHH	M	2.59	2.66	3.08	2.52	2.53	2.68
		N	165	165	165	165	165	165
		SD	1.244	1.068	1.104	0.948	1.166	0.94915
	Total	M	2.81	2.85	3.15	2.53	2.63	2.794
		N	330	330	330	330	330	330
		SD	1.165	1.023	1.059	1.016	1.114	0.90469

Source: Primary Data.

Table 12.11 shows the QOL indices indicating mental health among the selected tribal communities. The Kanikkar FHHs (2.23) and the Mulla Kuruman FHHs (2.69) recorded the lowest average denoting difficulty in exercising control over emotions. Among the MHHs, females belonging to Paniyan MHHs (2.47) had the lowest mean, implying greater difficulty in controlling emotions. Across tribe type and headship type, total average Figures displayed a lower mean score of control over emotion in FHHs (2.59) in comparison to MHHs (3.02). As regards the ability to think/learn/concentrate, the Kanikkar FHHs recorded the lowest mean (2.35) across the 8 subcategories of households. Females in Paniyan MHHs (2.37) displayed low mean ability to think/learn/concentrate. Considering aggregate mean, FHHs (2.66) recorded lower ability when compared to MHHs (3.03). Regarding happiness, the lowest mean was observed among females in Paniyan MHHs (2.34), followed by those in Kanikkar FHHs (2.46). Between the headship types, FHHs were observed to be less happy than MHHs. Aggregate mean happiness score of FHHs was 3.08 as against mean of MHHs (3.22). The feeling of loneliness was highest among Mulla Kuruman FHHs (1.92), followed by episodes of loneliness being reported the most in Kanikkar FHHs (2.62). The episodes of delusion or hallucination were reported the most among the Mulla Kuruman FHHs (1.92). Kanikkar FHHs also reported high incidence of delusion/hallucination (2.50).

The lowest indices of mental or emotional health across the 4 selected communities was recorded in the Kanikkar community (2.53) followed by Paniyan community households (2.69). The FHHs of Mulla Kuruman community noticeably had the highest incidence of episodes of hallucination and loneliness since they commonly reported cordial marital relations and the deprivation of the male head had much bearing on the disposition of female in FHHs, thus causing mental despair. The cause of absence of male heads was mostly due to death of the male that had a profound negative impact on their emotional health. Comparison of MHHs and FHHs showed a lower index of mental health among FHHs in all selected communities except Paniyan community. The overall index of mental health was 2.68 among FHHs and 2.90 among MHHs.

Social Quality of life

To ascertain the social quality of life, the respondents were asked questions related to Ostracization, threat by anti-socials, Theft/Robbery, Relationship with In-laws, Victimisation, Social connect, Societal support, Support from friends and family and Social Participation.

Kanikkar FHHs (2.46) and Mavilan FHHs (2.68) reported to be victims of social ostracization to a great degree. Kanikkar FHHs (2.31) and Mavilan FHHs (2.85) were the household sub categories that reported increased threat from anti socials. With regard to instances of theft or robbery, Kanikkar FHHs (2.31) and Mavilan FHHs (2.82) had observed that they were often the victims of theft or robbery. As with the relationship with in laws in the family, Kanikkar FHHs (2.23) and Mavilan FHHs (2.71) had observed that they had strained relations with in laws. Kanikkar FHHs (2.62), and Mavilan FHHs (2.94) had observed that they felt victimised in several spheres of life. Social Connectedness was least among Paniyan FHHs (2.09) and Kanikkar FHHs. Societal Support was lowest among Kanikkar MHHs (2.38) and Mavilan FHHs (2.38). Kanikkar FHHs (2.46) and Mavilan FHHs (2.59) had the least support from friends and relatives. Kanikkar FHHs (2.31) and Mavilan FHHs (2.53) were the household categories that had the least social participation.

Table 12.12: Social Quality of Life across tribe and headship type

Tribe name	*MHH/ FHH*		*Ostracization*	*Threat by Antisocials*	*Theft/ Robbery*	*Inlaws Relation-ship*	*Victimi-sation*	*Social connect*	*Societal support*	*Support from friends and family*	*Social Partici pation*	*Social connect Index*
Paniya	MHH	M	3.35	3.19	3.37	3.11	2.85	2.28	2.57	2.91	2.8	2.94
		N	79	79	79	79	79	79	79	79	79	79
		SD	0.77	0.833	0.754	0.577	0.753	0.831	0.812	0.485	8.463	0.45171
	FHH	M	3.21	3.27	3.38	2.97	2.99	2.09	2.46	2.95	2.92	2.93
		N	79	79	79	79	79	79	79	79	79	79
		SD	0.963	0.858	0.867	0.751	0.809	0.754	0.797	0.45	0.829	0.55169
	Total	M	3.28	3.23	3.37	3.04	2.92	2.18	2.51	2.93	2.86	2.9294
		N	158	158	158	158	158	158	158	158	158	158
		SD	0.869	0.844	0.81	0.671	0.782	0.797	0.804	0.467	6.067	0.50409
Kani	MHH	M	3.04	3.42	3.15	2.65	3.04	2.65	2.38	2.85	2.85	2.8923
		N	26	26	26	26	26	26	26	26	26	26
		SD	0.916	0.643	0.543	0.629	0.528	0.629	0.697	0.543	0.543	0.47555
	FHH	M	2.46	2.31	2.31	2.23	2.62	2.15	2.85	2.46	2.31	2.2992
		N	26	26	26	26	26	26	26	26	26	26
		SD	1.303	1.289	1.087	0.815	1.098	0.784	0.967	1.104	0.838	0.93243
	Total	M	2.75	2.87	2.73	2.44	2.83	2.4	2.12	2.65	2.58	2.5958
		N	52	52	52	52	52	52	52	52	52	52
		SD	1.153	1.155	0.952	0.752	0.879	0.748	0.878	0.883	0.75	0.79165
Mulla kuruman	MHH	M	3.6	3.76	3.79	3.32	2.88	2.44	2.56	3	3	2.9519
		N	26	26	26	26	26	26	26	26	26	26
		SD	0.5	0.523	0.415	0.476	0.726	0.651	0.583	0.408	0.511	0.85443
	FHH	M	3.27	3.58	3.62	3.27	3.12	2.42	2.85	3.19	3.04	3.1496
		N	26	26	26	26	26	26	26	26	26	26
		SD	0.827	0.504	0.496	0.452	0.711	0.703	0.732	0.402	0.344	0.32915
	Total	M	3.43	3.67	3.7	3.29	3	2.43	2.71	3.1	3.02	3.0508

(Contd...)

		N	52	52	52	52	52	52	52	52	52	52
		SD	0.7	0.516	0.463	0.46	0.721	0.671	0.672	0.413	0.428	0.6488
Mavilan	MHH	M	3.5	3.41	3.42	3.18	3.35	3	2.97	3.03	3.34	3.24
		N	34	34	34	34	34	34	34	34	34	34
		SD	0.508	0.5	0.502	0.392	0.485	0.426	0.46	0.388	7.065	0.35617
	FHH	M	2.68	2.85	2.82	2.71	2.94	2.76	2.38	2.59	2.53	2.6956
		N	34	34	34	34	34	34	34	34	34	34
		SD	1.319	1.132	0.999	0.76	0.886	0.741	0.779	0.988	1.051	0.86809
	Total	M	3.09	3.13	3.12	2.94	3.15	2.88	2.68	2.81	2.94	2.97
		N	68	68	68	68	68	68	68	68	68	68
		SD	1.075	0.913	0.844	0.649	0.738	0.612	0.701	0.778	5.02	0.69923
Total	MHH	M	3.37	3.36	3.41	3.09	2.99	2.51	2.62	2.94	3	3.03
		N	165	165	165	165	165	165	165	165	165	165
		SD	0.728	0.725	0.655	0.571	0.692	0.755	0.72	0.466	6.735	0.52578
	FHH	M	2.99	3.08	3.13	2.85	2.94	2.29	2.41	2.84	2.76	2.798
		N	165	165	165	165	165	165	165	165	165	165
		SD	1.124	1.03	0.985	0.786	0.867	0.789	0.855	0.751	0.862	0.71469
	Total	M	3.18	3.22	3.27	2.97	2.96	2.4	2.51	2.89	2.85	2.95
	N=330	SD	0.963	0.901	0.848	0.696	0.784	0.779	0.797	0.627	4.813	0.63405

Source: Primary Data

A comparison of overall QOL indices shows that FHHs had poor social ties when compared to the MHHs, the former recording a mean score of 2.79 and latter recording a higher score of 3.03. Social connectedness was lowest among the Paniyan FHHs since they were always aloof from the main stream society and only ventured out and interacted with the larger community when in need of work or debts. Most of them being uneducated, lacked social skills and shied away from interactions. Overall, the Kanikkar FHHs (2.29) and Mavilan FHHs (2.69) had the lowest score in the social domain.

Economic Quality of Life

To ascertain the economic quality of life, the respondents were asked questions related to access to income generative resource, problems in getting regular work, difficulty in credit availability and liability left by husband/in laws. The Mulla Kuruman community had the lowest index (2.628) in the economic domain implying that they had lesser access to income generating resources, had greater difficulty in credit availability, encountered more problems in getting regular work and suffered from enhanced liability created by husband or in laws. The Mulla Kuruman had very traditional value system wherein the man in the household was the custodian of most assets.

Table 12.13: Economic Quality of Life across tribe and headship type

Tribe name	*MHH/FHH*		*Access to income generative resource*	*Problems in Getting regular work*	*Difficulty in credit availability post shock*	*Liability left by husband/in laws*	*Index*
Paniyan	MHH	M	2.33	2.83	2.52	2.64	2.58
		N	79	79	79	79	79
		SD	0.492	1.1	1.043	1.151	0.98634
	FHH	M	2.9	2.86	2.25	2.89	2.725
		N	79	79	79	79	79
		SD	1.118	1.136	0.894	0.994	0.81127
	Total	M	2.615	2.845	2.385	2.765	2.653
		N	158	158	158	158	158
		SD	1.059	1.115	0.971	1.018	1.24562
Kanikkar	MHH	M	3	2.54	3.35	2.33	2.805
		N	26	26	26	26	26
		SD	0.752	1.104	1.071	0.577	0.80388
	FHH	M	3.23	2.77	3.5	2.31	2.953
		N	26	26	26	26	26
		SD	0.815	0.587	0.827	0.928	0.72951
	Total	M	3.115	2.655	3.425	2.32	2.879
		N	52	52	52	52	52
		SD	0.801	0.883	0.957	0.946	1.33627
Mulla Kuruman	MHH	M	2.00	2.95	2.32	3	2.568
		N	26	26	26	26	26
		SD	1.03	1.161	0.995	0.816	0.4615
	FHH	M	2.61	2.58	2.27	3.29	2.688
		N	26	26	26	26	26
		SD	1.076	0.945	1.12	0.806	0.73489
	Total	M	2.305	2.765	2.295	3.145	2.628
		N	52	52	52	52	52
		SD	1.06	1.052	1.047	1.138	1.00769
Mavilan	MHH	M	2.29	2.79	3.62	3.38	3.02
		N	34	34	34	34	34
		SD	1.799	0.82	1.098	1.598	0.96852
	FHH	M	3.17	2.12	3.03	3.39	2.928
		N	34	34	34	34	34
		SD	1.642	1.25	1.267	1.286	1.28489
	Total	M	2.73	2.455	3.325	3.385	2.974
		N	68	68	68	68	68
		SD	1.683	1.105	1.215	1.337	1.29654

(Contd...)

Total	MHH	M	2.405	2.778	2.953	2.7625	2.7247
		N	165	165	165	165	165
		SD	1.47	1.124	1.156	1.323	0.9082
	FHH	M	2.978	2.583	2.953	2.97	2.7758
		N	165	165	165	165	165
		SD	1.303	1.119	1.106	1.063	0.95515
	Total	M	2.692	2.681	2.953	2.8675	2.7503
		N	330	330	330	330	330
		SD	1.321	1.122	1.136	1.112	1.25324

Source: Primary Data

Since the women ventured out less, they had difficulty in finding work unless the job was available nearby. Since the life standards of the MK were better, the needs also increased which were met by loans. This explains the increased liability among them. However, FHHs were better off within the community in the economic domain. In the Paniyan community, except difficulty in credit availability, FHHs were better off than counterpart MHHs. Except in case of Mavilan community, all FHHs in their respective communities were better off than their counterpart MHHs. Overall index of economic domain indicating quality of life was 2.7503 which suggests the relative deprivation of tribal households.

Quality of Life in Child Nurturing

To ascertain the quality of life in child nurturing, the respondents were asked questions related to child obedience, neglect of children's education, dependence on others for rearing children and problems caused by children

In case of child obedience, Paniyan FHHs recorded the lowest mean score of 2.10 followed by Mavilan FHHs (2.14) implying high levels of disobedience. Children's education was much neglected in Kanikkar FHHs recording the lowest mean score (2.08) across the eight sub categories of households. Kanikkar FHHs (2.12) and Mavilan FHHs (2.29) depended excessively on others for rearing their children. Paniyan FHHs (2.13) and MHHs (2.14), followed by Kanikkar FHHs (2.20) reported greater instances of problems caused by children against comparison with other community tribal households.

The index of child nurturing was the lowest in Kanikkar FHHs, depicting the low mean score of 2.245, followed by Paniyan MHHs (2.37). Across the four tribes, the Paniyan community households recorded the lowest child rearing and nurturing index of 2.41.

Table 12.14: Quality of Life in Child Nurturing

Tribe name	*MHH/FHH*		*Child Obedience*	*Neglect of child(ren) education*	*Dependence on others for rearing children*	*problems caused by children*	*QOL Index*
Paniyan	MHH	M	2.29	2.69	2.35	2.14	2.37
		N	75	75	75	75	75
		SD	0.95	1.182	5.031	0.873	1.62599
	FHH	M	2.10	2.66	2.83	2.13	2.43
		N	69	69	69	69	69
		SD	0.958	1.214	1.028	1.095	1.30032
	Total	M	2.25	2.68	2.59	2.13	2.41
		N	144	144	144	144	144
		SD	0.956	1.201	3.565	0.987	1.4885
Kanikkar	MHH	M	2.68	2.5	2.75	2.75	2.67
		N	25	25	25	25	25
		SD	1.249	0.707	1.092	1.258	1.02451
	FHH	M	2.58	2.08	2.12	2.2	2.245
		N	26	26	26	26	26
		SD	1.349	1.283	1.327	1.327	1.44009
	Total	M	2.63	2.29	2.44	2.48	2.46
		N	51	51	51	51	51
		SD	1.286	1.243	1.215	1.299	1.24966
Mulla Kuruman	MHH	M	3.35	3.67	4.59	4.87	4.12
		N	26	26	26	26	26
		SD	0.489	1.155	0.59	0.344	1.00005
	FHH	M	3.52	3.55	4.12	4.68	3.967
		N	23	23	23	23	23
		SD	0.918	1.438	0.881	0.748	0.9917
	Total	M	3.44	3.61	4.35	4.78	4.04
		N	49	49	49	49	49
		SD	0.755	1.387	0.788	0.592	1.08859
Mavilan	MHH	M	2.52	2.17	2.62	2.71	2.51
		N	31	31	31	31	31
		SD	0.829	1.329	1.049	1.15	1.20484
	FHH	M	2.14	2.79	2.29	2.46	2.42
		N	28	28	28	28	28
		SD	1.044	1.25	1.084	1.138	1.62773
	Total	M	2.33	2.48	2.46	2.59	2.47
		N	59	59	59	59	59
		SD	0.951	1.408	1.07	1.141	1.43057
Total	MHH	M	2.71	2.76	3.078	3.12	2.847
		N	157	157	157	157	157
		SD	0.968	1.301	3.524	1.07	1.38006
	FHH	M	2.585	2.77	2.84	2.868	3.0818
		N	146	146	146	146	146
		SD	1.065	1.28	1.153	1.247	1.3939
	Total	M	2.647	2.765	2.96	2.994	2.85
		N	303	303	303	303	303
		SD	1.019	1.282	2.604	1.163	1.40761

Source: Primary Data

Quality of life in level of independence and satiation

To ascertain the quality of life in level of Independence and satiation, the respondents were asked questions related to dependence, self-efficacy satisfaction, satisfaction with self-care activities, work capacity rating, self-esteem and self-confidence.

Table 12.15 shows the index of the level of independence and satiation. Mavilan FHHs (2.29) and Paniyan MHHs (2.38) reported high levels of dependency. Dependency levels were higher among the female in FHHs in comparison against the counterparts in MHHs in all communities except in the Paniyan community. Across the eight sub categories of households, the Mavilan FHHs reported the lowest mean score (2.09) indicating low levels of satisfaction in self-efficacy.

Table 12.15: Quality of life in level of independence and satiation across tribe and headship type

Tribe name	*MHH/ FHH*		*Dependence*	*Self-efficacy satisfaction*	*Satisfaction with self-care activities*	*work capacity rating*	*Self-esteem*	*Self-confideence*	*QOL Index*
Paniyan	MHH	M	2.38	2.34	2.78	2.66	2.52	2.63	2.5529
		N	79	79	79	79	79	79	79
		SD	1.017	0.83	0.842	0.783	0.731	0.771	0.62328
	FHH	M	2.54	2.49	2.76	2.53	2.58	2.49	2.5672
		N	79	79	79	79	79	79	79
		SD	1.141	0.815	0.755	0.845	0.794	0.815	0.60725
	Total	M	2.46	2.42	2.77	2.59	2.55	2.56	2.5601
		N	158	158	158	158	158	158	158
		SD	1.08	0.823	0.797	0.814	0.762	0.794	0.6134
Kanikkar	MHH	M	2.85	2.62	2.38	2.81	2.65	2.58	2.6473
		N	26	26	26	26	26	26	26
		SD	0.834	0.852	0.697	0.694	1.018	0.809	0.6542
	FHH	M	2.69	2.54	2.08	2.69	2.46	2	2.41
		N	26	26	26	26	26	26	26
		SD	1.011	0.948	0.628	0.838	0.761	0.8	0.71916
	Total	M	2.77	2.58	2.23	2.75	2.56	2.29	2.5287
		N	52	52	52	52	52	52	52
		SD	0.921	0.893	0.675	0.764	0.895	0.848	0.69113
Mulla Kuruman	MHH	M	3.48	2.76	3.04	2.72	2.64	2.6	2.7246
		N	26	26	26	26	26	26	26
		SD	0.586	0.723	0.455	0.843	0.638	0.577	0.83241
	FHH	M	2.92	2.44	2.68	2.16	2.48	2.44	2.3854
		N	26	26	26	26	26	26	26
		SD	0.909	0.712	0.748	1.068	0.653	0.768	0.89797
	Total	M	3.2	2.6	2.86	2.44	2.56	2.52	2.555
		N	50	50	50	50	50	50	52
		SD	0.808	0.728	0.639	0.993	0.644	0.677	0.87422

(Contd...)

Mavilan	MHH	M	2.56	2.36	2.39	2.27	2.33	2.3	2.2897
		N	34	34	34	34	34	34	34
		SD	1.236	1.113	1.029	1.008	0.89	0.918	1.07258
	FHH	M	2.29	2.09	2.44	2.12	2.12	2.03	2.1229
		N	34	34	34	34	34	34	34
		SD	1.338	1.19	9.842	1.149	1.149	1.114	1.1498
	Total	M	2.43	2.22	2.42	2.19	2.22	2.16	2.2063
		N	68	68	68	68	68	68	68
		SD	1.285	1.152	7.072	1.076	1.027	1.024	1.10673
Total	MHH	M	2.82	2.45	2.65	2.62	2.53	2.53	2.55
		N	165	165	165	165	165	165	165
		SD	1.053	0.89	0.844	0.841	0.804	0.787	0.77937
	FHH	M	2.61	2.39	2.49	2.38	2.41	2.24	2.37
		N	165	165	165	165	165	165	165
		SD	1.141	0.919	3.543	0.965	0.867	0.897	0.81981
	Total	M	2.72	2.46	2.57	2.47	2.5	2.39	2.46
		N	330	330	330	330	330	330	330
		SD	1.097	0.904	3.271	0.91	0.836	0.851	0.80083

Source: Primary Data

Paniyan community FHHs was the only community in which FHHs reported higher self-efficacy satisfaction compared to MHHs. Kanikkar FHHs (2.08) and Kanikkar MHHs (2.38) reported the lowest levels of self-care satisfaction. Mavilan FHHs (2.12) and Mulla Kuruman FHHs (2.16) reported to have the lowest work capacity. Across community headship types, the difference in the scores of work capacity was highest among the MHHs (2.72) and the FHHs (2.16) of Mulla Kuruman community. Mavilan FHHs (2.12) and MHHs (2.33) reported the lowest self-esteem levels. Within the two types of headship in the community, self-esteem scores showed that FHHs (2.58) fared better than MHHs (2.52) only in the Paniyan community. Kanikkar FHHs (2.00) and Mavilan FHHs (2.03) had least levels of self-confidence. Mavilan community had lowest score of self-confidence. The lowest score of independence and satiation was observed among the Mavilan community (2.206). Mavilan FHHs (2.12) and MHHs (2.28) had the lowest levels of independence and satiation.

Quality of life in General awareness and Banking habits

To ascertain the quality of life reflected in general awareness and banking habits, the respondents were asked questions relating to news awareness, awareness about poverty alleviation schemes, and visit at the bank.

Paniyan MHHs (1.71) and FHHs (1.8) had the least awareness of news among the selected communities. A comparison of MHH and FHHs, revealed that only in the Paniyan community, a higher mean score indicating better news awareness was observed among the females in FHHs (1.80)

Table 12.16: Quality of life in General awareness and Banking habits

Tribe name	*MHH/FHH*		*News awareness*	*awareness about poverty alleviation schemes*	*visit at the bank*	*Awareness Index*
Paniyan	MHH	M	1.71	1.70	1.97	1.79
		N	79	79	79	79
		SD	0.736	0.463	0.158	0.13405
	FHH	M	1.8	1.78	1.99	1.86
		N	79	79	79	79
		SD	0.853	0.414	0.113	0.14821
	Total	M	1.75	1.74	1.98	1.825
		N	158	158	158	158
		SD	0.796	0.44	0.137	0.14231
Kanikkar	MHH	M	2.15	1.88	1.85	1.96
		N	26	26	26	26
		SD	0.675	0.326	0.368	0.11974
	FHH	M	2.08	1.85	1.62	1.85
		N	26	26	26	26
		SD	0.484	0.368	0.496	0.05435
	Total	M	2.12	1.87	1.73	1.906
		N	52	52	52	52
		SD	0.583	0.345	0.448	0.0928
Mulla Kuruman	MHH	M	2.92	1.36	1.92	2.067
		N	26	26	26	26
		SD	0.997	0.49	0.277	0.3973
	FHH	M	2.84	1.36	1.83	2.01
		N	26	26	26	26
		SD	0.987	0.49	0.381	0.4052
	Total	M	2.88	1.36	1.88	2.04
		N	52	52	52	52
		SD	0.982	0.485	0.331	0.39748
Mavilan	MHH	M	2.73	2.67	2.18	2.526
		N	34	34	34	34
		SD	0.977	0.479	3.573	0.76678
	FHH	M	2.24	2.82	2.27	2.443
		N	34	34	34	34
		SD	1.017	0.387	0.387	0.14723
	Total	M	2.48	2.745	2.23	2.485
		N	68	68	68	68
		SD	1.02	0.438	2.563	0.55183
Total	MHH	M	2.38	1.90	1.98	2.086
		N	165	165	165	165
		SD	0.96	0.472	1.608	0.40401
	FHH	M	2.24	1.97	1.928	2.046
		N	165	165	165	165
		SD	0.932	0.441	0.442	0.20405
	Total	M	2.31	1.935	1.95	2.065
		N	330	330	330	330
		SD	0.945	0.457	1.185	0.31964

Source: Primary Data

against the females in MHHs (1.71). Mulla Kuruman MHHs and FHHs had the lowest awareness on poverty alleviation schemes (mean score of 1.36 each). Kanikkar FHHs (1.36) reported the lowest frequency of bank visits of all 8 sub categories of households.

Among the groups under study, Paniyan community households recorded the lowest average indicating lowest general awareness and banking habits (1.825). This was clear from the very aloof and alienated nature of the tribes. The test of quality of life among the 8 sub category household groups revealed that except in the case of physical health, all QOL indices showed lower values among tribal households, with FHHs being more disadvantaged.

The Paniyan FHHs came across as the most deprived of the eight sub categories studied. The persistent illiteracy makes them the least empowered when compared to all the other sub categories of households. Thus, the feminization of poverty argument is substantiated among FHHs based on static measures of poverty.

Section V: Conclusion

This study was an attempt to understand the poverty dimension and emphasis on qualitative life perception of the tribal women belonging to FHH and MHHs in Kerala. The study had two objectives, the first objective was to understand the socio economic status of female headed tribal households against their male counterparts, the indicators used being income, occupation, education, etc. The analysis of the same proves the comparative deprived position of FHHs to MHHs. This is also indicative of the possible lower qualitative life of the females in the FHHs. The second objective was to undertake a comparative assessment of qualitative life of the women in both tribal household categories. The various tribal categories recorded low values in all indices except physical health. The QOL indices prove that women in FHHs were more disadvantaged than counterparts in MHHs. Hence it can be drawn from the study that women living in FHHs are at a higher risk of health fails than women in MHHs. Here we can reminisce the studies across the world on FHHs that women in such households are indeed one of the most vulnerable to excesses of life due to their hardship of single-handedly caring for and earning to maintain households. To conclude, it is imperative to frame specific policies to reduce the stressors that contribute to reducing the well-being of FHHs especially those belonging to tribal groups. An inclusive policy that aims to mitigate and empower the tribal population with distinct emphasis on distressed FHHs must be formulated in Kerala.

References

1. Arias, E., & Palloni, A. (1999). Prevalence and patterns of female headed households in Latin America: 1970-1990. Journal of Comparative Family Studies, 257-279. Retrieved from http://www.jstor.org/stable/41603629

2. Brunner EJ, Marmot MG. Social organisation, stress and health. In: Marmot MG, Wilkinson RG, eds. Social determinants of health. Oxford: Oxford University Press, 1999.

3. G Haffary, Karimi. Aasnd Nowrezi, H. (2012) Trend study of Quality of life in Iran .Social Studies and Research in Iran, 1(3), 107-134.

4. Group. W (1998). Development of the WHOQOL-BREF Quality of life assessment. Psychological medicine 28(03), 551-558.

5. Kennedy BP, Kawachi I, Glass R, Prothrow-Stith D. Income Distribution, socioeconomic status, and self-rated health in the United States: multilevel analysis. BMJ 1998; 317: 917-21.

6. Lynch JW, Davey Smith G, Kaplan GA, House JS. Income inequality and mortality: importance to health of individual income, psychosocial environment, or material conditions. BMJ 2000; 320: 1200-4.

7. Michael Marmot, Richard G Wilkinson Psychosocial and material pathways in the relation between income and health: a response to Lynch et al., BMJ 2001;322:1233–6

8. René Landero Hernández, Benito Estrada Aranda, Mónica Teresa González Ramírez (2009), Depression and quality of life for women in single-parent and nuclear families Spanish Journal of Psychology. 2009 May; 12(1):171-83. doi: 10.1017/s113874160000158x.

9. Ryan, R. M., & Deci, E. (2001). On happiness and human potentials: A review of research on hedonic and eudaimonic well-being. Annual Review of Psychology, 52, 141–166.

10. Ryff, C. D., & Singer, B. (1998). The contours of positive human health. Psychological Inquiry, 9(1), 1–28. Sandvik, E., Diener, E., & Seidlitz, L. (1993).

11. Sims J, Butter M. Health and environment: moving beyond conventional paradigms. In: Sen G, George A, Ostlin P, eds. Engendering international health: the challenge of equity. Cambridge MA: The MIT Press, 2002:195–220.

12. Stephan klasen, Tobias lechtenfeld, Felix Povel A Feminization of Vulnerability? Female Headship, Poverty, and Vulnerability in Thailand and Vietnam, https://doi.org/10.1016/j.worlddev.2013.11.003

13. Shahnaz Rimaz, Maryam Dastoorpoor, Samira Vesali, Narges Saiepour, Saharnaz Nedjat, Masoumeh Sadeghi, Effat Merghati Khoei(2015):Investigation of relationship between social capital and quality of life in female headed families, Medical Journal of the Islamic Republic of Iran (MJIRI), Iran University of Medical Sciences

14. Sirgy, M. J. (1998). Materialism and quality of life. Social Indicators Research, 43, 227–260

15. Tahmasebi, A. (2006). Quality of life and well-being of women heads of households covered the area south of Tehran and its relationship with personal and family (pp. 8-35). Welfare and Rehabilitation Sciences.

16. World Bank (2011). World development report 2012: Gender equality and development. Washington, DC: The World Bank.

Part V
Economic Burden of Diseases

13

Vector Borne Diseases in Kerala: An Analysis of Economic Burden at Family level

K. Anitha

Those golden days
The perfect way
Let us-(s) pray
The mess today! – Reiter

Vector Borne Diseases (VBDs) are illnesses caused by infectious microbes that are transmitted to people by arthropods. They have long impacted human affairs and remain influential to this day. VBDs affect all countries, claim lives and put stress on the health systems of all economies. VBDs have not only adversely affected the health of the people in a region but also impeded over all socio-economic development (La Beaud AD and Aksoy S, 2010). They have emerged as a substantial public health concern leading to serious social and economic costs. Over the 17th through the 20th century, human morbidity and mortality due to VBDs outstripped that from all other causes combined (Gubler, 2018)). At present VBDs account for more than 17 percent of all infectious diseases, causing more than 7,00,000 deaths annually. They continue to be a major public health concern throughout the tropical and subtropical regions of the world (WHO, 2020). The economic and public health impacts of VBDs are looming despite the fact that most of these diseases are preventable through protective measures and community mobilisation.

Multitudinous VBDs are prevalent in India. In India, the challenge VBDs pose is serious because the increase in geographic distribution of vectors and VBDs have the potential to affect 90 percent of the population (WHO, 2014). The major VBDs prevalent in India are Malaria, Filariasis, Dengue, Chikungunya, Kala-azar and Japanese Encephalitis. People suffer from a significant disease burden from these diseases in local and focal areas of India, which is reflected in the form of morbidity and mortality (NVBDCP, 2020). Malaria, dengue and other VBDs were estimated to account for 1.6 percent of India's total disease burden (WHO, 1998). VBDs represent a substantial burden in many low and lower middle income countries, including India. They result in loss of productivity, school absenteeism, deeper impoverishment, higher health care costs and subsequent burden in public health services (WHO, 2014).

In India, about 95 percent population resides in malaria endemic areas and 80 percent of malaria reported is confined to areas consisting 20 percent of population residing in tribal, hilly, difficult and inaccessible areas (NVBDCP, 2020). Dengue has been very common in India since the last two decades. It can affect everybody irrespective of their age and gender (www.nhp.gov.in). The global picture of dengue in India is currently that of an endemic country (Chakravarti et al, 2012). India experiences cyclic epidemic of dengue over the years and the infection imposes for the leading cause of hospitalisation and death among children in the country (www.searo.who). The problem of under reporting of dengue cases from India has come into focus recently and validated that the real burden of dengue in the country is heavily ignored (Shepard et al, 2014). Conjointly, filariasis, kala-azar, Japanese encephalitis and chikungunya are posing hazards to the health scenario in the country.

Kerala has been under the threat of VBDs for quite a long time. Traditional ones like malaria and filariasis have been wiped out or brought under control by successful governmental interventions. But later years witnessed the re-emergence of a number of the traditional variety. The last few years have made Kerala a showcase of heterogeneous breeds of VBDs and contributed substantially to the morbidity and mortality of the state. Over the recent years, some of the VBDs like dengue have assumed such alarming proportion making it difficult for the public authority to combat these diseases. The major burden of VBDs in Kerala comes from dengue; a situational analysis of dengue in Kerala over the last few years reveals that the state has been recording accelerated incidence of dengue cases.

VBDs thus remain a major public health concern in the country and particularly in the state even then, there is a gap in research on the impact of VBDs. The estimation of the economic burden imposed by these diseases can be evaluated by estimating the cost of treatment of illness. An accurate estimation of the cost of illness is essential in the formulation and prioritisation of policies in the health sector and allocation of resources to the sector. Cost of illness measures medical and other costs resulting from a specific disease or condition. This provides decision makers information on the economic burden of a disease, which offers a sense of how big the problem is. The determination of the cost of illness tells us how much the society is spending on a particular disease and by implication the amount that would be saved if the disease were abolished and identifies the different components of cost (Byford et al). A number of studies has illustrated that much of the burden of ill-health falls on households. The households have to bear the soaring treatment cost on VBDs and that appears as a domain of distress. The present study employs unit level data for Kerala from the NSS 71st round on health to analyse the cost of treatment of VBDs in Kerala. It is complemented by assessing the impact of dengue in Thiruvananthapuram district of Kerala by focusing on individuals with clinically confirmed dengue and their families.

WHO recognises health as a fundamental right to be enjoyed without distinction of race, religion, political belief, economic or social condition (www.who.int) and this rightly includes availability, accessibility, acceptability and quality as its core components. Historically, the Indian commitment in tune with this right perspective relied on two principles- state responsibility for health care and free medical care for all. But with advocacy to reduce the role of state in health, people have been forced to switch to expensive private provisions of care (niti.gov.in). Particularly in Kerala, the public health care system was at the helm in the provision of care due to its intrinsic characteristics like high quality, low cost etc. But of late, public facilities exhibit a tendency of non-delivery and accordingly more preference is shown towards private provision of health care. The present study also probes into the cost differences associated with both providers of care to comprehend and compare the burden each provider imposes on the VBD afflicted in the state and in Thiruvananthapuram district.

The present study employs unit level data from NSS 71st round on health to estimate the cost of VBDs in Kerala, specifically the data is analysed to get at the cost differences of VBD treatment between public and private providers of care. Besides, the study focuses on dengue afflicted in Thiruvanthapuram district by collecting data from the infected and compares the cost differences in public and private care settings.

Methods

The first section of the study draws data from NSS unit level data pertaining to Kerala from the 71st round on Social Consumption: Health, 2014. The NSS data consists of information on the cost of treatment of VBDs as divulged as total expenditure for hospitalisation during the last 365 days. Majority of reported VBDs require hospitalisation. VBDs are the most common cause of febrile illness in hospitalised patients in India (Robinson et al, 2018). Hence the hospitalisation details of VBD afflicted have been utilised for the analysis. Further, the 71st round laid special emphasis on medical treatment received as inpatients of medical institutions during the last 365 days and expenses thereof. Any ailment reported for the last 15 days and expenses only for inpatients of medical institutions were considered in the NSS survey. The legitimate perception of the cost of VBD treatment could only be recognised by taking the reference period of last 365 days as it gives an accurate comprehension. The providers of care were branched as public and private providers. For each, the components of cost were isolated as medical and non-medical. Medical expenditure of treatment comprised of items like package component, doctor's fee/surgeon's fee, medicines, diagnostic tests, bed charges and medical expenses such as attendant charges, physiotherapy, personal medical appliances, blood, oxygen etc. Non-medical expenditure included transport for patient and other non-medical expenses incurred by the households on food, transport for others, expenditure on escort, lodging charges etc. Average cost incurred for VBDs was calculated in both the settings and total average cost was arrived at accordingly.

The study on the cost of dengue was compiled from the dengue affected in Thiruvananthapuram district in 2014 by cleaving cases as those seeking hospitalised care and ambulatory care and is presented in Section II of the present study. Treatment of dengue many a times requires hospitalisation because of the severity of the disease. For diagnosis and disease monitoring, patients visit ambulatory care also. The present study used patient level data to calculate costs of hospitalised as well as ambulatory treatment of dengue inflicted in Thiruvananthapuram district. The data source was the State Surveillance Unit, Integrated Disease Surveillance Project, Directorate of Health Services, Kerala. Adopting stratified random sampling, the dengue affected in the district were delineated as public care seekers and private care seekers. Systematic random sampling technique was wielded to select from both kinds of care seekers and the sample of public care seekers were identified as 210 and that of private care seekers, 90. Costs of treatment for hospitalisation were segregated under the heads:

- Medical expenses whose components were doctor's fee/registration fee, costs of medicine, cost of diagnostic tests, room rent, cost of medical devices, costs on blood, oxygen etc, food and other materials and other medical expenses which were incurred on the patient during hospitalisation. For treatment after discharge, the cost expended on doctor's fee/registration fee, diagnostic tests and medicines and any other medical expenses were considered as medical expenses.
- Non-medical or other expenses which covered elements like transportation charges during hospitalisation and follow up treatment, lodging, other food charges of escorts and other expenses allocated for non-medical components.

The average charges per hospitalisation were calculated separately for public and private hospitals considering all these ingredients and finally, the average cost for treatment for dengue in hospitalised environment was arrived at.

The cost components of ambulatory care too were cut off into medical and non-medical expenses. The medical items of expenditure were composed of medical items included in hospitalisation except room rent, blood, oxygen and other medical items. The non-medical constituent had only one element, transportation cost.

To arrive at the average cost of dengue in Thiruvananthapuram district, the indirect cost of dengue was added to the cost on hospitalisation and ambulatory care. Indirect cost was defined as the value of patient's or family members' days lost or adversely affected by the illness.

Results

(1) Source of treatment

Table 13.1 presents the distribution of VBDs in Kerala between public source and private source of Kerala. The vast majority of vector borne affected in Kerala that is 66.2 percent, relied upon private sources of care for treatment. This goes perfectly in tune with the tendency of the population to rely on private sources of care.

Table 13.1: Distribution of respondents by source of care

Source of care	*Number*	*Per cent*
Public	147	33.8
Private	288	66.2
Total	435	100

Source: Computed from Unit Level Data, NSS, 71st round

(2) Treatment costs of VBDs

Table 13.2: Average cost incurred on vector borne diseases

Components	*Cost per source of care (in Rs.)*		
	Public Hospital	*Private Hospital*	*All Hospital*
Package component	493.33	8426.32	7344.55
Doctor's fee/surgeon's fee	228.57	1177.92	1153.39
Diagnostic tests	336.85	1033.93	889.63
Bed charges	590.95	1615.48	1540.52
Other Medical expenses	167.25	1411.87	1160.25
Total average medical expenditure	849.07	7406.62	5672.32
Transport for patient	288.42	359.51	334.45
Other non-medical expenses	655.46	797.21	749.24
Total average cost	1437.78	8320.37	5994.53

Source: Computed from Unit Level Data, NSS, 71st round.

Table 13.2 presents the average expenditure on VBDs per hospitalisation in public care settings vis-a-vis the private care settings. It can be seen that, for hospitalised treatment of VBDs, more amounts were spent by patients in private hospitals (Rs 8320.37) than in public hospitals (Rs 1437.78). In fact, the total average treatment cost in private hospitals was 5.8 times greater than the cost in public hospitals. The greatest difference could be observed in the medical component of treatment, in a private hospital a VBD afflicted have to bear Rs 849.07 as medical expenditure whereas Rs 7406.62 had to be expended for the same component in a government hospital - the difference being 8.7 times. The difference in cost of treatment spent on non-medical constituents between the providers was inconsiderable compared to the medical overheads. Overall, an average of Rs 5994.53 was spent by VBD afflicted for treatment on hospitalisation in 2014.

Burden of Dengue at the family level

The household cost of dengue was categorised into direct and indirect costs. The direct costs comprised the expenses incurred on the treatment of the disease while the indirect cost is the economic value lost by households due to illness and productivity loss to household members and caretakers.

(1) Cost of Hospitalised Treatment

Data collected from dengue infected in Thiruvananthapuram conveys that of the sample of 300, 221 patients were hospitalised (73.7 percent) while the rest 79 (26.3 percent) sought outpatient care. Another striking contradiction against the general trend was that 70 percent of the inflicted sought care from public providers. This is on the ground that surveillance system captures mainly data from the public sector.

On an average, a hospitalised dengue patient spent Rs 5987.15 for hospitalisation. Of this, 81 percent was spent on the medical component of hospitalisation. The cost comparison between public and private hospitals reveals that the expenses in the latter were six times more than the former. On all components of expenditure, the private health care seeker had to expend more than the public care seeker. The maximum spent on private hospitals was on room rent. Certain items like doctor's fee/registration fee and medical devices were absent for the public seeker of care. Between medical expenses and non-medical expenses in public and private hospitals, the treatment cost differences were 6.6 times and 5.2 times respectively.

Table 13.3: Average cost of hospitalization for dengue patients

Items of expenditure	*Average expenditure incurred in*		
	Public Hospital	*Private Hospital*	*All Hospitals*
Medical expenses			
Doctors fee/Registration Fee	0	302.52	79.39
Medicines	228.13	1470	554.05
Diagnostic tests	212.5	1199.95	471.65
Room rent	245.83	7719	2207.11
Medical devices	0	64.29	16.87
Blood, Oxygen etc	104.17	554.76	222.42
Food and other materials	1171.88	1376	1225.49
Other medical expenses	0	285.71	74.98
Total Medical Expenses	1962.51	12972.42	4851.99
Non Medical expenses			
Transportation charges	319.79	2280.91	834.47
Lodging and food Charges of escorts	214.53	542.86	300.69
Total non-medical charges	534.32	2823.71	1135.16
Total average charges for hospitalization	2496.83	15796.13	5987.15

Source: Primary data

(2) Cost of Ambulatory care

The average amount spent for outpatient treatment of dengue in Thiruvananthapuram district was Rs 1751.35. The average expenses in public hospitals was Rs 1203.34 and in private hospital, Rs 2556.25. The cost difference was about two times. The maximum inequality was observed in the medical component; between public and private hospitals the disparity was 2.4 times.

Table 13.4: Average cost of ambulatory care for dengue patients

Items of expenditure	*Average expenditure incurred in*		
	Public Hospital	*Private Hospital*	*All Hospitals*
Medical expenses			
Doctors fee/Registration Fee	0	225	91.14
Medicines	166.67	725	392.83
Diagnostic tests	90	425	225.69
Medical devices	0	93.75	37.97
Food and other materials	650	712.5	675.32
Total Medical Expenses	906.67	2181.25	1422.96
Non Medical expenses			
Transportation	296.67	375	328.39
Total average expenses for ambulatory case	1203.34	2556.25	1751.35

Source: Primary data

(3) Indirect cost of Dengue

Indirect cost covered days lost at work or school both by the sick and the care givers. Table 13.5 presents estimates of indirect cost of dengue. More days were lost when care was obtained from a public provider. It was found that a student lost 7.6 days and 6.8 days of school in case of seeking public and private care respectively. Comparison of days of work lost for the dengue patients between public and private care seeker revealed that those who sought public health care lost an average of 9.43 days of work and those who approached private providers lost 7.4 days of work. The loss of work days for the care taker was 2.99 days and 1.9 days respectively for the public seeker and private seeker.

Table 13.5: Average Loss of school/work days for dengue patients

Category of patients	*Average loss of days for*		
	Public Seeker healthcare	*Private health care seeker*	*All*
Student	7.6	6.8	7.2
Adult	9.43	7.4	8.82
Caregiver	2.99	1.9	2.6
Total	6.67	5.37	6.23

Source: Primary data

The average loss of income due to dengue infection as reported by the respondents was calculated as Rs 15588.08. These income losses were reported only by the public health care seeker only.

(4) Economic burden of Dengue at the family level

The costs of dengue for hospitalisation, ambulatory care and indirect costs were added to arrive at the economic burden of dengue at family level. Combining all costs, the average cost of treatment of dengue in Thiruvananthapuram district was calculated as 8850.10.

Table 13.6: Average Total cost incurred by dengue patients

Components	*Average cost incurred in*		
	Public Hospital	*Private Hospital*	*All Hospitals*
Medical cost			
Hospitalised care	1962.51	12972.42	4851.99
Ambulatory care	906.67	2181.25	1422.96
Total average medical cost	2869.18	15153.67	6274.95
Non-Medical cost			
Hospitalised care	534.32	2823.71	1135.16
Ambulatory care	296.67	375	328.39
Total Average Non-medical cost	830.99	3198.71	1463.55
Indirect cost	1588.08	0	1111.60
Total average cost	5288.25	18352.38	8850.10

Source: Primary Data

Table 13.6 reveals that wide discrepancies could be noticed in all the costs between government and private hospitals. The total average cost in government facilities was Rs 5288.25 which included direct cost of Rs 3700.17 and indirect cost of 1588.08. Cost of dengue treatment in private hospitals involves an average sum of Rs 18352.38 which was around 3.5 times higher than the cost in government hospitals.

Contrasting the cost differences between public and private hospitals, medical costs were 5.5 times larger in private hospitals. Tremendous difference was observed in hospitalised care in this respect; medical costs in private hospitals were more than five times than that in government hospitals. In case of hospitalised care, non-medical component of cost too was larger than the cost borne in public hospitals.

Discussion

The present study endeavoured to appraise the cost of VBD in Kerala and dengue in Thiruvananthapuram district and weigh the cost borne by the ailing in the public sector against the private sector providers of care.

The sick in Kerala count more on private providers of care for the treatment of VBDs and private facilities dominate the health care services, even with improved quality of services at public sector. It has been argued that private facility offer lesser waiting time and speedy service delivery (Musinguzi, 2013). This reiterates that affordability and physical access to health care in less developed countries should also include a focus on emotional dimensions of utilisation (Ergler et al, 2011). The high non-medical expenses in the present study vouchsafe this finding.

For VBDs in Kerala, people spent a hefty amount on the medical components particularly in the private care settings. The medical component absorbs 90 percent of total cost in private hospitals and 59 percent of total costs in public hospitals. Persons seeking care from public hospitals had to spent more amounts than the private care seeker in transportation, food, lodging charges of both the patients and care givers. This proves that the persons seeking care in public hospitals are from far off places whereas inpatient health care facilities are mostly located in towns and cities.

Overall, private hospital in-patients experience higher total costs than those treated in public hospitals. The cost in private hospitals is about six times larger than that of the public hospitals. The cost comparison in all the components between public and private hospitals discloses that in all the ingredients of costs, a patient had to pay more amounts in a private hospital than if he were in a public hospital. The highest difference could be observed in the package component; the difference was to the tune of 17 times. Apart from medical expenses, a public care seeker had to spend the maximum amount on other non-medical expenses implying amounts expended on food, transport for others, expenditure on escort, lodging charges etc. The absolute difference in this regard of both the sectors is small. But for the public seeker this is huge and reinforces that for person seeking care in public hospitals, escort charges occupy a major portion of the total costs. Other charges involved in medical treatment between the two providers of care too significantly differ, which amounts to 8.4 times in the private hospitals. Altogether, private hospital in-patients experience higher total cost for treatment of VBDs than those treated in public hospitals. The cost of treatment in private hospitals was about six times the cost in public hospitals. The total average cost on the treatment of VBD was estimated at Rs. 5994.53. Comparing this to the per capita monthly income of Kerala in 2014, which was Rs. 8652, the burden imposed by VBDs on households, appears enormous- it consumes 70 percent of the monthly income. Given the low income of the population, this may result in people receiving in adequate treatment or no treatment at all, particularly for the poor who spent relatively more of their income on health.

The dengue infected in Thiruvananthapuram district were examined in the present study. About three fourth of them had to resort to hospitalised treatment which goes against the usual trend of relatively high rate of utilisation of outpatient services in Kerala (Levesque et al, 2006). This could be due to the severity of the disease as severe dengue often requires hospitalisation (www.cdc.gov).

The average total cost of treatment of dengue in Thiruvananthapuram district was found out as Rs. 8850.10 including direct and indirect costs of both hospitalised and ambulatory care in public and private hospitals together. Cost of treatment in private hospitals was about 3.5 times bigger than the cost spent on government hospitals. With higher inclination towards private providers of care in the state, such huge sums on treatment could be catastrophic. It could invigorate the poverty ill-health link. Provided that the private sector complied with accurate data recording of dengue infection, the cost of treatment on dengue would have been far greater than the one that had been estimated in this study.

The up-scaled average cost for dengue is mainly contributed by the medical cost incurred in private hospitals or hospitalisation. Non-medical costs in all settings were meagre. The indirect cost of dengue, that is number of days lost, were more for the public health care seeker emphasising the cost aspect involved in private in-patient health care seeking. The proposition evolved from the study that none of the private care seekers reported loss or diminution of income due to dengue, proposes that care from private hospitals might have been sought by the well-off section of the society.

A disease of the magnitude of dengue imposes heavy burden on households. It consumed about 87 percent of the average per capita monthly income. Gravity is added to this, when the fact is taken into consideration that the national surveillance system in the country captures only 0.35 percent of annual number of clinically diagnosed cases in India and for each reported case, 282 clinically diagnosed dengue cases actually exist (Shepard et al, 2014). If such an estimate is taken into account the total cost of dengue treatment in the state could present a distressing picture.

The present study captures the VBD scenario in Kerala with special attention to dengue in Thiruvananthapuram district. The cost difference between public provider of care and private provider of care is apparent from the study. High cost of treatment imposes heavy burden on the households, more so for those households relying on private sources of care. VBDs though universal, disproportionately affect the poorest population (Valenzuela et al, 2018). The care obtained from the private hospitals could put a regressive burden on poor households and drag them to a poverty trap. In the extreme situation this can even prevent them from accessing proper care and jeopardise the health for all agenda. This calls for effective intervention by the government to ensure a health care system which is available, accessible, acceptable and of good quality. The state has to remain in mainstay for wider access to health care for all without undue burden.

References

1. Anita Chakravarti, Rohit Arora, Christine Luxemburger, Fifty Years of Dengue in India. Transactions of the Royal Society of Tropical Medicine & Hygiene, Volume 106,Issue 5, May 2012, pp. 273-282
2. Conard Musinguzi , Patient waiting time and associated factors at the Assessment Center, General out-patient Department Mulago Hospital Uganda, https://www.researchgate.net/publication/271726117
3. D.S. Shepard, Y.A. Halasa, B.K. Tyagi, S.V. Adhish, D. Nandan, K.S. Karthiga, *et al.* **Economic and disease burden of dengue illness in India**Am J Trop Med Hyg, 91 (6) (2014), pp. 1235-1242
4. Ergler CR, Sakdapolrak P, Bohle HG, Kearns RA. Entitlements to health care: why is there a preference for private facilities among poorer residents of Chennai, India? *Soc Sci Med.* 2011; 72(3):327-337. doi:10.1016/j.socscimed.2010.09.042
5. Gubler DJ. Resurgent vector-borne diseases as a global health problem. Emerging Infectious Diseases. 1998; 4(3):442–450.
6. https://niti.gov.in/planningcommission.gov.in/docs/reports/genrep/bkpap2020/26_bg2020.pdf
7. https://www.nhp.gov.in/dengue-fever_pg
8. https://www.who.int/mediacentre/news/statements/fundamental-human-right/en/
9. Jean-Fre´ DE´ Ric Levesque, Slim Haddad, Delampady narayana Pierre Fournier, Outpatient care utilization in urban Kerala, India,, *Health Policy and Planning*, Volume 21, Issue 4, July 2006, Pages 289–301.
10. Jesus g Valenzuela and Serap Aksoy, Impact of vector biology research on old and emerging neglected tropical diseases, Plos Negl Trop Dis,2018 May, 12(5)
11. LaBeaud AD, Aksoy S.Neglected funding for vector-borne diseases: a near miss this time, a possible disaster the next time. PLoS Negl Trop Dis. 2010 Oct 26; 4(10): e847.
12. Matthew L. Robinson, Dileep Kadam, Sandhya Khadse, Usha Balasubramanian, Priyanka Raichur, Chhaya Valvi, Ivan Marbaniang, Savita Kanade, Jonathan Sachs, Anita Basavaraj, Renu Bharadwaj, Anju Kagal, Vandana Kulkarni, Jonathan Zenilman,George Nelson,Yukari C. Manabe,Aarti Kinikar,Amita Gupta

and Vidya Mave , Vector-Borne Disease is a Common Cause of Hospitalized Febrile Illness in India, Am. J. Trop. Med. Hyg., 98(5), 2018, pp. 1526–1533.

13. National Vector Borne Disease Control Programme (2020) Magnitude of the Problem accessed from nvbdcp.gov.in > Index4
14. Sarah Byford, David J Torgerson, James Raftery, Cost of Illness Studies, BMJ, V 320(7245),2000 May 13
15. WHO dengue fact sheet. http://www.searo.who.int/entity/vector_borne_tropical_diseases/data/data_factsheet/en/.
16. WHO. World Health Report 1998. Geneva, Switzerland: WHO; 1998.
17. World Health Organisation (2014) World Health Day 2014 Small Bite: Big Threat Vector-borne diseases in India, An analysis from a health systems approach.
18. World Health Organisation (2020) https://www.who.int/news-room/fact-sheets/detail/vector-borne-diseases
19. www,cdc.gov>dengue.symptoms

14

Extend and Depth of Catastrophic Health Care Expenditure due to Non Communicable Diseases in Kerala

Manju S. Nair & Manjusha P.

Within India, the state of Kerala is noted for its own unique pattern of development. With low levels of income, Kerala has achieved laudable progress in social development indicators. Regarding health, Kerala has achieved commendable progress, almost comparable to that of developed countries, the widely accepted health indicators like crude death rate, infant mortality rate, life expectancy evidence this. Hence, Kerala was held up to the world as a model of 'good health at low cost' implying that it was possible at low level of resources to achieve laudable health status, at least by measure of mortality and gross morbidity. Kerala became a model for the right kind of social policies to be pursued by developing societies which would ensure balanced and equitable development and steady improvement in health indices. However, even by 1984, serious doubt was being expressed as to the desirability of the Kerala model of health. Many surveys found that even though mortality was low in Kerala, the prevalence of morbidity was found to be quite high.

Kerala is now on the third stage of epidemiological transition since modern life style diseases are on the increase in the state (Navaneetham et al., 2009). Hence Kerala has to confront with the rising prevalence of non communicable diseases including diabetes, cancer and cardiovascular diseases. Added to this, road accidents/injuries in the state is showing an increasing trend in recent years. As per the NSSO surveys, Kerala has the highest share of out of pocket expenditure and catastrophic health expenditure among the states in India. The percentage of medical expenses to total monthly per capita expenses is as high as 9.75 and the percentage of medical expenses to total monthly per capita non food expenses is as high as 15.1 in Kerala for 2011-12. (Sinha, R.K. et al., 2014). These Figures are also reflected in the health financing data which shows that Kerala state has the highest private expenditure (90.3 percent) compared to any other state in India. (Kumar, A.K. et al., 2011) Since the relationship between out of pocket expenditure, non communicable diseases and catastrophic health expenditure has been long established (WHO, 2005), these findings are to be expected considering the high prevalence of non communicable diseases and their risk factors in the state. (Gupta, R. 2007; Thankappan, K.R. et al., 2010 and Sugathan, T.N. et al., 2008)

Catastrophic health care expenditure has been documented as the major cause of impoverishment for people suffering health shocks. The experience of catastrophic healthcare expenditure differs for people belonging to different socio-economic categories. Factors relating to the pre health shock period like being from lower socio economic status, past financial losses etc., factors relating to the event including diagnosis, expenditure for treatment and hospitalization and post event factors like loss of employment and distress financing determine the magnitude of catastrophe incurred. These factors determine the pathways to catastrophic health care expenditure and consequent poverty. Delving in to the trends of extent and depth of catastrophic health care expenditure over time across different asset groups and quantifying the incidence, intensity, becomes imperative to have a proper understanding of the whole scenario of catastrophic health care expenditure and its impact on living standards. The increasing prevalence of non communicable diseases in the disease pattern accentuates catastrophic health care expenditure spread over a long period of time. Tracking the pathways to poverty as a result of catastrophic health care expenditure from non communicable diseases requires evaluation over a span of time which needs micro panel data. This is necessary in order to facilitate an understanding of where and when the different strategies to address catastrophic health care expenditure are to be targeted. Based on this background, the article using micro panel data intends to unravel the extent and depth of catastrophic health care expenditure due to NCDS in Kerala

The rest of the paper is organized into five sections. Section one gives the objectives of the study and elaborates the methodology. Section two and three focuses on the expenditure details of households during the pre-health shock and health shock situation and section four provides an analysis of the extend and depth of catastrophic expenditure due to non-communicable diseases and section five provides the conclusions.

Section I: Objectives and Methodology of the study

1. To understand the extent and depth of catastrophic healthcare expenditure due to major health shocks (in terms of Non Communicable Diseases) over a span of time.
2. To understand how households financed health shocks and the extent of Distress Financing.

Methodology

The study intends to unravel the extent and depth of catastrophe and its effects on living standards. Non Communicable Diseases (NCDs) impose a greater burden on out of pocket expenditure and is considered as major health shock. Data shows that the out of pocket expenditure for a single hospital stay for a non communicable disease was nearly double than that of other health conditions. (World Bank, 2009) Expenditure incurred for cardiovascular diseases and major accidents/injuries is significantly higher compared to other non communicable diseases. It is a recognised fact that private medical expenditure is significantly higher than public medical care treatment, since the public sector subsidises the cost of treatment. Since non communicable diseases require major surgeries and lifelong monitoring and medication, availing facilities even from the public sector turns out to be catastrophic, particularly for the poor. The effect of medical care expenditure on living standards while availing treatment for NCDs from public sector is not examined in detail by the available literature and hence the researcher focuses on health expenses incurred by NCDs and resulting catastrophe while availing facilities from the public sector. Within non communicable diseases, the share of public sector hospital stays was highest for cardio vascular diseases and accidents/injuries (World Bank, 2009). Hence the researcher has selected two major non communicable diseases i.e. cardiovascular diseases and accidents/injuries to understand catastrophic health expenditure and its impact on living standards.

Within India, the state of Kerala stands apart because of the high human development status, particularly the health status as measured by indicators of mortality and fertility. However the morbidity prevalence in Kerala reported by all NSSO rounds is appalling since Kerala reveals the highest morbidity rate among Indian states. Kerala has the highest prevalence of cardio vascular diseases and stands first in the country in terms of accidents/ injuries. Added to this, the low public health spending and steep rise in health care costs especially for NCDs has put Keralaties under huge pressure. Moreover, even though public facilities are said to subsidise health treatment, availing care from tertiary level hospitals for NCDs involves lots of cost[12] (Ekbal, 2006). Thus, on the one hand Kerala is in the advanced stage of epidemiological transition which compounds the problems with NCDs like cardiovascular diseases and accidents/injuries becoming prevalent and on the other hand the rising cost of treatment has increased the catastrophic share of health expenditure. Kerala state was selected for understanding the different dimensions of catastrophic health expenditure considering the above said aspects.

Kerala's health care system in the public sector is divided into three levels, primary, secondary and tertiary levels. At the tertiary level there are five Medical Colleges located at Thiruvananthapuram, Alappuzha, Kottayam, Thrissur, and Kozhikode. Of the five Medical Colleges, Thiruvananthapuam Medical College is the first established and the largest multi specialty hospital in South Kerala having 3000 beds. The researcher has selected Thiruvananthapuam Medical College as the location for identifying samples.

Data

The study on the impact of catastrophic health care expenditure on living standards is based on micro panel data. In micro panel data, the same cross sectional unit is surveyed over time, hence it has space as well as time dimensions. By combining time series of cross section observations, panel data give 'more informative data, more variability, less collinearity among variables, more degrees of freedom and more efficiency' (Baltagi, 2005). Micro Panel data is better suited to study the dynamics of change and the researcher decided to collect micro panel data on the above said considerations.

Micro Panel data collected helps to understand the process and pathways by which people fall into catastrophic health care expenditure and its implication on quality of life and impoverishment as a result of health shock. Since non communicable diseases[13] completely or partially disables the sufferer and follows a lifelong cause of increasing dependency on the family, manifold impact can be understood only if the patients are continuously tracked. Micro panel data becomes justified in this scenario, data is collected from 120 patients, 60 belonging to cardiovascular disease category and 60 belonging to accidents/injuries category. Cardiovascular diseases and accidents/injuries were selected, since among the NCDs these are the two categories which have the highest prevalence rate. Also both these require prolonged hospital stay and cause the highest per capita out of pocket spending (NSSO, 2004). From the Cardiology Department of Medical College, 60 patients were selected by simple random method, from among the 200, who have succumbed to Myocardial Infarction (heart attack) and underwent medical intervention, in the form of angioplasty or bypass surgery September 2016.

Regarding accidents/injuries, discussion with Medical Officers revealed that orthopedic surgery becomes necessary for majority of the severe accidents/injuries cases. As per the advice of the orthopedic surgeons in Medical College, the researcher considered patients requiring orthopedic intervention due to accidents/injuries for analyzing the impact of catastrophic health expenditure on living standards. Out of the 200 patients who succumbed to accidents/injuries and underwent surgery and were admitted in the orthopedic unit one of Medical College during September 2016, 60 were selected, by simple random method for analysis.

The researcher met them two times, during the time of surgery and six months after discharge from hospital. Hence data pertaining to three points of time could be collected.

1. Data pertaining to the period before health shock - Pre Health Shock
2. Data at the time of health shock - Health Shock
3. Data after six months of discharge from hospital - Post Health Shock

Details regarding socio-economic conditions, health expenditure, conditions of quality of life etc. was collected using interview schedule.

Quantitative Techniques

1. Catastrophic Payment

The data required is at the household/individual level containing information on both health care payment (say H) and living standards. Living standards is also be measured by an "ability to pay" variable (say Y) such that,

Y = I - D (I), where I represents consumption expenditure and D (I) represents necessary or non-discretionary expenditure on items such as food.

The sample of households/individual is said to have incurred catastrophic payments on healthcare when the fraction, H/Y exceeds a pre-specified threshold, say Z. This sample of individuals represents the catastrophic payment headcount. Now we define an indicator E such that E=1 if / > Z and zero otherwise.

The catastrophic payment headcount which measures the extent of catastrophe is,

$$\text{HCR} = = \frac{1}{N}\sum_{i=1}^{n} \text{Ei}$$

where N is the sample size.

Incidence and intensity of catastrophic impact: (depth of CHCE)

Another measure, the catastrophic payment gap which reflects depth of catastrophe captures the average degree by which payments as a proportion of income exceeds the threshold, Z.

Now we define the excess or overshoot as = ((/)-Z), i.e. the amount by which the payment fraction / exceeds the catastrophic threshold Z.

The catastrophic payment gap is given by, $G = G = \frac{1}{N}\sum_{i=1}^{N} Oi$

Thus while H only captures the incidence of any catastrophe occurring, G also captures the intensity of the occurrence.

Section II: Expenditure details in the Pre-Health Shock Situation

Section II examines the pre-health shock situation of the households in terms of Monthly Per Capita Food Expenditure, Monthly Per Capita Non Food Expenditure, Monthly Per Capita Health Expenditure, Monthly Per Capita Expenditure and Catastrophic Health Care Expenditure.

Table 14.1: Monthly per capita expenditure details of Cardiovascular disease patients

		MPFE	*MPNFE*	*MPHE*	*MPCE*
APL	M	1048.36	1497.69	147.28	2546.05
	N	30	30	30	30
	SD	365.80	1245.20	110.84	1336.40
BPL	M	831.76	963.66	110.00	1795.42
	N	30	30	30	30
	SD	236.54	918.02	88.34	913.17
Rural	M	860.24	1405.02	552.50	2265.25
	N	40	40	40	40
	SD	287.74	1309.25	456.96	1390.71

(Contd...)

Urban	M	1099.71	881.98	610.00	1981.69
	N	20	20	20	20
	SD	342.07	373.09	291.36	634.23
Low	M	1019.00	748.67	260.00	1767.67
	N	4	4	4	4
	SD	496.39	402.58	84.85	898.97
Average	M	888.73	975.93	104.17	1864.67
	N	44	44	44	44
	SD	305.85	745.01	81.32	776.37
High	M	1101.96	2325.37	174.58	3427.33
	N	12	12	12	12
	SD	337.64	1717.25	130.57	1765.10
Total	M	940.06	1230.67	128.63	2170.73
	N	60	60	60	60
	SD	**322.09**	**1108.67**	**100.29**	**1187.63**

Note: MPFE- Monthly Per capita Food Expenditure, MPNFE- Monthly Per capita Non. Food Expenditure, MPHE- Monthly Per capita Health Expenditure, MPCE- Monthly Per capita Consumption Expenditure, M- Mean, N- Number, SD- Standard Deviation.

Source: Estimated from primary data.

The mean monthly per capita consumption expenditure of the cardiovascular disease patients before the onset of disease comes to Rs. 2170.73 of which 940.06 (43.31per cent) falls on food expenditure and 1230.69 (56.69 percent) falls on non-food items. There exist differences in Monthly Per Capita Expenditure on food and non food items between the sample based on place of residence, poverty level and asset classification. The Monthly Per Capita Expenditure on food and nonfood is Rs. 831.76 and Rs.963.66 for BPL and Rs. 1048.36 and Rs.1497.96 for their APL counterparts. The rural urban mean Monthly Per Capita Expenditure levels of food and non-food items for the cardiovascular disease patients are Rs.860.24, Rs.1099.71, Rs.1405.02 and Rs.881.98 respectively. Based on asset classification, the expenditure on non-food items is as high as Rs.2325.37 for the high asset group against Rs.748.67 and Rs.975.93 for the low and average group. Average monthly per capita health expenditure was Rs.147.28, Rs.110.00, Rs.552.50, and Rs.610.00 for the APL, BPL, rural, and urban categorization.

For the accidents/injuries patients also there exist differences between the groups based on all back ground characteristics. Their monthly per capita food expenditure, monthly per capita non-food expenditure, and monthly per capita consumption expenditure are Rs.873.82, Rs.715.15 and Rs.1588.97 respectively. The APL families have 22.11, 11.35, and 17.33 percent high consumption of food items, non food items and total items than their BPL counterparts, the corresponding percentages for the urban sample is 94.39, 112.13 and 102.37 as against the rural sample. Based on asset classification the high asset group have Rs.1234.00, Rs.1039.55 and Rs.2273.55 as their Monthly Per Capita Consumption Expenditure on food, non food and total items whereas for the lower asset group the values are Rs.657.17, Rs.481.07 and Rs.1138.24.

Table 14.2: Monthly per capita expenditure details of Accidents/Injuries patients

		MPFE	*MPNFE*	*MPHE*	*MPCE*
APL	M	1029.68	773.67	64.75	1803.35
	N	20	20	20	20
	SD	274.22	333.56	59.21	546.97
BPL	M	795.89	685.89	76.49	1481.78
	N	40	40	40	40
	SD	431.04	526.01	109.39	893.81
Rural	M	821.83	665.16	330.71	1486.99
	N	56	56	56	56
	SD	278.67	363.80	401.65	549.78
Urban	M	1601.67	1415.00	650.00	3016.67
	N	4	4	4	4
	SD	1157.30	1298.72	777.82	2456.02
Low	M	657.17	481.07	138.91	1138.24
	N	14	14	14	14
	SD	151.12	127.85	170.71	222.29
Average	M	858.03	716.07	52.35	1574.09
	N	36	36	36	36
	SD	434.30	543.37	49.09	909.30
High	M	1234.00	1039.55	52.50	2273.55
	N	10	10	10	10
	SD	248.08	265.80	31.12	331.38
Total	M	873.82	715.15	72.57	1588.97
	N	60	60	60	60
	SD	**397.03**	**466.45**	**94.66**	**800.02**

MPFE- Monthly Per capita Food Expenditure, MPNFE- Monthly Per capita Non Food Expenditure, MPHE- Monthly Per capita Health Expenditure, MPCE- Monthly Per capita Consumption Expenditure, M- Mean, N- Number, SD- Standard Deviation
Source: Estimated from primary data

Even before the onset of a chronic disease, a family may spend money on health treatment including preventive treatment, treatment of acute disease etc. If living standards are measured by monthly per capita consumption expenditure, ability to pay is obtained by subtracting non discretionary expenditure (food expenditure) from the consumption expenditure.

The average health expenditure incurred by the household as percentage of ability to pay is given in Table 14.3.

Table 14.3: Average health expenditure as a proportion of ability to pay - Pre Health Shock Period

	Cardiovascular disease			*Accidents/Injuries*		
	M	*N*	*SD*	*M*	*N*	*SD*
APL	15.10	30	14.62	13.68	20	20.04
BPL	23.27	30	26.32	18.39	40	23.85
Rural	17.76	40	23.16	15.56	56	20.84
Urban	22.03	20	17.87	34.44	4	46.65
Low	58.51	4	48.80	35.70	14	33.84
Average	17.69	44	18.27	12.48	36	15.74
High	11.57	12	7.86	6.04	10	4.14
Total	**19.18**	**60**	**21.32**	**16.82**	**60**	**22.42**

Note: M- Mean, N- Number, SD- Standard Deviation

Source: Estimated from primary data

On an average, patients who were affected later with cardiovascular disease (CVD) problem spend 19.18 percent of their non food income on health expenditure, for the BPL families it is 23.27 percent, for the urban families it is 22.03 and for the low asset category it is 58.51 percent. For the accidents/injuries patients, on an average they spend 16.82 percent of their non food income as health expenditure, the values for the BPL, urban and low asset group are 18.39, 34.44, and 35.70 percent respectively.

Catastrophic Health Payments in the Pre Health Shock Period

A sample of households is said to have incurred Catastrophic Payment on health care if health expenditure as a percentage of discretionary expenditure (H/Y) exceeds a pre specified threshold level say Z. We consider three pre specified threshold levels i.e., 20 percent, 30 percent and 40 percent.

Suppose an indicator E such that E=1, if H/Y exceeds Z and 0 other wise i.e.

Case I E=1, if H/Y > 20%, = 0 otherwise

Case II E=1, if H/Y > 30%, = 0 otherwise

Case III E=1, if H/Y > 40%, = 0 otherwise

Even before the onset of health shock, the cardiovascular disease households were spending 19.18 percent and the accidents/injuries households 16.82 percent of their discretionary income on health. Head count ratio at different catastrophic threshold levels shows that 100 percent of the low asset category of the CVD patients was spending more than 20 percent of discretionary income as health expenditure. The head count ratio at 20 percent threshold is 26.6 percent for APL, 3.3 percent for BPL, 25 percent for rural and 27.27 percent for average asset category. For the accidents/injuries patients the head count ratio is 20 percent for APL, 30 percent for BPL, 25 percent for rural, 50 percent for urban, 42.8 percent for low asset group and 5.56 percent for average asset group.

Table 14.4: Catastrophic head count and catastrophic health count ratio of respondents in the Pre Health Shock

	Cardiovascular disease				*Accidents/Injuries*			
	HC 20%	*HCR 20%*	*HC 30%*	*HCR 30%*	*HC 20%*	*HC R 20%*	*HC 30%*	*HC R 30%*
APL	8	26.67	2	6.67	4	20	2	10
BPL	10	33.33	8	26.67	12	30	6	15
Rural	10	25	8	20	14	25	6	10.71
Urban	8	40	2	10	2	50	2	50
Low	4	100	2	50	8	57.14	6	42.86
Average	12	27.27	8	18.18	8	22.22	2	5.56
High	2	16.67	0	0	0	0	0	0
Total	**18**	**30**	**10**	**16.67**	**16**	**26.67**	**8**	**13.33**

Note: HC20%, HC30% etc. implies Head Count at 20%, 30% threshold etc. respectively.

HCR 20%, HCR 30% etc. implies Head Count Ratio at 20%, 30% threshold etc. respectively.

Source: Estimated from primary data

Section III: Expenditure details in the Health Shock Period

As already mentioned, both the cardiovascular disease and accidents/injuries patients were admitted in Thiruvananthapuram Medical College during September 2016. The cardiovascular disease patients had myocardial infarction and medical intervention was done either as angioplasty or as bypass surgery. Both these interventions were costly. As for angioplasty, the stents that were implanted in the heart were to be brought from outside and bypass surgery involved costly investigation and operation. Regarding accidents/injuries patients, costly surgery was done in the orthopedic department and these patients had to remain in hospital for prolonged period of time. All these involved sudden financial shock for the household. Added to this, caretakers attending these people were not able to go for employment.

The economic costs of illness generally are divided into direct costs and indirect costs. Direct costs represent the value of resources used for detection & treatment of health impairment or its effect. Indirect costs represent the value of output lost due to illness.

Direct Costs

Direct costs of treatment include medical and non-medical components. Medical direct costs are related to diagnosis and treatment and include payment of doctor's fees, expenditure towards medicines, hospitalization charges and expenditure for pathological tests. Non-medical direct costs include transportation cost to health care, cost of special foods, lodging charges for other members accompanying and other expenses. Thus the direct cost of illness includes

1. Payment of doctor's fees
2. Expenditure towards medicines
3. Hospitalization charges
4. Expenditure for special food
5. Expenditure for pathological tests
6. Lodging charges (stay charges) for other members accompanying and
7. Other items

The various components of direct expenditure incurred by the respondents while availing treatment due to health shock and their relative share in total expenditure is analysed in Table 14.5.

Table 14.5: Direct cost of Health Shock

Item	*Cardiovascular disease*		*Accidents/Injuries*	
	BPL	***APL***	***BPL***	***APL***
Hospital charges *	700.0 (0.61)	1550.0 (1.05)	1000.0 (1.19)	1400.0 (1.19)
Room rent	436.0 (0.38)	1420.0 (0.96)	500.0 (0.60)	1200 (1.02)
Doctors fee/ registration fees	2000.0 (1.73)	4625.0 (3.12)	2250 (2.68)	3280 (2.78)
Payment to medicine	28262.8 (24.47)	36833.3 (24.84)	17000.0 (20.27)	19800.0 (16.79)
Pathological tests	20310.1 (17.59)	30733.3 (20.72)	13500.0 (16.10)	16200.0 (13.73)
Operation charges	48174.7 (41.72)	60080.0 (40.51)	38500.0 (45.91)	60250.0 (51.08)

(Contd...)

Cost of food	4703.3 (4.07)	4120.0 (2.78)	3110.0 (3.71)	6130.0 (5.20)
Transportation cost	1120.0 (0.97)	1073.3 (0.72)	1350.0 (1.61)	1370.0 (1.16)
Care taker's cost	5073.3 (4.39)	4673.3 (3.15)	3650.0 (4.35)	4470.0 (3.79)
Other expenditure	4700.0 (4.07)	3200.0 (2.16)	3000.0 (3.58)	3850.0 (3.26)
Total	**115480.2 (100.00)**	**148308.2 (100.00)**	**83860 (100.00)**	**117950 (100.00)**

Note: * Hospital charges implies tips/bribes given to nurses, attenders and all other charges incurred with in connection with hospitalization.

Source: Estimated from primary data

On an average, the BPL category in the cardiovascular disease group had to spend Rs.115480 for the health shock against Rs.148308 for their APL counterparts. The BPL section in the accidents/injuries group on an average spent Rs.83860 whereas the APL group had to spend Rs.117950. Operation charges form the major item of direct cost of health shock, followed by payment to medicine and expenses for pathological tests. Out of the total direct cost of health shock for the BPL group in cardiovascular disease group, 41.72 percent is as operation charges, 24.47 percent is as payment to medicine and 17.59 percent is for pathological tests. The corresponding values for the APL group are 40.51 percent, 24.84 percent, and 20.72 percent. In the accidents/injuries group the BPL category spent 45.91 percent, 20.27 percent and 16.10 percent for operation charges, payment to medicines and expenses as pathological tests respectively. The corresponding values for APL group are 51.08 percent, 16.79 percent and 13.73 percent respectively. Transportation cost formed around 1 percent and caretakers cost around 3.5 percent.

Indirect Costs

Indirect costs represent the value of forgone earnings from lost productivity including value of work loss of currently employed individuals and income loss of care takers.

Indirect cost = (Daily income of the sick person × No. of working days lost due to sickness) + (Daily income of care takers × No of working days lost due to care taking)

On an average, an amount of Rs.9822 and Rs.8655 is the monthly indirect cost of health shock. This includes loss of income of the respondent as he was unable to go to work and also the loss of income of the caretakers. The difference in indirect cost due to health shock according to background characteristics show that in the cardiovascular disease group, APL category lost Rs.11281, BPL Rs. 6741, rural category Rs.8598, urban Rs.10795, low asset category Rs.1700, average asset category Rs. 6856 and high asset category Rs. 15293. The corresponding values in the accidents/injuries group are Rs. 10376.67, Rs.6380.71, Rs.8982.42, Rs. 9265.24, Rs. 5556.19, Rs. 6068.63, and Rs. 15960.00. Definitely the indirect cost of illness is high for APL, urban and high asset group, since they used to earn more in the pre health shock situation.

Table 14.6: Monthly income lost due to Health Shock

	Cardiovascular disease	*Accidents/ Injuries*
APL	11281.82	10376.67
BPL	6741.03	6380.71
Rural	8598.04	8982.14
Urban	10795.24	9265.24
Low	1700	5556.19
Average	6856.14	6068.63
High	15293.33	15960.00
Total	**9822.22**	**8655.17**

Note: CVD- Cardiovascular disease, A&I- Accidents/injuries

Source: Estimated from primary data

Table 14.7: Source of financing medical expenditure during Health Shock

Item	*Cardiovascular disease*		*Accidents/ Injuries*	
	F	*Percent*	*F*	*Percent*
Own saving	24	40.0	16	26.7
Out of job income	22	36.7	16	26.7
Borrowing from friends and relatives	26	43.3	42	70.0
Borrowing from institutions and money lenders	30	50.0	38	63.3
Sold/pledged property/ornaments	32	53.3	44	73.3
Donations from NGO's/ charitable institutions	2	3.3		
Other source	2	3.3	2	3.3

Note: F- Frequency

Source: Estimated from primary data.

When experienced with a health shock, households try to mobilize their fund from different sources immediately. Selling or pledging ornaments and property form a major source of financing health shocks, (53.3 percent did so) fifty percent went for borrowing from institutions and moneylenders, whereas 43.3 percent borrowed from friends and relatives. Own saving, job income etc. are other form of mobilizing finance. In the initial period of health shock, families have not resorted to cutting down family expenditure.

Table 14.8: Amount of financing Health Shock

	OS	*OJI*	*BFR*	*BML*	*S/P P/O*	*C*	*NGO*	*Total*
Cardiovascular diseases								
BPL	19000 (15.89)	11550 (9.66)	1000 (0.84)	35500 (29.69)	34000 (28.44)	6000 (5.02)	12500 (10.46)	119550 (100.0)
APL	30000 (20.20)	6550 (4.41)	21250 (14.31)	52000 (35.02)	38700 (26.06)			148500 (100.0)
Accidents/Injuries								
BPL	3000 (3.28)	2300 (2.52)	8500 (9.30)	42500 (46.52)	32060 (35.0)	3000 (3.28)		91360 (100.0)
APL	15000 (12.61)	5140 (4.32)	12000 (10.09)	52310 (43.98)	3450 (29.00)			118950 (100.0)

Note: Figures in bracket denote percentage to total, OS- Own Saving, OJI- Out of job income, BFR- Borrowing from friends and relatives, BML- Borrowing from money lenders, S/P P/O- Sold/pledged property/ornaments, C- concession , NGO- Donations from NGO's/charitable institutions

Source: Estimated from primary data.

The average amount mobilized by the families for health shock financing is given in Table 14.8. Borrowing from money lenders and selling or pledging ornaments or property formed the major source of financing both for the APL and BPL category. The BPL category in the cardiovascular disease group met 29 percent and 28 percent of their finance from money lenders and by selling or pledging ornaments/property. The corresponding percentage for their APL counterparts is 35.02 percent and 26.06 percent respectively. Thus altogether 57 percent and 61 percent funds was distress financing. The APL families could mobilize 14.31 percent from friends and relatives. Non distress financing for the cardiovascular disease patients in the BPL group was 40.97 percent, whereas for the APL group it was 38.92 percent.

Regarding the accidents/injuries patients also the same trend is discerned, selling or pledging property/ornaments and borrowing from moneylenders form the major item of finance. The BPL families mobilized Rs.425000 and Rs.32060 from moneylenders and selling or borrowing assets respectively. The corresponding values for APL groups are Rs.52310 and Rs.34500 respectively. Non Distress Financing formed only 18.33 percent of the total for the BPL families and 27.02 percent for the APL families.

Health Insurance

Out of the total 70 BPL, 62 opined that they received concessions in treatment. Those who received concessions possessed Rashtriya Swasthya Bima Yojana (RSBY) health insurance card. They got concessions in medicine, lab & investigation and operation charges. The total insurance coverage under RSBY was only around Rs. 30,000. Many of the respondents had already availed this facility earlier and hence could use only lesser amount than Rs. 30,000 for this particular health shock. Regarding the APL patients, majority did not have any health insurance schemes. Only four government employees had taken health insurance policy of government.

Section IV: Catastrophic Health Care Payment: Extent and Depth in the Post Health Shock Period

This section enquires into the extent and depth of catastrophic health care payment in the post health shock period I. Post health shock period I is considered here as the period after six months of discharge from the hospital. The patients, both cardiovascular diseases category and accidents/injuries category were visited and details regarding their health expenditure, sources of meeting this expenditure, extent and depth of CHCE etc. were collected and this section provides the details of the analysis in the post health shock period I.

Table 14.9: Monthly cost of health care in Post Health Shock Period

	Cardiovascular disease		*Accidents/Injuries*	
	APL	*BPL*	*APL*	*BPL*
Cost of drug	4291.00 (58.75)	3151.67 (60.25)	3541.00 (41.43)	2780.00 (48.93)
Hospital charge *	1400.00 (19.17)	800.33 (15.30)	3350.00 (39.20)	1190.00 (20.95)
Food on hospitalized	280.00 (3.83)	260.00 (4.97)	295.00 (3.45)	462.50 (8.14)
Transportation	723.33 (9.90)	713.33 (13.64)	975.00 (11.41)	844.00 (14.86)
Others	610.00 (8.35)	305.67 (5.84)	385.00 (4.51)	405.00 (7.13)
Total	**7304.33 (100.00)**	**5231 (100.00)**	**8546 (100.00)**	**5681.5 (100.00)**

Note: * Hospital charges imply tips/bribes given to doctors, nurses, attenders and all other charges incurred in connection with hospitalization.

Source: Estimated from primary data

Main reason for financial burden is that health expenditure tended to be very high even after six months of health shock. The monthly health expenditure for the patient, both component wise and aggregate, which represents the direct cost of treatment is provided in Table 14.9.

Both for the BPL and APL group, expenditure incurred in procuring medicine is the dominant item. Within the six months of discharge from the hospital, these patients had to visit the hospital for checkup and investigation, this item, given in the table as hospital charge form the second major item of expenditure. In order to take these people to hospital, transportation charges are incurred which form the third component. On an average Rs. 7304.33, Rs. 5231, Rs. 8546, Rs. 5681.5 was spent respectively every month by cardiovascular disease APL, cardiovascular disease BPL, accidents/injuries APL, and accidents/injuries BPL respectively as expenses for health care.

Table 14.10: Employment status of the respondents in the Post Health Shock Period

	Cardiovascular disease		Accidents/Injuries	
	Frequency	**Per cent**	**Frequency**	**Per cent**
Yes	18	30.0	6	10.0
No	42	70.0	54	90.0
Total	**60**	**100**	**60**	**100**

Source: Estimated from primary data.

Table 14.10 shows that only 30 percent of the cardiovascular disease patients and 10 percent of the accidents/injuries patients have started going for employment. This involves financial distress on the households, since on the one hand the income generated by the respondents are nil or meager and on the other hand the expenditure is very high.

Continuous medical and related expenditure associated with the illness has had its effects on their living standards. The following section provides the details of the Monthly Per capita Food Expenditure (MPFE), Monthly Per capita Non Food Expenditure (MPNFE) and Monthly Per capita Health Expenditure (MPHE) of the sample respondents.

Table 14.11: Monthly per capita expenditure details of Cardiovascular disease patients in the Post Health Shock Period

		MPFE	MPNFE	MPHE	MPCE
APL	M	801.85	1983.05	1640.02	2784.89
	N	30	30	30	30
	SD	297.36	725.34	651.24	770.44
BPL	M	574.67	1759.60	1599.49	2334.27
	N	30	30	30	30
	SD	200.26	576.80	558.27	578.30
Rural	M	614.79	1935.84	1679.12	2550.93
	N	40	40	40	40
	SD	218.47	693.36	632.61	702.43
Urban	M	835.21	1742.29	1501.04	2577.49
	N	20	20	20	20
	SD	325.87	578.69	526.85	755.38
Low	M	900.25	1835.62	1656.87	2735.88
	N	4	4	4	4
	SD	328.45	983.76	759.26	1312.21
Average	M	617.03	1758.86	1558.70	2375.88
	N	44	44	44	44
	SD	239.73	584.49	568.89	614.39
High	M	878.79	2295.61	1831.25	3174.40
	N	12	12	12	12
	SD	300.80	760.91	719.34	598.94
Total	**M**	**688.26**	**1871.32**	**1619.76**	**2559.59**
	N	**60**	**60**	**60**	**60**
	SD	**274.58**	**653.84**	**596.35**	**707.47**

MPFE- Monthly Per capita Food Expenditure, MPNFE - Monthly Per capita Non Food Expenditure

MPHE- Monthly Per capita Health Expenditure, MPCE- Monthly Per capita Consumption Expenditure

M- Mean, N- Number, SD- Standard Deviation

Source: Estimated from primary data

Table 14.12: Monthly per capita expenditure details of Accidents/ Injuries patients in the Post Health Shock Period

		MPFE	MPNFE	MPHE	MPCE
APL	M	674.03	1915.57	1705.83	2589.60
	N	20	20	20	20
	SD	151.36	925.11	809.64	948.49
BPL	M	533.78	2410.99	2250.32	2944.77
	N	40	40	40	40
	SD	176.41	1321.34	3389.59	1214.2
Rural	M	525.45	1805.07	1627.31	2330.52
	N	56	56	56	56
	SD	175.92	1060.52	1023.33	1117.33

(*Contd...*)

Urban	M	1351.67	8416.67	8250.00	9768.33
	N	4	4	4	4
	SD	803.75	10818.73	10771.59	11622.48
Low	M	465.86	1892.69	1805.36	2358.55
	N	14	14	14	14
	SD	109.34	1860.69	1867.15	1922.88
Average	M	589.72	2294.81	2125.12	2884.53
	N	36	36	36	36
	SD	380.59	3465.46	3449.66	3792.64
High	M	708.00	2564.00	2235.00	3272.00
	N	10	10	10	10
	SD	108.20	814.66	753.66	829.91
Total	**M**	**580.53**	**2245.85**	**2068.82**	**2826.38**
	N	**60**	**60**	**60**	**60**
	SD	**308.37**	**2810.14**	**2792.69**	**3062.88**

MPFE- Monthly Per capita Food Expenditure, MPNFE- Monthly Per capita Non Food Expenditure, MPHE- Monthly Per capita Health Expenditure, MPCE- Monthly

Per capita Consumption Expenditure, M- Mean, N- Number, SD- Standard Deviation

Source: Estimated from primary data

The impact on living standards is first examined by examining the Monthly Per capita Consumption Expenditure, Monthly Per capita Non-Food Expenditure, and Monthly Per capita Food Expenditure of the sample households. The average Monthly Per capita Consumption Expenditure incurred by the cardiovascular disease patients, is Rs.2559.59, the Monthly Per capita Consumption Expenditure on food being Rs. 688.26 and Monthly Per capita Non-Food Expenditure being Rs. 1871.32. The corresponding amount for the accidents/injuries patients are Rs.2826.38, Rs.580.53 and Rs.2245.85 respectively. There exist differences between APL/BPL, rural/urban, low/average/high in food expenditure, non-food expenditure and total expenditure both in the case of accidents/injuries and cardiovascular diseases patients.

The MPNFE remains high for all background characteristics because of the very high health expenditure.

Average health expenditure as a proportion of ability to pay in the Post Health Shock Period

Health expenditure is said to be catastrophic when it exceeds a threshold percentage of discretionary income (which is the difference between total expenditure and food expenditure). This threshold is often taken as 10 or 20 percent, i.e., health expenditure is said to be catastrophic if it exceeds

10 percent or 20 percent of discretionary income. Analysis shows that health expenditure, forms a dominant share i.e., on an average as high as 86.22 percent for the cardiovascular disease patients and 89.93 percent for the accidents/injuries patients. The rural urban difference in this regard is insignificant, but a visible trend of increasing catastrophe is seen as we move from APL to BPL and from high asset group to average to low asset group. The APL group spends 82.14 percent and 89.34 percent (cardiovascular disease and accidents/injuries) and the BPL group spends 90.29 and 90.23 percent (cardiovascular disease and accidents/injuries) of their discretionary income as health expenditure. For the low asset group, the Figures are 92.46 percent and 92.93 percent for the cardiovascular disease and accidents/injuries patients respectively. Thus the discernable pattern emerging from the table is that a very dominant part of income is spend on health by all groups with increasing Figures for the households belonging to BPL and low asset groups, leaving virtually nothing for consuming other nonfood items.

Table 14.13: Average health expenditure as proportion of ability to pay in the Post Health Shock Period

	Cardiovascular disease			**Accidents/injuries**		
	Mean	**N**	**SD**	**Mean**	**N**	**SD**
APL	82.14	30	7.48	89.34	20	5.05
BPL	90.29	30	6.28	90.23	40	6.80
Rural	86.42	40	8.63	89.88	56	6.04
Urban	85.82	20	6.80	90.69	4	11.42
Low	92.46	4	8.19	92.93	14	5.56
Average	87.59	44	6.47	89.67	36	6.72
High	79.10	12	9.65	86.69	10	3.46
Total	**86.22**	**60**	**7.95**	**89.93**	**60**	**6.20**

Note: M- Mean, N- Number, SD- Standard Deviation

Source: Estimated from primary data

Catastrophic Health Expenditure: Extent

The extent of catastrophic health care expenditure captured by incidence is measured by Head Count Ratio (HCR) at different thresholds.

Household's incurring catastrophic health care payments at threshold levels 70 percent, 80 percent and 90 percent is given below. All the households spend more than 70 percent of their discretionary income for health care, hence the head count ratio at 70 percent is 100 percent. For the cardiovascular disease patients HCR is as high as 36.67 when the catastrophic rate is 90 percent whereas the corresponding Figure for accidents/injuries patients is 50. The HCR is 60 percent for BPL and 13 percent for APL at 90 percent threshold for cardiovascular disease patients whereas it is 50 percent for both categories for the accidents/injuries patients. For the asset category in the cardiovascular disease group, the HCR is 50 percent and 45 percent for the low and average group respectively, whereas it is zero for the high asset group. 57.14, 55.56 and 20 percent is the HCR for the accidents/injuries patients belonging to low, average and high asset group when 90 percent is considered the catastrophic threshold. Thus, it is striking to note that after six months of health shock, the families are finding it difficult to spend on any other non food item since health expenditure is carving away around 90 percent of the discretionary expenditure for more than 50 percent of the households.

Table 14.14: CHCE head count ratio at different thresholds for Cardiovascular disease patients in the Post Health Shock Period

	Cardiovascular Disease						
	N	*HC 70*	*HCR 70*	*HC 80*	*HCR 80*	*HC 90*	*HCR 90*
APL	30	30	100.00	20	66.67	4	13.33
BPL	30	30	100.00	30	100.00	18	60.00
Rural	40	40	100.00	32	80.00	16	40.00
Urban	20	20	100.00	18	90.00	6	30.00
Low	4	4	100.00	4	100.00	2	50.00
Average	44	44	100.00	40	90.91	20	45.45
High	12	12	100.00	6	50.00	0	0.00
Total	60	60	100.00	50	83.33	22	36.67

Note: N- Number, HC70, HC80, HC90 implies Head Count at 70%, 80%, 90% threshold levels respectively, HCR implies corresponding Head Count Ratio.
Source: Estimated from primary data.

Table 14.15: CHCE head count ratio at different thresholds for Accidents/ Injuries patients in the Post Health Shock Period

	Accidents/injuries						
	N	*HC 70*	*HCR 70*	*HC 80*	*HCR 80*	*HC 90*	*HCR 90*
APL	20	20	100.00	20	100.00	10	50.00
BPL	40	40	100.00	38	95.00	20	50.00
Rural	56	56	100.00	54	96.43	28	50.00
Urban	4	4	100.00	4	100.00	2	50.00
Low	14	14	100.00	14	100.00	8	57.14
Average	36	36	100.00	34	94.44	20	55.56
High	10	10	100.00	10	100.00	2	20.00
Total	60	60	100.00	58	96.67	30	50.00

Note: N- Number, HC70, HC80, HC90 implies Head Count at 70%, 80%, 90% threshold levels respectively, HCR implies corresponding Head Count Ratio.
Source: Estimated from primary data.

Catastrophic Health Expenditure: Depth

Catastrophic payment gap captures the intensity of catastrophe, it is the average degree by which payments as a proportion of income exceeds the threshold Z. Excess or overshoot is defined as = [(/Y_i) -Z] i.e., the amount by which the payment fraction exceeds the catastrophic threshold Z

The Catastrophic payment gap is given by

$$G = G = \frac{1}{N}\sum_{i=1}^{N} Oi$$

While H captures the incidence of any catastrophic occurring G also captures the intensity of the occurrence.

Catastrophic overshoot (Gap) at different threshold levels

Table 14.16: Catastrophic overshoot (Gap) at different threshold levels for Cardiovascular disease patients

		O30	O40	O50	O60	O70	080	O90
APL	M	52.14	42.14	32.14	22.14	13.30	6.66	0.25
	N	30	30	30	30	28	20	4
	SD	7.48	7.48	7.48	7.48	6.18	3.20	0.13
BPL	M	60.30	50.30	40.30	30.30	20.30	10.30	4.89
	N	30	30	30	30	30	30	18
	SD	6.28	6.28	6.28	6.28	6.28	6.28	2.28
Rural	M	56.42	46.42	36.42	26.42	17.50	9.70	4.34
	N	40	40	40	40	38	32	16
	SD	8.63	8.63	8.63	8.63	8.63	5.63	2.99
Urban	M	55.82	45.82	35.82	25.82	15.82	7.31	3.25
	N	20	20	20	20	20	18	6
	SD	6.80	6.80	6.80	6.80	6.80	5.20	2.38
Low	M	62.46	52.46	42.46	32.46	22.46	12.46	8.25
	N	4	4	4	4	4	4	2
	SD	8.19	8.19	8.19	8.19	8.19	8.19	0
Average	M	57.59	47.59	37.59	27.59	17.59	8.72	3.62
	N	44	44	44	44	43	40	20
	SD	6.47	6.47	6.47	6.47	6.47	5.60	2.52
High	M	49.10	39.10	29.10	19.10	11.76	7.22	0
	N	12	12	12	12	11	6	0
	SD	9.65	9.65	9.65	9.65	7.95	3.68	0
Total	**M**	**56.22**	**46.22**	**36.22**	**26.22**	**16.92**	**8.84**	**4.04**
	N	**60**	**60**	**60**	**60**	**58**	**50**	**22**
	SD	**7.95**	**7.95**	**7.95**	**7.95**	**7.08**	**5.49**	**2.77**

Note: O30, O40......O90 implies overshoot at catastrophic threshold levels 30%, 40%,...... 90% respectively, M- Mean, N- Number, SD- Standard Deviation

Source: Estimated from primary data

Table 14.17: Catastrophic overshoot (Gap) at different threshold levels for Accidents/Injuries patients

		O30	*O40*	*O50*	*O60*	*O70*	*O80*	*O90*
APL	M	59.34	49.34	39.34	29.34	19.34	9.34	3.60
	N	20	20	20	20	20	20	10
	SD	5.04	5.04	5.04	5.04	5.04	5.05	1.70
BPL	M	60.23	50.23	40.23	30.23	20.23	11.19	5.49
	N	40	40	40	40	40	38	20
	SD	6.81	6.81	6.81	6.81	6.81	5.44	2.89
Rural	M	58.88	49.88	39.88	29.88	19.88	10.54	4.58
	N	56	56	56	56	56	54	28
	SD	6.04	6.04	6.04	6.04	6.04	5.01	2.52
Urban	M	60.69	50.69	40.69	30.69	20.69	10.68	8.76
	N	4	4	4	4	4	4	2
	SD	11.43	11.43	11.43	11.43	11.43	11.42	0
Low	M	62.93	52.93	42.93	32.93	22.93	12.92	6.99
	N	14	14	14	14	14	14	8
	SD	5.55	5.55	5.55	5.55	5.55	5.55	2.85
Average	M	59.67	49.67	39.67	29.67	19.67	10.71	4.44
	N	36	36	36	36	36	34	20
	SD	6.71	6.71	6.71	6.71	6.71	5.22	2.02
High	M	56.69	46.69	36.69	26.69	16.69	6.69	.67
	N	10	10	10	10	10	10	2
	SD	3.46	3.46	3.46	3.46	3.46	3.46	0
Total	M	59.93	49.93	39.93	29.93	19.93	10.55	4.86
	N	60	60	60	60	60	58	30
	SD	6.20	6.20	6.20	6.20	6.20	5.29	2.65

Note: O30, O40……O90 implies overshoot at catastrophic threshold levels 30%, 40%,… 90% respectively, M- Mean, N- Number, SD- Standard Deviation

Source: Estimated from primary data

The depth of burden of disease as given from the table indicates that average catastrophic overshoot is as high as 56.22 percent for cardiovascular disease patients and 59.33 percent for accidents/injuries patients when 30 percent is considered as the threshold level. It means that when 30 percent is considered as threshold, on an average the cardiovascular disease household's spending on health exceeded 30 percent by 56.22 percent and for the accidents/injuries the excess percentage is 59.33 percent. The economic burden is disproportionately more for the economically backward category as the overshoot is higher for the BPL category against their APL counterparts, for all threshold levels, both for the cardiovascular disease and accidents/injuries households. Similarly the burden increases as one move from the high asset category to the low asset category at all threshold levels both for the cardiovascular disease and the accidents/injuries households. The overshoot is 62.46 percent, 57.59 percent and 49.10 percent respectively for the low, medium and high asset group in the cardiovascular disease category at 30 percent threshold level and the corresponding Figures are 62.93 percent, 59.67 percent and 56.69 percent for the accidents/injuries patients. The catastrophic overshoot is positive even at an extreme high threshold after their subsistence consumption is spent for meeting health expenditure. This definitely shows the intensity of catastrophic health expenditure.

Source of financing treatment expenses

96.67 percent of the cardiovascular disease and 80 percent of the accidents/injuries patients opined that they have reduced their family expenditure for mobilizing money for treatment expenses. Twenty percent of the cardiovascular disease patients have resorted to borrowing from institutions and moneylenders and also sold/pledged property and ornaments, whereas 56.67 percent of the accidents/injuries patients have borrowed from institutions and money lenders and 23 percent have sold/pledged ornaments.

Table 14.18: Source of financing expenses in the Post Health Shock Period I

Item	*Cardiovascular disease*		*Accidents/injuries*	
	F	*Per cent*	*F*	*Per cent*
Own saving	8	13.33	6	10
Out of job income	34	56.67	6	10
Borrowing from friends and relatives	4	6.66	10	16.67
Borrowing from institutions and money lenders	12	20	34	56.67
Sold/pledged property/ornaments	12	20	14	23.33
Cutting down or reducing any other family expenditure (food/education/housing/other)	58	96.67	48	80

Note: F- Frequency

Source: Estimated from primary data

Table 14.19: Amount of source of finance in the Post Health Shock Period I

Item	*Cardiovascular disease*			*Accidents/injuries*			*Total*		
	Mean	*N*	*SD*	*Mean*	*N*	*SD*	*Mean*	*N*	*SD*
OS	4220.00	8	1697.23	2233.33	6	2396.25	1198.86	14	1693.02
OJI	3949.77	34	2462.04	3310.00	6	2549.18	3853.80	40	2417.33
BFR	4000.00	4	2828.43	1920.00	10	898.33	2514.29	14	1703.36
BIML	5333.33	12	2089.66	9652.94	34	16103.50	8526.09	46	13905.11
S/PP/O	6500.00	10	1658.31	4771.43	14	2651.86	5491.67	24	2372.36
CDRFE	2517.99	60	1904.37	2521.63	48	1209.74	2519.61	108	1618.48

Note: M- Mean, N- Number, SD- Standard Deviation, OS- Own saving, OJI- Out of job income, BFR- Borrowing from friends and relatives, BIML- Borrowing from institutions and money lenders, S/PP/O- Sold/pledged property/ornaments, CDRFE- Cutting down or reducing any other family expenditure

Source: Estimated from primary data

The amount of mobilization of funds for treatment expenses during the first six months of discharge from hospital is given in Table 14.19. Borrowing from institutions and money lenders form the major item of source of finance. On an average, an amount of Rs. 9652.94 and Rs. 5333 was borrowed by accidents/injuries and cardiovascular disease patients respectively during the first six months of discharge from hospital. By selling or pledging property, an average amount of Rs. 6500 was mobilized by the cardiovascular disease patients and Rs.4771 by the accidents/injuries patients. Other major sources of funds include cutting down family expenditure.

Section V: Conclusion

The article examined the extent and depth of CHCE arising out of two NCDS. The experience of CHCE differs for people belonging to different socio economic categories and understanding the micro economic impact of CHCE requires panel data from people belonging to different socio economic categories affected with NCDs. As such, the researcher collected panel data from 120 patients admitted in the Thiruvananthapuram Medical College, 60 from the cardiology department and 60 from the orthopedic department. This is because the researcher has identified CVD and accidents/injuries as the two major NCDs in Kerala since both of these require long hospitalisation, protracted treatment and huge costs. All these patients were interviewed two times - during the health shock and after six months of health shock, hence data pertaining to three points of time were collected (a) data pertaining to the period before health shock - pre health shock, (b) data at the time of health shock - health shock, (c) data after six months of discharge from hospital - post health shock

Living standards is examined by the expenditure details of the households. Monthly Per Capita Consumption Expenditure (MPCE), Monthly Per Capita Food Expenditure (MPFE), Monthly Per Capita Non-Food Expenditure (MPNFE) and Monthly Per Capita Health Expenditure (MPHE) of the households before the onset of ill shock provides an understanding of the pre health shock situation of the households. On an average the CVD patients spent Rs. 940.06, Rs. 1230.67 and Rs. 128.68 as MPFE, MPNFE and MPHE in the pre health shock situation whereas the corresponding Figures for the accidents/injuries patients are Rs. 873.82, Rs. 715.15, and Rs. 72.57. The APL, urban and high asset group definitely have higher levels of food and non food expenditure. Even before the onset of health shock, the CVD patients spent 19.18 percent of their ability to pay (defined as monthly per capita consumption expenditure minus non-discretionary food expenditure) on health, the corresponding values for accidents/injuries patients was 16.82. It was the low asset group in the CVD group who spent 58.51 percent and in the accidents/injuries group which spent 35.70 percent on health. Any health expenditure greater than 20 percent of ability to pay is treated as catastrophe in literature. Even in the pre health shock situation, 30 percent of the CVD patients and 26.67 percent of the accidents/injuries group were incurring catastrophic health expenditure.

The economic cost (both direct and indirect) of the health shock is also examined. Direct costs are divided into hospital charges, room rent, doctors fee/ registration fees, payment to medicine, pathological tests, operation charges, cost of food, transportation cost, care taker's cost and other expenditure. The BPL group received concessions in registration fees, payment to medicine, pathological tests and operation charges, however for the particular illness episode the BPL CVD patients on an average spent Rs.115482 and the accidents/injuries patients an amount of Rs.117950 the corresponding values for the APL group are Rs.148308.2 and Rs.117950. The major components of direct health expenditure fell on operation charges, payment to medicine and pathological tests. Indirect cost is worked out as the value of forgone earnings from lost productivity including value of work loss of currently employed individuals and income loss of care takers. On an average there was an indirect loss of Rs.9822 for the CVD patients and Rs.8655 for the accidents/injuries patients.

The cost of NCDs is not limited to immediate health treatment, NCDs require protracted treatment and lifelong medication. This imposed severe financial stress on the households and the probability of health payment to be catastrophic among different socio economic categories tends to be very high. Per month, the APL CVD category had to spend Rs.7304 and BPL category Rs.5231 for health. The corresponding values for the accidents/ injuries patients were Rs.8546 and Rs. 3681 respectively. Expenditure on procuring medicines forms the major item of health expenditure. The MPFE and MPNFE net of health has declined in the post health shock period. The source of financing treatment expenditure is mainly cutting down family expenditure followed by borrowing from institutions and money lenders. Coping up strategies mainly focused on increase in debt, reduction of non food item, sale of jewels, land etc. To conclude, catastrophic health care expenditure due to major health shocks are driving people into poverty and deteriorating their quality of life. Breaking this vicious circle require concerted efforts from all stakeholders and involves reducing the likelihood that the event will take place, mitigating the deleterious impact on individuals and households due to health shock and helping households in coping up.

15

Burden of Non-Communicable Diseases in Kerala: An Analysis Based on Chronic Kidney Disease

Seena K.M

Every disease exerts a deep influence on the decision of infected households, the decision becomes traumatic in the case of Non-Communicable Diseases (NCDs) because NCDs affect individuals over an extended period of time with implications on huge health care costs cause socio-economic burden to the individual, family, and nation. As per WHO statistics 2017, NCDs kills 41 million people each year, equivalent to 71% of death globally and this throws light on the huge cost that NCDs inflict on global population. NCDs threaten progress towards the agenda for sustainable development which includes a target for reducing premature death from NCDs by one third by 2030(WHO, 2017). Chronic Kidney Disease (CKD) which is one of the major NCDs shows a rising trend during the last few decades (Bloom *et al.,* 2012). CKD may also be caused by the prevalence of other NCDs like diabetes, blood pressure etc. which elevate the seriousness of the disease (Thankappan *et al.* 2010; Couser *et al.* 2011) End Stage Renal Disease (ESRD) is treated either by dialysis or kidney transplantation. Dialysis involves using machines to filter out waste from the body and placing clean blood back to the body and transplantation involves removing the affected kidney and placing a functioning donated organ inside the body. Both these treatment processes are highly expensive and takes a long duration of associated medication. Along with the financial catastrophe resulting from treatment of CKD, daily life choice of the patients and their families are affected by the disease (Luyckx, 2018). Against this background, the study examines the dynamics of kidney transplantation arising from End Stage Kidney Disease with a particular focus on the economic implication and daily life. Kerala occupies the first rank in health index report published by NITI Ayog in 2018 and has a long tradition of well-established health system compared to all other states in India. However, Kerala has a high prevalence of lifestyle diseases like diabetes mellitus and hypertension which can cause some serious health damage to the population. According to the reports on disease burden profile of Kerala from 1990 to 2016, Chronic Kidney Disease (CKD) is the fourth major cause of death after heart disease, stroke, and suicide in Kerala (Institute for Health Metrics and Evaluation (IHME), 2018). The study focuses on End Stage Renal Disease patients in Kerala and tries to understand the burden of the disease, in terms of economic and non- economic cost.

The article is divided into three sections. First section deals with the objectives and methodology of the study. Section II analyses the economic burden of kidney transplantation and Section III analyses the source of income for transplant and other effects of transplantation.

Section I: Objectives and Methodology

Ojectives

1. To examine the direct and indirect cost of kidney transplantation associated with Chronic Kidney Disease
2. To understand the source of financing in relation to kidney transplantation and other costs

Methodology

The state of Kerala faces the highest prevalence of non-communicable diseases including cardiovascular diseases, cancer, chronic pulmonary disease, CKD etc. Two main risk factors identified for CKD are diabetes and hypertension and within the Indian state, Kerala tops the list in both these risk factors and is an indication of the high prevalence of CKD in the state. CKD may lead to complete failure of renal activities which is referred to as the End-stage renal disease. The two main treatment possibilities of ESRD are dialysis or kidney transplant, both demanding high financial cost. If the kidney transplant is opted, till the time of transplant, dialysis has to be continued draining the resources of the family. To understand the economic implications of CKD the researcher has selected ESRD and the medical solution of the kidney transplant, since this transplant involves cost of economic and non-economic dimensions including finding an available donor whose kidney matches the recipient, identification of hospitals where the surgery can be performed, mobilizing finance for the transplant, complication after the surgery, adjusting the changed situation both for the donor and recipient, follow up activities both medical and non-medical etc.

Kidney Federation of India (KFI) is an NGO which works with the aim of providing network and support for kidney transplantation in Kerala. They also engage in activities including spreading awareness regarding kidney and related diseases, kidney donation, and formation of kidney bank an initiative to gather people willing to donate their kidneys. It is understood that the majority of patients who are in need of kidney transplantation contact KFI and register their name for availing volunteer donors. However KFI has criteria for selecting the patients that they can support, the major criteria being socio-economic status. Discussions with the authorities of KFI reveal that only 30% of the needs of kidney transplantation are met by KFI. Others who are not receiving help from KFI find donors from their family or go for cross donation or go for paid donors and continue dialysis or in the worst case are not able to find any of these and meet with death. The researcher relied upon the data source available within KFI for selecting the samples. KFI was formed in the year 2009 and a total of 2617 people have registered with KFI for kidney transplantation during the 9 years. The researcher classified the years into 3 categories - those who are registered 3 years back, 3-6 years back and 6-9 years back each of the category forming 48%, 40 % and 12% of the total. Samples of fifty kidney transplant patients were selected applying the same proportion and hence 24, 20 and 6 kidney transplanted persons were selected randomly from their representative groups. An interview schedule was prepared based on review of literature, expert advice and current NGO reports. Questions on their socio-demographic profile, and disease details and health expenditure and impact of disease on their life were included. Donor's details were also included in the questionnaire. For obtaining secondary data, various journals and publications were used.

The economic cost of CKD and kidney transplantation is estimated by working out the direct and indirect cost.

Direct Cost

Direct cost I: Cost before transplantation which includes the cost of dialysis and lab/scanning charge

Direct cost II: Cost of kidney transplantation

(a) Medical expenditure which includes special package amount cost of drugs, and scanning charge

(b) Non-medical expenditure which includes the cost of room rent, cost of food and transplantation charge

Direct cost III: Current expenditure on treatment

Indirect Cost

Indirect cost I: It includes the salary lost because of illness

Section II: Economic Burden of Chronic Kidney Disease

This section analyses the expenditure incurred before kidney transplantation and the medical expenditure for transplantation. As a prelude, the initial symptoms and medical causes of Chronic Kidney Disease is also provided.

Initial symptoms of Chronic Kidney Disease

Chronic kidney disease (CKD) usually gets worse slowly, and symptoms may not appear until kidneys are badly damaged. In the late stages of CKD, as patients are nearing kidney failure, they may notice symptoms that are caused by waste and extra fluid building up in their body. This is because the body is able to cope up with a significant reduction in the kidney function.

Table 15.1 indicates the initial symptoms faced by people affected with chronic kidney diseases. Signs and symptoms may include fever, headache, muscle cramps, back pain, urine problems, swelling in feet and ankle, fatigue etc. Twenty percent of the respondents approached doctors with high fever and another 20 percent with recurring nature of headache. This is followed by nausea and vomiting, urine problem, swelling in feet and ankle. Feeling fatigue always is an important symptom that respondents experience as the disease progress.

Table 15.1: Initial Symptoms of Chronic Kidney Disease

Initial symptoms	*Frequency*	*Percent*
Muscle cramps	2	4
Fever	10	20
Nausea and vomiting	6	12
Back pain	4	8
Urine problem	6	12
swelling in feet and ankle	6	12
Headache	10	20
Fatigue	6	12
Total	50	100

Source: Primary Data

Causes of Kidney Failure

Medical studies show that the major causes of Chronic Kidney diseases which lead to end- stage renal disease are diabetes and blood pressure. Too much glucose, also called sugar, in blood damages kidneys' filters. Over time, the kidneys can become so damaged that they no longer do a good job filtering wastes and extra fluid from the blood. Often, the first sign of kidney disease from diabetes is protein in the urine. When the filters are damaged, a protein called albumin, which people need to stay healthy, passes out of blood and into the urine. A healthy kidney doesn't let albumin pass from the blood into the urine. High blood pressure can damage blood vessels in the kidneys so they don't work as well. It can also be caused by genetically and urinary tract problems. Heavy doses of some medicines like painkillers, drugs for leptospirosis can also damage the kidney.

Table 15.2 examines the major causes reported among the patients who were treated for the CKD. 40 percent of the respondents were having high blood pressure which is followed by 36 percent with diabetic problems. CKD is prevalent among respondents who took painkillers or some other heavy dose medicines. For some, it happened genetically as there were some CKD patients in their lineage.

Table 15.2: Causes of Kidney Disease

Causes	*Frequency*	*Percent*
Blood pressure	20	40
Diabetes	18	36
Genetic	2	4
Urinary tract problem	2	4
Medicinal impact	8	16
Total	50	100

Source: Primary Data

Total Amount Spent Before Transplantation

Table 15.3 examines the average of the total amount spent on medical treatment for chronic kidney disease before renal transplant. The average value of total medical expenditure for the sample prior to kidney transplantation is Rs. 1,45,200. Initial treatment for CKD includes expensive dialysis which costs above Rs.1000 for one dialysis and other lab/scanning and medical check-ups. Many of the patients have to take a number of dialysis in a week itself. Average amount spent for the initial period shows difference between BPL and APL families. APL families spend a higher amount for accessing initial treatment. More than that, some of the medical concessions given to the BPL families are also a reason for the difference between these two categories.

Table 15.3: Total Amount Spent before Transplantation (amount in Rs)

Background characteristics		*Mean*	*N*	*Std. Deviation*
APL/BPL	APL	156250	36	64174.24
	BPL	125555.6	18	49272.49
Hospital type	Government	93333.33	6	30550.51
	Private	152272.7	44	59994.59
Time gap between diagnosis and transplant	Up To One Year	92500	16	21213.2
	One To Two Years	163636.4	22	51239.19
	Two To Three Years	181666.7	12	68239.77
Total		**145200**	**50**	**60077.73**

Source: Primary Data

There is a significant difference between spending in the government hospital and private hospitals. Patients who sought treatment from the government hospital had to pay less than the patients who were treated in a private hospital. Patients who have undergone treatment up to one year before transplant spend less than those who took two to three years. This reveals the financial burden experienced by patients if the transplant is postponed due to various reasons.

Days of admission in the hospital for transplant

Table 15.4 examines the number of days patients were admitted in hospitals for the kidney transplant. Patients need to be under medical observation for preparing them for the transplant. People who belong to the APL category prefers to be admitted in the hospital for more days for better treatment.

Table 15.4: Days of admission in the hospital for transplant

Background characteristics		*Mean*	*N*	*Std. Deviation*
APL/BPL	APL	17	32	4.70
	BPL	16.22	18	3.30
Hospital type	Government	14.33	6	2.51
	Private	17.04	44	4.31
Years after surgery	Up To Three	17.5	24	4.14
	Three To Six Years	16.5	20	4.81
	Six To Nine Years	14.33	6	0.57
Total		**16.72**	**50**	**4.19**

Source: Primary Data

Private hospitals admit patients for more days than in government hospital. It is also evident that people who were treated before six years were in hospitals for a few days than people who received medical support recently.

Special Package for Kidney Transplantation

Majority of the private hospitals provide their services as a package which includes operation charge, anti-rejection injection and other medicine and check-up charge for the surgery, food, and consumables for the patient, donor, and one bystander. Eighty eight percent of the patients revealed that treatment expenses were in the form of this special package facility. There is a wide variation between the minimum and maximum package amount in private hospitals for the transplant service. It varies between 3,50,000 to 7,00,000. People who received Karunya benevolent fund or RSBY benefit need not pay the full amount and the amount would be deducted from the total package cost. As this package is provided by private hospitals only, and it includes almost all the same services, this large variation is a sign of exploitation of patients in private hospitals. There is no unanimous package amount in private hospitals in Kerala for the kidney transplant

Total Medical Spending For Transplant

Table 15.5 analyzes the total cost associated with renal transplant which patients had to incur. This expenditure includes special package amount, cost of drugs and lab/scanning charges for the first three to four months when patients were under regular consultation with the doctor.

Table 15.5: Total Medical Spending for Transplant

Background characteristics		*Mean*	*N*	*Std. Deviation*
APL/BPL	APL	553125	32	127107.2
	BPL	372222.2	18	56519.42
Hospital type	Government	300000	6	50000
	Private	513636.4	44	125529.2
Years after surgery	Up to three	437500	24	128142.3
	Three to six years	565000	20	120300.5
	Six to nine years	433333.3	6	152752.5
Total		488000	50	137900.9

Source: Primary Data

The table shows that kidney transplantation is a costly affair which amounts an average of Rs. 4,88,000. As BPL families get some concessions for some of the medical services, they had to pay less than the APL families and the gap between the total medical expenditure between them is very clear in the table. However, BPL families also had to spend an amount which is not less than the normal cost for treatment. There is a high possibility of infection and rejection of transplanted kidney as their immunity power is reduced after the transplant. In such cases, patients have to pay extra for all the complications after the transplant.

There is also a very large deviation in the expenses for the treatment in government hospitals and private hospitals. Whereas people have to pay an average amount of Rs. 3,00,000 in the government hospital for accessing the service, people who were treated in a private hospital incurred an average amount of Rs.513636.

Cost of Drugs for the Initial Months after Transplant

Table 15.6 examines the cost of drugs for the months immediately after transplant, because patients have to take some costlier medicines after the transplant, for these months are very critical for them.

Table 15.6: Cost of Drugs for the Initial Months after Transplant

Background Characteristics		*Mean*	*N*	*Std. Deviation*
APL/BPL	APL	33812.50	32	6901.38
	BPL	33666.66	18	9178.77
Hospital type	Government	26000.00	6	14000.00
	Private	34818.18	44	6138.37
Year after surgery	Up to three	36916.66	24	7354.13
	Three to six years	33000.00	20	5395.47
	Six to nine years	23666.66	6	7094.59
Total		33760.00	50	7606.35

Source: Primary Data.

On an average Rs.33760 was spent as the cost of drugs for the initial months after transplant. There is no much difference between the amount spent on drugs by BPL and APL categories. Although they get the benefit of some of the government schemes for transplantation, the treatment expenses after transplantation is a burden. In addition to that, the procedure and duration for claiming reimbursement of drug cost by those who didn't receive any concession for transplant, takes time. However, the difference in spending on drugs in government and the private hospital is very visible. When an average amount of Rs.26000 is spent in the government hospital there is an average difference of Rs.8818 between government and private hospitals.

There is also variation in the expenses on drugs during different years. The table shows an increase in the payment for drugs among people whose surgery was done before six to nine years, three to six years and three years.

Rented Room

Table 15.7: Rented Room

Rented Room	*APL/BPL*			*Type of hospital*			*Years after surgery*			
	APL	*BPL*	*Total*	*Govern-ment*	*Private*	*Total*	*Up to 3*	*3-6*	*6-9*	*Total*
Yes	24 75%	16 88.9%	40 80%	4 66.7%	36 81.8%	40 80%	20 83.3%	18 90%	2 33.3%	20 80 %
No	8 25%	2 11.1%	10 20%	2 33.3%	8 18.2%	10 20%	4 16.7%	2 10%	4 66.7%	10 20%
Total	32 100%	18 100%	50 100%	6 100%	44 100%	50 100%	24 100%	20 100%	6 100%	50 100%

Source: Primary Data

Patients require anti-rejection medications to suppress their immune system so their body doesn't reject the transplanted kidney. Because their immunity power is suppressed, they are prone to infection especially during the first three to six months of transplant. They have to seek medical reference in a regular interval which can be two to three times a week. They are made to believe that they cannot refer any other doctors or hospitals. So people arrange a house or flat near to the hospitals to meet the doctor. The decision to take a room depends on the distance between hospitals and their home and their care for health. 80 percent of the respondents rented house or flat outside the hospitals for three to six months.88.9 percent of the BPL families and 75 percent of APL families took house or flat on rent. The expenditure on the room is one of the major factors which contribute to the high expenses.

Non-Medical Expenditure

Table 15.8 analyses the non-medical monthly expenditure incurred by the patients upto three to six months after the transplant period. There is a significant difference in monthly expenditure on food and transportation among BPL and APL families. While APL families spent higher on food and transport, BPL families spent less. However, spending on room rent shows a reverse pattern. Patients are compelled to take room near hospitals because of constant medical check-ups.

Table 15.8: Non-Medical Expenditure

Background characteristics			***Cost of food***	***Room rent***	***Trans-portation Charge***
APL/ BPL	APL	Mean	6937.50	12875.00	4718.75
		N	32	32	32
		Std. Deviation	14382.71	9618.55	2366.21
	BPL	Mean	3777.77	17444.44	2444.44
		N	18	18	18
		Std. Deviation	2108.18	8308.29	1810.46
Years after surgery	Up to three	Mean	8250.00	17416.66	3500.00
		N	24	24	24
		Std. Deviation	16527.52	9129.95	2679.89
	Three to six years	Mean	4250.00	14200.00	4600.00
		N	20	20	20
		Std. Deviation	1585.52	8256.98	2221.11
	Six to nine years	Mean	1166.66	4000.00	3166.66
		N	6	6	6
		Std. Deviation	2020.72	6928.20	2020.72
Total		Mean	5800.00	14520.00	3900.00
		N	50	50	50
		Std. Deviation	11539.78	9265.16	2415.22

Source: Primary Data

As there is a high possibility of infection they should live in a clean environment, so they rent the house or flat even at the higher cost with an average amount of Rs. 17,444.4. The location of the hospital also has an influence on high rent. There is large deviation among APL families in payment of rent. The average amount spent on food, room and transportation increases over time. There is a difference of Rs. 7083.4 in expenditure on food among people who were under therapy before 6 years and those who have completed only 3 years.

Frequency of hospital visit

Table 15.9: Frequency of hospital visit

Background characteristics		*The frequency of visit per month*			
		1	*2*	*3*	*Total*
APL/BPL	APL	18 56.30%	12 37.50%	2 6.30%	32 100.00%
	BPL	2 11.10%	16 88.90%	0 0.00%	18 100.00%
Total		20 40.00%	28 56.00%	2 4.00%	50 100.00%
Hospital type	Government	0 0.00%	6 100.00%	0 0.00%	6 100.00%
	Private	20 45.50%	22 50.00%	2 4.50%	44 100.00%
Total		20 40.00%	28 56.00%	2 4.00%	50 100.00%
Year after surgery	Up to three	4 16.70%	18 75.00%	2 8.30%	24 100.00%
	Three To Six Years	14 70.00%	6 30.00%	0 0.00%	20 100.00%
	Six To Nine Years	2 33.30%	4 66.70%	0 0.00%	6 100.00%
Total		20 40.00%	28 56.00%	2 4.00%	50 100.00%

Source: Primary Data

The table shows the frequency of hospital visit by the patients currently. Everyone (100%) needs a regular consultation with the doctor even after years of transplant. Majority of them visit the hospital at least once a month. There are patients who meet the doctor even three times a month. The age structure of the kidney patients shows that the prevalence rate of kidney failure is high among middle-aged people and there is a high probability of disease as people get older. The major causes of kidney problem are lifestyle diseases such as high blood pressure and diabetes which require lifelong care.

Monthly cost on drugs at present

The table indicates the monthly cost on drugs incurred by kidney transplanted patients. Patients who were treated in government hospitals pay less than the patients whose surgery was in a private hospital. It also reveals a reduction in the cost of drugs as the years are passing. Patients whose surgery was before six to nine years spend only an average of Rs. 5500 while people who have undergone transplantation treatment prior to three to six years spent an average amount of Rs.10300 in a month. Patients of BPL category spend less since they get some of the benefits of different government schemes. Some of the patients who didn't receive Karunya benevolent fund for the surgery receive it for medicine. The cost of monthly medicines will be deducted from that allowed amount

Table 15.10: Monthly cost on drugs at present

Background characteristics		*Mean*	*N*	*Std. Deviation*
APL/BPL	APL	9481.25	32	4299.49
	BPL	11777.77	18	4730.95
Hospital type	Government	9500.00	6	5220.15
	Private	10418.18	44	4525.02
Years after transplant	Up to three	11516.66	24	5499.88
	Three to six years	10300.00	20	2507.76
	Six to nine years	5500.00	12	2291.28
Total		**10308.00**	**50**	**4503.32**

Source: Primary Data

Job Loss

The poor health of the people results in job loss which may adversely affect every walks of their life. After kidney transplantation, patients are not able to go for work for more than 20 months. A period of more than one-month job loss after the surgery is enough to impoverish the already downtrodden families. People take this long gap either due to the suggestion of doctors or because of consciousness or fear of consequent health problems. Patients are requested to take complete rest for some period of time after transplant. There is no significant difference in the period of time people take the test or remain as unemployed after transplant. Majority of them took more than one year to do any job. They had either difficulty to find a job that needs less physical capacity or their care for their health compelled them to take a sufficient gap in occupation.

Table 15.11: Job loss in months loss

Background characteristics		*Mean*	*N*	*Std. Deviation*
APL/BPL	APL	20.06	32	13.00
	BPL	21.33	18	12.80
Hospital type	Government	27.00	6	8.18
	Private	19.63	44	13.05
Years after transplant	Up to three	19.00	24	11.67
	Three to six years	21.40	20	15.60
	Six to nine years	23.66	6	7.09
Total		**20.52**	**50**	**12.67**

Source: Primary Data

Income loss

A long period of rest after the kidney transplantation results in a huge amount of income loss for those who are working and it is high for the APL families. They lost an average of Rs.23625 while BPL families lost Rs. 6777 per month because of the illness. There is no much difference between income loss among those who are treated in government or private hospitals.

Table 15.12: Income loss per month

Background characteristics		*Mean*	*N*	*Std. Deviation*
	APL	23625.00	16	14008.92
	BPL	6777.77	9	3632.41
APL/BPL	Total	17560.00	25	13970.44
Hospital Type	Government	18333.33	3	18929.69
	Private	17454.54	22	13741.58
	Total	17560.00	25	13970.44
	Up to three	13833.33	12	15068.53
Years after transplant	Three to six years	20800.00	10	12236.55
	Six to nine years	21666.66	3	16072.75
Total		17560.00	25	13970.44

Source: Primary data

Section III: Source of Income for Transplant and Other Effects of Transplantation

Mobilizing money for meeting the health expenditure is always a cumbersome task for people. Every disease has a lot of impacts on the life of patients. Illness can influence every walk of life including his/her plan for the future. They may be exposed to the question of survival again and again in each and every aspect even after it is cured. This section analyses source of income for transplant, how the Kidney transplantation affected their financial stability, its physical and psychological impacts and how much they are able to be back to the normal life.

Source of Income for Transplant

The table explains the different source from which kidney patients mobilized resources for transplant. It is observable that none of the BPL families could spend anything from their savings as they were not able to save due to various reasons. One of the major reasons that they reveal is their expenditure on pre-transplant medical expenditure, especially for dialysis.

Table 15.13: Source of Income for Transplant

Background characteristics		***Source of income for transplant***							
APL/BPL		***Savings***	***Borrowing from friends /family***	***Borrowing from money lenders***	***Sold or pledge d property or ornament***	***Gift or remittance***	***Health insurance***	***Donation from NGO/ charitable institutions***	***Committee***
APL	Mea	175000	250000	75000.	612000	671000	133200	350000	562500
	n						.		
	N	18	8	4	30	20	10	10	16
	Std.	143527	191485	35355.	652251	120773.	153333	217944.94	206587
	Deviation	.00	.42	33	.04	84	.62		.92
BPL	Mea		50000	87500	458571	378333.	212500	123428.57	525000
	N				.42	33		4	
	N		4	4	14	12	8	14	16
	Std.		0.00	88388.	555290	359467.	62915.	77517.43	243486
	Deviation		0	34	.57	19	28		.57
Total	Mea	175000	183333	81250.	563181	561250.	168444	217833.33	543750
	N	.00	.33	00	.81	00	.44		
	N	18	12	8	42	32	18	24	32
	Std.	143527	180739	55433.	614060	969363.	122420	184829.07	218993
	Deviation	.00	.22	89	.53	19	.49		.91

Source: Primary Data

Majority of families sold or pledged their properties for accumulating the money irrespective of the categories. APL families could mobilize a larger amount by borrowing from friends and relatives. Both APL and BPL families have availed of health insurance. But the number of persons who received it is less. Majority of them were the beneficiaries of Karunya benevolent fund, a health insurance scheme of Kerala government which gives a benefit up to 2 lakh only.

An important fact here is that patients received immense support from the society which gives credence to the compassion of our society. People received donation from various sources. Total of 72% patients received money collected through committees which were formed by people in their locality. People rarely did consider their past financial status in such cases. They form these committees including their local representatives with a wide support from all sections of the society.

Number of families Shifted from APL to BPL

The table shows one of the major socio-economic effects of kidney transplant.50 percent of the APL families shifted from APL to BPL and the total percentage of BPL category increased to 68 percent. There is a provision for changing their ration card if there is anyone under treatment after the kidney transplant or continuing dialysis in the family under some rules and regulations.

Table 15.14: Number of families Shifted from APL to BPL

APL/BPL	*Sift to APL/BPL*		*Total*
	APL	*BPL*	
APL	16 50%	16 50%	32 100%
BPL	0 0%	18 100%	18 100%
Total	16 32%	34 68%	50 100%

Source: Primary Data

Source of Income for Meeting Consumption Expenditure

The best way to understand people's current financial position is to analyze how they meet their consumption expenditure. This table examines the various sources from which people mobilize money for meeting their consumption. The largest percentage (62.5%) of people belonging to the APL category now depend on their income and take loan to meet their needs, whereas people belonging to the BPL category depend on all the sources including money lenders, borrowing from friends and relatives, The total of 29.4 percent BPL families use the borrowed money from money lenders and banks for meeting their expenditure.

Table 15.15: Source of Income for Meeting Consumption Expenditure

Background characteristics		*Income*	*Borrowing from friends/ relatives*	*Loan from banks*	*Borrowing from money lenders*	*Depend on other family members*	*Total*
BPL/APL	APL	10	0	2	0	4	16
		62.5%	0.0%	12.5%	0.0%	25.0%	100.0%
	BPL	12	6	6	4	6	34
		35.3%	17.6%	17.6%	11.8%	17.6%	100.0%
Total		22	6	8	8	10	50
		44.0%	12.0%	16.0%	8.0%	20.0%	100.0%
Hospital type	Govern- ment	2	0	0	0	4	6
		33.3%	0.0%	0.0%	0.0%	66.7%	100.0%
	Private	20	6	8	4	6	44
		45.5%	13.6%	18.2%	9.1%	13.6%	100.0%
Total		22	6	8	4	10	50
		44.0%	12.0%	16.0%	8.0%	20.0%	100.0%

(Contd...)

Years after transplant	Up to three	6	2	4	4	8	24
		25.0%	8.3%	16.7%	16.7%	33.3%	100.0%
	Three to six years	10	4	4	0	2	20
		50.0%	20.0%	20.0%	0.0%	10.0%	100.0%
	Six to nine years	6	0	0	0	0	6
		100.0%	0.0%	0.0%	0.0%	0.0%	100.0%
Total		22	6	8	4	10	50
		44.0%	12.0%	16.0%	8.0%	20.0%	100.0%

Source: Primary Data

The table also shows that there is the dependency on other family members by the two categories. People who were treated in government hospitals had to pay less compared to private hospital charges. So they don't depend on money lenders or banks for the present consumption. There is also a difference in the use of the various source of income among people who were in treatment in different years. Patients whose surgery was carried out in recent years depend more on bank loans and money lenders than the people whose operation was done years ago.

Other effects

Health shock has a lot of impact on the individual and family. It can even devastate the socio- economic status of a family by affecting the whole decisions of other family members also. As kidney transplant is a costly affair in Kerala it has a deep influence on life after transplant.

The table reveals that it increases the financial dependency of the patients and the case is the same for both APL and BPL. It is because of the fact that they are either not working now or they work at less pay. Those people who left the occupation after their health shock are difficult to find a job that suits their present health condition. More than that, many of them cannot work for long hours. So they are ready to work at less salary and it amounts to the dependency of the patients. Another fact is that people who were treated in private hospitals are highly dependent (77.3 %) on others. As they cannot refer any other doctors or hospitals, their frequent visit to private hospitals makes them financially dependent on others. They need their doctor's recommendation even for taking pills for fever.

The table points out to the fact that there is a difference in the level of reduction in the consumption of food expenditure. The main reason for the reduction of food expenditure is that they cannot eat all the foodstuff as some of them can cause negative effects. They have to follow strict diet pattern, but it varies from person to person.

Majority of the people reduced non-food expenditure irrespective of their category. Non- food expenditure here includes spending on clothes, entertainment, and other consumer durables. It is clear from the table that 93.3 percent of the people who were in the APL category reduced their non- food expenditure. People who are under the observation of doctors in private hospitals lowered it (95.5 %) than the people in government hospitals (66.7%).

Table 15.16: Other Effects

Effects of transplantation	*APL/BPL*		*Hospital type*		*Years after transplant*		
	APL	*BPL*	*Govern-ment*	*Private*	*upto3*	*Three to six*	*Six to nine*
Increased financial Dependency	22 68.8	12 (66.7)	0 0.0%	34 77.3%	16 66.7%	16 80.0%	2 33.3%
Reduced food expenditure	16 50.0%	12 66.7%	2 33.3%	26 59.1%	12 50.0%	16 80.0%	0 0.0%
Reduced non-food expenditure	30 93.8%	16 88.9%	4 66.7%	42 95.5%	24 100.0%	20 100.0%	2 33.3%
Reduced saving	30 93.8%	18 100.0%	4 66.7%	44 100.0%	24 100.0%	20 100.0%	4 66.7%
Increased debt	28 87.5%	18 100.0%	4 66.7%	42 95.5%	22 91.7%	20 100.0%	4 66.7%
Diversification of employment of the family member	6 18.8%	4 22.2%	2 33.3%	8 18.2%	6 25.0%	2 10.0%	2 33.3%
Sale of land	16 50.0%	8 44.4%	4 66.7%	20 45.5%	12 50.0%	12 60.0%	0 0.0%
Sale of jewels	32 100.0%	18 100.0%	6 100.0%	44 100.0%	24 100.0%	20 100.0%	6 100.0%
Sale of home	4 12.5%	2 11.1%	0 0.0%	6 13.6%	0 0.0%	4 20.0%	2 33.3%
Sale of other assets	2 6.3%	0 0.0%	0 0.0%	2 4.5%	0 0.0%	0 0.0%	2 33.3%

Source: Primary Data

The analysis of their saving and debt status can best reflect their current financial status. Hundred percentage of the people in BPL category, patients of private hospitals, and people whose surgery was done before six years reduced their saving level and 93.8 percentages of the patients who belonged to the APL category also cut down savings. The matter of debt is also not different from this. The debt level of everyone in the BPL category increased after treatment and there is variation among the patients of private hospitals and government hospitals. Whereas the debt level of 95.5 percent in private hospitals shows an increase, it is 66.7 percent for people in the BPL category.

There is diversification of employment of other family members in some families. The reasons for diversification is that patients need a long duration of care after transplant, so some quit their job for caring for them and do other works now. People always seek different ways to meet the two ends of their life. The table explains that everyone sold their jewels for mobilizing money for their treatment and there are patients who are forced to sell their house and land for money.50 percent of APL families and 44.4 percent of the BPL families sold their land. Some sold their other assets like animals and vehicle for having medical assistance. Thus, the impact of CKD on the life of the patients is very high in terms of the financial and non-financial burden that is created.

Section IV: Conclusion

The central issue discussed in the article is the evaluation of the burden of the Chronic Kidney Disease. Health status of the individual has immense implications on every walk of life. Once a person gets ill, financial and emotional security of the whole family will be adversely affected. Non-communicable diseases are caused mainly through the change in the lifestyle and their major risk factors are blood pressure, diabetes, use of tobacco, alcohol etc. among which BP and diabetes have a greater implication on the Chronic Kidney Disease. End stages Kidney disease has only two solutions either kidney transplantation or dialysis. Both are costly affairs in India and the article unravels the burden of Kidney transplantation in Kerala.

The initial symptom of CKD usually appears at the later stages because the body is able to cope up with a significant reduction in kidney function with other renal parts. A severe headache and fever are a major symptom of kidney failure. Nausea, vomiting, urine problem, fatigue are also the initial symptoms of kidney problem. The major cause of Kidney failure is usually blood pressure and diabetes.

On an average, a patient spends Rs.145200 for initial treatment of CKD. Patients often require two or three dialyzes in a week which costs high in addition to other costly medicine. There is a difference between the amount paid by APL and BPL categories but this difference is not very large, but there is wide variation in the amount paid in government and private hospitals. The period between dialysis and transplantation, lead to the rise in the cost because patients who have undergone transplantation within a short span after diagnosis spend less.

Majority of the private hospitals provide organ transplant facility in the form of special package which includes operation charge, medicine, and check-up expenses, food and consumables for the patient, caretakers and donor. Eighty eight percent of the surgery was under this package facility but this package amount varies in between Rs.350000 to Rs.700000.

Patients need costly drugs after the transplantation. On an average, Rs. 33760 was spent on drugs for six months to one year. There is a difference in the cost in private hospitals and government hospitals and patients who had undergone surgery six years ago pay less than the patients whose surgery was before one year which indicate the rise in the cost of drugs year after year. The total cost of kidney transplantation on an average isRs.488000 in Kerala. Private hospital charges a higher amount for the transplant.

Non-medical expenditure which includes room rent, transportation charge and expenditure on food also contribute to the higher amount of expenditure. Patients have to seek medical reference many times a week, so they rent a flat or house near the hospital. Their immunity power will be reduced to prevent rejection of transplanted kidney which demands a living in a clean and tidy environment. Hence they rent highly paid rooms.

They mobilize resources for the transplant through various sources. None of the BPL families were able to spend out of savings. They received massive support in the form of gift or donation. Many of them received financial support from committees organized for helping them. Even the patients of APL families also received such assistance from the society which is a clear sign of compassion and humanity in the society. Both APL and BPL families were beneficiaries of Karunya Benevolent Fund, a health insurance scheme of Kerala government which gives a benefit of Rs. 2 lakh.

Patients require lifelong medication after Kidney transplantations. Majority of them visit hospitals at least once a month and the amount they spent on drugs get reduced after years.

Indirect cost is found by analyzing the years and income loss after surgery. It takes more than one year for them to be back in jobs and there are patients who quit the job after the operation and hence they lost a large amount of income. There is a shift from APL to BPL families because of kidney transplantation. People who belong to the APL category depend on their income or other family members for meeting consumption expenditure whereas a large number of BPL families depend on borrowing from money lenders, friends or relatives. People who were treated in government hospitals do not depend upon money lenders because they had to spend less compared to the private hospital counterparts. Patients whose surgery was carried out in recent years depend more on bank loans and money lenders than people whose operation was years ago. There are patients who quit the job after surgery and many of them have changed occupations which require less physical hard work.

Kidney transplantation leads to the increase in financial dependency of the patients either due to the shift to less paid, less hardworking occupation or unemployement.77 percent of the patients who were treated in private hospital are financially dependent.

Financial problem compels them to minimize spending on non-food expenditure like entertainment, other consumers durable also. The debt level of both APL and BPL family increased after transplantation. Everyone sold their jewels and 50% of APL families and 44.4% of BPL families sold their land and which adversely affect the asset level of families. It can be hence discerned that the burden on disease created by End Stage Renal Transplantation is very severe in terms of financial and non-financial burdens and requires interventions at the policy levels.

References

1. Bloom, D. E., Cafiero, E., Jané-Llopis, E., Abrahams-Gessel, S., Bloom, L. R., Fathima, S., ... & O'Farrell, D. (2012). The global economic burden of noncommunicable diseases (No. 8712). Program on the Global Demography of Aging.
2. Couser, W. G., Remuzzi, G., Mendis, S., & Tonelli, M. (2011). The contribution of chronic kidney disease to the global burden of major noncommunicable diseases. Kidney international, 80(12), 1258-1270.
3. Institute for Health Metrics and Evaluation (IHME). (2018). Findings from the global burden of disease study 2017.
4. Luyckx, V. A., Tonelli, M., & Stanifer, J. W. (2018). The global burden of kidney disease and the sustainable development goals. Bulletin of the World Health Organization, 96(6), 414.
5. Mondal, S., & Van Belle, S. (2018). India's NCD strategy in the SDG era: are there early signs of a paradigm shift? Globalization and health, 14(1), 39.
6. Thankappan, K. R., Shah, B., Mathur, P., Sarma, P. S., Srinivas, G., Mini, G. K., ... & Vasan, R. S. (2010). Risk factor profile for chronic non-communicable diseases: results of a community-based study in Kerala, India. Indian Journal of Medical Research, 131(1), 53.
7. Thankappan, K. R., Shah, B., Mathur, P., Sarma, P. S., Srinivas, G., Mini, G. K., ... & Vasan, R. S. (2010). Risk factor profile for chronic non-communicable diseases: results of a community-based study in Kerala, India. Indian Journal of Medical Research, 131(1), 53.
8. Upadhyay, R. P. (2012). An overview of the burden of non-communicable diseases in India. Iranian journal of public health, 41(3), 1.

9. Vupputuri, S., Kimes, T. M., Calloway, M. O., Christian, J. B., Bruhn, D., Martin, A. A., & Nichols, G. A. (2014). The economic burden of progressive chronic kidney disease among patients with type 2 diabetes. Journal of Diabetes and its Complications, 28(1), 10-16.

10. Wang, V., Vilme, H., Maciejewski, M. L., & Boulware, L. E. (2016, July). The economic burden of chronic kidney disease and end-stage renal disease. In Seminars in nephrology (Vol. 36, No. 4, pp. 319-330). WB Saunders.

11. World Health Organization. (2013). Global action plan for the prevention and control of noncommunicable diseases 2013-2020. World Health Organization.

12. World Health Organization. (2017). Tackling NCDs: 'best buys' and other recommended interventions for the prevention and control of noncommunicable diseases (No. WHO/NMH/NVI/17.9). World Health Organization.

List of Contributors

1. **Dr. V. Raman Kutty**
   Honorary Chairman, Health Action by People
   Ex- Professor, Sree Chitra Tirunal Institute for Medical Sciences and Technology, Former Head, Achutha Menon Centre for Health Science Studies, Trivandrum

2. **Dr. Manju S.Nair**
   Professor
   Department of Economics
   & Hon. Director
   Centre for Agroecology and Public Health
   University of Kerala

3. **Dr. S.S. Santhosh Kumar**
   Associate Professor &
   Deputy Superintendent
   Government Medical College
   Thiruvananthapurm

4. **Dr. Manjusha P.**
   Research Associate
   Kerala State Planning Board
   Government of Kerala

5. **Dr. Aruna S.Anand**
   Assistant Professor
   Department of Economics
   Maharaja's College
   Ernakulam

6. **Dr. K.Anitha**
   Associate Professor
   Department of Economics

Government Arts College
Trivandrum

7. **Dr. Megha Radhakrishnan**
Assistant Professor
Department of Economics
S.N.College, Varkala

8. **Dr.Anupama Augustine**
Research Associate
Centre for Agroecology and Public Health
University of Kerala

9. **Dr. Sajeev M.V.**
HSST Assistant
Government of Kerala

10. **Tanita Eloo Philip**
Research Scholar
Department of Economics
University of Kerala

11. **Shameer V.K.**
Research Scholar
Department of Economics
Government College for Women
Thiruvananthapuram

12. **Ancy John**
Research Scholar
Department of Economics
University of Kerala

13. **Merin Joy**
Research Scholar
Mahatma Gandhi University
Kottayam

14. **Kavya Nair P.J.**
Research Scholar
Department of Economics
University of Kerala

15. Seena K.M.
Former M.Phil Scholar
Department of Economics
University of Kerala

Index

C

G

H

I

L

M

N

O

P

W

Y

Z